# WORD PROCESSING HANDBOOK

# WORD PROCESSING HANDBOOK

**IVAN FLORES**

**Computer Consultant**
**Professor of Computer Methodology**
**Baruch College, City University of New York**

VNR VAN NOSTRAND REINHOLD COMPANY
NEW YORK  CINCINNATI  TORONTO  LONDON  MELBOURNE

Library of Congress Catalog Card Number: 82-2727
ISBN: 0-442-22526-1

Published by Van Nostrand Reinhold Company Inc.
135 West 50th Street, New York, N.Y. 10020

Van Nostrand Reinhold Publishing
1410 Birchmount Road
Scarborough, Ontario M1P 2E7, Canada

Van Nostrand Reinhold Australia Pty. Ltd.
17 Queen Street
Mitcham, Victoria 3132, Australia

Van Nostrand Reinhold Company Limited
Molly Millars Lane
Wokingham, Berkshire, England

15 14 13 12 11 10 9 8 7 6 5 4 3 2 1

**Library of Congress Cataloging in Publication Data**

Flores, Ivan.
   Word processing handbook.

   Includes index.
   1. Word processing (Office practice)   2. Office
practice—Automation.   I. Title.
HF5548.115.F55   651.7   82-2727
ISBN 0-442-22526-1   AACR2

# Preface

This handbook attempts to give a complete coverage of how to use word processing (WP) systems and how they work. It tells you all you need to know about the hardware and the software, the programs that run the WP systems. It tells you what WP systems can do and what they can't do. It tells you how to operate the major WP systems—not the details—but what buttons you press to get the desired results.

Who will benefit by reading the handbook?

**Managers who consider installing a WP:** To deal with the WP sales representatives, you have to understand the jargon—RAM, ROM, floppy, minifloppy, dot matrix printer, n-key rollover, etc. How the terminal, printer, computer, and other components work is described in Chapters 2 through 5. If you are in a hurry, there is a large glossary at the end of the book defining the jargon in simple language.

**Managers who want to capitalize on existing WPs:** If you are a busy and creative executive who hasn't experienced how WP can expedite and supplement your own talent by eliminating time-consuming intermediate steps, you may become convinced to give it a go. Chapter 1 gives some personal incentives.

**Vendor sales, marketing, and product planning personnel:** You may know all about your company's machine, but what about competitive WP systems? You can't fight the opposition unless you know what their machines do and why they do it. For instance, what are the advantages to the operator of seeing a full page on the display and how can these advantages be overcome for a partial page display (Section 7.4).

**Consultants:** Data Pro and Auerback system reports and vendor's spec sheets are simply not enough to evaluate the specific needs of your clients. For instance, the variety of methods for dealing with columnar reports which require calculations is hard to find put together in one place (see Chapter 11).

**Operators:** Whether you are experienced on a particular machine or seeking to learn what WP is all about, you will see how powerful the systems are, yet tame to your touch. For simple editing, WP systems differ very little. (They differ considerably on the complex tasks they do and how easy they are to request.) Knowing how to do basic operations on different machines, as described in Chapters 6 through 9, will give you the confidence to take over a new machine when the opportunity arises.

**EDP installation managers:** Your installation may have plenty of computing power, but can it do record processing? Can you use record processing to advantage in your office? Chapter 12 explains what might be done with this feature.

This handbook is intended to serve a wide range of needs. Some explanations are basic to establish definitions of such words as "platen"; others are technical, such as the difference between the two kinds of justification and how each is calculated by the software. Both types of explanations are printed in smaller type.

A WP system consists of a computer and other devices (hardware) and a program (software), which together help you do your writing, editing, and printing. Most WP systems are put in a pretty package and can go into an office to replace one or more typewriters. But you should keep in mind that this is not the only way that WP capability is available. Three kinds of WP installation are available:

1. A standard WP system intended primarily for WP office applications *may* also be able to do accounting and simple record handling.
2. A data processing system with a large computer to which is attached terminals to do the WP chores.
3. A small personal computer in the home or small business which not only solves a range of problems but also does WP.

This book describes *primarily* the standard office WP system. However, the similarities of WP systems are much greater than their differences. Information specifically about WP systems using personal computers or using mainframes is put in smaller type in the book.

How to Read This Book explains the sequence in which each kind of user might read the book. Chapter 1 introduces the **WP** system, its effectiveness and power, coupled with its simplicity. The development of the **WP** system from the memory typewriter and magnetic card system provides a historical perspective. Then the large electronic components of the **WP** are examined, along with alternatives for putting them together.

Part I, Chapters 2 through 5, is devoted to the computer system. Chapter 2 is an overview of the computer and the programs which run it. Then the main hardware components which comprise a computer are discussed in terms of their need in the WP system. These include the computer itself, the keyboard and display, by which the operator communicates with the computer. Finally we describe equipment needed for communication between a central WP computer and a remote terminal or remote computer. This is the basis for the WP network, electronic mail, and other goodies.

Chapter 3 examines printers which create the document: printing techniques; moving paper; positioning the print element; justifying output; and automated paper handling.

Chapter 4 is devoted to external storage, the means for storing electronic documents in computer readable form. A simple view of magnetics is presented. The various media, magnetic disk, card, and tape are examined. Both floppy disks and hard disks are scrutinized. The format and location of data and programs on the disk are investigated. The meaning and interpretation of disk drive specifications are described.

Software consists of directions (programs) which tell the computer what to do. Chapter 5 describes operating systems, drivers, files, catalogs, programs, programming languages, and utilities. Most of these are "invisible" to the user but they have an effect on response time, free disk space, and so on.

With this background, Part II deals with how you operate a WP and how it works. All the features that might be found on almost any WP (but not one single WP) are examined here. Of most importance are the variations among the WP features and the ways each vendor implements them. What kind of help does the WP provide to expedite and simplify editing? For example, the WP might provide different kinds of hyphenation assistance:

1. Fully automatic—it's done for you
2. Semiautomatic—the WP provides a hot zone or a soft hyphen, but you say where the hyphen goes.
3. Manual—it is up to you to note where lines are *too* short, where to break the word, and where to move it.

How good is the automatic feature? If it is right only half the time, we may be better off without it.

Chapter 6 examines the basic activities that all WP systems must provide to create and edit the electronic document. Even the simplest things, such as where the input you enter appears on the screen is subject to considerable variation: some vendors use a *typing line* on which text *must* be entered; for others; text may be entered *only* at the cursor. Chapter 7 views formatting—how the WP helps you organize your document on the screen and then duplicates this organization as the text is printed out. Chapter 8 looks at full and partial documents to see how they are manipulated within memory and stored on external storage. Chapter 9 examines how more advanced edit features improve accuracy, reduce total work expended, and allow the use of less skilled workers to keep cost low while maintaining the overall work flow in its original form.

Entering a different specific item, such as name and address, into fixed positions of each new copy of a document, assembling boilerplate automatically, and entering names and dates into papers are only some of the labor-saving features discussed in Chapter 10. That feature is the basis for the automatic form letter.

Preparing financial documents requiring calculations and handling larger forms are the topics of Chapter 11. Incorporating both calculations and data management functions into the WP system is becoming increasingly available. Chapter 12 discusses record processing, the most advanced DP capability furnished by the vendor. First, the concepts of records, fields, and files are considered. Various ways files may be processed are examined. Then subfiles, their need and definition, are pursued in Section 12.3. How to generate reports and documents from the subfile is described in Section 12.4. Then attention is given to user programs in BASIC and to vendor packages.

Part III is about the need and expectation for integrating WP into the office system. First, in Section 13.1, the intelligent typewriter is considered. Then the larger process of getting your thoughts delivered and put down onto a decent document is examined in Section 13.2, along with the human and mechanical aids for doing this. Section 13.3 brings up many matters you should consider in setting up and/or expanding your WP installation. Finally, Section 13.4 ponders what advances are in store for WP in general and the larger picture of what other ways the office may change vis-a-vis WP.

**Acknowledgments.** This enterprise was sparked by the encouragement of Larry Hager of VNR. Mary-Ellen Quintana helped me in the initial work of writing to an audience unfamiliar to me. Naomi Mendelsohn read all the drafts I gave her, no matter how bad, and helped make the rough places plain. Patricia Seybold made innumerable useful comments and would steer me back when I would go off into the technical blue. Paul Abrahams supplied guidance in putting my words more accurately on target. Marilyn Carp raised important practical questions about the usefulness of many discussions. As always, Arlene Abend's gorgeous cover wraps it all up.

IVAN FLORES

# Contents

## II. WORD PROCESSING

# WORD PROCESSING HANDBOOK

# How to Read This Book

This book is intended for a wide range of readers—from those with no previous knowledge about WP to experienced operators, managers and sales personnel. What each might need is different.

The book, as described in the Preface, consists of three parts; the parts and, as much as possible, each chapter, is an independent unit. As a consequence, there is some repetition. The first chapter is introductory. I suggest that all readers start with it.

The first part describes the hardware and software of the WP computer. It provides background information for all those with some technical or managerial experience in WP. It makes the technical details of Part II more accessible. Part I should be skipped by the novice on the first reading.

Part II describes how the WP is used for creating, editing and printing documents in Chapter 6 and 7. After Chapter 1, these two should be read next by the novice, skipping the small print. More advanced features are introduced in succeeding chapters of this part. The experienced practitioner will profit from the contrast of capabilities of existing WPs presented here.

All kinds of WPs, including those no longer in production, are examined and sometimes used as examples. This equipment may still be found doing useful although less efficient work in offices than that of newer models.

Details in fine print in all chapters should supplement the knowledge of the technically inclined person: sales and account representatives, technical liason, designers and engineers.

Advanced features described in Chapters 8 through 12 are of interest to all who wish to take advantage of these features in their companies or to sell them to others. Here the differences among WPs are most obvious and the advantage of proper selection is most significant.

Part III may be of some use to the manager who must select and plan for acquisition or expansion. It should alert you to pitfalls and omissions which might be costly. It predicts the evolution of some aspects of WP technology that might influence your present choice for acquired equipment.

Don't neglect the glossary. It is there to provide definitions, especially when a term is defined in an area of the book which is remote from your current reading.

# 1
# Introduction

## 1.1 THE LURE AND INEVITABILITY OF WORD PROCESSING

In my opinion the comparison between word processing and typing is equivalent to the comparison between writing with pen and ink and ancient hieroglyphics. Since 1960 I have written a total of 18 books. The first draft of *Data Base Architecture* was written on a typewriter. Only the final draft used the word processing machine. I can truly say that my attitude and approach to writing has changed markedly since I've had the opportunity to work with a WP system. (Hereinafter WP is used to represent either "word processing" or "word processor".)

What I find most important is the ability to rework whole sections of material without undue effort. To change a couple of pages out of 20 takes only the effort required to revise those 2 pages. Moving them around is no work at all.

The second factor which improves operation so markedly is that the WP helps the uninitiated adapt to unfamiliar terminology. Almost every profession has a jargon which is unfamiliar to outsiders and which contains words that are difficult to spell (such as "byte"). My assistants are part-time employees. They tend to be occupied with other activities and may even be seeking full-time employment elsewhere. With a WP system, I am able to direct them in productive work immediately. Once they realize that a misspelled word is not a problem (because it takes just a second to edit), they're willing to take a guess at the word they hear on a recorded tape to make the first draft. This makes their time more efficient and gives them the knowledge that they are being useful even in an area unfamiliar to them.

A third advantage is the ease with which people take to the WP system. I interview people for typing jobs without telling them beforehand that they will be using a WP system. Perhaps it is my air of confidence that they will master it without any trouble that encourages them. With only a few minutes of instruction, I get productive work from them and I can evaluate their typing ability.

The WP system is easy and even fun to use. I'm a fair typist and I don't mind sitting down to edit a number of pages if I have time. I even enjoy it. Sometimes I compose text right at the terminal. My typing speed has improved, because I don't have to worry about making mistakes. I can type as fast as I like and go back and correct any errors. Or my spelling program will find mistakes for me.

## The Operator's View

How can we evaluate the effect of a WP system on one who uses it? There's been a lot of talk about computers and other machines as having dehumanizing influences. The effect of a machine or an invention depends entirely on how people put either to use. To me, nothing could be more dehumanizing than the work of a scribe in medieval times who sat around all day copying text from one document to another.

Are there bad WP installations? Of course there are, just as there are bad typing installations. A WP pool and a typewriting pool are equally dehumanizing. Some offices have been reorganized when WP systems were brought in because it seemed more efficient to provide a pool to keep a steady supply of work for the operators. And now capital equipment is involved! If this replaces a more personal relation between a typist and a single individual or a small group, it may be counterproductive and demoralizing. It is *people* who make the decision about how to use the equipment.

Will operators be replaced? The sale of 30 million typewriters last year, despite a booming WP market denies an immediate demise of the office staff. As the number of WPs increase, more and better paying jobs will become available. The aim of WP is to make frequent changes and reorganization of a manuscript easier and to produce a perfect copy. Only secondarily does WP increase the efficiency of the operator, and by only a small percentage. The number of documents produced is increasing too fast for the small improvement in operator efficiency to have any effect. Typists will not be eliminated—because many or more people will be needed to cope with document entry—only their skill and earning power will be upgraded.

One of the biggest problems in creating a felicitous working environment may be the attitude of office managers to capital equipment. Managers may not be used to dealing with such an expensive machine. The feeling is that to make the equipment cost effective, it has to be used constantly. There is a tendency to see efficiency in terms of key strokes rather than production of perfect (error free) copy.

There is a negative carryover from the large computer environment. Here a lot of keypunch operators are employed to enter hard copy by keying it into terminals. Their effectiveness is measured in key-stroke productivity and error rate. The copy they work with is often meaningless to them. The WP system should not be abused in this way; it should be integrated into the office environment in much the same way the typewriter is.

## The WP Advantage

The attitude of the WP manager is so important to the novice first getting on the system. If the manager knows the machine and is truly confident of its usefulness and of the fun of using it, the novice absorbs this attitude and immediately take to the machine. (I explain my theory of training in the last chapter.)

The most frustrating aspect of typing is correction. Whether it be with white-out, with rubber erasers, or with erasing tape, the action of exorcising those bad letters annoys me greatly. Then you have to get the correct letters properly placed to overwrite the corrected area. And they never look quite right. After spending years as a typist, what a joy it is to face a day with no erasures!

Most people take pride in their work. With the WP system you can actually produce a perfect document. That is an accomplishment you can feel good about.

If you see that a sentence or a group of sentences is in the wrong place when you are composing, you can move them about in a few seconds just to see how they look in another position. Put them back where they were if you want, with the same dispatch.

Then there are repetitive letters, contracts, sections of manuscript, and so forth. Once they're stored in the WP system, you don't have to type them ever again; just bring them up electronically and paste them in electronically where they belong.

I have never met a WP operator who would prefer to go back to typing. They are the industry's best advertisement.

## The Technological Imperative

I have heard it said that it is impossible to live in California without a car. It certainly is impossible to be a company executive if you refuse to fly. Technology moves at an incredible rate and we must keep up with it. Can you imagine an office with handwritten letters? Most professors require their students to type their papers. Carbon paper is on its way out because of the copying machine.

The office has not been able to stay free from the march of technology. Now computers are here. The first commercial computer, the ENIAC, occupied the space of an average apartment. Now that same computing power can be put in a package the size of a book and sold at a price that is within the range of most office budgets. This power can be brought to bear in the office setting to relieve us of drudgery and to make our productive hours enjoyable.

Then why do we resist? Certainly it must be fear—fear of the new, fear of learning something at which we are not initially proficient. Perhaps just a fear of the impersonal element of the computer. We've been brainwashed.

It is the nature of technology that if you don't keep up with it, you may fall by the wayside. Some offices cannot afford to overlook the potential of WPs to improve the output and the satisfaction of their employee. There is hardly a large law office that does not have WP capability. Once you have assembled a legal document from a number of source paragraphs in a matter of a few minutes, you realize how much time you would waste by typing the document from beginning to end. In the legal area it is simply not cost effective to use a typewriter.

If you are involved in extensive writing and editing, a WP system is a must. Proposals for grants and government contracts seldom are less than half an inch thick. The time and money required for typing such a document is many times more than the cost of the WP equipment.

## The Needs of Today's Office Management

Those who are concerned with managing office staff and equipment must become knowledgeable in WP equipment. They must be aware of its capabilities and effectiveness. They must understand what features are available, why they are needed, how they are used and, to some degree, how they are implemented.

To acquire a thorough background in this wide range of technology, two approaches are essential:

1. Hands-on experience. That is, you play with the equipment, understand it and do productive work on it to gain complete familiarity.
2. Awareness of the competitive market. Understanding and operating a single piece of equipment does not suffice if you have to negotiate the purchase and installation of such equipment for your office. You should know what else is available. Some features which are absolutely necessary in one office environment can be done without in another, and vice versa.

## 1.2 THE EVOLUTION OF WORD PROCESSING

### Aim

The mechanical typewriter had been around since the turn of the century. It became an office fixture by the middle of the century. With a careful and vigilant operator and considerable time and effort, it could be used to prepare a neat, clean and acceptable document for office correspondence. Regardless of the competency of the operator, there were still problems with the typewriter that technology would be able to overcome. Improvement was necessary to provide capability for:

- simple correction, in that 80 percent of the errors that a typist makes are noted immediately and could be corrected at once if a good mechanism to do this were provided,
- reasonable changes in the document during creation,
- major changes in the document without the need for retyping.

The point of reference to these changes is the mechanical typewriter. It was the first popular mechanical typing device with formed letters that produced neat, clean output with a minimum of training and skill.

**Separation of Input from Output**

The original mechanical typewriter is a device which takes the force provided by the operator and applies it to mechanical linkages to place an image of the character at the next position on the paper in the machine. The operator hits the key on the keyboard on which the letter to print appears. The force with which the key is hit is transmitted directly through a series of mechanical linkages to a type bar. This type bar flies through the air and hits the ribbon against the paper to cause the impression. The harder you hit a key, the darker the impression.

Electric typewriters are almost identical in concept. The difference is that the electric typewriter provides a "power assist." This is very much like power steering or power brakes in an automobile. You direct the mechanism and it applies the force in the direction you indicate. However, the force applied is not your mechanical output. Instead, your touch is only an indicator converted by the mechanism into a strong and uniform force as you direct.

For the electric typewriter, the letter selection you make activates an electric arrangement. The type bar is still sent to hit the ribbon against the paper. However, the force with which it hits the paper does not depend upon how hard you hit the key. There is a separate adjustment, so that when you are making multiple copies, the type bar or golf ball hits the paper with greater force. The electric typewriter is a considerable improvement over the manually operated typewriter because it means that the appearance of the document is independent of the force provided by the operator. Since fingers are not equally forceful and since operators differ with respect to the strength of their fingers, the document looks the same and is of uniform darkness regardless of such factors.

The important feature to note about both the mechanical and electric typewriter is that the action (printing) happens almost immediately after the choice is made (hitting the key). The quest was for some way to break this relation so that something could be done between the time a key is hit and the information is printed.

*Intermediate Storage*

Then the problem was this: enter keystroke information at the keyboard and store it on some medium externally and then later take the information from this medium and have it operate the typewriter. We were content in the first devices to prepare the information on the typewriter, provided that another copy in some alterable form was available externally; the saved information could be altered easily before it was reproduced.

The first technique provided is illustrated, in terms of its philosophy, in Figure 1.2.1. Here we see the following activities:

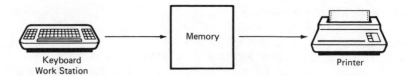

Figure 1.2.1. Memory typewriter schematic.

A. Input
   1. Collect stroke information.
   2. Convert each key stroke into a code.
   3. Store the information on external medium.
B. Storage
   1. The external medium holds the information.
   2. The information can be altered by some physical or electric means.
   3. The altered information can be kept in tact for some later use.
C. Output
   1. The codes from the external medium are extracted and sent over to the printer.
   2. The codes are converted into electric form.
   3. The electric form of the code is used to activate the type bars mechanically and print the document.

**Paper Tape**

The 1950s saw the beginning of computer evolution. Computers seemed to eat up data as fast as we could generate them. The operator could key a maximum of about ten characters per second. Computer input rates were almost limitless. For large installations, the initial solution was punchcards. These ubiquitous items are still around. They speed up the input process considerably. However, the reader for the cards is fairly expensive.

A more economical source for computer input appeared, called the Flexowriter. Figure 1.2.2 illustrates how it is used. This device consists of an electric typewriter to which a small paper tape punch is attached. As you key information at the keyboard, the electric typewriter prints it. During this action, each key stroke is also converted into a set of electric impulses, as described above. These

Figure 1.2.2. The Flexiwriter stored keystroke information on punched paper tape.

impulses are also fed to the paper tape punch. For each key you hit, a set of holes is punched into an endless stream of paper tape. So as you create your document, you also create a piece of paper type containing the same information as the document.

The paper tape produced at the Flexowriter was primarily to make computer input faster; the computer did not have to stop while the operator keyed in data. This keying was **off line**, that is, it did not involve the computer. Several operators could prepare tape for one input session. The tape was read at full speed, a hundred times faster then the operator could read it.

For office use, you play back the paper tape on the typewriter. There is a paper tape reader attached to the typewriter. To replay the electronic document, simply enter the paper tape into this reader and put a piece of paper into the typewriter. When you start it up, the paper tape reader produces character codes which operate the typewriter exactly as you did while typing to create the tape a little while ago.

### Immediate Corrections

Suppose during the course of typing that you keyed "Teh" instead of "The." You stop immediately and back up the paper punch two characters. Then you hit the delete key twice, a special key on the Flexowriter. It punches a set of 1s to replace each character that you are deleting. In other words, wherever the paper tape has a character consisting entirely of holes, this signifies a deleted character which does not print. Now you return to your typing and type "he" to replace the "eh" which you deleted. As you can see, the document you are typing at the typewriter has gotten messed up. However, the tape reflects the typing to be produced; when it is played back it produces a perfect document. What you are typing serves only as a draft.

### Cut and Paste

You can do editing with the Flexowriter by cutting and pasting. And the action actually *is* cutting and pasting; what you are cutting and pasting is the paper tape, a messy job. You can create a paper tape insert by simultaneously typing the insert on the typewriter and punching the tape. The insert you have created is a length of tape. To alter your original tape, you play it back with the tape reader (typing out at the same time) to the insertion point and mark this point. Then take the tape out of the reader, cut it there and paste in the insert.

Deletion is done similarly. Find the area in the paper tape which is to be deleted by reading it into the typewriter and marking the tape accordingly. Once you have marked the area, simply snip it out and join the tape, omitting this excerpt.

*Reproduce*

Another way to do editing with the Flexowriter is to produce a new tape from an old tape and the typewriter. Place the old tape in the paper tape reader. There is fresh tape in the punch. Play back the document through the typewriter and the punch, up to the point where you wish to make a change. Turn off the reader and enter information at the keyboard. The new information is inserted only in the new paper tape in the punch.

To delete information, turn off the punch and continue to read information, printing it on the typewriter, until the matter to be deleted has printed. Then continue the reproduction.

*Use*

As you can see from the description, the Flexowriter is not nearly as convenient as are present day machines. In fact, there were few, if any, offices that adopted these machines. Instead, they were used mostly in the computer environment and by direct mail firms. It is essential to get correct information and programs into the computer. The amount of energy spent in creating a perfect document is definitely worth the trouble.

The tape produced by this method could be read into the computer at rates of a thousand or more characters per second. This enables the computer to gobble up the data at a rate more appropriate to it. Programs that had to be entered over and over again use this reliable method for entry.

Direct mail firms and business service bureaus used paper tape to duplicate many hundreds or even thousands of form letters with much less human effort. A form letter is easily produced as a paper tape. Stop codes are entered into the paper tape where distinctive information is to be entered. Thus the name and address is entered at the keyboard and the rest of the letter is produced from the paper tape. Typewriters operate at maximum speed and human operators are required only to enter the variable information.

**Internal Memory**

If the document could be stored internally in a form which made it immediately available, this improvement would help considerably. Internal memory provides a means for holding the document and altering it while there, so that changes in editing can be done easily and quickly. Memory is called internal memory when it is within the computer and is not in a visible form such as paper tape, which can be moved about physically. The document stored in internal memory or external memory for that matter is referred to in this book as an **electronic document (ED)** to distinguish it from **hard copy**, the document in printed form.

The diagram of the word processor now takes the form of Figure 1.2.3. As the document is keyed in, it is placed in memory and also printed on the typewriter. Changes made in the electronic document are made directly into memory. As each change is made, it may also be displayed on the copy produced in the typewriter. When the ED is assumed to be perfect, it can be played back on the typewriter for verification; when the operator is satisfied, the document can be stored on the external medium for later editing or playback.

**External Medium**

The most important desirable feature for an external medium is that it be reusable, as the punched tape was not. The medium is **reusable** when it will store new information where the old information used to be. It is impossible to replace holes punched out of the paper tape. Magnetic media are reusable. A whole chapter of this book is devoted to them. The three important media for the evolution of word processing are:

- the magnetic tape cassette,
- the magnetic card,
- the floppy disk.

These media allowed the WP field to advance in leaps and bounds.

*Magnetic Tape*

A cassette of magnetic tape such as that used in an ordinary home recorder was adapted to store many pages of text. Its use made editing of an existing document considerably easier than was the case in the past.

To edit a short document, simply read the document from the tape into memory and then rewind the cassette to receive the new copy of the document. The ED now in memory can be edited by using the help of the program and keyboard. Once the new document is found to be satisfactory, hard copy can be produced and/or the document can be rerecorded onto the cassette.

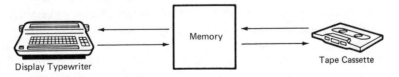

Figure 1.2.3. The word processor components.

*Magnetic Card*

A plastic card, coated with a magnetizable material and about the size and shape of a punchcard was used in early word processing systems. The card holds up to a full single-spaced page of text. It is used just as is the cassette: read the document back; edit it; return the revised document.

*Floppy Disk*

In the mid-1970s, IBM developed the floppy disk to hold small operating system programs to be loaded into its computer. The medium was an immediate success, and copiers of the device and the floppy disk sprang up all over the world. What makes the medium so appealing for word processing use is the ability to go to any part of the disk and extract information without reviewing the entire disk.

For instance, if you have a 10 page document and want to make a correction only on the third page, you can go directly to that page with your word processor, extract the text, alter it and return it without the overhead time required to process the entire document.

## Visual Display

Without a display, every time you want to make a small correction or edit an electronic document you must have the typewriter produce hard copy which is not actually usable. What is needed is a reusable visual medium, that is some presentation which the operator can look at and use for altering the document, but which does not use up any resource. The answer is a visual display.

Visual displays were available in the 1960s in the form of the **video display terminal (VDT)**. Displayed on the screen of a television tube is textual information which constitutes the electronic document. A keyboard is generally attached, but we disregard it for the moment. The VDT was invaluable to the computer operator, the one who works the EDP installation computer. It became a popular way for programmers to work with computers.

Now almost every programmer has a VDT at his desk by which to enter and check programs and data. VDTs of this type cost $2,000 to $4,000, considerably more than the cost of a typewriter. The office environment was loathe to acquire such an expensive piece of equipment, when document output was clearly still limited by the attached typewriter at a slightly higher speed than that of the human operator.

The other visual output device of interest is called the **light emitting diode (LED)**. You are probably most familiar with this device in the digital wristwatch. The display produces an illuminated visual image of the time when you press a button. A set of similar devices are used in connection with intelligent type-writers to display part of a line (see Chapter 13). However, they were not economically feasible until the mid-1970s.

### Printers

Until the early 1970s, there were only two actual choices for hard copy computer printout:

- the low speed, high quality typewriter,
- the high speed, low quality, high priced line printer.

Line printers produce great quantities of output in a hurry, but the quality of this output can not be used for correspondence. In fact, many EDP printers are equipped to print only uppercase letters, which is usable for drafts but at a price far beyond the reach of most offices.

For many years the search was on to find a compromise in cost and speed which would not detract from the attractiveness of a document used for correspondence. Only in the early 1970s was the daisy wheel printer developed. It was immediately attractive to the word processing field because of its fully formed high quality printing. Initially, it printed 35 characters per second; current speeds of 60 characters per second provide the same corresponding quality as does the electric typewriter.

In the early seventies, there was no economical way to use the VDT. With the addition of the daisy wheel printer, the VDT became more appealing, because printing could proceed at a much higher rate. A printer working at top speed could print output for three efficient operators. Three terminals could share one printer, accommodating the output of three operators.

There were further developments at the end of the seventies which made possible fast and accurate printing at a higher price. These were the ink jet printer and later the laser printer. The laser printer can produce all the documents required for a fairly large office installation. The problem is that of integrating such a high capacity printer into the office system.

### Microprocessors and Internal Memory

One further development was necessary in the electronic technology area, that of large scale integration (LSI), which made available high powered computing capability and considerable amounts of internal memory at a fairly low cost. All the necessary components to put an economical word processing system together were available. Figure 1.2.4 is a block diagram of such a system.

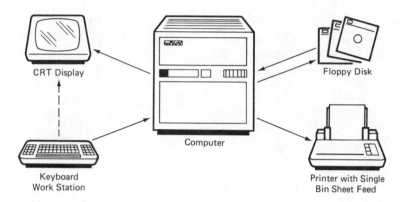

CRT Display

Floppy Disk

Keyboard
Work Station

Computer

Printer with Single
Bin Sheet Feed

Figure 1.2.4.  The VDT based WP.

The main task of this book is to set forth the various relations of these components and the capability acquired through their use.

### Intelligent Typewriters

In the middle and late seventies, word processing separated into two camps. The capability already available was provided to the office secretary at a modest cost. Millions of intelligent typewriters have been and will be sold. What these devices can do is limited in scope and in speed. However, they serve a useful purpose, especially if they are properly integrated into the office environment. In the last chapter of this book we examine what they are and how they are integrated into the procedures of the modern office.

To keep this volume down to a reasonable size, we direct attention to only the VDT based WP outlined in Figure 1.2.4.

## 1.3 CONFIGURATIONS

### Kinds of Components

A word processing system consists of components which fall into three general categories: hardware, software and people. Put them together with procedures and you have a system. All these are of interest to us and all are discussed in this book:

- Hardware consists of mechanical, electric and structural components placed in a cabinet. Open up the cabinet and we can see and touch them; they are "hard." Chapters 2 through 4 discuss hardware components.

- Software consists of the programs, which are sets of instructions to run the computer. Programs are the power behind the word processor. The computer cannot operate without a program. The details are described in Chapter 5.
- People use the system. Without people, the system sits idle. Both the people that use the system and those that receive their results have to be pleased with the system. Most users are pleased with WP.

Much space in this book is devoted to hardware. It is the substantial and visible part of the system. The hardware consists of a number of components—printers, terminals, consoles, and so forth. Hardware systems are fabricated by putting together different types and quantities of these components to make a configuration which differs considerably in price and capability from other alternatives.

**Minimum Needs**

The following hardware items are the bare minimum required to provide word processing capabilities above those of the memory typewriter:

- The keyboard is the means by which you communicate with the system; you enter both text and editing commands there.
- The display presents the portion of the text which you are now editing, showing how it is currently recorded.
- A computer manages input, accepts commands and temporarily stores text, when you direct it to do these word processing chores.
- Memory in the computer stores the current piece of text that you are working on and the editing and printing programs to serve the WP needs.
- External storage accepts the text that you have created at the terminal and stores it permanently so that you can work with it again at some later point. External storage is needed because, when you turn off the computer, everything stored in its temporary memory disappears.
- A printer converts the text that you have created into a document.

A **configuration** is a number of components tied together to satisfy your needs. Configurations differ from one to the next according to the number and type of components they have and the specifications of each component. Before we examine some of these configurations, let us pause a moment to define them:

**Stand alone**—a complete word processing machine which is self-contained, independent and sometimes in its own cabinet, except perhaps for the printer,

**Shared resource**—multiple stations which share one or more pieces of common equipment, such as a printer,

**Shared logic**—multiple stations which share computing power as well as perhaps other resources.

**Mainframe**—a large computer to which one or more stations is hooked up by means of wires, a local net or telephone lines,

**Microcomputer**—a small, inexpensive computer from which a word processing machine may be assembled by adding other components and a WP program.

### Stand Alone

The stand alone WP is so called because it is independent and "stands alone." If any of the other equipment in the office breaks down, this has no effect on the unit. However, documents prepared and stored on disks in one stand alone unit can be transferred and edited and/or printed in another similar unit of the same vendor, should the first unit fail.

The stand alone unit consists of two or more modules or cabinets. One of these is the printer which produces the output documents; the other contains the computer and the hardware needed to make the unit function. A single plastic cabinet may house the microcomputer, the keyboard, the display and the disk drives. This makes the unit look like a television set with a keyboard pasted on. Displays can vary as to length and height; some are wider than they are high, and vice versa. There is one or, more often, two slots with small doors to accommodate floppy disks which hold the documents in electronic form or programs to run the computer.

Another alternative is to keep the keyboard and display in one unit; the other module holds the computer and the disk drive(s). The entry keyboard resembles a typewriter keyboard, but it has additional keys for telling the word processor what editing functions you want. Sometimes the keyboard is movable, being attached to the display by a cable; you can situate it to be most comfortable.

Vendors have made an attempt to provide comfortable workplaces for the operator to use; they might do more!

### Shared Resource

It has become clear that some expensive equipment which is part of the WP system does not get as much use as does the rest of the equipment. The printer is in use only when it is printing out a document. You ask it to print out a document only when you have finished composing it. While you are composing and editing a document, the printer sits idle. Some other station could be using this printer.

One printer sometimes serves several stations. What the system must do is:

A. Connect several stations to the same printer.

B. Make sure that printing from one station does not interfere with a request from a second. There is a computer-organized waiting line (queue) for the printer. As requests come from different stations to use the printer, they are put on the waiting line and serviced in the order of their arrival. It would not do to intermix text from one station with that of another. Each document must remain separate from all other documents.

If one resource is to be shared among a number of stations, it is generally the printer. However, there is another resource which some larger systems have. This is the hard disk, which is like a very large file cabinet full of documents which a number of people might share. It is a fine place to store less-active documents to be used by several stations. For the more modest WP installation, we occasionally find floppy disk systems shared among several users.

### Shared Logic

The microcomputer in the word processor is very fast and adept. It can perform a million operations in a single second. Most of the time that you are entering the text, it is idle and has nothing to do. There are only certain times when you can keep it fully occupied, such as when you repaginate a document or find a document on the disk. Since the computer is so powerful, it can usually service a number of stations simultaneously. Vendors saw this possibility and some of them provided equipment where one computer services several stations. Generally, there is no interaction between the stations. The computer is occasionally fully occupied working for one operator and the other stations have to wait. This is more or less of an inconvenience depending on the frustration tolerance of the operator.

The computer is, itself, indispensable to shared word processing activity. If it becomes faulty, all stations connected to it are inhibited, if not disabled.

More recently, the cost of the microprocessor chip has become almost inconsequential. There is no problem in incorporating a computer into each facility, and shared logic has gone out of vogue. Its main advantage, reducing overall costs, has all but disappeared.

### Microcomputer System

All the hardware required to produce a WP system can be purchased as separate modules. It is very much like the situation which existed a decade or so ago in the high fidelity field. Sound buffs who wanted systems which met their exact specifications would buy separate components—loudspeakers, turntables, receivers and so forth. When these were connected together, the overall system was expected to provide just the feature the buff desired. The problem lay not only in selecting the components so they would match but also in hooking the components together so that they would work properly.

It is the same case in the computer field. You can buy separate components. But will they match? And how do you put them together? And what if they don't work properly? Who is responsible then? Who is going to maintain and guarantee the equipment?

All the necessary components for a WP system are available from a different class of hardware vendors. Some are of the same quality as you find in the office system, but there is considerable variation in quality. They are lower in price. They are very reliable, but they do occasionally require maintenance.

Very few offices have gone in the direction of mixing components. Consultants who know how to select and purchase separate components and organizations who supply the equipment are not generally known in the office community, nor do they look for business there.

*Summary*

We restrict the rest of this book to WPs popular in the office and exclude, for the most part, mainframes, personal computers and intelligent typewriters. The programs to run the word processors that are available in the separate component field are in the forefront of design and will hold their own with any of the commercial vendors.

### Mainframes

Many larger offices which were the first to purchase word processing equipment were part of organizations that used large computers. All that computing power could have been brought to bear in the office. The problem was that the people needed to make the arrangements and select the equipment were missing. The data processing organization did not want to be bothered with the office people, and there was little conversation, if any, between the two parts of the big organization.

A computing facility has tremendous power. It also has considerable storage and probably a high speed, poor quality printer. What is needed to tie into such a facility is a terminal. A dumb terminal relies totally on the intelligence of its host, the central computer. A smart terminal provides some editing and format capability within its own box. A terminal can be hooked to the computer by wiring it in, hooking it into a local net or using telephone lines.

The trouble with using a centralized computing facility is manifold:

1. It breaks down.
2. During periods of high use, its response slows down. Sometimes you have to wait to connect up with and use the computer; then when you key data or commands at the terminal, it responds sluggishly.
3. The proper advice and help is not available to hook you in.
4. The printing is often at a different location, which is remote, and the printing may be of low quality.
5. The printing within your office may be slowed, if not impeded entirely, by the response time it receives from the central computer.
6. Most central sites are overloaded with EDP applications.

In the not too distant future it may be possible to take the best of the two worlds: to hook in completely independent word processing stations to the main computer facility and benefit from the power that it can provide and the data stored there and yet remain independent of it.

# I
# SYSTEM COMPONENTS

# 2
# The Computer System

**What is the computer system?**

A computer system consists of three things. First, there is the mechanical and electric equipment. It is tangible; it can be touched and seen and sometimes even smelled when an electric problem arises. It is called **hardware** in computer jargon, perhaps because of its tangibility.

The second component of a computer system consists of directions to the hardware telling it *exactly* what it is to do. These directions *are* the **program**. While it is running in the computer the program is not visible; it is less tangible than the hardware and hence is called **software**. Programs are written by **programmers** trained in this discipline. The program is specific to an application, making the computer behave as though it were designed to solve only a particular problem.

The third element of the system combines **people** and **procedures**. People operate terminals and keyboards and perform procedures to supply data to the computer system. The hardware, software, people and procedures should fit together to produce the information and communication needed in the office environment.

This chapter introduces the hardware and enables someone in a managerial position to understand the overall interaction of the components. With this background, a manager may then talk cogently to salespeople and engineers who wish to install or modify equipment in the office environment.

**A First View of Hardware**

Figure 2.0.1 illustrates the components which constitute most computer systems. A square box at the center represents the computer, often referred to as the **central processing unit** or, more briefly, the **CPU**. It is examined in Section 2.1.

At the left of the CPU is the **keyboard** where you enter data and commands for the computer. At the bottom of the figure is the **display**, with a screen where the computer presents information to the operator. This is the same kind of screen we are familiar with in the television set; it works differently when used with the computer, as described in Section 2.3.

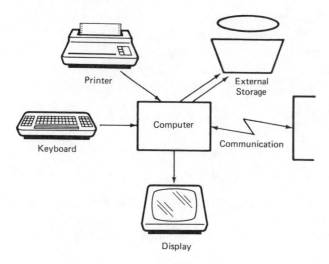

Figure 2.0.1. Components of the WP computer.

Sometimes a display and a keyboard are built into a single terminal. Although housed together, these units do not interact directly; each is connected separately to the computer. It seems as though what you key in is immediately displayed, but the data are actually first verified and accepted by the computer. You see *only* what the computer has accepted.

The **printer** (top) is a device to put the document on paper. Printer speeds vary considerably from a few characters a second to many pages per second for the very large and expensive computer systems. Most offices are concerned only with printers that produce high quality work for the least possible cost.

**External storage** (upper right) saves documents safely, even when the computer is turned off. In the past few years the cost of storing information on convenient magnetic disks has plummeted. Hundreds of thousands of characters can be stored on a disk that looks like a 45 rpm record and costs only a few dollars. It can store 50 to 100 pages of written material. A new set of documents is immediately available simply by changing disks. More about this later.

Today, several powerful computers not only serve our needs but they can also talk with each other to deliver messages, both written (electronic mail) and oral (electronic voice mail). Either cables or regular telephone lines connect computers together (lower right).

In Section 2.1 we look more closely at how the computer works. Keyboards are the topic of Section 2.2. Displays are then examined in Section 2.3. Section 2.4, which ends the chapter, is a discussion of telecommunication and an explanation of how computers talk to each other or to their components, whether near or far.

Printers appropriate to the office environment are covered in Chapter 3. Included there is a discussion of features which add to the power and flexibility of the WP. External storage is so important and so large a topic that all of Chapter 4 is devoted to it. Chapter 5 covers programs of all sorts.

## 2.1 THE CPU

The CPU in Figure 2.1.1 appears as the central cube to which several devices connect. Each device, display, keyboard, printer, etc., is shown as a trapezoid. The double line represents a cable, a number of wires which connects a device to the CPU.

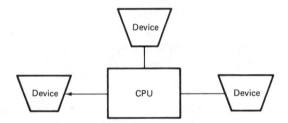

Figure 2.1.1. Devices connected to the CPU.

Figure 2.1.2 shows what is inside of the CPU:

- The memory stores information which is immediately available for use.
- The processor works on this information as directed by the program.
- The bus is a set of wire that interconnects all the units.

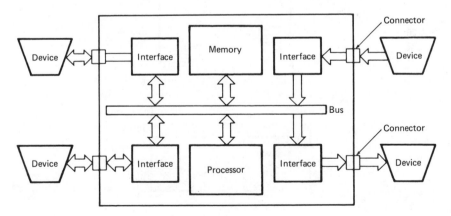

Figure 2.1.2. What's in the CPU.

• The interfaces connect the bus to an external receptacle into which a device cable is plugged.

### Data, Programs and Memory

Two kinds of things are stored in **memory**, the program and data (Figure 2.1.3). The **program** is directions to the computer about what actions to take. **Data** consists of letters and numbers to be processed by the computer.

*Data*

All data in the computer consists only of **0s** and **1s**, or states called **on** or **off**. These units of information are called **bits**, a contraction for binary digits. But the printed page has letters, numerals and punctuation on it. A sequence of bits, called a **code**, represents each input character on the keyboard. The number of bits in each code depends upon the number of characters in the **alphabet** incorporated into the computer by the manufacturer. For the WP system, each code usually consists of seven bits to provide 128 unique combinations.

The code is an assignment of a combination of bits to a character; viz., assign 1000001 to A. The collection of code assignments made to all characters in the alphabet is called a **code set**. There are several standard code sets. One of these, the American Standard Code for Information Interchange, or **ASCII** for short, uses seven bits. It is most often found in WP applications. Another code set that you might encounter is called **EBCDIC** for Extended Binary Coded Decimal Interchange Code.

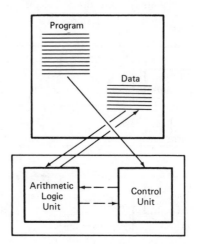

Figure 2.1.3. Program and data in memory.

Computers prefer to manipulate data in terms of 8 bits; that unit is called a **byte**. That's fine, because this leaves an extra bit for the ASCII code set to check the transfer of data and to make sure that a character code has not been altered improperly as it is moved about.

*The Program*

The program is held in memory. Figure 2.1.3 shows the program and data in memory, each with its own space. The computer gets it directions from the program area only. Should it stray and try to interpret the data as instructions, trouble is bound to arise. A further look at programs is postponed until Chapter 5.

*Memory*

Memory is rated in bytes—eight bits which hold a single character code. Since memories are large, we speak of **kilobytes**, kilo here meaning 1024, or approximately 1000. Thus 16K of memory means 16,384 bytes. Notes that a single spaced standard 8 1/2 by 11 inch page has about 3 to 4K bytes (letters and spaces) on it.

Memory comes in several forms:

**RAM** is **random access memory**. It can be read from or written into. The **access time** is the time to get at a piece of data; typical access time is 250 nanoseconds (billionths of a second). The memory is called "**random**" because any cell chosen at random can be accessed in this same time. Data or a program put in RAM, unless written over stays there as long as the power stays on. When the power is turned off, data and programs in RAM disappear. Hence, modern memory is called **volatile**.

**ROM** is **read-only memory**, which cannot be written into or modified except at the factory. But it is not volatile! Hence it is sometimes used to hold programs with the assurance that they will be there after the computer is turned on and off.

## The CPU

The CPU consists of two smaller units as shown at the bottom of the figure. At the left is the **arithmetic logic unit**, or simply **ALU**, which processes data when requested with arithmetic or editing operations; at the right is the **control unit**, which finds out what has to be done next by examining the program in memory.

*Control Unit*

The control unit reacts to the commands in the program by delegating them to other units to get the job done. A **command** is a request to move data about, do arithmetic or make a decision. Each command is obtained from memory sequentially. Getting a command is called **fetch**. The control unit figures out what must be done and then asks the ALU to do it. A typical command might *move* data from a keyboard memory area into the document work area. In this way an insertion is recorded in the document during editing. Sometimes a command in the program is directed to a device such as the printer or disk drive. For simplicity this is not shown in the figure.

Once the ALU (or a device) is delegated a request, it performs the action requested during the **execute** cycle. If data are required from memory, they are obtained as part of this cycle. The ALU (or device), when done, returns a signal to the control unit, indicating completion of its assignment. Now the control unit can fetch another command and delegate it as described.

### Interface Control

As the control unit scans the program for directions, it encounters requests for processing which it delegates to the ALU; requests to send data out or bring them in activate devices. All requests, data and directions for where they go are sent between units and devices on the bus. In some cases computing and input or output may take place simultaneously. However, for most small computers, processing is suspended while data come in or go out of the computer memory. Then when a device is done it simply returns a signal to the control unit to proceed with the next fetch cycle.

### What's Inside

Figure 2.1.4 shows a typical computer chasis, one made by Morrow Designs. At the bottom left is the disk drive mechanics—notice the drive door and the motors. At the left is the motherboard which contains common interface circuitry. At the back center are slots for printed circuit boards which optionally provide for more memory; another printer; a hard disk controller; and so forth. The power supply is inside left and connectors to devices are behind it.

## 2.2 KEYBOARDS

### Purpose

The **keyboard** is the only way to talk to the computer. You give all your directions from the keyboard. You also use it to key in the document and new text for insertion and modification.

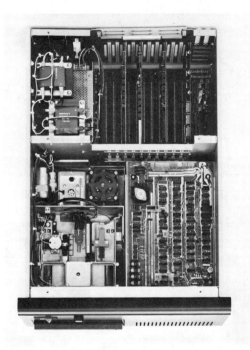

Figure 2.1.4. A typical computer with the case removed. (Courtesy of Morrow).

The computer manipulates data in bytes, sets of 8 bits; each byte represents one letter or number internally. The keyboard generates these bytes or codes as input. Each key, when pressed, produces a code which is passed onto the bus for the computer to acquire. Figure 2.2.1 shows the characters and their ASCII codes.

There are two keyboard design extremes: provide one key for each code, or 128 keys; provide two keys, one each for 1 and 0 and let the operator use eight key strokes for each character. Neither is desirable. The keyboard should be designed to make it easiest for the operator to use.

A glance at the ASCII code set of Figure 2.2.1 shows on the left a number of combinations labeled communication codes; there is no corresponding character on the printing device for this code. Therefore, each is also called a **nonprinting code**. Each serves an important use by representing operator requests which are then easily distinguishable from data.

A **control code** represents an operator request, not data. If it also represents a character, a conflict might easily arise. A control code is thus usually nonprinting.

| | | | | | | COMMUNICATION CODES | | PRINTABLE CHARACTERS | | | | | |
|---|---|---|---|---|---|---|---|---|---|---|---|---|---|
| b7 | | | | | | 0 | 0 | 0 | 0 | 1 | 1 | 1 | 1 |
| b6 | | | | | | 0 | 0 | 1 | 1 | 0 | 0 | 1 | 1 |
| b5 | | | | | | 0 | 1 | 0 | 1 | 0 | 1 | 0 | 1 |
| Bits b4 | b3 | b2 | b1 | Column → Row ↓ | | 0 | 1 | 2′ | 3 | 4 | 5 | 6 | 7 |
| 0 | 0 | 0 | 0 | 0 | | NUL | DLE | SP | 0 | @ | P | | p |
| 0 | 0 | 0 | 1 | 1 | | SOH | DC1 | ! | 1 | A | Q | a | q |
| 0 | 0 | 1 | 0 | 2 | | STX | DC2 | " | 2 | B | R | b | r |
| 0 | 0 | 1 | 1 | 3 | | ETX | DC3 | # | 3 | C | S | c | s |
| 0 | 1 | 0 | 0 | 4 | | EOT | DC4 | $ | 4 | D | T | d | t |
| 0 | 1 | 0 | 1 | 5 | | ENQ | NAK | % | 5 | E | U | e | u |
| 0 | 1 | 1 | 0 | 6 | | ACK | SYN | & | 6 | F | V | f | v |
| 0 | 1 | 1 | 1 | 7 | | BEL | ETB | ' | 7 | G | W | g | w |
| 1 | 0 | 0 | 0 | 8 | | BS | CAN | ( | 8 | H | X | h | x |
| 1 | 0 | 0 | 1 | 9 | | HT | EM | ) | 9 | I | Y | i | y |
| 1 | 0 | 1 | 0 | 10 | | LF | SUB | * | : | J | Z | j | z |
| 1 | 0 | 1 | 1 | 11 | | VT | ESC | + | ; | K | [ | k | { |
| 1 | 1 | 0 | 0 | 12 | | FF | FS | , | < | L | \ | l | : |
| 1 | 1 | 0 | 1 | 13 | | CR | GS | - | = | M | ] | m | } |
| 1 | 1 | 1 | 0 | 14 | | SO | RS | . | > | N | ˆ | n | ~ |
| 1 | 1 | 1 | 1 | 15 | | SI | US | / | ? | O | — | o | DEL |

Figure 2.2.1. ASCII code set.

### Keyboard Requirements

It is important *not* to confuse the keyboard with a **terminal** of which it may be a part. The terminal is a combination of two devices, one to send, such as the keyboard, and the other to receive, such as a one line crystal display or a display screen. When you use the terminal, the characters which you type immediately display on the screen, so there seems to be an interconnection. But there is actually no *direct* connection. As mentioned earlier, all characters entered at the keyboard go first to the computer before they are sent to the screen to display. This is important to realize.

The essential requirement for the keyboard is that when you strike a key, the 8 bit code for the character engraved on the key top is transmitted to the computer. Shift and control keys multiply the number of codes produced.

There are several other characteristics of the keyboard which we investigate:

- keys and key placement,
- control keys and control information,
- rollover.

### Keys and Key Placement

Alphanumeric keys, namely, the letters and numerals, have an established place on the typewriter which is carried over to the computer input keyboard. That is, the numbers appear in order in the first row: 1, 2, 3 . . .; the next row has the letters q, w, e, r, . . .; and so forth. These positions are maintained to achieve transfer of training from the typewriter.

Manufacturers, occasionally make changes, especially in the personal computer field, with regard to the position of punctuation and special symbols. Thus for some keyboards such things as the colon, exclamation point, etc., may turn up in odd places. This detracts from the transfer of training and lowers your speed initially. Key placement for the office WP keyboard is standard except for additional function keys, i.e., delete, etc.

The position in which a key appears, its distance from its neighbors, the tilt of the keyboard and its feel are all important. These vary from one keyboard to the next; the most preferred keyboard is closest in appearance and feel to the common typewriter. Because of similarity of arrangement, touch, appearance and sound some are called "Selectric" keyboards.

*Alternatives*

Keyboard layout depends on what key appears on the keyboard. Figure 2.2.2 shows one generalized scheme; shaded areas are for additional keys which do not appear on all keyboards. Figure 2.2.3 shows the keyboard arrangment for the Wang Office Systems series. Figures 2.2.4 and 2.2.5 show VDTs furnished respectively by Lexitron and Royal.

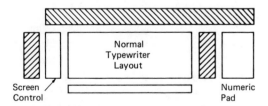

Figure 2.2.2. Typical WP keyboard layout.

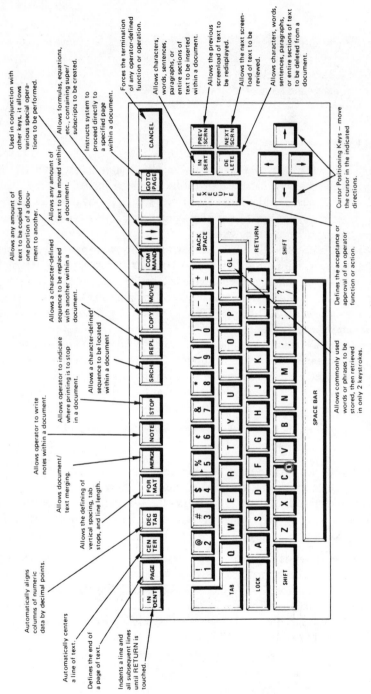

Figure 2.2.3. Keyboard layout for the Wang Office System. (Courtesy of Wang).

32

Figure 2.2.4. The Lexitron VDT. (Courtesy of Lexitron).

Figure 2.2.6 shows a VDT manufactured by Ann Arbor Terminals. It has a detachable and movable keyboard. This type of VDT might be used in a more expensive personal computer.

### Shift

Typewriters have a shift key and a shift lock. On a manual typewriter the **shift key** (designated <u>shift</u> here after) actually shifts the carriage up vertically so that a different part of the type bar—the part with the upper case letter—hits the paper. When the shift key is pressed along with a character key, the computer keyboard generates the code for the uppercase character. When there are two symbols, such as punctuation, on the same key, depressing the shift key at the same time sends the code for the upper symbol to the computer. The **shift-lock** on the conventional typewriter, once set, causes all keys which are pressed to print as when the shift key is also pressed. The WP keyboard also has a shift lock.

Figure 2.2.5. The Royal VDT. (Courtesy of Royal).

*Alpha Lock*

A computer keyboard used for entering programs works in a slightly different way, using the **alpha-lock**. When it is set, all letter keys produce uppercase character codes. However, the numerical and punctuation keys are not affected. The computer then receives a mixture of uppercase and numerical codes and whatever symbols are found in the lower part of punctuation keys. The shift key *still works* to change numerals to symbols, etc. The purchaser of a WP system which uses a personal computer should know whether he is getting a shift lock, an alpha lock or perhaps something different. However, for commercial word processing systems the shift lock is standard.

**Standard, Nonprinting and Control Codes**

Several keys on the WP keyboard have no corresponding symbols on the printer or typewriter. The number and function of these keys vary from one keyboard

Figure 2.2.6. The Ann Arbor terminal. (Courtesy of Ann Arbor).

design to another. Here is a list of four types of control keys with examples of each:

| | |
|---|---|
| Typewriter oriented | return |
| | tab |
| | rub |
| Screen oriented | clear |
| | home |
| | break |
| Special multiplier | control or code |
| | escape |
| | command |
| Editing | delete |
| | insert, etc. |

Names for keys appear underlined throughout the text.

Return, tab and rub perform mechanical or electrical functions on the type-writer. For the WP keyboard, each of these keys produces a code sent to the computer to inform the WP program, respectively, that you have finished a paragraph or wish to tab or backspace.

Screen-oriented commands keys produce codes which the program interprets in connection with the display. Clear (not on most WPs) causes the screen to go blank; home moves the entry point for data and the cursor as described in Section 6.3; break creates a communication code.

### Control Keys

Some keys do not produce a printing character code; instead, they produce a control code—a single nonprinting code (there is no character at the printer corresponding to this code). A control code is really a command to the WP: it tells the (WP) program what to do; it is not data.

You are concerned with how easy it is to tell the WP what to do. One way provides a separate key for each function you might need (function key). But the sophisticated WP provides so many functions that the keyboard would have to triple in size.

Another approach is to have a multiplier key (code or control). Hit this key in conjunction with one (or more) conventional (alphanumeric) key and you give a command. Which command you give depends on that extra letter(s). And that's the catch. You have to remember which letter or number is associated with which functions. Some WPs inscribe the *additional* function on the skirt of the key. Thus if code d means "delete," the word "delete" is on the vertical wall of the key facing you called the **skirt**. (It may be hard to see.)

A combination is most popular. Assign individual keys to frequent functions such as delete, insert, page, etc. Use control combinations for the others.

Let us take a closer look at control codes. Several types of control codes and the way that they are produced deserve attention:

- **Universal keys** appear on *most* keyboards and produce a fixed code.
- **Function keys** unique to a vendor's keyboard produce its control codes. codes.
- **Programmable function keys** on commercial keyboards are set to a particular code by software or mechanical adjustment of the keyboard.
- A **control key** or **code key** may be pressed *with* another key to create a control code.
- A **program key** produces a sequence of codes.

*Universal Keys*

An example of a universal key is <u>rub</u>. The WP has no carriage to move backward. When you hit <u>rub</u>, the WP program removes a character from the text you are editing and shows this on the screen. (See *backspace correction.*) Rub produces a universal (nonprinting) code. When the WP program gets this code, the action it takes depends on the WP system design.

Some keys communicate functions desired by the user to the program; hence the name function key. Each key carries a label in full or abbreviated such as <u>delete</u>, <u>word</u> or <u>para</u> (for paragraph), making evident its representation. It generates a control code; there is *no* standard for these codes; vendors use different bytes for the same purpose. We use italics to represent function codes and underlines for function keys: when you press <u>delete</u> you generate *delete* (a code for "delete" for this WP).

*Programmable Keys*

Some keyboards on VDTs of mainframe terminals and personal computers have a row of unmarked keys at the top. These may be labeled as required by an application program. By setting switches or using some other technique, the bits or code generated when this key is pressed are then set into the keyboard. Labels may be prepared and pasted on each key to remind you of their function.

*Control Keys*

Many keyboards have a key labeled <u>control</u>, which multiplies the action of the other keys similarly to the shift key. On some WPs this is labeled <u>code</u>. It is sometimes indicated in this book with the character ^ . It works in *one* of two ways, depending on the vendor's design:

- as a multiplier, like <u>shift</u>,
- as a prefix to a control sequence.

*Multiplier*

Here <u>code</u> produces no code when hit alone; if it is pressed along with one letter or symbol key, a control code is generated.

For example, consider the h key.

- <u>h</u> alone produces the code for h;
- <u>shift h</u> produces the code for H;
- <u>code h</u> produces a control code different from the code for h or H.

You may wonder if there is a fourth case—what happens for code shift h? This requires some finger acrobatics and is not considered legal for most WPs. CPT (a WP vendor) uses three keys for subscripts and superscripts. Press control shift 0 to start a superscript.

Just as the shift key doubles the number of unique codes the keyboard generates, the control key changes this to a factor of 3 (or sometimes 4). That is, one key can produce four codes; one each when it is pressed:

- alone,
- with the shift key,
- with the control key,
- with both shift and control.

*Code as a Prefix*

Other WPs use code in a different way; you convey some commands with a sequence of key strokes, only the first of which is code. For Syntrex, you inform the WP program to "undo" the last activity with code 2 and to put a page break in the text with code p. Code says that what comes next is a command. The program expects a symbol after it receives code.

Thus code alerts the program that at least one more character is forthcoming. Some WPs follow code or the like with several keystrokes for a long command. For example, one way to mark an area for editing is to press mark followed by strokes that state what is to be marked. Press mark and follow it by one (or more) word stroke to mark a block of several words. This produces one code for mark and one for each word.

*Combination*

Most WPs use a combination of these techniques:

- a typewriter keyboard for alphanumerics,
- function keys for frequent edit requests,
- code or control as a multiplier or a prefix (not both) for less-frequent action requests.

**Rollover**

A keyboard should provide a unique code whenever the operator presses a single key. But the operator is human and potentially fallible. What if more than one key is pressed or if a second is pressed before the first is released? How should the keyboard respond?

Unless the keyboard is specially designed, pressing two keys produces a code different from what is expected from either. This is not acceptable. The solution is called **rollover**, which works as follows. When two keys are pressed, one after the other, nothing happens until one of them is released. The keyboard generates the code for the key released first. When the next key is released, its code is generated. This is an effective solution for an important problem.

Occasionally three or more keys may be pressed at the same time. Some keyboards handle this case too. The solution is called **multikey rollover**. A code is produced as each key is *released*. Hence, if several keys are pressed, codes are produced only as each successive key is released. The manufacturer may or may not specify the maximum number of keys for which the multikey rollover applies. It is up to the purchaser to find out this information.

## 2.3 DISPLAYS

### Physical Appearance

The display consists of a **cathode ray tube (CRT)** such as in the home TV and the associated electronics in a neat housing, such as that shown in Figure 2.2.2. The visible portion of the CRT is referred to as the **screen**. The effectiveness of the display depends to a large extent on the physical appearance of the CRT as well as the characters look. You may spend many hours at the terminal—the display and the keyboard—so it is important that you are comfortable and content with the physical surroundings.

The description which follows considers the qualitative rather than the quantitative aspects of the display.

### Size and Shape

Standard CRTs are rated according to their diagonal size—the distance along the diagonal from one corner to the other. There is a standard **aspect ratio**—the ratio of height to width—which is usually about 3 to 4. The common TV CRT is rectangular, with the width being greater than the height—just the opposite of the conventional page.

CRTs are manufactured with a diagonal size anywhere from 3 to 26 inches. The former is tiny and useful only in portable TVs that you would take to the seashore; the latter is immense and may be found in a luxury living room as an impressive TV console. CRTs in computer displays range from 8 to 15 inches in diagonal size. Most commonly they are 10 or 12 inches. The size of the characters depends on the overall size of the screen. It is easier to read text on a 15 inch screen than on a 10 inch one.

Because of its aspect ratio, only a portion of the page can be displayed on the *standard* CRT. Even if it is turned on its side, it does not provide the proper height for the desired width. Still, many WPs use them for the sake of economy.

Some displays present a full page at once. Special CRTs are made to order to provide this function. This adds to the WP cost but provides a more realistic display. Other displays provide more width, so that you can see all 132 characters of a computer printout or a wide page at once.

*Phosphor*

The beam of electrons produced within the CRT is directed by the electronics to hit the screen at a spot which then glows and emits light. The inner surface of the glass is coated with a **phosphor** which **fluoresces** (emits light) when the electron beam hits it. The light produced is monochromatic (is a single color). The color may be green, blue or orange, or phosphors may be mixed to produce a white light. Opinions differ about which is the most pleasant phosphor. Studies have been conducted, but preference is still a matter of opinion.

Besides color, another quality of the phosphor is **persistence**. After the beam of electrons is turned off, the spot continues to emit light for a period of time. For a **low persistence** phosphor, it is impossible for the human to detect the short period for which the light continues to be emitted (the spot seems to disappear immediately). For a **high persistence** phosphor, the spot may continue to emit light for minutes or even hours. Thus, it would be impossible to change the display immediately. Hence, we do not see high persistence phosphor in office applications.

Though very low persistence phosphors are useful in some kinds of work, we do prefer the light to continue for several milliseconds so that the operator does not see any flicker (still classified as a low persistence).

The image of the text is projected on the screen like a movie at the movie house. It is made by projecting many almost-identical frames. If the rate is too slow, the result is annoying flicker and perceptible changes in brightness, which can make some people jittery. This can be cured by increasing the rate only slightly or increasing the number of frames per second. Unfortunately, both increase the cost of the display.

*Other Factors*

There are other factors to be considered in selecting a display, some of which include:

- A movable and adjustable display can suit operators of different heights.
- A display that tilts also accommodates to the physique of the operator.

- Brightness and contrast should be adjustable to the operator's preference (as on your home TV).
- Treating the outside of the CRT with a special compound or adding a light filter can reduce glare considerably.

*Black on White*

Some vendors contend that since black print on white paper is what we are used to, the display should and does conform to this. Studies seem to show that there is a benefit to black print on a white background. Hence, for example, CPT makes the CRT background white and the letters black as though you are dealing with white paper and black print. Most vendors supply the conventional terminal, where white or colored letters appear on a black background. A few vendors let you choose either alternative.

**Display Layout**

Figure 2.3.1 shows a typical CRT screen layout. For discussion, the screen is broken up into horizontal rectangular **rows**. It is also broken up into vertical rectangular areas, called **columns**. Where a row and a column intersect is a **cell**, one of the places on the screen where a letter or a character may be displayed. The **capacity** of the screen is the number of cells resulting from this division; it is the number of rows times the number of columns.

Small personal microcomputer systems sometimes provide displays with a capacity of 16 × 60 (16 lines of 60 characters). This is too small for the office environment. A more-standard screen capacity is 24 × 80. About the right width for most documents is 80 columns. A standard 8 1/2 × 11 inch sheet of paper at 10 characters per inch would be 85 characters wide without any margins. With

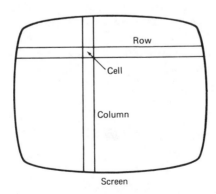

Figure 2.3.1. The display screen.

a 1 inch margin, we get 65 characters or columns per line, so 24 rows provides for about 1/3 to 1/2 a page. Although many word processors have this restriction, vendors claim that this is all the text that you need to see as you enter and edit material.

When the layout of a page is important, you might need to see a complete page displayed on the screen. Therefore, some word processing systems provide a 66 X 80 format.

Furthermore, displays sometimes provide one or two extra lines at the top or bottom of the screen to display control and status information. Therefore, other screen sizes are 25 X 80, 68 X 80 and 68 X 102. Xerox 8010 (Star), Vydec 2400 (not in production) and the Lexitron 1300 use double-page screens.

*Two Sizes*

The biggest problem encountered with the full page screen is that the characters are small; but with the partial screen, where the letters show up well enough, you can't see what the page looks like. Why not have two character sizes and get the advantages of both with the defects of neither?

The Xerox 860 has a full page screen, but you can magnify a portion of the text. When you start editing, you get a format menu where you can elect:

**zoom line**, which doubles the size of the line containing the cursor, the one you are working on;

**zoom screen**, which doubles the size of all text displayed but limits the displayed portion (containing the cursor.)

Should you wish to change the character size of the displayed text at any time, press format. The format menu returns to the screen and you can make a new choice.

The Lexitron 1303 has a partial page display. If you want to see the makeup of a page press full-page; the screen shows in miniature what you will get. You see how the text will appear when printed; you can *almost* read it (it is small)! But it effectively allows you to alter the appearance of the page. When done, press full-page again and full size characters return.

**The Cell**

A cell is the small area in which a character may appear. The character may be formed in two ways:

- a matrix of dots,
- a set of strokes.

When a number of small dots are placed close together in the cell, this array of dots, called the **dot matrix**, produces a clearly recognizable character. This method, to which we give full attention, is most pervasive in WP systems.

Another technique puts a number of **strokes** (line segments) into the cell to compose the letter. It is still used for **graphic displays**, putting sketches and graphs on the screen, in personal and large scale computers, but it is out of favor for WP systems.

Dot matrix definition, the presence of detail in the letters, is determined by numbers—the number of horizontal dots and the number of vertical dots in each cell. Typical dot matrix sizes are 5 X 7 (5 dots long by 7 dots high), 7 X 9, 7 X 11 and 9 X 14. The larger matrix size provides more detail in the letter on the screen. For simplicity below, we examine only the 5 X 7 matrix.

The matrix is composed of a grid of horizontal and vertical lines; a dot may or may not appear at the intersection of any two lines. If a dot appears, it is referred to as a **dot**; if no dot appears at the intersection of a horizontal and vertical line, I sometimes call this an **undot**. Hence, the letter is composed of dots and undots.

Now let us look at one cell on the screen. Where a horizontal line intersects a vertical line, we find a **spot**. The electron beam is turned on at this spot to create a dot of light; the beam may be turned off to create an undot (no light).

The electron beam sweeps out each line of the cell and is turned on or off as it reaches each spot to create the dots and undots which make up a letter. The motion of the beam as it sweeps over the *entire* screen is called a **scan**.

At the left of Figure 2.3.2 we see a 5 X 7 grid and dots and undots which make up the letter E.

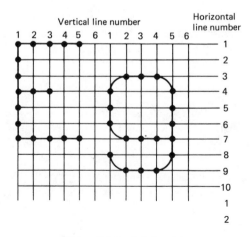

Figure 2.3.2. A dot matrix.

*The Character*

Some displays and printers put all letters, whether lowercase or uppercase, within a rectangular boundary. Some lowercase letters do not look right when displayed this way. Part of the letter should go below the imaginary line upon which the letter sits. The part of the lowercase letter (such as "p" or "g") which goes below the line is called a **descender**. To include the descender, the matrix has to be lengthened somewhat. A 5 × 7 matrix actually consists of 10 horizontal lines, as shown on the right on Figure 2.3.2. The top seven lines are for uppercase letters and lowercase letters that have no descenders. Two additional lines are for the descender; the tenth line separates the bottom of characters in one row from the top of characters in the next successive row. All office WP displays and printers show good quality characters with descenders.

### Display Memory

Built into the display is a **display memory** which holds 1 byte (8 bits) for one character code for each cell on the screen. The standard display with 24 rows of 80 characters uses 1,920 bytes of memory. When the display is turned on, each byte of display memory is set to the null code; for the null character, no dots display; hence the display appears blank.

The computer transmits a character to the display by sending over the code for that character. These codes are placed into successive positions of display memory. In most cases, display memory is loaded sequentially, as the discussion below reveals.

*Cursor*

The **cursor** is a distinguishing mark which appears on the display to show the operator the next position in the text where a character entered on the keyboard will be placed. Several ways to show this are:

- an underline,
- a rectangle with reverse video,
- a blinking character (which may be underlined) or a blinking underline or rectangle.

Sometimes the cursor appears superimposed over a character. As you enter text, the cursor moves to the next (blank) position on the screen. When you edit text, you move the cursor into existing text and usually on top of an existing character. Reverse video shows the cursor position clearly, but does not obliterate the letter it sits on. The white rectangle would blot out the character entirely if it were not for **reverse video**, which makes the square appear white and the character within it black. Some displays let you choose from these methods how you want the cursor to appear.

Reverse video displays a black character on white where the cursor is positioned by reversing foreground and background. Suppose that the dot matrix for each character stores 1s and 0s for white and black, respectively, on a black background. To get reverse video, the display electronics simply changes the meaning of the bits: use 1 for black and 0 for white now. The space between letters is also 0 for white in the black-on-white display.

As described, reverse video applied to a black-on-white presentation achieves a similar effect. Here the cursor shows a character as a white on black.

## Display Procedure

Displays commonly employ low persistence CRTs. Characters written on the display fade in a fraction of a second. To maintain the text on the screen, all characters must be **refreshed**, that is, rewritten many times a second. The common rate is 60 times a second. This is easy to achieve, since it is the same frequency as that used for the common ac plug available in the home or office. This is well past the flicker rate, so that you cannot see a character being rewritten, even when a new character takes its place.

When the screen is refreshed, it is always rewritten in the same order. The scan starts at the upper left-hand corner and writes all the characters in the first row in sequence; the scan continues thus until the whole screen is written and then starts all over again.

The center of Figure 2.3.3 shows display memory for the standard display with 24 rows of 80 characters. Each memory position contains the 8-bit code for the character which should appear in the corresponding position on the screen. Where blank space appears on the screen, (between words and at the end of the last line in a paragraph), nulls are recorded in display memory.

During the scan, a display counter keeps track of the position of the cell where a character should next appear. This same pointer therefore records the position in display memory where the character code is stored. As the scan reaches each cell, the display memory is consulted and the character code is brought forth.

Now the character is created on the screen in the cell where it belongs: dots and undots are placed into the right positions so as to light up the screen in the form of the desired letter.

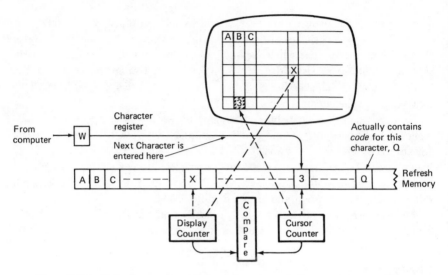

Figure 2.3.3. Refresh memory contains a character code for every screen position.

### Creating a Character

This description is actually oversimplified. Characters are not displayed a cell at a time. Instead, one line segment from each character in each cell of the row is written all the way across the screen. A **scan line** is one complete horizontal beam motion across the screen from the extreme left to the right. The top portion of all the 80 characters in one row is written as the first scan line of that row. Then the beam goes back and writes the second line segment for each of the 80 characters; this continues for all 10 scan lines of the row (the last line being blank). Although the latter description is accurate, it is complicated and not really necessary to understand the overall operation of the display.

### Cursor Position

The cursor is presented to the operator by one of the techniques mentioned earlier. The **cursor counter** records the position of the cursor relative to display memory and corresponding to its row and column. During each refresh cycle, but before each character is presented on the screen, the display counter is incremented by 1 and then compared with the cursor counter. When the two are equal, this position should display the cursor.

The display notes that the counters contain the same quantity and alters the screen so that the cursor appears as:

- an *underline,* to display the character as usual but add a horizontal segment in the eighth line;
- *reverse video,* to interpret 0s and 1s from the character generator for each horizontal line segment of the character as 1s and 0s, respectively, so that black and white are reversed;
- as a *blink* to cause the character (or underline) to appear for some number of cycles (typically 60 cycles, or 1 second) and disappear for another such set of cycles.

## Entering Data

When you hit a key at the keyboard to enter a character, that character code is transmitted to the computer. If this is a data code during a data input sequence, the program should display it on the screen. That same code is then transmitted by the WP program to the display. The display receives the character and enters it into the **character register** at the upper left of Figure 2.3.3. The character remains there until it is needed. The code in the character register enters display memory and is simultaneously displayed on the screen, but only when the cell pointed to by the cursor counter is reached by the scan.

In Figure 2.3.3 the code for *M* is currently stored in the character register. The display counter is at that portion of the scan where *X* is being displayed. The scan continues until the display counter and the cursor counter are equal. This represents the position on the screen where the *M* should be shown. Display memory is also addressed at that position. Now the code from the character register is entered into display memory and is also displayed on the screen.

Thereafter the cursor counter is advanced by one position and a **flag**, a hardware indicator, is set to tell the computer that a new character may be sent to the character register of the display if the computer should wish to do so.

## Cursor Movement

Cursor positioning is requested at most keyboards using keys marked with arrows: up, down, left and right. (Other alternatives are described in Section 6.3.) When you press an arrow key, a control code goes to the computer. The keyboard passes the code to the WP program, which takes note that a directional cursor key was pressed. The WP program then calculates the new position of the cursor, which is now transmitted to the display along with a control signal to distinguish the position from data. The display picks up this position and enters it into the cursor counter.

Thus, each times the left arrow on the keyboard is pressed, a control code is sent to the WP program, which decrements the position counter that the WP program keeps. The new cursor counter position is sent to the display to the cursor counter. Pressing the up arrow decrements the counter's position by 80 instead of 1.

It is common during editing to move the cursor along from one end of the text to the other, making changes as you go. A character entered at the terminal when you stop the cursor is picked up by the program and put into the text in memory at a position corresponding to the cursor position. The character code is also transmitted to the display, which enters the code into the display memory at the cursor position. In this way a single character may be altered in the middle of the text. The rest of the text remains unchanged. The cursor advances one position because the cursor counter has been incremented.

If data update were done directly at the display without a signal going to the computer, then the WP program would not record the new cursor position. Data entered thereafter would be recorded as being elsewhere, and things would really get messed up.

## Fonts and Alphabets

The pattern for each character of the available alphabet is stored in a ROM called the character generator. For the more elaborate displays, such as that on the Xerox STAR, there are several different fonts provided. Each has its own ROM character generator. The WP program sends a signal to the display to switch form on font to the next. This activates another ROM.

This is only worthwhile in a more expensive display with electronics that provides more lines per screen and hence more detail in each letter. Very little detail results from the 5 X 7 matrix; at least 10 X 14 is needed to make multiple fonts distinguishable.

*Graphics*

A code for which there is no character on the printer is a nonprinting character. This code may call forth a pattern from the character generator. When this pattern does not correspond to a letter, number or punctuation mark, it is called a **graphic**; a triangle, square, circle or other geometric pattern is a common graphic.

Graphics are often used by the WP program to show special functions you have called for, such as <u>return</u>, the boldface prefix, sub- and superscripts and so forth. You also find them as switch codes and other special functions. The graphic must be built into the ROM to display; if there are several ROMs, all must include the graphic patterns.

*Emphasis*

You can get emphasis with italics, boldface, underscore or a different font. A separate ROM generator is used. The WP program switches ROMs in the terminal by sending a control signal or control sequence. This would be of little use if the printer cannot later be set to print in this form.

*Size*

Magnifying or reducing the size of the characters in the display is most easily achieved by switching to a different character generator. This also changes the size of the dot matrix used and alters the number of rows on the screen, using more or less lines per row. Magnified letters use more lines per row and show more detail; reduced letter use fewer lines per row and show little detail.

**Other Functions**

Your word processing display may be able to provide many other functions. Some of these require the display to show two or more kinds of data such as:

- a **split screen**, which enables you to view two electronic documents at once and move information from one to the other;

- a **menu**, which provides you with a choice of alternative functions to request;
- a **status line**, which shows the document name, page number, line number, character number on the line and other parameters, etc.
- a **typing ruler**, which shows the margins and tab stops.

These functions seem to be provided by the display. They are not! Except for the split screen, they depend entirely on the program which is currently in the computer. This section describes only the facilities provided within a display; other facilities are implemented in the WP program and are invoked from the keyboard, only later to be presented in an altered display.

## 2.4 COMMUNICATION

**Need**

For a small office, a small stand-alone WP suffices. Shared resource or shared logic with a number of work stations is viable in a medium-sized office. For a large office, it may be useful to have several systems which can converse. A company with two or more branches might want their WPs to communicate. For all but the smallest facility, communication is an important consideration.

Communication is also a necessity within the computer system. At the lowest level, it takes place between the components which constitute the computer. When a computer component is given additional capability and "intelligence," it is sometimes able to operate on its own for a period of time. Then, after collecting, editing and formatting information, a component, such as a terminal, communicates to supply the central computer with what it has collected and to get new directions about how to continue.

More complex systems consist of several computers. One—named the **host**, or **master** computer—is usually in command of the situation. Other computers—known as **satellites**, or **slaves**—report to it. Again, there is a need for the host to talk to its satellites and for them to talk to it.

Finally, where a number of computers are equal in status, such as communicating WPs, we call them **peer** computers. When any two of the computers can talk to each other, this is called **networking**.

This is the case with communicating word processors. They could be used to pass about small or large chunks of text. In the former case, with many WPs participating, we have the makings of an electronic mail system; in the latter, a document exchange.

### Distance

The way that components are connected depends upon the distance separating them. We distinguish three degrees of distance and discuss communication in the section according to distance:

- a few feet;
- within the same office or building for distances up to a few hundred feet;
- long distances, perhaps over public telephone lines.

*Method*

The simplest way that data flows between components is by a direct connection—wires pass between them. A character or symbol is represented by a code: the aggregate of bits which compose the code is a byte. When a separate wire is furnished for each bit of the byte, there is **parallel** transmission. If we convert each byte into a series of bits so as to transmit 1 bit at a time sequentially on a single pair of wires, we have **serial** transmission. Although bits are transmitted one at a time, which is slower, only two wires connect the components.

When the transmission distance is long, conditioned cables with amplifiers connect the components. An alternative connection is by private lines which pass around an office or building. Finally, there is the public carrier, or telephone line.

### Short Distance

Only a few feet separate components in the typical WP system. The terminal may be on top of a desk, with the computer underneath the desk or in a different box. A number of signals pass in parallel between the two. A cable, consisting of separate wire for each signal is acceptable for distances of up to about 10 feet.

When components are separated by greater distances, even though they are still in the same general area, a simple cable is no longer viable. The signals are degraded by the resistance of the wire and become susceptible to all kinds of electronic and magnetic noise present in most office settings.

One solution provides an amplifier for each wire to increase the size of each signal. Each may travel unmolested through the noisy environment. But this is costly.

Another solution **serializes** the signals, that is, converts them from parallel to serial form. Then only two wires are needed to carry them. A single amplifier suffices to provide noise immunity. This arrangement is shown in Figure 2.4.1. The receiving equipment reconverts the serial signals back to parallel form using

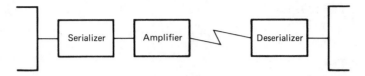

Figure 2.4.1. Serialize, amplify and deserialize as required for communication.

a **deserializer**. If signals pass in both directions, then amplifiers are required at both ends of the line. Also, each end must have its own serializer and deserializer.

### Medium Distance

Consider data transmission among components or computers in a large office or building. Although slow communication is tolerable between a computer and a component such as a terminal, computers should talk to each other more rapidly. The technique described for short distances is not satisfactory at faster rates. It is necessary to serialize the signals or to use other techniques, but transmission must take place rapidly and over a special line.

Medium distance transmission lines comprise **local networks** which are not standardized. One example is the Ethernet, marketed by Xerox. Transmission uses a coaxial cable. Each computer or component is hooked into the line through a **gateway**. When the cable is not busy with a message, a transmitting station may send a message which bears the identity of the would-be receiver. The message is placed on the line and is available to all other stations attached to it. However, like a party-line telephone, only the intended receiver picks up the phone and accepts the message. This is illustrated in Figure 2.4.2.

Should a sender have a message while the line is in use, the gateway puts the sender on hold until the line becomes clear. Then the line becomes available to requesting users on a priority basis. This system is suitable for distances up

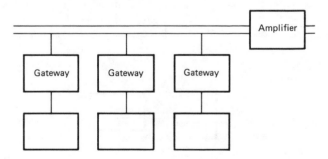

Figure 2.4.2. Local network such as Ethernet.

to about a mile. It is also possible to add an amplifier, as shown in the figure, to double or triple this distance.

### Long Distance

It is possible to transmit data around the world using telephone and microwave lines, optical fibers and satellites. Communication is a study unto itself, so this discussion is necessarily brief. One generalization is possible though: communication over distance uses serial signals.

**Line capacity** is the rate at which information is transmitted; greater capacity costs more. To transmit large amounts of information fast requires expensive lines, such as the coaxial cable used for television. Given its high cost, these lines are used only in special cases.

At the other end of the spectrum we find telephone lines, which cost the same whether they carry voice or digital communication. Line capacity is limited to a few hundred characters per second.

*Conversion*

Telephone lines do not carry on/off, or binary, information directly. One technique converts binary information into the presence or absence of a tone. But when no tone is present, the line is susceptible to noise. Hence, a better method employs two tones: one tone stands for a 1; the other stands for 0.

Figure 2.4.3 shows the equipment required to tie into a telephone line. The computer produces data in parallel form. This goes to a serializer which converts the data to a series of 0s and 1s. This passes to a **modem**, a device which converts pulses into one or another tone of a tone pair. Electrical engineers call this con-

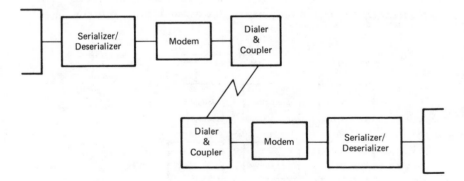

Figure 2.4.3. Typical communication hardware requirement.

version **modulation**. The opposite action of converting tones into bits is **demodulation**. Modem is a contraction for modulator-demodulator. The final box in the figure shows the dialer and the coupling from the transmitter to the telephone line.

When a terminal and a computer or two computers talk, it is most convenient for them to be able to talk and answer simultaneously. One pair of transmission lines is used in each direction (call them A and B): one talks on A and listens on B; the other computer talks on B and listens on A. This is called **full duplex**.

Sometimes a terminal and a computer can manage with a single line. One talks and the other listens until such time as the roles reverse. Then one computer switches the hardware around. This is called **half duplex**.

Full-duplex operation with a *single* pair of wire lines is possible and most common: *two pairs* of tones are provided. Before communication begins, you decide which tone pair is used at each station. The station which uses the lower-frequency pair is in **originate mode**. The other station is in **answer mode**. The tones used are standard:

- The low frequency pair operates at 1270 Hertz for mark and 1070 Hertz for space.
- The high frequency pair is 2225 Hertz for mark and 2025 for space.

**Mark** is communication jargon for on, while **space** means off. Once the *mode* is set, the hardware reacts as required without the need to reset it when the transmission direction is changed.

In a **dial-up** network, there is one host computer which one of the many remote users may dial into via the telephone. It is customary for the remote user to be in originate mode. It is less expensive to get a modem which accommodates only one mode. For only a slightly higher cost, one can get a switchable modem.

### Rates

The rate at which data are sent or received is given as bits per second (**bps**). Another common term in communication circles is the **baud**, the number of marks and spaces per second. In the **synchronous** case, bps and bauds are the same. Bits of the characters are sent at fixed time intervals, in accordance with a clock. This is common when two computers talk to each other.

When data is generated by a human operator at a keyboard, key strokes occur irregularly and additional pulses are required to indicate the start and end of a character. This is called **asynchronous** communication and here 1200 baud may be equivalent to 900 or even 600 bps.

It is important that data sent are received accurately. Various techniques are used to ensure this. One of them is called **parity**. An additional bit is appended to each byte so that the number of 1s is always odd (or even, whichever the rule is). Upon receipt, each character is checked to make sure that its code contains an odd number of 1s. All characters received are so checked.

Another technique, called **check sum**, verifies the accuracy of a group of characters. A check sum is calculated as the data are transmitted; it is calculated at the other end as the data are received. Then the first check sum is transmitted and should agree with that calculated on the *receive* end, or else retransmission is requested.

### Protocol

For two systems to talk with each other, each must follow a correct sequence of steps that the other is acquainted with and verifies. This is called a **protocol**. It assures not only that data are transmitted correctly, but also that they are interpreted properly. Several transmission protocols are described in the literature, but there is no single standard.

A protocol assures that a block which contains an error is retransmitted so that eventually a correct transmission is assured—not withstanding hardware failure.

# 3
# Printers

### 3.0 INTRODUCTION

The printer creates the printed document. We discuss four kinds of printers important to WP in Section 3.1 and also take a look at new technology of emerging importance. Then we examine how the printer puts the characters on the paper in Section 3.2. This determines how the WP program can provide the desired format upon the document. One such format requirement is *justification* which we explain in Section 3.3. We look at other format features in Section 3.4. Section 3.5 examines automatic single-sheet paper feeds. Bear in mind that this chapter examines only *hardware*. WP programs to format and print are covered in Chapter 7.

### 3.1 TYPES OF PRINTERS

Seven types of printers generally encountered in the office environment are:

1. the augmented electric typewriter,
2. the dot matrix printer,
3. the daisy wheel and thimble printers,
4. the laser printer,
5. the ink jet printer,
6. the electrostatic printer and
7. the line printer.

These are introduced briefly and then each is described in more detail.

The earliest printers used for automating the office were based on the electric typewriter. In the typewriter's original form, the operator hit a key to activate a mechanism which was electrically propelled to cause printing. To make this usable for word processing, a computer is interposed between the keyboard and the printing mechanism. The electric typewriter was designed for an operator whose maximum speed never exceeded 15 characters per second. This is the limit for the output rate of the typewriter even when it is computer-driven.

The dot matrix printer is important because of its relatively high speed obtained at a rather low cost. It prints at rates from 40 to 500 characters per second and costs between $600 and $3500. Until recently, its print quality was low, so it appeared to be acceptable only for drafts in some offices. Higher quality is available now, and the acceptability of less well-formed characters will depend on the trade offs.

The daisy wheel printer is by far the most popular WP device. It provides high quality output at a medium speed and a moderate cost. It prints 20 to 60 characters per second (cps) and costs about $3000.

The line printer is so-called because it prints one line at a time. Several copies of a complete alphabet of type slugs are imbedded in a moving circular arrangement alternatively called a **chain**, **train** or **belt**, according to its design. It covers the print area of one line, which can then be printed in one set of operations. The line printer produces anywhere from 300 to 3000 lines per minute (**lpm**) with prices starting in the $3000 range and extending up to the hundreds of thousands of dollars.

Finally, the subsection on recent technologies covers jet, electrostatic and laser printers.

**Modified Typewriter**

Figure 3.1.1 shows the Selectric$^{TM}$ typewriter. A **platen**, present in all printers, is the horizontal rubber cylinder against which the paper is pressed by the **paper bail**. The platen rotation advances the paper (**line advance**) upward past the carriage when one of the knurled knobs on the platen is turned by the operator or when the carriage return is activated by the computer. The **carriage** (sometimes called the **carrier**) holds the ribbon cartridge, the print element and part of the print mechanism. As each character is printed, the carriage moves to the next print position.

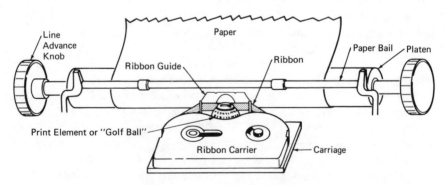

Figure 3.1.1. The golf ball typewriter.

The removable **print element** does the printing and is dubbed a **golf ball** because of its shape (Figure 3.1.2). Upon this "globe," four rows of characters are arranged at different "latitudes" parallel to the "equator." The ball:

- turns halfway round to get to uppercase characters and symbols;
- turns around its axis to one of many character positions in either direction in addition to the half revolution, when present;
- tilts forward or backward to one of the four rows.

Hitting a key, perhaps accompanied by a shift, when used by an operator, causes the ball to position so that the desired character is directly above the paper; then an electrically energized hammer hits the ball. The type bangs against the ribbon to leave an ink impression at this position on the paper.

This typewriter can be "computerized" in two ways. The first is an add-on solenoid arrangement which is cheap, but unreliable and unsuitable to an office environment. It consists of a number of electrically activated picker fingers, one for each key. This is installed beneath the typewriter. It depresses the keys in the correct order as directed by the print program. The second incorporates circuitry in the modified typewriter to convert the character codes sent by the computer into impulses which substitute for those created by the operator when a key is pressed. But the machine was designed for human use and has an inherent speed limitation of about 15 **characters per second (cps)**. When run at this speed, higher than any realistic continuous human output rate, it is prone to frequent mechanical failure.

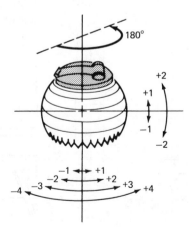

Figure 3.1.2. Motion of the golf ball.

## Dot Matrix Printer

The principle of developing the character pattern for the dot matrix printer is similar to that for the CRT display. The carriage sweeps out one row of characters at a time; the characters are created by printing a matrix of dots. The layout of these dots and undots are kept in binary form in ROM (read-only memory) in the printer called the **character generator.** The wires print a vertical line segment, one column of a character at a time. For the 5 × 9 matrix, each character consists of five verticals.

A character consists of a number of dots laid out in a matrix. Although other matrix sizes are used, we examine only the 5 × 9 matrix displayed in Figure 3.1.3. The top seven rows (horizontal) are used for all uppercase letters and lowercase letters without descenders. Rows 3 through 9 print letters with descenders; the tenth row (not shown) is a nonprinting separator between single spaced lines.

The carriage shown in Figure 3.1.4 carries the ribbon cartridge and a **print element** or **print head,** which consists of nine rigid **print wires** arranged *vertically.* Behind each wire is a tiny fast-acting hammer which may hit that wire against the ribbon to make an ink dot on the paper. These wires are shown from the side in Figure 3.1.5 as they print the third vertical of the letter *E.* This action as it appears from the front is shown at the bottom of the figure.

Figure 3.1.6 shows how the print head is positioned in front of the paper. Figure 3.1.7 shows the ballistic[TM] print head manufactured by Lear Siegler Inc.; at the left are magnets which, when energized, sharply pull down the clappers or hammers. These, in turn, send the wire (center) to hit the ribbon and make the impression. Figure 3.1.8 shows more detail. The print needle is spring loaded

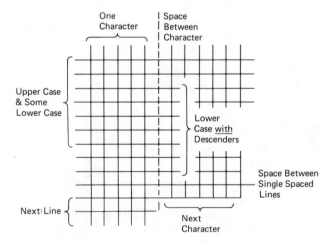

Figure 3.1.3. A 7 x 9 matrix for a printer.

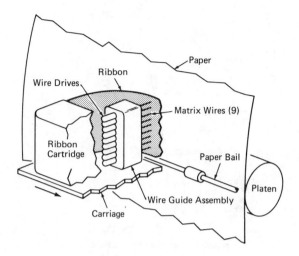

Figure 3.1.4. The dot matrix printer carriage.

away from the paper (a) until the electromagnet is energized. This moves the clapper to hit the needle and make a dot on the paper (b). Figure 3.1.9 shows the print head installed in the printer and actively printing.

A line of characters to be printed is sent by the computer to a **print buffer** in the printer. If there is only one buffer, printing cannot start until it is full,—which is why some printers supply two or more of such buffers—one can fill while the other is used to print from. The print buffer now contains codes for all the characters that are to be printed on this line.

The carriage starts its fast trip across the paper, horizontally; it will not stop until it reaches the other side (or the end of short line). As the carriage arrives at the next character position, the circuitry gets the character code from the print buffer for that character.

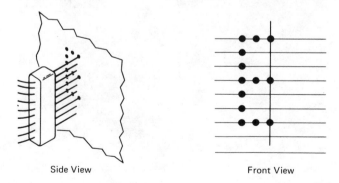

Side View                Front View

Figure 3.1.5. Printing the middle vertical of "E" with the dot matrix printer.

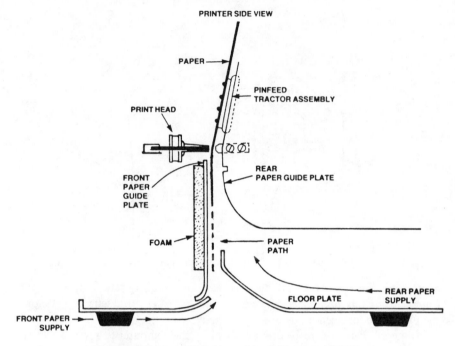

Figure 3.1.6. A printhead in position. (Courtesy of IDS).

Figure 3.1.7. A ballistic printhead. (Courtesy of Lear Siegler).

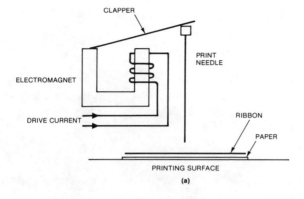

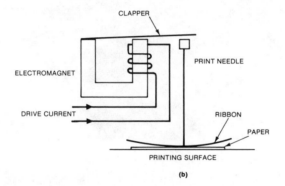

Figure 3.1.8. The print needle before(a) and after(b) hitting. (Courtesy of Anadex).

The circuitry requests the character generator to describe the first vertical position. The character generator supplies a set of 1s and 0s corresponding to the wires to hit to produce the first vertical segment of this character. This set of bits is put into a 9 bit **hammer register.** The carriage moves until it is exactly aligned at the first column of the character. Where there is a 1 in the hammer register, a hammer hits the corresponding wire to print the first vertical. The carriage moves through four more vertical positions. At each position the character generator is interrogated. A set of 9 bits for each different vertical element which makes up the character is put into the hammer register sequentially. Hammers hit the print wires as those positions are swept out.

Figure 3.1.9. Printhead actively printing. (Courtesy of Anadex).

*Characteristics*

These printers produce draft-quality output at a rate of 50 to 500 cps. Prices vary from $600 to about $3000. Less expensive ones have a single typeface, but this can be printed in compressed or expanded format (fewer or more characters per inch), as shown in Figure 3.1.10. More expensive ones (such as those manufactured by Malibu) have several fonts as well as multipass capability. Figure 3.1.11 provides samples of printout from a Malibu printer.

*Multipass*

There are multipass printers on the market in the $2000 to $4000 range which send the printhead back and forth across the same line several times, moving it down the page only slightly to offset the second set of dots produced for the same character vertically. Later scans also offset the dots horizontally. In this way, good quality output can be achieved at an appreciable loss in speed. How-

NORMAL

! "£$%&'()*+,-./0123456789:;<=>?@ABCDEFGHIJKLMNOPQRSTUVWXYZ
[\]^_`abcdefghijklmnopqrstuvwxyz{|}¯ſ
! "#$%&'()*+,-./0123456789:;<=>?£ABCDEFGHIJKLMNOPQRSTUVWXYZ
ÄÖÅÜ_éabcdefghijklmnopqrstuvwxyzäöåüſ


NORMAL ELONGATED

! "£$%&' () *+,—./0123456789:;<=>?
@ABCDEFGHIJKLMNOPQRSTUVWXYZ[\]^_`
abcdefghijklmnopqrstuvwxyz{|}¯ſ
! "#$%&' () *+,—./0123456789:;<=>?
£ABCDEFGHIJKLMNOPQRSTUVWXYZÄÖÅÜ_
éabcdefghijklmnopqrstuvwxyzäöåüſ


PROPORTIONAL

!"£$%&'()*+,-./0123456789:;<=>?@ABCDEFGHIJKLMNOPQRSTUVWXYZ
[\]^_`abcdefghijklmnopqrstuvwxyz{|}¯ſ
!"#$%&'()*+,-./0123456789:;<=>?£ABCDEFGHIJKLMNOPQRSTUVWXYZ
ÄÖÅÜ_éabcdefghijklmnopqrstuvwxyzäöåüſ


PROPORTIONAL ELONGATED

!"£$%&'()*+,—./0123456789:;<=>?@ABCDEFGHIJKL
MNOPQRSTUVWXYZ
[\]^_`abcdefghijklmnopqrstuvwxyz{|}¯ſ
!"#$%&'()*+,—./0123456789:;<=>?£ABCDEFGHIJKL
MNOPQRSTUVWXYZÄÖÅÜ_éabcdefgh:
ijklmnopqrstuvwxyzäöåüſ

Figure 3.1.10. Compressed and expanded dot matrix printing. (Courtesy of IDS).

# Malibu Dual-Mode 200 Character Sets

Titan 10 LQ prints 10 characters per inch at 42 cps to provide letter perfect output for business correspondence.

Standard 10 DQ prints at 165 cps and is ideal for data processing requirements and draft printing.

Titan 12 LQ prints 12 characters per inch at 50 cps and is ideal for business correspondence.

Gothic 12 LQ prints at 50 cps and provides crisp, highly readable characters for reports and technical manuals.

*Italics 12 LQ prints at 50 cps and is perfect for emphasizing text or use as a script-like font.*

Standard 12 DQ prints at 200 cps and is ideal for data processing requirements and draft printing.

OCR-A LQ PRINTS AT 42 CHARACTERS PER SECOND TO PROVIDE MACHINE READABLE OUTPUT FOR MANUFACTURING AND RETAIL OPERATIONS.

Greek/Math and APL sets are available and print these characters at 42 cps for special applications:

Greek/Math:  πο{}}∫÷[₊≢'/~Α⁰¹²³⁴⁵⁶⁷⁸⁹⁻"Π≢±/∑∇∞Ψ◆←<∧Π↑>≋↓∂( )ℓ
             ΓΘΣ→Ξ∠ΔΩΤ≈√>≠•`∥αβΨΦ∈~λη⊥≡κω{ναρΥΘστξ×δχυζ●]<α

APL:  ¨)<≤=>]ν≠≢,+./0123456789([;×:\∣α⊥∩ℓ∈∇Δ∘'□∣το≋
      ?ρ⌈~↓∪ω⊃↑c←↦→≥-◇*ABCDEFGHIJKLMNOPQRSTUVWXYZ{¬}$*

Pitch 17 LQ provides condensed print for compact reports with 17 characters per inch at 70 cps.

Pitch 17 DQ provides 17 characters per inch and 198 cps for volume data processing and draft printing.

In addition to these, Malibu offers foreign character sets, as well as proportional sets for special word processing applications. If what you are looking for isn't here, please ask us about it. We may be working on it already, or we may be able to design a custom set to fit your needs exactly.

Figure 3.1.11. Multipass dot matrix printout. (Courtesy of Malibu).

ever, the speed for draft quality is 150 to 400 cps. Good-quality printing is producted at 40 to 60 cps or more. The printer can still be used in the single-pass mode suitable for fast rough drafts and lower quality printout. Often, several different typefaces can be built into the printer (as removable ROMs) and selected by the computer program. Figure 3.1.11 shows samples produced on such a printer, manufactured by Malibu. Watch for more developments in this area!

### The Daisy Wheel Printer

The **daisy wheel printer** is so-called because its print element is a small disk from which spokes radiate. At the end of each spoke is a circular area on which is stamped a character, as shown in Figure 3.1.12. The element looks like a flower whose petals are the type slugs. There are as many petals as characters to be printed—usually 96 or 128. Figure 3.1.13 is a photograph of a daisy wheel made by Qume.

The print element is centered in a carriage which also carries the ribbon as it moves across the paper horizontally. The print buffer stores codes for the characters for the line to be printed. The carriage is in motion while a line is printed. After printing one character, the carriage is on its way to the next character position; the code is brought from the next position of the print buffer. Then the daisy wheel is rotated to the position which has that character.

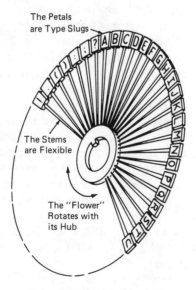

Figure 3.1.12. A daisy wheel.

Figure 3.1.13. Photo of a daisy wheel. (Courtesy of Qume).

Choose one petal on the daisy wheel as the **home** position. The **petal table** in the electronics stores the petal number of each character, counting from the home position on the daisy wheel. The **petal register** stores the petal number of the last character printed. The number of petal positions to move the daisy wheel to the selected petal is the difference between the number in the petal register and the number of the desired petal. The electronics looks up the petal number of this character in the petal table and then finds the difference, call it D.

The electronics sends D pulses to rotate the daisy wheel to the selected character. A fast stepping motor moves the daisy wheel one petal position for each pulse sent it. The selected petal is thus positioned while the carriage moves. When the carriage arrives where the letter should print, the hammer behind the daisy wheel hits the choosen petal against the ribbon to make the ink impression.

The petal stepping motor is bidirectional. Knowing both the present and desired petals, the electronics determines which way to rotate the daisy wheel to use the least number of pulses; the wheel need never rotate more than half a revolution.

Daisy wheel printers are made by Ricoh, Diablo, Qume and NEC (using a thimble instead) and sell for $1800 to $4000. They produce letter-quality output at speeds between 20 and 60 cps.

The daisy wheel is removable; it comes in a variety of typefaces and is made in different materials, two of which are notable. Plastic wheels are less expensive and print at top speeds but wear out after several million impressions, degrading in the process. Metal wheels provide a better impression from the start and last several times longer than plastic, but they cost more. A metal wheel does not print at as high a speed as does a plastic wheel because it is heavier.

*Two Heads are Better than One*

Some printers have two independent printheads in a wide carriage. The two heads share the work and hence may as much as double the print speed. They are employed in two ways.

1. Each head carries a different font such as:
   normal and italics
   normal and math symbols
   Print speed is the same as for the single head, but two sets of characters are available without manual intervention.
2. Both heads carry the same font: one head prints the left side of the page; the other, the right. Together they print in half the time.

Coordination of the two heads is a software task. The program to drive the printer is necessarily more complex, especially when bidirectional printing is used.

*Print Wheel*

The daisy wheel or thimble is easy to replace or change. It takes only a few seconds to remove one and mount another. In a single-head model italics or a different font can be employed several times on the same page with operator intervention twice for each change. With a "don't print" feature (Chapter 11), you can print the whole page with one wheel and then go back and print it again with the second wheel.

**The Line Printer**

The **line printer** is so-called because it seems to print a line at a time. Its printing rate, measured in **lines per minute (lpm)**, is generally much higher than those discussed so far. Printing speeds range from 300 to 3000 lpm or more. (High end dot matrix printers are becoming competitive.) Line printers are found in medium and large computer installations and usually print only uppercase characters. They print faster this way, but *can* print lowercase too, at a speed sacrifice, if you change the chain. If your WP can connect to such a printer, you may want to use it to make drafts and take the load off local printers.

At the center of the line printer is a mechanism which carries a set of engraved type slugs. There are several ways to mount and carry the slugs along the paper, named the chain, train and belt.

For the **chain**, each type slug is independently mounted and hooked together with a pivot arrangement. At the top and bottom of each slug is a sprocket hole. The result looks like a chain, moved by two sprocket drives, as shown in Figure 3.1.14.

For the **belt**, each slug is cemented to a polyeurethene and fiber glass belt. This carries the slugs at high speed as driven by a pair of spindles at either end.

### Printing Arrangement

The printing arrangement is shown in Figure 3.1.15. The "endless" circular belt of type slugs moves continuously at high speed. In front of the belt is a ribbon the length of the paper. Behind the ribbon is the paper.

Within the circumference of the belt is a set of hammers. There is one hammer for each print position along the paper. Each hammer can be separately activated. When a character on the belt is aligned at a print position where it should print, a hammer hits the slug sharply against the ribbon which deposits ink on the paper, thus producing the desired character.

### Transmitting the Line

A line to print is transmitted by the computer. The character codes received by the printer are put in the **print buffer,** shown in Figure 3.1.15. Printing does not begin until the line image is put in this buffer.

The **chain buffer** records the character slug which occupies each position on the belt. As the belt moves, this buffer is updated; it always records which character is at each print position. The print buffer and the chain buffer are compared.

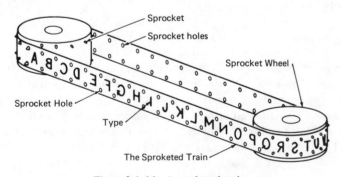

Figure 3.1.14. A sproketed train.

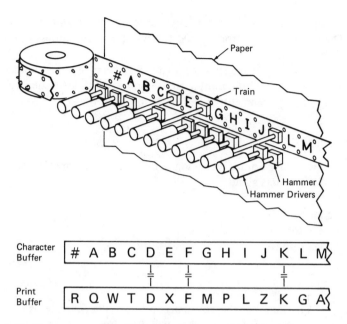

Figure 3.1.15. Hammers are driven forward when codes in the character and print buffers correspond.

When character codes in the two coincide, the corresponding hammer driver is activated.

When the chain arrives at the print position, the hammers are already on their way to hit the slugs and make an impression for those characters which should print. In the figure, the hammers are printing D, F and K. Note that each time the slugs get to a print position, none, one, several or all the slugs may be hit.

### Print Complete

The maximum time to print a line occurs when for some print position, the proper letter has just passed by. We have to wait for another copy of that character to appear at this print position. However, the chain may have several copies of the alphabet on it, so that the maximum time to print a line might be a half or a quarter of a revolution.

The minimum time occurs when the message to be printed is a sequence of characters identical to that on the print chain, an uncommon occurrence. Usually the message is printed in less than the maximum time. We cannot predict when the printer will finish. To assure that the printer becomes available to print the next line as soon as this line is printed, we keep track of whether each character in the message has been printed. An extra bit in the print buffer is set when the character in that position has printed. Printing is complete when this bit is on for all characters in the print buffer.

When properly maintained, line printers produce good quality printing at high speed. They range in cost from $5000 to several hundred thousand dollars, according to speed and size.

As the price decreases and shared resource WPs become more popular, an efficient office may tie in draft printing to line printers with lower quality but very high speed. Quality documents may still use the daisy wheel.

### Other Technologies

There are three other printer technologies that are used in large WP systems. We now present some facts about:

- the ink jet printer,
- the electrostatic printer,
- the laser printer.

### The Ink Jet Printer

This printer functions like the dot matrix printer: the character is formed from a matrix of ink dots. Because of the spread of the ink dot, characters look good. However, only one copy is possible on this type of printer. The source of each dot is a jet of fine ink droplets. There is one jet for each dot which might appear along one of the vertical lines constituting a character. An electronically driven generator to create each ink jet includes an ink supply and a tiny crystal which vibrates because a high frequency voltage is applied to its sides. This breaks off tiny droplets, which then eject toward the paper.

As each ink jet travels toward the paper, it passes through a charged grid. For an "undot," the grid is charged with a voltage to deflect the jet into a reservoir; it never hits the paper. An uncharged grid allows the jet to reach the paper as a dot.

As with the dot matrix printer, the line to print is stored as character codes in a print line buffer. As the print element approaches a new print position, the code for the character to be printed in that position is brought from the ROM character generator. The pattern of 0s and 1s corresponds to the dot pattern for one of the vertical line segments which comprise the character.

This bit pattern is stored temporarily in a register. The 1 activates the grid so that the jet produces a dot; undots are produced by 0s.

The ink jet printer has the same speed range as the dot matrix printer, 50 to 200 characters per second. However, it produces a higher quality print at a higher cost. The IBM 6640 has an automatic feeder which handles several sizes of paper and envelopes and includes two hoppers from which the computer can choose to feed paper (or envelopes). It is furnished as part of Office System 6 and costs about $23,000.

*The Electrostatic Printer*

The electrostatic printer resembles the dot matrix printer. The printhead may even look the same: a number of fine vertical wires create the dots. The expensive printer uses a paper width bank of wires in a fixed, full width printhead. However, the wires are not hit. Instead, each wire is charged with a voltage for a dot and uncharged for an undot. Again a character generator determines the wires to charge. The charge is transferred to a small restricted area on the paper.

No visual impression is yet formed on the paper, which then passes beneath a spray of find carbon particles. Particles adhere only to the charged area. Now the dots are visible but they are not permanent and thus could be brushed off under rough handling. The paper is chemically treated to fix the particles to adhere to the paper.

*The Laser Printer*

Instead of the electron beam found in the CRT display, the laser beam sweeps from one side of the paper to the other. It is turned on and off to produce dots and undots. The beam prints by heating the paper.

This was an expensive device previously found only in large-computer environments. However, it is now within reach of the office WP system. We have the IBM 6670 and the Xerox 5700 (under $29,000), and Hewlett Packard has a product for its minicomputer. A number of different character generators can be referenced for boldface, italics and additional character fonts to be mixed in the same line.

The laser beam is turned on for a dot and off for an undot. Its heat alters the paper chemically, but not visibly. The paper is passed through a toner, which produces the black image and makes it indelible.

Laser printers cost up to $350,000 and print at speeds from 12 pages (8½ × 11) per minute to 5.5 pages per second.

## 3.2 MOTION IN THE PRINTER

Motion is required to put the right character on the paper in the right position. What moves?

1. The print element moves along the paper horizontally.
2. The paper moves up or down vertically from one line or page to the next.
3. The ribbon passes beneath the print element to provide fresh ink.

These are examined in the order listed.

### Print Element Advance

During printing, the paper is held fixed between the platen and the paper bail, as shown in Figure 3.1.1. The carriage moves the print element to the desired print position. The print element creates an image of the correct character. (For line printers, printing occurs only at fixed positions along the line; for the others, character positions may be varied in discrete increments.)

*Fixed*

The golf ball usually and chain/train printers always position the type at fixed column positions along the width of the paper. The golf ball advances one position after each strike. For the chain, the proper slug is aligned in a column position before the hammer strikes it.

*Variable*

For the dot matrix and daisy wheel printer the carriage moves in **increments** (of 1/120 inch). The number of increments that the carriage moves is controlled by the computer. **Horizontal pitch** is rated in characters per inch (**cpi**), or simply **pitch**. There are two standard pitches, 10 and 12. Pitch is sometimes controlled locally within the printer and is set for 10 or 12 per inch. Sometimes a pitch of 15 cpi is provided. This allows the WP to print a large table on a page without turning it one quarter of the way around. Proportional spacing and justification are controlled by the print program by varying the spacing between print positions.

*Bidirectional*

The typewriter moves the carriage rightward as each key is pressed. It is returned to the left margin when you hit return. This full line reverse motion of the carriage takes only a small fraction of the time spent moving forward—and besides, who can type backward?

Since the WP printer speed, 20 to 60 cps, is so fast, the time for the return of the carriage is now a large fraction of the forward printing time. All that reverse time can be saved if it prints also from right to left. And why not? The print mechanism couldn't care less which way the carriage is moving.

The problem is the sequence of the text. You keyed in each line from left to right. That is the way the text editor stores it, displays it and records it on disk. We see in Chapter 7 how the print formatter reverses alternate text lines as it sends them to the printer to take advantage of the speed gained by **bidirectional printing**.

**Line Advance**

**Line advance** is the movement of the paper vertically so that another line on the paper may be readied for printing. There are three types of paper feed mechanisms:

- friction feed,
- pin feed,
- tractor feed.

*Friction Feed*

For the friction feed found on typewriters, the paper is held between the platen and paper guide. The platen is made of rubber or a similar compound with a high coefficient of friction. The metal paper guide is slippery; when the platen is moved, it takes the paper for a ride because of friction alone: the friction between the paper and platen transmits the vertical motion; the low friction between the guide and the paper allows it to slide by.

The friction feed allows printing of separate pages with ease. However, when it comes to handling continuous stock, it is impossible to maintain alignment by friction alone for more than a few pages.

*Pin Feed*

A **pin feed** printer has a platen with pins projecting radially at both ends, as shown in Figure 3.2.1. It handles continuous stock which has holes punched in both margins. The pins on the platen fit into the holes in the stock and as the platen turns, the paper is advanced positively, maintaining its alignment indefinitely. But since the pins are built into the platen, they are set a fixed distance apart and only one width of continuous stock can be used.

Figure 3.2.1. Pin feed platen. (Courtesy of NEC).

The **tractor feed** overcomes the requirement for fixed width stock found with the pin feed drive. It is adjustable over a large range of paper stock and can handle forms from a couple of inches in width to the maximum width for the platen.

In Figure 3.2.2, as the paper emerges from the paper guide, it passes over the tractor feed. Two sprocket hole guides at opposite ends of the feed may be moved in either direction horizontally and clamped in place with thumb screws. Pins in the guides are set into the holes in the paper, once the separation of the guides has been set. A hinged clamp holds the paper against the guide and keeps the pins in the sprocket holes. When the printer gets a line feed signal, a stepping motor geared to the sprocket wheels advances the paper one line space as set on the printer control panel or dictated by the computer signals.

> *Note:* The friction feed should always be disengaged when either the pin feed or tractor feed is in use; otherwise the feed holes will get mangled and alignment will be altered or feeding interrupted.

Usually the tractor is removable so that single sheets may be handled with the friction feed. To permit single sheets and even envelopes to be handled like continuous forms, some paper suppliers take the single sheets you furnish, such as your letterhead, and affix them to a continuous backing with feed holes in it.

Figure 3.2.3 shows a number of platens of different sizes, a tractor feed (left), two daisy wheels with daisy (bottom right) and a ribbon cartridge (bottom left).

Figure 3.2.2. Tractor feed. (Courtesy of NEC).

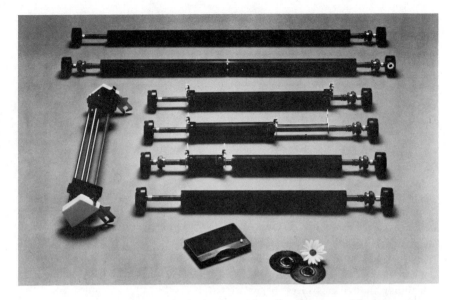

Figure 3.2.3. Daisy wheel printer paraphenalia. (Courtesy of Qume).

*Quantity and Direction*

The user generally views the separation between lines in terms of lines per inch (**lpi**) with 6 and 8 lpi being standard on the typewriter. However, most printers provide a much finer granularity, with 48 vertical units per inch being common. The number of vertical units per line is under WP program control. Your WP may allow you to select intermediate line heights to achieve a more attractive page makeup. Now you have almost continuous control of line spacing and can get 1½ or 1¼ line spacing.

If the computer can control the *direction* of line spacing and the printer can also move the paper backward, a number of important features can be easily implemented, as described later, including subscripting and one kind of multicolumn formatting.

### Ribbon

The line printer uses a wide ribbon, usually of a single color, so color is not generally under computer control. The other three impact printer types use ribbon cartridges. Ribbon in them is of three varieties:

- Inked cloth ribbon of one color winds from one spool to another until the end of the first spool is reached. Then the spool mechanism is reset automatically to wind in the other direction. The ribbon is thus reused many times until someone notices that the impressions are faint and changes it.

- Inked cloth of two colors works the same way, but the print color can be changed between black and red by the computer.
- The "multistrike" cartridge contains Mylar plastic ribbon coated with carbon material, which makes an excellent dark impression when struck but cannot be reused. With each strike the ribbon is advanced a fraction of a character width. When the spool is wound completely to one end, no further printing may be done. An alarm notifies an operator to change the ribbon.

Except for the line printer, ribbon is furnished in a cartridge (much like the typewriter ribbon cartridge) which you can load quickly without dirtying your hands. Figure 3.2.4 shows a ribbon cartridge being replaced. There is no standard shape or size for the cartridge and they are *not* interchangeable between different manufacturers or models. Cartridges cost from $5 to $25 each and seem to disappear quickly. Because of their expense, an industry has risen up which replaces the ribbon in used cartridges for 60 percent of the cost of a new one. Some vendors now seal their cartridges to prevent reuse.

Figure 3.2.4. Ribbon cartridge being replaced. (Courtesy of Anadex).

## 3.3 JUSTIFICATION

There are many features that owe their implementation to variable carriage motion. By far the most important of these is justification.

Justification prints text with uniform margins on both the left and right side, and not with jagged righthand edges as is the case with copy produced on the standard typewriter. It can be achieved in two ways:

- by changing the spacing between each word to fill out the line;
- by changing the spacing between all characters in the line.

Sometimes these methods are combined.

**Procedure**

There is enough text available in memory to the WP print program for several lines of print. The text editor has already assembled lines of text with word wrap (see Chapter 6) so that:

- the line may have some blanks at the end;
- it does not have enough room to hold the first word on the next line.

Each line consists of two parts:

- the text between the first and last letter on the line and including the spaces between words, T;
- the extra space between the last letter of the line and the right margin, X.

To justify the line, the extra space, X, has to be spread out over the line so that: the first letter of the line is on the left margin; the last letter of the line is on the right margin.

The Linotype machine has a way to do this. Each blank between words is expandable. Letter slugs are put into a line until it is full, using a method similar to the WP's word wrap. Then the blanks are allowed to expand to take up the slack. Hot metal is poured into this mold to create a "line of type."

The WP works with the printer to get the same result. The print program takes the space, X, and divides it up into as many portions as there are gaps between words; it adds one portion of space into each blank between words. These blanks act as though they were spring-loaded and take up the slack. This loading is done digitally by a calculation. The WP program calculates the right size for the space, and tells the printer how far to advance between words. This is **interword justification**.

*Between Letters*

The WP has the ideal workhorse available—fast calculating power. It is quick and easy to make any calculation desired. WP designers have seen that the WP could just as easily spread out X in any way desired. One way is to divide X into portions allocated to each and every letter on the line. This is sometimes called **intra-word justification**, or **microjustification.**

With microjustification, an otherwise short line is spread out to a large extent and each word is considerably longer than that of the original. It is said to be less readable and attractive, but no conclusive studies show its readability in contrast to the other alternatives.

**Proportional Spacing**

Some printers, notably of the daisy wheel type, provide print wheels for which the character width varies from character to character. A character such as M prints wide; the i and the period print quite narrow. This is **proportional spacing.** Several widths of characters make for a particularly attractive line.

The daisy wheel printer is ideal for proportional printing because printing and carriage advance are independent operations. The laser printer is even better; it has no carriage, so advance is controlled electronically. And a wide choice of fonts are available to be chosen from by the computer without human intervention. The work of driving the printer is left to the print formatter program in the WP. The text editor does some additional calculations to figure out line composition unless the display is responsive to proportional spacing (see Section 7.4). The brunt of the work falls on the print formatter program. Luckily, character widths for most proportionally spaced fonts are standard. A single table tells the print formatter how far to advance the carriage for each character it encounters in this mode. The spacing of Table 3.3.1 is standard.

Proportional spacing may reduce print speed because many carriage advance signals are sent with the text to the printer. What slows things down is the mechanical action which may take place between each character printed to alter the distance moved.

**Proportional Spacing and Justification**

Both proportional spacing and justification can easily be combined. Either justification method is feasible. Changing the gaps between characters or the space between words does not affect the character width.

### Table 3.3.1. Widths of Proportionally Spaced Characters.

| Character | Size | Character | Size | Character | Size |
|-----------|------|-----------|------|-----------|------|
| A | 14 | a | 10 | 1 | 10 |
| B | 12 | b | 10 | 2 | 10 |
| C | 14 | c | 10 | 3 | 10 |
| D | 14 | d | 10 | 4 | 10 |
| E | 12 | e | 10 | 5 | 10 |
| F | 12 | f | 8 | 6 | 10 |
| G | 14 | g | 10 | 7 | 10 |
| H | 14 | h | 10 | 8 | 10 |
| I | 6 | i | 6 | 9 | 10 |
| J | 10 | j | 6 | 0 | 10 |
| K | 14 | k | 10 | ! | 6 |
| L | 12 | l | 6 | '' | 8 |
| M | 16 | m | 16 | # | 12 |
| N | 14 | n | 10 | $ | 10 |
| O | 14 | o | 10 | % | 16 |
| P | 12 | p | 10 | & | 14 |
| Q | 14 | q | 10 | ' | 4 |
| R | 14 | r | 8 | ( | 6 |
| S | 10 | s | 8 | ) | 6 |
| T | 12 | t | 8 | @ | 16 |
| U | 14 | u | 8 | + | 10 |
| V | 12 | v | 10 | * | 10 |
| W | 16 | w | 14 | ; | 6 |
| X | 14 | x | 10 | : | 6 |
| Y | 14 | y | 10 | , | 6 |
| Z | 12 | z | 10 | . | 6 |
| ¼ | 12 | ½ | 12 | / | 8 |
| ? | 10 | = | 10 | | |

## Definitions

Before we examine how to justify, we make a few definitions. Assume that the carriage can advance along the line in **unit** increments (1/120 inch is standard for the daisy wheel printer); then define character and intercharacter length, as shown in Figure 3.3.1, in terms of unit increments:

C is the width of each character (or the escapement value).
G is the letter space gap or intercharacter space.
P is each character or print position size.
L is the number of units (carriage advance increments) in the line.

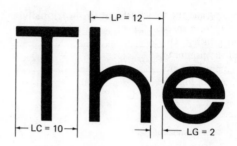

Figure 3.3.1. Escapement value, letterspace and character position.

C depends on the character font installed in the printer, its pitch and the gap size. The default value for the gap, G, is 2 units, but it is under the control of the WP. It may be reset by the user to extend or compress areas of text. A character position consists of the character found there plus the gap. Then we have

$$P = C + G \qquad (3.3.1)$$

Pitch is defined as characters (positions) per inch. An inch is 120 units. Define $P_{10}$ as position size for 10 pitch and $P_{12}$ as position size for 12 pitch. Then,

$$P_{10} = \frac{120}{10} = 12 \text{ units} \qquad (3.3.2)$$

and

$$P_{12} = \frac{120}{12} = 10 \text{ units} \qquad (3.3.3)$$

## Word Justification

For interword (or simply word) justification, the extra space, X, is distributed among the word spaces. We have

W words on this line,
X extra space positions left over at the end.

However, for W words, there are W – 1 spaces between words within the text line; for 10 words there are 9 spaces between words. Call S the new size of each space after justification. Then,

$$S = P + \frac{X \times P}{W - 1} \qquad (3.3.4)$$

## Word Space Example

Consider 10 pitch lines of 60 print positions (12 units each). Suppose that a line to be printed has four extra character positions at the end and that there are nine words in the line. Then the new length of each word space is given by (3.3.4) as

$$S = 12 + \frac{4 \times 12}{9 - 1} = 12 + \frac{48}{8} = 18 \qquad (3.3.5)$$

Characters are 10 units long and the computer tells the printer to move 12 units after hitting each character. However, for a space nothing is printed, so we advance the carriage an additional 18 units without printing. Or to put it another way: after the character is printed at the end of a word, tell the printer to advance 30 units to get to the next printing character. The printer advances 12 units for most characters and 30 units at the end of a word. Such a line being justified is shown in Figure 3.3.2.

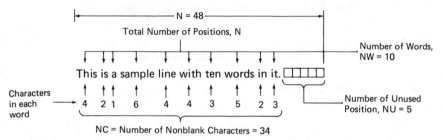

Figure 3.3.2. A line to be justified.

### Fractional Units

The last example comes out even; S was an integer because the division in (3.3.4) works. It does not usually come out even; let us examine such an example.

Again assume a pitch of 12 and a 60 character line; now these are 11 words (W = 1) and there are 4 spaces left over (X = 4). Then,

$$S = 12 + (4 \times 12)/(11 - 1) \tag{3.3.6}$$

Division does not come out even, so we have

$$S = 12 + 48/10 = 16.8 \tag{3.3.7}$$

This won't work, since we do not have fractional units.

### Algorithm

We can now go to a systematic procedure (which is called an **algorithm**). There are many such algorithms which one might employ. Let us look at one example which is dynamic: calculations are made as each line is examined. First note that S in (3.3.4) consists of a fixed and a variable part for each line. This could vary within the line. We then have

$$S = P + A \tag{3.3.8}$$

where A is the additional unit added to a space to get an even line. Now let us calculate A dynamically as we scan the line. Here is the algorithm:

Call L the space left to allocate on the line and R the remaining words. If L/R has no remainder, use it for A for the rest of the line. If L/R has a remainder, use the next larger integer for A. Then the new value of L is L - A and for R is R - 1; start with L = P × X and R = W - 1.

Let us see how this works in the example with 11 words and 4 blanks at the end of the line. Start with L = 4 × 12 = 48 and R = 11 - 1 = 10.

$$L/R = 4.8 \quad A = 5 \tag{3.3.9}$$

Now $L = 48 - 5 = 43$ and $R = 10 - 1 = 9$ and we have,

$$L/R = 43/9 \quad A = 5 \tag{3.3.10}$$

Then $L = 38$ and $R = 8$, so that

$$L/R = 38/8 \quad A = 5 \tag{3.3.11}$$

We keep getting values for A of 5 until there are only two words left. Then we get,

$$L/R = 8/2 = 4 \quad A = 4 \tag{3.3.12}$$

So we use $A = 4$ for the last two words. Note that 8 words have spaces of 17 units between them and the last two have spaces of 16 units, which works out fine.

### Proportional Space Calculations

When you create (or edit) text, the text-edit program provides word wrap, described in Chapter 6, so that you are not bothered with line makeup. For proportional spacing the length and content of each line is calculated based on a character table which gives the width of each character in units. (See Table 3.3.1.)

It makes little difference whether or not line content is reviewed at print time. Assume that we start after line allocation so that the text to be printed is now determined; how is justification done?

The line width occupied by the text is a function of which letters comprise the line and is not a simple product of the number of letters and the position width in units. No matter— the space occupied by the text, in units, call it T, is the sum of the widths of each character to be printed, including the gap. Call the space left over (in units) X. Then we have

$$N = T + X \tag{3.3.13}$$

where N is the number of units in the line. So the calculation of spaces between words is the same; divide X up into equal chunks to add to each blank between the words. If X does not divide evenly, use an algorithm. The varying size of the characters has no effect on justification. The algorithm described earlier is equally effective here.

### Bidirectional

To print bidirectionally, the print program need only activate the printer properly. When printing left to right, the program transmits text from the electronic document in sequence, interspersing control codes to the printer with the text. These codes are occasionally single bytes; usually commands are distinguished by a control sequence which begins with an escape code [es]. A control sequence tells the printer to change horizontal distance traveled to the required size to get the space needed for justification.

Once a left-to-right line is printed, the carriage is sitting on the right. There is no need to return it—in fact, returning it only wastes time. Simply send over material to be printed as the carriage returns right to left. But characters are printed in the order received by the printer as it travels leftward. Hence the print program has to reverse the order for this line. No problem. The print program finds the right end of the line and sends characters in the order found as it scans backward to the start of the line.

The justification algorithm is applied as letters are transmitted; control signals set blanks between words to the correct width. This even has a beneficial effect. Recall that the al-

gorithm puts larger blanks at the start of lines and smaller ones near the end. When applied in reverse, this too is reversed. It prints out less messy and really looks better.
Justified bidirectional proportional spacing uses all the actions we have just described.

## 3.4 OTHER FEATURES

This section describes *hardware* features of printers only. The same features reappear later in connection with editing, display and the print format program in Chapter 7.

### Underscore

Underscore, printing a line beneath a set of characters, is usually achieved by the printer with a second pass of the line containing the underlined letters. That is, after printing a line, the paper is *not* advanced. The carriage passes over the line again, this time printing only the underscore for those characters where it belongs.

Another way to get the same result is to suppress carriage motion after printing a character at an underscore position. Then print the underline and advance. The difficulty is that this requires starting and stopping the carriage for each underline. A second pass turns out to be faster, even for only a couple of words.

Double underscore puts *two* lines under a set of characters. This requires the double underscore character on the print wheel but it is otherwise the same as single underscore. If the underscore is applied to spaces and symbols in the set of characters, this is a solid underscore: otherwise, if there is no underscore in the spaces between words, it is a broken underscore.

### Overstrike

Printing two (or more) characters in the same print position is called overstrike. A "not equal" sign is made by overstriking = and / to print $\neq$. To kern is used to reduce the spacing between characters. The spacing between overstruck symbols is 0.

### Boldface

Boldface characters stand out because they are darker and thicker, even though they are the same shape as their counterparts. This is achieved with WP printers by overstriking with the same character. There are three variations:

1. Simply hit the same character twice (or three or four times) without carriage advance. This is called shadow printing.

2. Advance the carriage one or two increments (1/120 inch) between strikes.
3. Repeat step 2 more than once.

Without carriage advance, only a slight emboldening results. The carriage displacement between the two strikes really makes a heavier character impression. When this is repeated, the effect is strange. Some WPs let you specify which boldface variation you want.

### Subscripts and Superscripts

Subscripts and superscripts are used extensively in scientific and mathematical texts. A **subscript** is one or more letter (or number) printed slightly below the line; a **superscript** is a symbol(s) printed slightly above the line, viz., $x^2$. Superscripted numerals are often used to designate footnotes.

The line increment advance feature accounts for both sub- and superscripts. To superscript, reverse line advance for a fraction of a line, print the characters which go above the line, and then line advance partially to resume printing the line. To subscript, advance incrementally, print the subscripts, and then reverse incrementally to resume printing.

### Multicolumn Printing

Statistical printing requires multiple columns of numbers aligned in different ways, as described in Chapter 11. For an accounting report, this is done by **tabbing** to the proper column. The WP just advances the carriage rapidly to the proper column—no great feat.

Multicolumn printing can be achieved in two ways:

- Print one column on the page and then reverse the paper and print the next column from the top, and so forth for each column.
- Rely on software entirely to organize the text and print one line from each column on each line of the page.

*One Column at a Time*

This is easier to program; it relies on the capability of the printer to back up the length of a page and print the record (and other columns) from the top. It is less desirable for two reasons:

- Printer reversal for an entire page is difficult; it may crease or tear the page and it is unreliable.
- For sheet feed, the paper *must* be reinserted, which demands operator intervention.

For this method the text editor program can take any text and reformat it for this purpose; the place where each column breaks can be inserted into the text for the print program. The latter creates each column with justification, bidirectionality and proportional spacing as requested. At the end of the column, the printer is commanded to reverse the length of the page. The next column follows, but it is moved over to the right.

*Line at a Time*

Here the document is presented and displayed as a multicolumn electronic document (ED). Several vendors provide two columns; three and four columns are available from the Lexitron 2202 and 2203, which have lots of memory (393K). The editing allows correcting and automatic text flow from one column to the next.

The print program sees the text as lines, each broken into column portions or line segments. Each segment is handled as a separate entity for justification and proportional spacing. Each line is treated bidirectionally by full line. No gymnastics are required by the printer. And human intervention is eliminated for single-sheet operation.

## 3.5 AUTOMATIC SHEET FEEDERS

**Feeding Paper**

We have seen two different ways that paper is fed by the printer. The first uses continuous fan fold paper with small holes on each side. The printer has either a pin feed or a tractor feed. The pin feed is built into the platen and handles paper of a fixed width. The tractor feed is detachable and adjustable. For manual feed you insert the paper and align it. The printer advances the paper and ejects the page when it is printed.

*Tractor Feed*

The tractor (and pin feed) have two advantages:

- No stopping is required between pages.
- A printer works continuously unattended.

The main disadvantages of the tractor feed are a limitation on the kind of paper stock which must be used and that processing is necessary after printing: tearing apart the sheets of paper, called **bursting**; triming the half inch with the feed holes from each side of each sheet. After this is done, the page still has slightly ragged edges on each of its four sides.

The stock you can use is limited to what paper suppliers make in the way of continuous forms. However, some suppliers will put *your* letterhead on continuous feed stock; it is processed after printing by simply peeling off the letterhead from the backing. Envelopes can be handled the same way.

### Manual

The manual feed has an advantage in that it takes most shapes of paper. You can use your letterhead or any kind of paper, form or stock. On the other hand, the manual printer requires the presence of an operator to:

1. put the paper into the printer and turn the platen to align the paper (some few printers advance the paper for you);
2. watch for completion;
3. remove the printed sheet and stack it.

Of course we are all greedy and would like all the advantages and none of the disadvantages of both techniques. Perhaps the automatic sheet feeder is a good compromise.

### Automatic Sheet Feed

The sheet feeder has one and sometimes two hoppers into which you place paper commonly used in your office for printing. Some feeders also take envelopes. The feeder has an output stacker into which printed sheets move.

Some expensive printers, such as the ink jet printer for the IBM Office Systems 6, come with their own sheet feeder. Some manufacturers supply sheet feeders to fit most vendor's printers. In the most common case, the WP system comes with a standard printer such as a daisy wheel made by Diablo, Qume, etc., and a sheet feeder is purchased as an option. The customer may then purchase a feeder from a different vendor and attach it to this printer.

*Attaching*

To attach the sheet feeder, you remove either the tractor feed or the printer platen. Where the sheet feed replaces the tractor, you now have three options on any job: the tractor feed, the sheet feed or manual feed.

Activation of the sheet feeder can be electronic, optical or both. For an electronic connection the feeder hooks into the signals which travel between the computer and the printer. Electronics contained in the feeder use these signals to activate the mechanism.

The second method uses a light and a photocell to watch what is happening to the paper as it passes through the printer. When the paper reaches the proper point, the feed mechanism is activated to remove the printed sheet, to place it into the stacker and then to move a new sheet from the paper hopper into the platen and up to the proper position to receive the first line.

Some feeders provide two hoppers for sheets of different sizes. If so designed, one hopper may be used for envelopes. Some printers require a special feeder for the envelope.

### Tractor Feed

Because an automatic sheet feeder can replace a tractor feed, it is essential to understand how the tractor feed works. In Figure 3.5.1 we see how the sprocket pins in the tractor feed fit into the sprocket holes in the paper. As the pins move upward, they carry the paper along with them.

The paper is perforated at intervals so that it is easy to tear into sheets. The spacing between the perforations is typically 11 inches so that sheets of 11 X 8 1/2 result.

Figure 3.5.1. The tractor feed advances paper positively. (Courtesy of Diablo).

The printer must be set up to correspond with the format of your document for the computer to operate it properly. For vertical motion, two settings are important:

- the number of print lines per vertical inch for single spacing (lpi);
- the number of lines per page to correspond to this lpi setting.

A typical setting is 6 lines per inch. Hence an 11 inch page has 66 lines on it.

*Operation*

At document creation time you choose the page format. Page length rarely changes throughout the document. For some printers you must reset switches on the printer manually to alter the number of the lines per inch and page length; for others, the WP program resets the printer without manual interaction. These settings usually remain constant for a particular office installation. Turn on the printer. The present position of the form registers as the official top of the form.

If the paper is not properly aligned, turn the platen to advance the paper so that the carriage prints on the top line of the form. There is a button to press so that the printer now registers *this* line as the current top of the form.

When you are ready to print a document, you go through the activities described in Chapter 7 to invoke the print format program. The format program sends text lines to the printer. At the end of each text line, the program additionally sends a line advance command. This causes the printer to move the paper vertically after printing each line. When the text for an entire page has been sent to the printer, the format program sends a final control code, a form feed. The printer then advances the tractor feed to move the paper for several more lines. It counts the number of lines until the total reaches the form length which you set it for. The form is ready to print on the first line of the new page. More line feeds are sent over by the format program for the top margin because you do not want printing to appear on the first line of the page.

**Automatic Feed Operation**

When the equipment is first attached it requires physical and electric connections. In some cases, physical connection means removing the platen and replacing it with one supplied by the sheet feed manufacturer. This platen has its own motor to move paper independently of the printer. The electric connection routes the incoming print signals to the feeder electronics so that it can detect and respond to the form-feed signal. Later, when a new sheet is positioned, the sheet feeder electronics returns an "acknowledge" signal to the printer electronics so that it will continue printing.

Each printer requires a differently designed feeder. This mechanism can be attached or removed in a matter of a few seconds. Figure 3.5.2 shows a sheet feeder mounted on the Ricoh printer; Figure 3.5.3 shows an automatic sheet feeder with two bins, either one of which can be activated, mounted on the Diablo printer for which it was designed.

To use the automatic sheet feed mechanism, we take the following steps:

1. Load the paper into the hopper.
2. Press the feed button.
3. The printer platen clutch disengages the printer motor from the platen.
4. The sheet-feed motor turns the platen so that the paper advances.
5. At the same time, paper is ejected from the hopper and is moved by friction by the platen.
6. A light beam and photoelectric sensor detect when the top of the paper has advanced far enough so that printing begins on the proper line. This function is settable and printing usually starts on line 7.

Figure 3.5.2. Single sheet feed mounted on Richo printer. (Courtesy of Rutishauser).

Figure 3.5.3. Double bin sheet feed on Diablo printer. (Courtesy of Rutishauser).

7. The feed motor stops and the printer clutch engages so that the printer has control of the platen.
8. The feed electronics now sends a signal to the printer (which would normally be generated internally) to indicate that form feed is complete.

Now the printer takes over. Printing begins and continues as required. When the next form-feed signal is sensed, the automatic sheet feed electronics takes over. The printed sheet now in the machine is advanced by the feed motor after the clutch is disengaged. The printed sheet goes into the stacker. Thereafter the sequence of events described above takes hold. In this way, a new clean sheet is taken from the hopper and advanced to the proper place. The printer is then given control and printing continues on the next page.

### Envelopes

Some automatic feeders accommodate envelopes in a hopper designed for them; some have two hoppers, one for sheets and one for envelopes. Do you interleave a letter with its envelope, if that is possible? Do you print two separate streams and then collate the letters and envelopes later? Suppose that a letter is corrected and redone; how do you suppress printing the envelope? Or do you print one anyway, to simplify things?

An alternative which eliminates these questions is the window envelope. When the letter is folded and inserted properly, its address shows through the window. No envelope is ever printed. It is a saving in time and materials. However, it does not have complete acceptance.

# 4
# External Storage

## 4.0 INTRODUCTION

**Need**

You create a document on your word processing system in a work area of memory. Memory for the modern computer is fast and inexpensive. It has one drawback; it is **volatile**: when you turn off the computer, whatever is in memory disappears. If this is a one-shot document which you prepare, print and never use again, that is alright. Most uses of the WP require at least one round of editing to get a finished document. Few WPs even print from memory. This means the WP system *demands* that you save your document on external storage. Then it is safe after the computer is turned off. Even if you expect to print it after composing it, you should save the document.

Even if main memory were nonvolatile, it is limited in size for two important reasons: the small computer was not engineered to accommodate memory large enough to hold many documents; it is more expensive than external storage.

**External storage** provides large amounts of inexpensive, reusable nonvolatile storage. It consists of two parts:

- a **medium** onto which electronic documents are written;
- a mechanism, the **disk drive**, for putting the document onto the medium and recovering the document from the medium any time later—in a few minutes or years.

To **write** is to place the electronic document onto external storage medium; to **read** is to recover the electronic document (ED) from external storage and put it into memory. Reading is **nondestructive**: you copy the document from external storage (into memory), but the original ED is still on the medium. It's like reading a book; after you read it, the pages are still there. The third action of external storage is to **hold** information: when we read the medium a minute, an hour, a day or a year later we will probably find the electronic document safe and sound.

I say *probably* because we have to take normal precautions to ensure safe-keeping of electronic documents, just as with paper documents. It is equally unlikely that floppy disks or paper archives can survive a flood.

Under normal conditions, we read the external medium to bring forth an electronic document into memory for further editing or for printing. A revised electronic document may then be written to the medium, either to replace the old copy or to put it under a new name.

## Media Characteristics

Let us examine some of the characteristics which make for a good medium for external storage.

*Permanence*

The medium should hold many electronic documents *securely* over long periods of time.

*Capacity*

The more electronic documents that a medium can hold, the more useful that medium is. A unit of a medium which may be installed on the drive at any given time has the technical name **volume**. Examples of a volume are a magnetic card, a cassette, a floppy disk and a disk pack (several disks in a removable unit for a large hard disk device). Some volumes are permanently mounted.

The difference in capacity is striking. A mag card generally holds a page of text; a floppy disk can hold 30 or 40 pages, but in the near future we expect capacities of up to 100 or more pages. Hard disks for WP hold 5 to 300 million bytes. **Gigabyte** (one billion bytes) drives are on the market. It is preferable to measure capacity in bytes, kilobytes or megabytes, since these are precise.

*Size*

The dimensions of a medium have an effect on its acceptability in the office. All the above are small relative to their capacity in bytes (a fraction to two or three cubic feet).

*Reliability*

If we cannot retrieve the electronic document without mistakes induced by the medium, then that medium is less attractive, if not totally unattractive. Reliability is measured by how many bits can be read, on the average, before one bit is read incorrectly. Reliability for the magnetic disk is in the order of $10^9$ to $10^{10}$. That's an error in reading one character out of 100,000,000 or so.

*Reuseability*

To record on some media, such as paper, the medium is permanently deformed. Perhaps "deform" is a strong word, but when paper has holes punched on it or has been written on, it is no longer usable as a medium for new information.

*Cost*

Magnetic media can be erased and reused with no effect on their reliability. Unit cost of the medium is important. This is less true when the medium is reusable, especially when its life is long. Most magnetic media are so inexpensive that their cost ($3 to $5 for a floppy) is hardly a factor. The high cost of hard disks is compensated for by their long life and reliability.

*Speed*

If you can request a document and within a few seconds have that document displayed on your CRT screen, then this medium is fast enough for the office environment.

*Accessibility*

Data may be stored on a physically sequential medium, such as paper or magnetic tape. Then you must pass through all the data from the beginning to the end if you need to get data at the end. A **random access medium** lets you go directly to the data you need without passing through the intervening "garbage."

### Media Choices

There are really just two choices for physical media to store electronic documents, paper and magnetic materials. Once a lot of paper was used with the computer to store information. It's still around today. We still see punchcards and punched paper tape. The trouble with paper is that once information is entered on it, it is very difficult to recycle it without sending it back to the manufacturer.

Cards and paper tape get a grade of F because neither is reusable.

Magnetic materials hold full sway today because they are compact, easy to use, fast, reliable, and perhaps most important of all, reuseable. A floppy disk, for instance, can be used hundreds of times before its performance degrades and it misses reading a character or two. Floppies are so inexpensive that we can throw them away when they become defective. Of course, we want to copy off and revitalize the information before we throw the floppy disk away. Utilities described in Section 8.5 do this. Hard disks are durable and their wear can be compensated for, as described later.

## 4.1 MAGNETIC RECORDING

**Principles**

The principles of magnetic recording apply to all magnetic media, regardless of their form or format. So this discussion is applicable to mag cards, floppy discs, magnetic tape (whether cassettes or reel-to-reel), and even to hard disks and removable multiple platter disks that are found on large computers.

*Medium*

A very thin coating of magnetic material stores the data. It is usually iron with perhaps a couple of other metals such as cobalt and manganese mixed in to get a nice set of magnetic properties. The coating is thin and of uniform consistency and thickness. The material is applied to a base which may be rigid or flexible. Each kind of base has its place and advantage. Most magnetic media on the WP scene, such as tape and floppy disks, are flexible. (Hard disks are rigid.)

The important property of the coating material is that it is magnetizible. If we place a magnet on or near the surface, that surface becomes magnetized. But even more important, the coating retains the magnetism when the magnet is removed from the vicinity. The magnetism is retained indefinitely without degrading. Yet the medium can be remagnetized to hold the new data. It is completely **reusable**.

*The Data*

Fortunately, magnets are **polarized**. One end of a bar magnet is the North pole and the other end is the South pole. It is easy to distinguish one pole from the other by using another magnet. Opposite poles attract; like poles repel. (A small compass tells you which pole is which; its South pole points to the magnet's North pole.)

The polarity of the magnet is the means for recording data. We don't want to just record magnets, we want to record 1s and 0s. The polarity of the recorded magnet lets us tell a 0 from a 1. The north pole of the magnet points one way for a recorded 1 and in the opposite direction for a 0, as shown in Figure 4.1.1.

To present a simplified view, entering bits onto the material is done by writing little magnets pointing in one direction or the other onto the coating. The material on which the film is coated (the **substrate**) must be in motion to recover

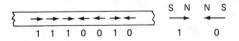

Figure 4.1.1. The polarity of recorded magnets designating 1s or 0s.

the data. The tape, mag card or floppy disk is moved at a constant speed to extract data from or enter data onto the medium.

The head which does the reading and the writing is a fraction of an inch wide. As the medium passes beneath the head, the head sweeps out an area called a **track**, regardless of the medium. The track is a thin long area, which may or may not fold back upon itself.

*Read*

The head is a soft iron bar which is bent around so that one end almost touches the other, as shown in Figure 4.1.2. It is in the shape of a circular horseshoe. The space between the two ends of the horseshoe is called the **gap**; the iron horseshoe itself is called the **core**. At about the middle of the core, wire wound about the iron is called the **coil**.

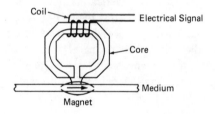

Figure 4.1.2.  A read and write head.

Let's see what happens when a magnet on the medium sits beneath the gap. The magnetism from the magnet, shown in the figure as lines of force, prefers to go through the soft iron than through the air. Many of the lines of force coming out of the North pole of the magnet are detoured through the core to return to the South pole of the magnet. They pass through the top of the core around a coil of wire. As long as these lines of force remain constant, they have no effect on the coil of wire. If they should change intensity, they generate a voltage in this coil.

When the little magnet on the medium sits still in the gap, nothing happens. When the medium is in motion, the number of magnetic lines passing through the core changes. This change in the magnetic field produces a voltage in the coil. The voltage is picked up and amplified by the electronics, which also extracts the 0 and 1 information originally recorded on the medium.

Since the coil responds only to a changing magnetic field, you see how important it is for the medium to move. If the motion is constant, it is easier to extract the 0 and 1 information from the voltages produced in the coil.

*Writing*

To write information on the medium, the arrangement is the same. In fact, the same head is used. Only the electronics is altered. Write electronics is switched in to replace the read electronics. The medium passes below the head. At the right time, a current sent through the wire produces a magnetic field in the core. When the field reaches the gap it would rather travel through the metal coating on the medium than through air. Hence, there is a strong magnetic field at this place on the medium. When the electric current stops, thus turning off the magnetic field, the magnet recorded on the medium remains there and can be read back at another time.

The direction of the electric current determines the direction of the magnetic field, which, in turn, determines if the magnet produced on the medium has a North pole which faces right or left for a 0 or 1.

**Shape of the Medium**

Figure 4.1.3 shows three important shapes which the medium may have. At the top we see a long, thin tape. In the middle is a disk. At the bottom is a flat rectangle.

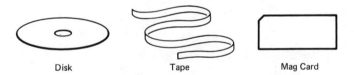

Disk                    Tape                    Mag Card

Figure 4.1.3. Shapes that magnetic media may take.

The tape at the top may contain one single track or a set of seven or nine tracks. The disk in the center has two surfaces on which either or both of many circular tracks may be placed. The rectangle at the bottom, the mag card, contains many parallel tracks going from left to right on one of its sides.

*Magnetic Tape*

The magnetic tape was the first external erasable computer-controlled storage medium. To store large quantities of information, wide tape is used. Width varies between 1/2″ and 1 inch. Even larger tapes have been used for special purposes.

A number of heads are spread out along the width of the track as shown in Figure 4.1.4. Usually they number either seven or nine. Nine bits records a byte and one additional bit for checking. Writing and reading is done a character at a time by examining all nine heads simultaneously. Such tapes are of little importance in word processing because the tape drives are expensive—$20,000 or more—well above the price of a full word processing system.

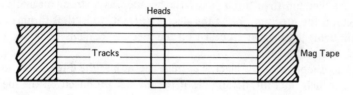

Figure 4.1.4. Magnetic tape.

Tape was one of the first magnetic media to be associated with word processing. The cassette shown in Figure 4.1.5 contains several hundred feet of magnetic tape 1/8 to 1/4 inch in width. Only one head records on or reads from the tape. Cassettes are inexpensive because they are used heavily in the audio field. To provide greater accuracy, a form of digital recording is used to write and to read from these cassettes.

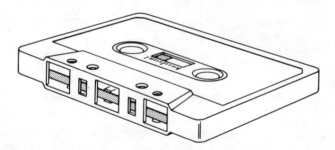

Figure 4.1.5. The cassette.

The first memory typewriters used mag cards or cassettes. When you hit a key, this may or may not activate a type bar; the code which the key produces is stored on the cassette (mag card). This cassette can be replayed later to drive the typewriter and type out the document. Correction is done by playing back the tape and reentering information over the old data.

New models of the memory typewriters have appeared recently in the $1,200 to $5,000 range. They provide some editing capability but not nearly enough for the kind of text processing which seems to be necessary in most office environments.

*Others*

The other two media, the floppy disk and the hard disk, are so important for the word processor that separate sections are devoted in this chapter to cover them.

## 4.2 DISK DRIVES

### Common Physical Features

The **disk** is the medium; the **disk drive** is the mechanical and electric device which reads from or writes onto the disk. Some drive units accommodate more than one disk. The disk or a group of disks which is accessible without operator intervention automatically is called a **volume**. For many drives you can remove the volume and store it elsewhere. The volume is **removable**. For other drives the volume is permanently associated with the drive and cannot be removed.

*The Disk*

Figure 4.2.1 shows two minifloppy disks (foreground) on top of a disk control-

Figure 4.2.1. A magnetic disk. (Courtesy of Micropolis).

ler board. Two drives in their cases are seen in the background accompanied by a connecting cable. Figure 4.2.2 shows a disk diagrammatically; it is like a 45 rpm phonograph record without grooves. Instead there are tracks, not visible to the eye. A rectangle in the figure represents a head which may move in either direction horizontally **(seek)**. The head moving mechanism is accurate, positioning the head precisely to a given horizontal position. As the disk rotates, a thin circular bank the width of the head gap and called a **track** passes beneath the head. The track contains all the data available at this horizontal position of the head.

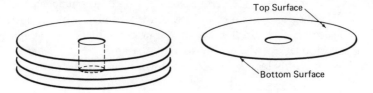

Figure 4.2.2. A multidisk magnetic volume, the disk pack.

The recording area starts at the outer edge of the disk but does not go to the center. The center area of the disk is not suitable for recording, just as is the case with a long playing record. Between the outer edge and the inner recording limit there are a number of tracks. This number, the **tracks per surface**, can vary from about 35 on minifloppies to 400 or more on large disks.

*Multiple Surfaces*

A volume, for some drives, consists of more than one disk. Each disk consists of two **surfaces**, a top and bottom. The volume shown in Figure 4.2.3 consists of four disks and eight physical surfaces. All surfaces are coated with magnetic material. However, sometimes not all are used for recording. The four disks shown in the figure may consist of only six **recording surfaces**. It is usual to find one head for each recording surface. It is then called a **head-per-surface drive**. Some very large and expensive drives have one head for every track.

The heads are mounted on an arm which moves in and out horizontally at the request of the computer. It moves accurately to a selected track; the movement

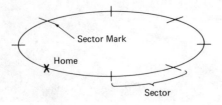

Figure 4.2.3. A track consists of sectors.

is called **seeking**. The time it takes for the arm to position a head from one track to another is called the **seek time**. Seek time is proportional to the distance between the tracks; it takes longer to go from track 1 to track 21 than it does to go from track 5 to track 10.

With multiple surfaces a single arm bears members, each holding one or two heads which move between adjacent surfaces. As the arm positions one head, it also positions the other heads. Thus, if the head on the first surface is on track 10, the heads for all the other surfaces are also on track 10. The set of tracks defined by each position of the arm is called a **cylinder**. Cylinder 16 for a 6 surface volume is track 16 of surface 1, 2, 3, etc.—a total of six tracks.

### Timing

The disk has circular tracks on it which seem to have no beginning or end. To make it possible to find specific areas of data, a timing signal originating from the disk itself establishes the start of each track.

When the timing signal occurs, this position is designated as **home**, a synthetic beginning of each track from which all data is referenced.

### Sectors

Secondary markers reference smaller amounts of data. **Sector markers** at fixed positions along the track separate the data into sectors as shown in Figure 4.2.4.

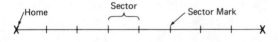

Figure 4.2.4. A track as a line segment.

A track is easier to visualize if we cut it apart at home and spread it out along the straight line, as shown in Figure 4.2.5. The track begins at home and contains a number of sector markers. A **sector** defines the data between two con-

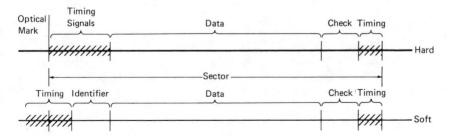

Figure 4.2.5. Makeup of a sector.

secutive sector marks. Sectors are numbered according to their position from home. The first sector is numbered 0, the second is numbered 1, and so forth.

*The Disk*

One way to mark a sector is with a small hole, as described in the next section. A sector timing signal results from a light and a photocell which detects the hole; this is called **hard sectoring**.

Another way to mark sectors is to write identifiers at the beginning of *every* sector on the disk. A disk formating program does this. Before a new volume is used, this program is run to **format the volume**. As the disk rotates, the program writes, at fixed intervals along the track, the sector and track identifiers for every sector and track on the disk. These identifiers may be rewritten at some later date, should the format program be rerun. They are not permanent, which is why this is called **soft sectoring**. Writing sector markers is only one of the things that the format programs does. Sometimes it also detects if writing may be done successfully on all tracks.

All volumes and disk drives associated with word processing use sectoring of some kind. Very large disks for large computer installations use other techniques to achieve timing.

### Data

The drive reads and writes data in units of one sector. Commands to request reading and writing come from the computer. Each sector to be read or written and every function to be performed needs a separate command. Reading or writing takes place only when the head is over the desired track and the sector arrives beneath the head. To identify the sector the drive must recognize:

- Which surface is desired when there are several surfaces;
- Which track is used;
- Which sector on the track is needed.

### The Sector

Figure 4.2.6 shows the general makeup of a sector. At the left, for hard sectoring only, the sector is announced by an optically sensed timing signal. Following this, a number of timing pulses are written to make sure that the electronics

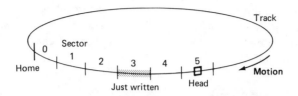

Figure 4.2.6. After writing section 3 the head may have moved to sector 5 when the next sector is ready to write.

is in synchronism with the signals coming from the head. Next an identifier, provided only for soft sectoring, lists this surface, track and sector number. Data follow and consist of bits grouped into bytes. A sector usually holds 128, 256 or 516 bytes of data.

Following the last byte of data are several additional bytes used for checking. This group of bits is called the **cyclic redundancy check** or **CRC**, discussed shortly. Following the CRC there is an area filled with timing pulses continuing past the beginning of the next sector. This area allows for changes in speed from one drive to the next when the volume is moved to another drive.

## Checking

It is essential to ensure the accuracy of the data. The electronic document that you wrote yesterday should be the same when you edit it today. Two kinds of checking are provided:

- A parity check bit is provided in each byte.
- The CRC provides a check of the data in the entire sector.

A parity bit checks each byte. Odd parity is standard. (It is possible to use even parity.) For **odd parity**, one bit is added to the seven bit ASCII code for every character to make it consist of an odd number of 1s. The bit added, the **parity bit,** is set to 1 or 0 so that whatever condition the other bits are in, this bit will always produce an odd number of 1s in the byte. If a character code is read with an even number of 1s, this is a **parity error** (since it was written with an odd number of 1s).

When data is sent to the disk drive, a standard but complex operation is performed on the bits as the data is *written* into the sector. This operation comes up with a set of 16 bits, the CRC. Later, when the disk drive *reads* the sector to recover the data, this same set of operations is performed on the data as it is read. The result is another set of 16 bits. If that set of bits is the *same* as the CRC recorded at the end of the sector, there is an excellent chance that the data is absolutely correct.

### Drivers, Blocks and Sectors

The disk drive is run by the **disk controller**, a part of the hardware (see Figure 4.2.1). After a sector is either read or written, control goes back to a program which activates the disk drive called the **disk driver**, (part of the operating system). The disk driver determines what action if any the disk drive should make next.

It takes time for the disk driver program to make a decision. In the meantime, the disk itself continues to rotate. The situation is shown in Figure 4.2.7. Here sector 3 of some track has just been written. While the disk driver program is making a decision about what to do next, the disk has rotated so that it is now over sector 5. If the disk-driver's decision is to write the next piece of data sequentially on the track after sector 3, then almost a full rotation will be required until sector 4 appears again.

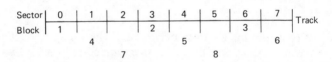

Figure 4.2.7. Skewing puts consecutive blocks in sectors to reduce elapsed time.

*The Block*

A **block** is a *quantity* of data identical to that held by a sector on the disk. The software which manages your file, the File Manager, views the file as sequential tracks each consisting of sequential blocks. Writing blocks in the same sequence and in the same positions as the sectors appear on the track reduces the timing efficiency of the hardware. To write into four sequential sectors might take four revolutions because of decision time of the disk driver program. By the time the driver reaches a decision, the next sector has passed beneath the write head; it takes a full revolution for the sector to return.

To reduce this time, a method of writing the blocks into sectors, called **skewing** or **interleaving**, is utilized. Skew is another word for offset. Instead of putting sequential blocks in sequential sectors, they are offset. The amount of the offset takes into consideration the longest decision-making time required by the disk-driver program.

Figure 4.2.7 shows a skewing scheme for an eight sector track. Sectors are numbered sequentially 0 to 7. Blocks are numbered 1 to 8, a more natural numbering system. Writing (reading) several sequentially numbered blocks into (from) the sectors assigned to them is definitely faster when skewing is employed.

Examine how to write blocks 2, 3, 4 and 5 in two revolutions. On command, the disk drive finds the desired track (the head seeks). For the next command the drive looks for sector 3 in which to write block 2. New the disk-driver program determines that block 3 is to be written in sector 6. Meanwhile the disk turns. Perhaps the head is in the middle of sector 5 when the disk drive is activated. That is fine, because sector 6 is coming up next. Both blocks 2 and 3 can be written on the same revolution of the disk; blocks 4 and 5 are written on the next revolution.

### Disk Software

There is considerable division of labor with respect to the tasks which are performed for **input** and **output** (other terms for reading and writing onto the disk). Figure 4.2.8 shows various agencies involved in simple input and output activity.

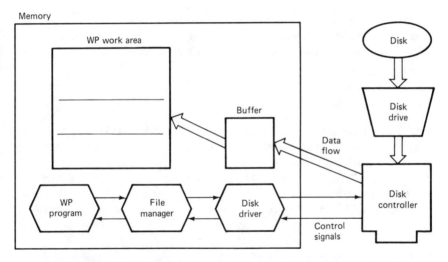

Figure 4.2.8. Disk software and hardware showing input.

In the box labeled "memory" we find two rectangles which represent work areas to hold text. There are three hexagons, each representing a program. The left hexagon labeled "WP" is one of the word processing programs such as the text editor or print format program. The other two are part of the operating system.

The center hexagon is the file manager as is labeled. It accepts requests from the word processor program in general terms and converts them into specific terms for the disk driver. This last operating system program converts the requests from the file manager into physical commands which cause movement in the disk drive.

The disk controller is a hardware component. It accepts commands for physical motion and electric action. It supervises these actions in the mechanical disk drive. Signals from the disk drive tell the controller what is happening and it issues further signals to complete the action.

Finally there is the disk. It contains the data. It is moved by the disk drive so that the data can be either copied from or entered onto the disk.

The disk controller takes care of only one command from the computer at a time. The hardware command may involve a number of simple mechanical actions within the drive. Signals go back and forth between the controller and the drive during the course of this command. A space in memory is set aside for data acted upon the drive. This space is called a **buffer**. A hardware command may either fill or empty this buffer (Figure 4.2.8). The device driver carries out the sequence of commands required to fill or empty the buffer. More details about file management are forthcoming in the next section and Section 5.3.

### 4.3 DISKETTES

The most popular WP external medium by far is the diskette. It is important to understand how the diskette is used and what specifications about it and its drive mean.

#### Physical Description

The **diskette** has several other names: sometimes it is called a **floppy disk** or simply a **floppy**; a small diskette is a **minifloppy**. Regardless of how you refer to it, here we simply call it a **disk** for brevity. The sandwich, consisting of a coated thin plastic disk between two sheets of thin cardboard is usually referred to as the diskette. It now comes in three sizes: 8, 5¼ and 3½ inch. The most popular for WPs is the largest, the floppy. The middle size, the minifloppy, is growing in use. The last is called a **microfloppy**—a new product put out by Sony to which we devote just a line in a table later on.

Both the floppy and the minifloppy disk are made of thin plastic coated on both sides with a magnetizable material. The disk is housed in a square envelope of thin cardboard, usually black on the outside. Its label bears either the manufacturer's or the vendor's name. There is room on the label for you to name the disk so that you can tell one disk from the next.

Both the disk and the envelope have a hole through their center. The hole in the disk is about an 1¼ inch in diameter, and that in the envelope is about 1½ inch. The drive mechanism grasps the disk and rotates it within the envelope which is held motionless. The inside of the envelope should provide little friction against the movement of the disk. It is coated with a smooth plastic on the inside to reduce friction.

Figure 4.3.1 shows a sketch of the disk and the envelope which contains it for both the floppy and minifloppy.

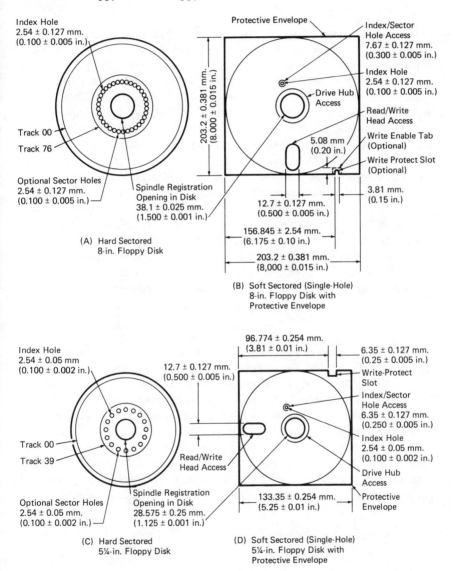

Figure 4.3.1. The floppy and minifloppy and their envelopes. (Courtesy of Mini-Micro-systems).

**Holes and Slots**

There are several holes and slots in the envelope and disk.

*Spindle Hole*

The hole in the center of the disk enables a cylinder, slightly tapered on the top, to penetrate this hole and position the disk precisely so that its center is the center of rotation, to ensure that it doesn't wobble. When the disk is seated properly and the head is positioned over a track, all of that track passes beneath the head. If the disk were off center, the track would wobble back and forth beneath the head like an off-center record on a turntable. If you insert the disk envelope so that the disk is slightly off center, the cylinder moves in and centers it properly when the drive is activated. It is amazing how well this works.

The hole in the envelope is larger than the hole in the disk to leave some of the disk showing. When the drive is turned on, a clutch is electrically activated. On one side of the disk is a continuously running drive platter; on the other side is a friction pad attached to a shaft which is free to rotate. The clutch moves the friction pad so as to push the central hub portion of the disk against the drive platter and thus start the disk moving. There is sufficient pressure and friction so that the clutch engages the drive platter. The motion of the platter is imparted to the flexible disk and brings it rapidly up to speed; the disk must be moving at a uniform speed for the data to be read or written accurately.

*Head Access Slot*

A slot along a portion of one diameter of the disk exposes the recording surface on one or both sides of the disk. If the disk is inserted properly, the head is above this slot. All the tracks are available to the head as it seeks back and forth. The head is moved in fixed steps; where it stops defines a track of the disk. Figure 4.3.2 shows the disk with the envelope removed and the head-positioning mechanism which moves the head to the desired track.

Before the head can read or write on the disk, it must be placed in contact with the disk. When no information is being transferred, the head is kept away from the disk to prevent wear. Only when data is being transferred is the head pushed toward the disk to make contact with it; this is called **loading** the head.

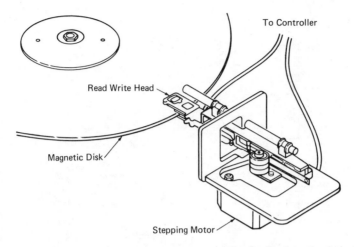

Figure 4.3.2. The stepping motor moves the arm to take the head to the desired track. (Courtesy of Mini-Microsystems).

*Index Hole*

There is a small hole in the envelope called the index hole. There is at least one hole in the disk at the same distance from its center. When the disk hole passes beneath the hole in the envelope, it signals the beginning of each track. When the index hole in the disk and the envelope are aligned, light passes from a source to a photocell, producing a timing signal indicating the home position on all tracks. At other times the disk interferes with this ray of light and no signal is produced.

*Sector Holes*

All disks have one index hole to designate the home position. Only hard sectored disks have sector holes at the same distance from the center. The same photocell and light source produce a sector signal as each sector hole passes through the light source. This is shown in Figure 4.3.3. The sector holes are smaller and produce a shorter pulse than that for the index hole.

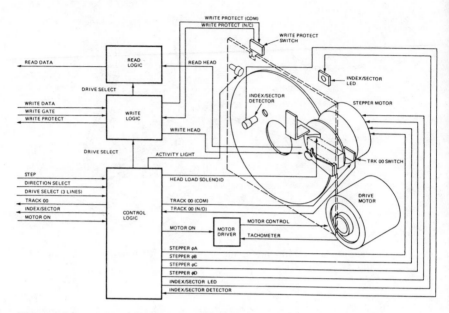

Figure 4.3.3. A photocell and light emitting diode detect the index and sector hole(s). (Courtesy of Mini-Microsystems).

*Protect Notch*

There is a slot or a notch in the cardboard in one of the corners of the envelope. No part of the disk lies beneath this slot; there is a clear path for a light ray to pass through this area. Another light source and photocell detect whether the slot is covered or uncovered.

For some reason the standards are different:

- For the minifloppy, you cover the slot to protect the disk from being written on and uncover the slot to write on the disk.
- For the floppy, you cover the slot to enable the disk to be written on and uncover the slot to protect the disk.

### Operating the Drive

*Inserting the Disk*

Your computer has one or sometimes two slots (**dual drives**) each of which can receive a disk. The slots may be vertical, which is usual, or sometimes horizontal. For a simpler orientation of the description, assume a horizontal slot. There are eight permutations for inserting the disk, determined by:

- which side of the disk is up,
- which corner of the disk goes in first on the left side (of course there are four corners).

You must follow the directions given by the vendor: inserting the correct surface facing up makes that surface available to the head; putting the proper corner in first aligns the slot to expose the surface of the disk to the head. The other three positions will not allow the head to contact the surface of the disk.

After inserting the disk, you close the door to activate the drive mechanism. If your drive has no door, a microswitch in the back of the drive turns on the drive when the disk is seated.

*Activating the Disk*

For the 8 inch disk, closing the door or pushing the disk in firmly activates the drive mechanism, engages the clutch and causes the disk to get up to speed. The drive circuitry may check out the disk to make sure that it can be read, align the head to track 0 and read in the first track, if you are "booting" the system. As long as the door is closed and the computer is on, the disk rotates. When the computer needs to write or read, it issues requests to the controller to position the head to the right track, load the head and check for home position. When the desired sector arrives, the controller begins to read or write information.

The minifloppy is driven by a DC motor which can get up to speed very quickly. When the disk is not being used, the motor is off and the disk is not revolving. To access the disk, the motor must first be activated; the disk needs time, several hundred milliseconds, to get up to speed. During this delay, the heads may position. The heads are loaded. The transfer of data is possible when the right sector arrives.

Another time delay in the minifloppy drive keeps the disk rotating for a short time after use. The philosophy is that if you have just used the disk, it is probable that you will use the disk again shortly. So the disk is kept rotating for several seconds. To use the disk within that interval, the mechanism simply loads the head, a matter of 50 to 100 milliseconds.

*Positioning Time*

How long does it take to find the data? This depends upon where you are. Let's start with the 8-inch floppy. If the disk has not been used recently, the head is not loaded; the head is sitting above the disk. Take the simplest case first. You want data on the track above which the head is sitting. The time to get to your data is the head load time plus latency. **Head load time** is the time to activate the mechanism which pushes the head against the disk; **latency** is the time required for the block of data that you need to arrive at the head. To prevent wear, the head is kept away from the disk when it is not needed. It takes about 40 milli-seconds for head load.

Once the head is loaded, you wait until the data appears beneath the head. The disk revolves at 360 revolutions per minute or 6 revolutions per second. One revolution takes 167 milliseconds. On the average you would have to wait for half revolution. **Latency**, the average time that you wait for data, is 83 milli-seconds.

Now suppose you have to **seek**—move the head to a different track. The disk drive has a stepping motor which moves the head one track at a time. The more tracks that we have to move the head over, the longer it takes to get to the de-sired track. Hence seek time depends on the number of tracks that the head moves. **Track-to-track positioning time** (time to move from one track to either adjacent track) is about 10 to 15 milliseconds. A seek can be performed with the heads loaded. If the heads have just been used previously, seek is performed while they are loaded. Otherwise, a seek is done as the heads are being loaded.

After the head arrives at the right track, it is all shaken up. The impulses in-duced by the stepping motor cause the head to vibrate; it needs time to settle down. The **settling time** (about 35 to 40 milliseconds) is the time for the head to stop vibrating before use.

To give you some idea of how long it takes to access data, the **average access time** is based on positioning the head over approximately one third of the tracks on the disk. It consists of:

- seek over the tracks,
- settle,
- load,
- latency.

This calculation of time in a typical case is illustrated in Table 4.3.1. The **track-**

**Table 4.3.1. Time for Floppy Disk Activities.**

| Item | Time in Milliseconds | | |
| --- | --- | --- | --- |
| | Range | Typical | |
| Track-to-track seek | 3–8 | 6 | |
| Seek 26 tracks | 78–208 | | 156 |
| Settle time | 10–15 | 13 | 13 |
| Load | 35–40 | 37 | 37 |
| Latency at 360 rpm | 83 | 83 | 83 |
| | | | |
| Track-to-track access time | | 139 | |
| Average Positioning time | | | 289 |

**to-track average access time** is calculated using the time to move to an adjacent track.

## Specifications

A number of quantities tell you how disk drives perform. Manufacturers and vendors provide quantitative figures to let you know what their drives can do. What does each parameter mean and how is it derived?

*Sides*

Disks are manufactured with a coating on both sides. Presumably, all disks *could* be recorded on either side. However, if they are checked out only on one side, they are single sided disks for a **single sided drive**.

When the disks are checked on both sides they are called dual sided disks for use in a **dual head** or **dual sided drive**. This drive has a pair of heads on the arm, one to read or write each side of the disk; you can read and write with either. Such a drive and disk doubles the storage capacity of a single disk. Also two tracks are available without a seek.

Dual sided disk drives came out at the end of 1979. They were released without complete life testing. Some of the drive designs were not perfect and the heads sometimes scored the disks, as shown in Figure 4.3.4. These defects have

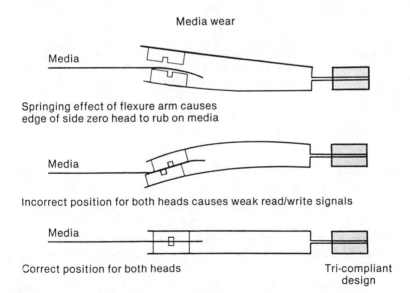

Figure 4.3.4. Double sided floppies had trouble with head designs. Note good and bad practice. (Courtesy of Mini-Microsystems).

been remedied and dual head drives are now very reliable. (Do not confuse **dual drives**—two drives in the same housing—with dual head drives.)

*Density*

**Density** refers to the number of bits packed per square inch of recording surface. This number depends not only upon the chemical composition of the coating but also on the design of the read/write head. The smaller the gap in the head, the smaller the spot where a bit is written. Figure 4.3.5 shows the evolution of the read/write head to the present day thin film head.

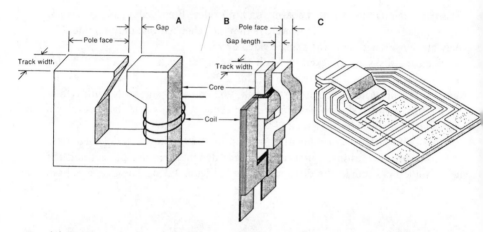

**(1)** Read/write heads are basically electromagnets **(A)**, and conventional heads are made of a ferrite core **(B)**. Much higher densities are achieved by thin-film heads **(C)**, which are made through photolithographic processes, and have higher resolution, higher permeability, and less noise.

Figure 4.3.5. Three implementations of the read/write head for the floppy disk drive manual file. (Courtesy of Mini-Microsystems).

Information is packed differently longitudinally—along the track created by the path of the read/write head—and between tracks. Hence there are two measurements of density. The size of the head gap determines how close tracks can be packed to one another without interference from its neighbor. One measure of density is the number of **tracks per inch** stored on the disk.

How close are bits written within the track? This measure of density is **bits per inch**. It determines for a given drive the number of **bits per track** and consequently the number of **characters per track**. These in turn depend on the track length. Note that the outermost track is longer than the innermost track. The limiting factor in determining bit density is the length of the innermost track. The track density in bytes per track (but not bits per inch) applies to every track, regardless of its position on the disk.

*Speed*

The speed of rotation for the disks is standard: 8 inch disks rotate at 360 revolutions per minute or 167 milliseconds per revolution. Minifloppies rotate at 300 revolutions per minute or 200 milliseconds per revolution.

*Transfer Rate*

The **transfer rate** is the rate at which data is passed between the disk and the computer. It is the product of the number of revolutions per second and the number of characters per track.

*Capacity*

The amount of data, whether program or text, that a disk can hold, the **disk capacity**, is the number of tracks times the number of characters on each track. Disk capacity is rated in characters per disk or per side.

Some WP vendors rate disks in terms of pages per disk. This may be misleading; you must know how big a page the vendor is talking about to make this estimate meaningful. Single spaced pages hold twice as much text as double spaced pages. Also, you must carefully distinguish between a memory page, as discussed later on, and a page of text on the printed document.

### Summary

Table 4.3.2 gives capacity information for the various forms of disks currently available, including microfloppies and high-density minifloppies by Tandon.

**Table 4.3.2. Floppy Disk Specifications.**

| Diameter: | 8" | | | | 5 1/4" | | | | | | | | 3.5" | |
|---|---|---|---|---|---|---|---|---|---|---|---|---|---|---|
| | | | | | | | | | | | | | Tandon | |
| Track/side | 77 | | | | 35 | | | | 35 | | | | 80 | 70 |
| Sectors/side | 26 | | | | HARD = 10 | | | | SOFT = 26 | | | | 10 | 9 |
| Density | S | | D | | S | | D | | S | | D | | D | D |
| Bytes/Sector | 128 | | 256 | | 256 | | 512 | | 128 | | 256 | | 512 | 512 |
| Sides | 1 | 2 | 1 | 2 | 1 | 2 | 1 | 2 | 1 | 2 | 1 | 2 | 2 | 1 |
| Capacity, K | 256 | 512 | 512 | 1024 | 89 | 179 | 179 | 358 | 71 | 143 | 143 | 287 | 819 | 323 |

## 4.4 DISK CONTENTS

At least 80,000 characters of text can be stored on a single small diskette. This could be the text of a single document. More commonly, there are many electronic documents on each volume. The contents of a volume is not restricted to electronic documents. It may contain programs and other things. Each entity on the volume is called a **file**.

### The File

The file is a quantity of information on the medium, allocated to and named by a user. The file is not immediately available until some application program such as the text editor asks the file manager to **open** the file. When finished with the file, the application program asks the file manager to perform an opposite action, to **close** the file.

There are many different kinds of files and file organizations. For some WPs, the entire electronic document (ED) comprises a file; for others the page of an ED is a file. The space which a program occupies on external storage is also called a file. Before it gets into memory, the text editor program is stored on a volume as a file. Parts of the operating system are stored as files before they get into memory.

### The Volume

There is a lot of space available, even on the smallest volume. It is important:

- to keep track of all the space
- and to be able to find a desired file immediately.

First, let us make some order out of the space. Begin with cylinders and number them from the outside in, starting from 0. Within a cylinder there are a number of tracks; number them according to the surfaces on which they appear, starting from surface 0. Within a track, number the blocks, starting with 0. If there is only one surface, number tracks and then blocks within the tracks.

In Section 4.2 we saw that blocks and sectors do not correspond exactly because of skewing. However, the driver converts the directions it receives in terms of blocks to sectors, so we need no longer concern ourselves with sectors.

*The Extent*

With the help of the driver, blocks (and tracks) numbered consecutively seem to be adjacent and we may regard them as so. A solid area consisting of a number of consecutive blocks in consecutive tracks is called an **extent**. An extent is a solid area in which there are no "holes" belonging to another file. It is convenient to handle a file which is in one solid area—a single extent. But if that were a requirement, it would interfere with the necessary growth of the file (an electronic document) as you add material to it during editing. If a file were limited to one extent, how would it grow without eliminating its neighbors? Hence, for most WPs, a file does not have to occupy one solid area; it may occupy several extents.

The file manager keeps track of the area occupied by a file, the extents it occupies. To make this possible, the file manager also keeps track of free, empty or unoccupied space to provide for growth of files during processing.

## Allocation Directories

Two directories are maintained on the volume by the file manager. These keep track of:

- free space on the volume which is not allocated,
- the space allocated to each active file.

The disk is an unwieldly shape. Let us change it into a rectangle. Think of the disk as being made of flexible material that can expand or contract at will. In Figure 4.4.1 we cut this disk along the home position and separate it. Now reform it, contracting the outside and stretching the inside so that it becomes a rectangle, as shown at the bottom of the figure. The blocks numbered 1 through 8 maintain the same relative position. Track 0, which is on the outside of the disk, is at the top of the rectangle. Track 35, which is on inside of the disk, now appears at the bottom of the rectangle.

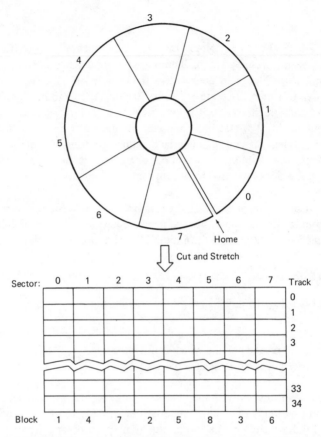

Figure 4.4.1. Cutting and stretching a disk so that it can be represented as a rectangle.

Now let us make a bit map as shown in Figure 4.4.2. This map keeps track of all space on the disk, telling us whether it is allocated or unallocated. For simplicity, let us keep track of tracks only. Actually, we could keep track of blocks, block pairs or any other intermediate subdivision. The left of Figure 4.4.2, the rectangle, shows blocks and tracks assigned to different files on this disk. At the right of the figure is a column with rows each consisting of one bit: that bit is set to 1 if the track it represents is assigned to some file; the bit is set to 0 if the space is free (not currently allocated to a file). Thus, only one bit keeps track of a whole track. This is an efficient way of monitoring free space.

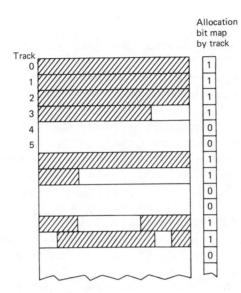

Figure 4.4.2. The bit map shows free and allocated tracks or sets of blocks.

We need another table to find any named file presently allocated space on the disk. One organization for such a directory is shown in Figure 4.4.3. Each entry in this directory begins with space for the name of a file of up to 11 characters. A number of bytes follow, each of which may hold a track number (in binary) of one of the tracks assigned to this file. Some files have only one track allocated, whereas others have several. Each byte position can contain a track number or 0. When 0 is encountered in scanning this entry, it indicates that no further tracks have been allocated to this file. Thus the file HELP.TXT is assigned only track 2, since all the other track number positions for this file are 0.

| LTR.1 | 18 | 19 | 0 | 0 | 0 | 0 |
|-----------|----|----|----|----|---|---|
| PROG3.BITS | 2 | 3 | 4 | 0 | 0 | 0 |
| HELP.TXT | 2 | 0 | 0 | 0 | 0 | 0 |
| SCHED.COM | 23 | 0 | 0 | 0 | 0 | 0 |
| RPT3 | 12 | 13 | 14 | 15 | 0 | 0 |

Figure 4.4.3. The allocation directory shows which areas are free and which tracks or sets of blocks are assigned to named files.

### Allocation Strategy

There are at least two **allocation strategies**—ways to assign space to files:

1. Provide a program called by a user to create and destroy files.
2. Have the file manager do the allocation as it works with each file.

For (1), when a user needs a file, he calls upon the allocation routine both to create the file entry and to allocate space to the file. However, this routine is called upon outside of the working program. It takes care of creating and disposing of the file. The application uses the file with the help of the file manager. A problem arises when the file space is used up. If the file manager cannot invoke the allocation routine, there is no easy way for the file to expand. A program is needed to get more space and to copy the file into the new, expanded area because the file cannot be extended dynamically. This strategy is unsatisfactory for word processing. When you create a file, you should not be expected to know its size.

For the second strategy, when you name a file, you get a minimum allocation for it. The file manager servicing your data requests is also in charge of allocation. As your file grows, the file manager keeps track of the remaining allocated space. When you reach the limit of your space, he immediately allocates more space for you and you continue to enter text without interference (unless there is no more space on the disk). (Since the file manager demonstrates some intelligence, I refer to it with a personal pronoun). The action of the file manager is unknown to you. In computer jargon, it is **transparent** (until the disk is full).

### Disk Layout

Figure 4.4.4 shows how the space on the disk might typically be used. It is standard to have the operating system at the beginning of the (system) disk (when

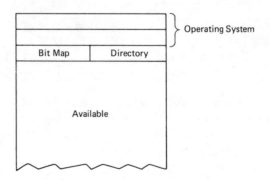

Figure 4.4.4. How disk space might be used.

the disk also houses programs). This facilitates bringing in the operating system, discussed in Chapter 5. At a standard position near the beginning we find the bit map followed by the file directory. Part of the file directory is unused, so that there is space to add entries for new files as they are created. The rest of the disk stores files—programs, text or other data.

## Using the Directory

The file manager uses the directory for:

1. Creating a new file,
2. Using an existing file,
3. Deleting (destroying) an existing file.

*Creating A File*

When a program, such as the text editor, needs to create a new file, it makes its request to the file manager. The file manager gets the bit map from the disk and brings it into memory. Then the file manager goes through the file directory on the disk to make sure that the new file does not already exist. If it does exist, then the creation request is invalid. The user is informed that "the file already exists."

With the bit map, the file manager finds an area on the disk, a track or number of blocks, which he allocates to this file. Then the file manager creates a directory entry using the name "supplied" to it by the text editor. The file manager puts the location of the first area allocated into the entry. As data is sent to the file manager to be written on to the disk, it is relayed to the disk driver, which activates the disk drive to write the data onto the medium. The data accumulates in a buffer until a complete block of data arrives. This block is then written.

The file manager keeps a close check on the quantity of data which he passes along to be written onto the disk. For instance, he may keep track of space by the block, even when space is allocated by the track. When the track is used up, the file manager examines the bit map and makes another allocation. As he does this, he enters the new allocation into the file directory entry. He also sets the corresponding allocation bit to 1 in the bit map to indicate that the track is now spoken for.

The file manager's action continues thus until the user program has completed the creation activity. Now the file manager has an updated bit map and a complete directory entry. Both are rewritten onto the disk at their assigned location for the next time a disk allocation is required.

For an existing file, the file manager finds and searches the directory, checking each entry for the file name. For a new file, he locates space within the directory. (If there is no space for the entry, additions to the disk can not be recorded.) Unused entries in the directory are flagged to indicate that they are available. For instance, they may contain blanks. The file manager writes the directory entry for this new file into the first blank entry that he encounters. The next time someone needs this file, the entry for it is in the directory.

Should the file already exist, after the new entry is written, the space it had occupied is released by flagging the old entry as empty.

### Using a File

First consider the simple use of the file without alteration. The program to print a file reviews (reads) the file from beginning to end without adding or deleting text; it makes no changes.

When you ask to print an ED, the operating system asks for the print program from the file manager, who finds it by looking up the program's file name in the file directory. The file manager needs only the directory entry. Since the file is read, not written, it cannot need more space.

Now the print format program takes over. You give it the name of the ED (file) that you want to print; he passes this to the file manager who gets the file entry from the directory and keeps it available in his work area.

As requests come from the print program, the file manager directs the disk driver to get the next block (or track, according to the file manager design) of information. The file manager keeps track of which track and block is being used. The last block in the file is distinguished by a particular mark, usually called the **end of file mark**. This tells the file manager that no more data is forthcoming and he informs the print program.

### Growth

A file which grows or contracts during use is a requirement for storing text in the word processing environment. There are several techniques to handle the growth process. These are deferred to Chapter 5.

### Deleting A File

The file manager accepts requests to delete files. It is important to understand that a file is never really destroyed. The file manager simply releases the space which the file presently occupies and removes the file entry from the directory by setting the file name in the entry to blanks. Later, if you ask for this file, since the directory entry is absent, the file manager cannot find the file. If you use a utility program to print out the contents of the disk right after you have deleted the file, you will see that the file is actually still on the disk.

In response to the delete request the file manager gets the bit map from the disk. Then he finds the directory entry. He notes where he got this directory entry. He writes blanks in place of the entry. The entry in the directory is now cleared and can be reused when another file is created.

The file manager refers to the copy of the directory entry which he has in memory. Each track listed in the entry corresponds to a part of the file. There should be a 1 in the bit map for each track which that file occupies. To delete all the space that the file occupies, merely set those bits in the bit map to 0. The directory entry tells the file manager which bit map entries to reset to 0. When the bit map is reset, write the bit map back onto the disk. Now the space previously occupied by the file is listed as "free." When space is needed at some later point for another file, the bit map lists the space that the file occupied as available. It may be written over for another user and under another file name.

## 4.5 WINCHESTER DRIVES

Anyone who has a WP and uses it for more than simply a casual letter or two understands the need for larger amounts of storage than that available with floppy disks. Drives are available which are variously called **Winchester drives, hard disks** or **rigid disks**. These seem to fill the bill because they have at least two advantages:

- They can store large amounts of data—from 5 megabytes to 100 megabytes or more.
- The transfer rate is about ten times faster than that for floppy disks, so a document can be brought into memory much more quickly than is the case with floppies.

The main disadvantage of the hard drive is that it is expensive compared with floppies, costing from one to several thousand dollars. However, the cost is going down every day.

Other advantages and disadvantages are discussed below.

### Characteristics

*Fixed*

There are a variety of hard disks and there are no real standards, since they are so new. However, there are some general statements which we can make about them. The first characteristic which is immediately notable is that the drive and medium are sealed together in a single unit; the medium, in most cases, is not removable. The disk is generally permanently attached to the drive (there are some exceptions which we cover later). It is this feature, that the drive and medium are sealed together in a single unit, which improves the reliability, packing density and speed of the unit. The big bugaboo is dust. A tiny grain of dust seems unimportant to us, but when compared with the size of a bit with high packing density, it is tremendous. If a speck of dust gets between the head and the disk, it can scrape out an area which amounts to many characters of the text. This might well be catastrophic. Figure 4.5.1 shows a 5¼ inch unit with the disks hermetically sealed. It occupies the same volume as a minifloppy drive.

Figure 4.5.1. A sealed 5.25 inch Winchester drive. (Courtesy of Shugart).

*Rigid*

One or more disks can be mounted on a spindle. Figure 4.5.2 is a photograph of a small unit opened up to show the bottom disk and the heads mounted on the arm. These disks are rigid: they are not flexible and do not bend. Before data can be transferred, the disks must get up to speed. They revolve continuously at a high rate. A standard speed is 3000 revolutions per minute or 50 revolutions per second. It takes some time to get the disk up to speed with the small motors provided in order to keep the units compact. A time delay is built into the drive so that you can not access data for one to two minutes while the disk is getting up to speed.

Figure 4.5.2. Winchester 8 inch disk showing one surface and a head. (Courtesy of Shugart).

A head must be positioned over the data before data can be read. Hard drives have one head for each recording surface. For a three disk drive we need six heads. Each head is mounted on an arm; the head assembly is moved as a unit; all heads go to the desired track. When the first head is positioned to track 19 on one disk, the other heads are positioned at the same track on the other surfaces. This means that a number of tracks are readily available without head movement within a cylinder.

*Air Cushion*

Since the disks are sealed within the drive, it is important to keep wear at a minimum. (It is expensive and difficult to replace hard disks.) To protect the disks, the heads are not in contact with the surface during reading or writing. The heads are kept a tiny fraction of an inch distance from the surface. This is hard to achieve, since both the head and the disk are rigid; there must be a totally uniform surface to keep a uniform distance between the two. Over the years a simple solution to this problem has developed.

After the disk gets up to speed, a thin film of air develops above each surface. If we lower the heads and let them float freely on this thin film of air, they stay at a uniform distance from the surface regardless of small irregularities in the surface. Thus for the hard disk, head loading consists of releasing the heads to float freely on the air film created by the revolution of each surface *after* the drive is up to speed.

Figure 4.5.3 is a sketch of the Winchester drive assembly. The arm on which the heads are mounted (center) can move in or out to seek to the right cylinder. The stepping motor at the right is activated by the controller to move it precisely. At the left is the drive motor which keeps the disks rotating at a constant speed.

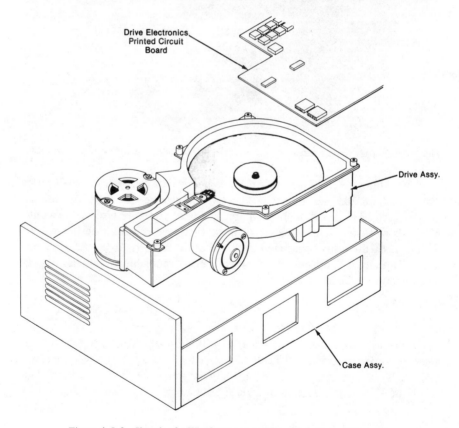

Figure 4.5.3. Sketch of a Winchester assembly. (Courtesy of Shugart).

Considerable electronics are required to control the drive. Figure 4.5.4 shows how the printed circuit boards are mounted on a hinged panel for easy access for service.

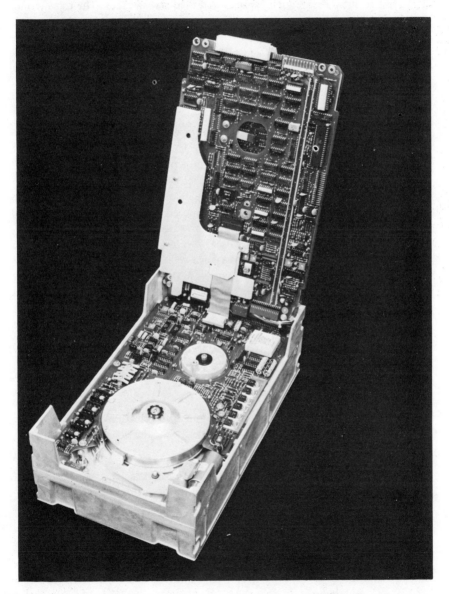

Figure 4.5.4. Hinged printed circuit board in an integrated design. (Courtesy of Micropolis).

## Specification

The two most important characteristics of hard disks, the ones that make them attractive to the user, are their capacity and their transfer rate. The transfer rate improves the response time of the word processor so that you do not have to wait to get new pieces of text for editing. These rates are fairly independent of the drive manufacturer and range from 500 to 800 kilobytes per second. This is at least ten times as fast as that for floppies.

### Size

The first hard disks used with word processors were furnished by the same manufacturers that supplied the large computers. The equipment was similar, except that all the frills were removed to put it in the price range affordable to the WP user. Hence, the first hard disks were 14 inches in diameters.

The size specification refers to the diameter of the disk, not the overall size of the equipment. A 14 inch drive may be housed in a cabinet which is 25 or 30 inches in its largest dimension. During the past two or three years, a war has developed in the electronics industry to see who can make the smallest hard drive with the largest capacity. Competitors have reduced the size of the disk to 8 inches and then to 5¼ inches. These smaller devices seem to be winning the battle; their overall size is small enough to fit into a desk top console. Yet they can hold 5 to 10 megabytes of text. As you might expect, the smaller the disk, the less storage capacity for the device. However, new technology is directed to the small devices, so they can hold proportionately more information than their older siblings.

### Electronic Specifications

Table 4.5 displays the range of values for some of the electronic characters of the hard-disk drives. Since the heads used are so much smaller and have a tiny gap,

**Table 4.5.  Hard Disk Drive Characteristics.**

| SIZE | 5¼" | 8" | 10½" | 14" |
|---|---|---|---|---|
| Transfer rate, Mbytes/sec | .5-1 | .5-2 | 1.9 | 3 |
| Kilobyte/linear inch | 7.6-9 | 6-18 | 9-15 | 8-20 |
| Tracks per inch | 254-400 | 200-500 | 700-800 | 600-900 |
| Average access time, Ms | 25-250 | 20-80 | 30 | 20-40 |
| Surfaces | 1-8 | 1-11 | 5-11 | 4-19 |
| Capacity, Mbytes | 5-12 | 7-110 | 85-475 | 10-630 |
| Price, $K | 1-1.5 | 2-15 | 4-8 | 5-40 |

information may be packed at a much higher density than for the floppy drive. This is responsible for the tremendous improvement in capacity. Also, the disks rotate at 3000 revolutions per minute, ten times faster than the floppies, so we expect a higher transfer rate.

The table also contrasts specifications of disk drives for the commercially available larger computer to give some idea about the state of the art.

### Other Considerations

Besides capacity, the larger drives differ from the smaller ones in these respects:

- They consume more power to keep the larger disks rotating at the high speed.
- They produce more heat.
- They produce more noise, sometimes to the point of being annoying.

Hard disks are very reliable because they are hermetically sealed. Dust is the villain which inflicts harm to the surface of the disk. If we keep dust out of the picture, we reduce the error rate considerably. Errors are still a problem when they arise, as we discuss shortly. The advantage of hard disks is that they make so much more text available and can make it available to several users. This feature brings along with it a problem—keeping track of a much larger number of documents. If the vendor does not furnish a good means for cataloging all these documents, the system tends to fall apart. Directory systems are considered later in Chapter 8 and 9.

### Drivers

The structure, format and circuitry of Winchester drives are different from those of floppies. They talk a different language, so to speak. The WP program cannot use the floppy driver to talk to a hard disk (see Section 5.2). A different driver program lets the WP program give the same kinds of requests to both types of disks. A different (hardware) controller is also needed. A hard disk driver (program) is written to let the WP program use the same commands as before; this driver activates the controller properly to run the hard disk.

#### *Internal Directory*

The method for keeping track of files and empty space described in Section 4.4 is still applicable with reservations. The hard disk has much space to keep track of, as well as many more files to monitor. Hence, the directory is substantially larger.

As with the floppy, the track is divided into sectors. But it does not pay to use 256 byte blocks (sectors). Track sizes, even for 5-1/4 inch disks, range from 8300 to 14K bytes. For the 14 inch drive, a track holds 20K or more. Hence, it makes sense to use 1K or 2K as a sector size. This effects the size of the bit map and the space allocated to the file directory but poses no problem. The amount of unused space allocated to a file also increases, but it is unimportant relative to the entire volume.

## Backup

What if something should happen to the hard disk? Would *all* the documents be lost? This is a scary thought. Hard disks are more reliable than are floppies yet there is a slight possibility of losing data on disks.

**Backup,** another copy of a document, is always an important consideration. But how do you backup hard disks? Some units have their own backup devices built in. For WPs, these are usually floppies, called archive disks. Backup can be done selectively or totally. For **selective backup** only, those documents which have been altered since the last backup are copied.

Total backup to floppies may take up to an hour or more. Hard disk manufacturers have sought alternatives:

- Streaming tape is a cassette of 1/4 inch tape which can copy an entire hard disk in a few minutes.
- Video tape is being used for backup too. The video cassette recorder (VCR) can be used for selective or total backup. It is faster but more expensive.
- Syntrex provides a complete duplicate disk drive. All writing is done on *both* drives. The two copies are constantly compared during reading. Should one disk drive fail, the other is automatically put into service and the first withdrawn; the field representative is automatically telephoned to fix the failed drive. When the repair person arrives, it may come as a surprise to you, since the system has not gone down!

## Error Detection and Recovery

*Not Like Floppies*

Hard disks are not like floppies simply because the medium is permanently attached. When you encounter difficulties with a floppy disk and you are sure that the disk is at fault, the remedy is simple. Copy all the files from the existing disk onto another disk. When you have done this, make sure that the file giving you difficulty has been corrected and brought up to date. Then you can simply throw away the bad floppy disk.

Floppies do go bad because the head contact with the disk causes wear. Wear causes particles of the magnetic material to be abraded away. When the material is missing from the disk, you cannot write there and you can not record information properly.

Although damage to hard disks is less frequent, consideration must be given to detecting and correcting errors of any sort.

### Detecting Hard Disk Errors

When you cannot read a file properly, this is not positive proof that the disk is at fault. There are many parts of the hardware and the software which may have malfunctioned. You can verify that an error is occurring only if you write and read back from the same area and check to see that what is read is the same as what is written. However, the user does not usually have this option in a WP environment. As a consequence, it is advisable to do a periodic checkout procedure.

### Hard Disk Checkout and Error Prevention

The first step in this procedure is to back up the entire disk. This means that all catalogued files on the disk are written to a backup medium such as a set of floppy disks or streaming tape. A utility performs this procedure for you.

Now the hard disk is thoroughly and totally checked by another utility. It writes a fixed pattern onto each sector of the disk, reads it back and compares it with the original pattern. This is repeated many times with different patterns to check every bit site on the disk. This procedure may take as much as a full day. However, it need not be attended; the computer can be run over the weekend and the checkout procedure will come up with the bad sectors.

The utility program collects a table of all the sectors which do not perform perfectly. Another utility is now run when the user returns, which takes the table created by the checkout utility and makes an invisible file out of it. This file is listed in the directory, so the user does not see it. The space this file occupies is not available to any real file. That is, bad areas on each disk are collected, chained together and put into the directory in such a way that the user is unaware of them. These sectors have been taken out of service, they will not be assigned to *any* user. A final utility takes the backup information and rewrites it on the hard disks. It is rewritten to make the best use of the available space and to provide the most free space for future use. You are now guaranteed that the files are in properly functioning sectors and that any new space assigned to new files will be from sectors that have been thoroughly checked out.

# 5
# Software

## 5.0 INTRODUCTION

**Software** consists of programs. One program is in control of the computer whenever it is running. There are different kinds of programs.

An **application program (AP)** performs work directly for a user:

- does text editing,
- makes numerical calculations,
- prints out a document,
- keeps track of money and materials,
- does forecasting,
- and so forth.

The word processor system includes one or more application programs which provide text editing and printing for the user.

An application program may perform large and complex functions which originally required the work of many people. For example, an accounts receivable program keeps track of all of a large company's clients. For each customer it monitors shipments, billing, invoicing, orders and payments.

There is a group of programs which helps run the computer; the **operating system** expedites and facilitates the running of application programs; it does not solve a user's problem directly. It is important to understand the need for the operating system and the function of its components. These components are introduced in this section and described in more detail in the other sections of this chapter.

### The Working System

Figure 5.0.1 shows a computer system with several devices attached. In the center is a view of the contents of memory. Each hexagon represents a program, or part of a program. Of immediate interest to the user is only the **application program**. All other components shown are parts of the operating system.

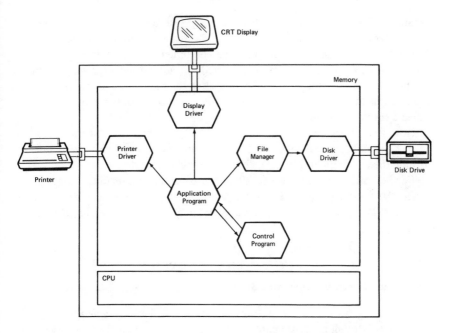

Figure 5.0.1. Computer system with several devices attached.

Around the periphery of memory we see three hexagons each labeled **driver**. Each driver runs one of the devices hooked to the system. At the bottom of memory is the **control program**. It accepts requests from the operator, the application program and other operating system components and meets their need whenever possible. The **file manager** manages the files and data which are kept on external storage.

These operating system components are called **resident** because they are stored in memory and are immediately available when needed. Other larger components, such as the translators and utilities employed in creating and copying programs and data, cannot be conveniently stored in memory. A copy of each is available on the system diskette.

Another occupant of memory shown in 5.0.1 is data operated on by the program. Some programs need only a little data—a few numbers, perhaps. For the WP, however, one or more pages of text is stored in memory for immediate editing.

**One-Piece Software**

The computer is sometimes run by a single package. The user or purchaser may be unaware of the contents of this package. The user often does not know what is in memory but is only aware of the amount of work space left over in memory because it limits the amount of text he may work on without invoking special procedures. This being the case, is it really necessary to know about the operating system? The supplier often provides the equipment as a complete system with little or no choice for the devices supplied, let alone for the program options. In this case, it is virtually impossible to alter the software without the help of the manufacturer. A system which is ready to work as soon as you *turn* it on is called a **turnkey system**.

However, understanding software requirements can help you make choices among systems and make it possible to talk more effectively with salespeople regarding the current and future capabilities of the system they offer.

Further, with more interest in WP/DP, programming is making inroads in the office. Vendors supply BASIC as an option. You should know what programming entails before you decide if it is something your office should get involved with.

## 5.1 THE OPERATING SYSTEM

### The Three Parts of the Operating System

The operating system can work most rapidly and effectively when it is resident in memory. But all resident components occupy valuable memory, which is then unavailable to application programs and as work areas. Hence, it is efficient to have part of the operating system remain on disk, from whence it may be brought in as needed. Utilities and translators and special programs for math, sorting, etc., which are not needed while an application is running, and which occupy considerable memory when active, are kept externally.

There are three parts of the operating system which are resident:

- the control program,
- the device drivers,
- the file manager.

How do those resident portions of the operating system get into memory? One way is for the manufacturer to supply them in read-only memory (ROM). Recall that ROM is **nonvolatile**—its contents do not disappear when the machine is turned off. Programs kept in ROM remain there and are immediately available as soon as the machine is turned on. Despite this important advantage, there is a disadvantage which makes this scheme less attractive. To revise a portion of the operating system requires that the manufacturer create a new ROM and furnish it to be plugged in by the user. Thus changes are more expensive and difficult to implement.

The other alternative is to keep a copy of the resident portion of the operating system on a disk. The operator brings in "the system" each time the computer is turned on. Most WPs work this way.

When you bring in the resident operating system components from the disk, you **boot** the system. This signifies that the system is pulling itself up by its own bootstraps. The components have been written onto the disk in fixed positions. The disk controller is the electronics which runs the disk drive. It has its own small ROM. When so directed by turning on the computer power, the disk controller reads the operating system and puts it at a preassigned position in memory.

When the computer is turned on, it first issues a signal to the disk controller to bring in the operating system. After this, the operating system begins to execute. The operating system then usually issues a prompt on the display for the operator to enter the first request. For the turnkey system, such as the WP, the operating system first brings in the application program and gives it (the WP program) control. That program prompts the operator for the first action, often with a menu.

### Control Program

The purpose of the control program is to simplify the job of the application program. Each application program needs at some time to:

- get data or commands from the keyboard,
- put information on the display,
- operate the printer,
- use a disk file.

The control program uses the device drivers extensively. The control program gets operator messages from the keyboard which it passes from the keyboard driver to the application program. The control program sends messages from the application program to the operator via the display driver and makes sure that it is presented properly.

Outside of the turnkey system, requests may be handled directly by the control program or delegated to the proper utilities, such as to:

- run a chosen program,
- display the contents of disk which is mounted,
- erase or copy a named file.

The control program not only makes use of the drivers, it also enlists the aid of the file manager to find files and programs on the disk as the operator or application program requests them. Normally then, the resident operating system consists of all the programs displayed in Figure 5.0.1 except the application program.

### Drivers

Each device which might be activated by the computer has a driver associated with it. The driver is always used in a predictable manner. Each action that a device might perform has a corresponding routine in the driver; to invoke an action, the application program or the operating system need only make a simple request. The driver chooses the built-in routine. The saving is threefold:

- All driver routines are prewritten.
- They need not be reprogrammed when needed.
- A simple request activates each.

Functions performed by the device and activated routines in the drivers are standard, but the devices themselves differ from one manufacturer to another. A driver is tailored to a particular vendor's device; it gives the control signals expected by that device and interprets signals returned from the device.

As an example, consider the printer. The application program assembles a complete line to send to the printer driver. Each driver is designed to accept the identical application requests, regardless of the physical device.

From Chapter 3, we are aware that printers differ, not only in the techniques they use to print a line, but also in their speed, capabilities and the control signals they respond to and status signals they generate. The driver for the Qume printer, for instance, is adjusted to the data and control signals for that printer; it may not work with the Diablo or Malibu.

When variable spacing is available, the printer driver issues all spacing sequences. When bidirectional printing is available, the driver directs the carriage which way to move. The driver may even be responsible for proportional spacing.

Supervision of a particular activity is not governed by a hard and fast rule. For instance, bidirectional printing may be activated and supervised by the application program, by the driver or within the device itself.

*Availability*

The driver is available (because it is resident) to both the application program and the control program. Sometimes the driver is reached indirectly through the control program by a call from the application program. To get to the driver program, the control program must first find it; the control program keeps a table giving the locations of each device driver.

*Tailoring*

Since a driver is device-specific, it is important to provide proper routines for a given physical device. Sometimes the manufacturer does this tailoring before the equipment ever reaches the installation. If all the user has to do is turn on the switch to get the system to work, this is a turnkey system.

In some cases, the system is tailored at the site. The control program has a setup routine which asks the operator or technician to describe his devices. The proper driver routines are obtained from the system disk and assembled to make the needed driver. This driver is then written into a new copy of the resident portion of the operating system and put on the system disk. When the computer is turned on, the drivers are immediately available. This scheme is most popular for WPs for personal computers.

## 5.2 PROGRAMS AND PROGRAMMING LANGUAGES

### The Application Program

The program is the directions to the computer to solve a problem. However, the only language that the hardware understands is **machine language**. A program which runs directly on the computer must be in machine language.

Machine language for any computer consists only of 0s and 1s. If one were to write a program in this language, one would have to write a sequence of 0s and 1s and be constantly aware of the meaning of each bit in each position. This is a formidable job and is rarely, if ever, done. Other languages are needed to make the programmer's job tolerable and efficient. The three types of language that one encounters are called:

- assembly language,
- procedure oriented language,
- higher level language.

*Assembly Language*

Assembly language is close to machine language. However, instead of using a sequence of 0s and 1s to constitute a command, the programmer uses an equivalent which is easier to remember, such as "A" for add, or "M" for multiply. The letter or set of letters is a **mnemonic**. One mnemonic produces one machine language command. Since the commands available in one computer are different from those in another computer, the assembly language commands for each computer are different.

*Procedure Oriented Language*

Procedure Oriented Languages (POL) are designed to make programming independent of a particular machine. The programmer converts the problem into a procedure which can be stated simply in the POL. The language is clearer to understand for the programmer. Once a POL program is written, it should be able to run on almost any machine. This is not entirely the case, for we find dialects of each POL suitable for machines made by particular manufacturers. A popular language for minis and micros is **BASIC**. Some WPs provide a BASIC capability as an option.

*Higher Level Languages*

There are other languages created to direct a computer to solve specific kinds of problems: architectural problems, financial reports, even text processing. They may or may not include a POL capability. For processing text, for instance, the user should not have to know anything about programming. He does have to know how to use the proper keys to tell the computer to put some characters in boldface and underline others.

### Writing and Translating

The most efficient program runs in machine language. This requires three steps, regardless of the program language used (which is called the **source language**). We itemize them below and then discuss them:

1. Write the program.
2. Translate the program into machine language.
3. Clear up any problems which prevent the program from running.

*Writing*

There are several ways to write and enter a program for translation. A long established method is first to write it in longhand and then to punch it into punchcards which are then fed into the computer.

A quicker and more effective way is to write the program interactively at a terminal, as shown in Figure 5.2.1. The statements are entered at the keyboard. An editor, much like that used in word processing, only less sophisticated, accepts the source language input. It allows you to alter, add, delete and renumber the statements of your program.

Keyed information is displayed on the CRT screen. While constructing the program, you can make changes necessary which then display on the screen. When

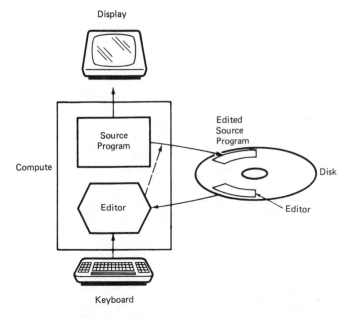

Figure 5.2.1. Writing a program interactively.

finished, the editor places the program on a disk for further processing. This file is shown in the figure as the **source program**—the program before it is translated.

*Translation*

The next action is to translate the source program into its machine language equivalent—MLP, Figure 5.2.2. To initiate this action, you tell the control program that you want to compile the source program stored as a named file. The operating system makes a request through the file manager to bring in the **compiler**, the translating program, from the disk. The control program installs the compiler in memory and gives it control.

Next, the source program is brought into memory to become the *data* with which the compiler works. The compiler examines the source program and creates the machine language program from it. Once the task is complete, the translation is placed in a file with a different name on a disk.

Few programs translate properly the first time. The compiler often encounters difficulties. Those are displayed to the operator on the CRT or are perhaps printed out. When the translation is not satisfactory, the program on the disk is not correct and should not be run. The errors detected by the compiler should be fixed and the program submitted again for translation.

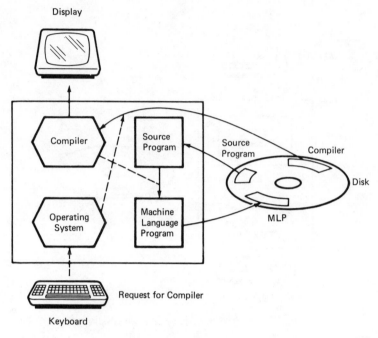

Figure 5.2.2. Translating the source program.

*Execution*

A directive to execute a translated program is entered at the keyboard. The control program installs the program, as shown in Figure 5.2.3, and starts it working. The program may require input from the keyboard or from another file; it may produce output at the display or the printer or as an output file.

*Fix*

The fact that a program was translated properly does not guarantee that it will execute correctly. The translator can detect errors and tell you about them, but only those in **syntax** (the grammar of the programming language). Thus, if you want to multiply by 3.5 but enter this in the programming language as 35, the compiler will not complain. But when you run your program, the results will be incorrect or at least not as you intended. All programs must be **debugged**, that is, checked out to determine if they produce the desired results for sample data which the programmer has verified.

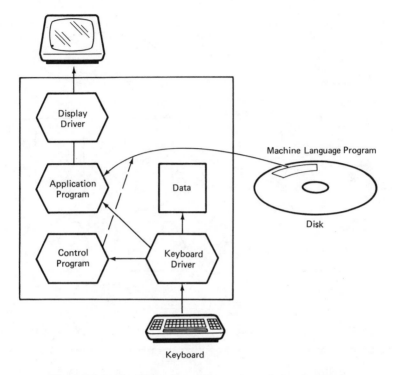

Figure 5.2.3. The CP installs an ML program and gives it control.

### The Interpreter

In some cases the user may prefer to use an **interpreter** which works directly with the source program. Its advantages become apparent below. No translator is needed.

The preparation of the source program proceeds as before, using the editor. The source program may be stored in memory or placed on a disk, as shown in Figure 5.2.4. When you are ready to run the program, or even a portion of it, you enter a request at the keyboard. This is accepted by the keyboard driver and passed to the control program, which asks the file manager to bring the interpreter into memory, if absent. The source program is also brought in. The interpreter is given control.

It scans the source program. Each command found there is *interpreted*. That is, the command is examined to find the key words which convey its intent. There is a **routine**, a small program, in the interpreter for each command type that might be requested in the POL. One of these routines, each shown as a little hexagon

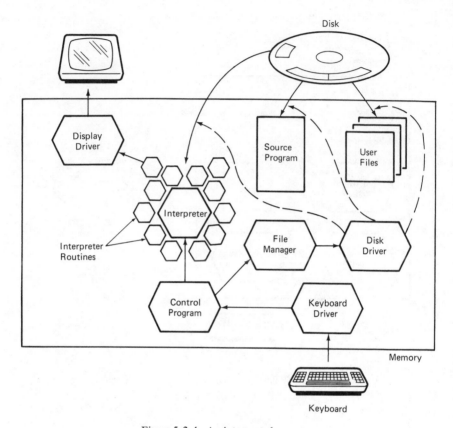

Figure 5.2.4. An interpreted program.

in the figure, is given control and executes a series of machine language commands, placing the results which it derives in labeled memory locations.

Some statements request input or output. These call in routines which, in turn, activate a driver or the file manager to fulfill the request.

The interpreter has the advantage that it can run a program immediately without any intervening steps. The user need not wait while the compiler translates the program and extra routines are linked to the translated program. Also, if many corrections have to be made, the user need not wait to complete the program after each change.

On the other hand, because a routine is invoked for *every* statement that the interpreter scans, execution can take ten times as long as for the machine language equivalent produced by the compiler.

## 5.3 SERIAL FILE MANAGEMENT

**Physical Medium**

When the first computers were developed, the only media available were restricted in the way that we could get information in and out of them. The principal medium to hold large quantities of data was magnetic tape. It is shown schematically in Figure 5.3.1. The magnetic tape is a **physically serial medium**: when positioned at the beginning of the tape and you need data from the other end of the tape, the only way to get there is to move all the tape, from one end to the other, past the head. All intervening data must pass beneath the head. This restriction arises from the physical nature of the medium.

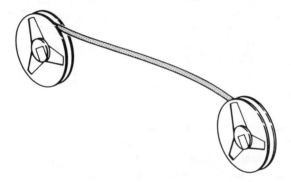

Figure 5.3.1. Magnetic tape is a serial medium.

The program to control input and output of data from a physically sequential medium is called the **serial file manager**. Because of the stringent restrictions in moving the medium, the file manager is simple to design and use.

The simplest serial media are **unidirectional**, that is, the magnetic tape cassette can be read by the computer in only one direction. It cannot be positioned in the reverse direction, except to rewind it. Once the tape has started moving forward, there are only two choices:

- continue to advance the tape, reading or writing as you go;
- rewind the tape and start again from the beginning.

The unidirectional medium is easy to manage, since choices are few.

For the **bidirectional file**, the file manager can move the medium in either direction. Some large tape drives can read and write only in the forward direction. They can position in the reverse direction in order to reread from a preassigned position. The most expensive tape drives, too expensive for word processing systems, can read and write in both directions and are truly bidirectional.

### Direct Access Media

The disk drive is a **direct access** (sometimes called a **random access**) device. It can be activated to position *directly* to any sector on any track of any surface. For instance, if the head is on track 5 examining sector 3, it is possible to move the head so that it positions directly to track 16. The head passes over track 6, 7, etc., but does not "see" the data there. At track 16 the drive waits until the desired sector arrives and then the reads it. This action is called "direct" because the passage from the old position (sector and track) to the new one does not necessarily pass through any of the intervening data. Section 5.4 examines file organizations based on this property.

Despite the fact that the disk can be used for direct access, it is often advantageous to organize data serially on it.

### Use of the Serial File

Serial file management is not restricted to physically sequential media. The disk can store a serial file just as well as the magnetic tape. What makes the file serial is how the file manager accesses it: the serial file manager reviews the file from beginning to end without reversing direction. This restriction lies within the file manager itself and not from the medium.

Many files are only intended to be used serially. For instance, all of a program must be in memory to be executed. Loading a program into memory, such as an interpreter or an application program, is quickest with a serial file. As the file is read from disk, it is written into memory at the same time. Consecutive bytes from the file go into consecutive bytes in memory.

Data to print onto a document are effectively handled as a serial file. Printing by nature is serial: characters are printed in succession on a line; lines are printed successively on the page. The electronic document is scanned from beginning to end and printed in exactly that sequence on the paper.

When the text editor is supplied with a large work area, small serial files are handled easily. As long as the electronic document is smaller than the work area, the total document is easily read in one action from a serial file. Once the ED is in memory, the text editor can skip around with ease. As you ask to view different parts of the document, the text editor supplies them as fast as the display can be altered.

The large electronic document does not fit entirely into the work area, but editing can still be effective. In Figure 5.3.2, the first part of the document labeled ED1 is brought in from the disk and put into the work area. You can edit

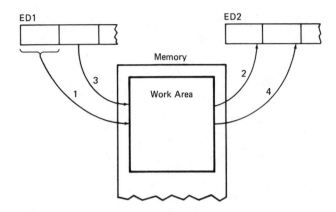

Figure 5.3.2. Using the serial medium.

any portion of this section of the document. When you are finished, the text editor writes the edited portion onto a new file, shown here as ED2. The next portion of the file is then brought into the work area. The limitation is the inability to get back to the first portion of the *edited* document on the new file ED2. The file manager writes forward onto that file starting from the beginning. It is not possible to move backward within that file without complications.

As long as you arrange to edit the part of the text which is in memory fully before moving ahead to the next part, you're OK. Even if you want to make some corrections in "the part that got away," all is not lost. Finish everything up and start all over again. Personal and EDP word processing systems use serial files and provide additional programs and techniques to get back to earlier edited material *within the same session.* These techniques are discussed in Chapter 8.

### Software Overview

Let us reexamine, in order, the components invoked in using a serial file starting from the user and going toward the medium. Figure 5.3.3 shows pictorially the flow of control and data.

1. A word processing program, the text editor or print formatter, makes a request for more data from the disk. (To put data onto the disk is similar.)
2. The file manager accepts the general request and changes it into a request for the next block(s) of the file. A block is described by its relative position within the file (e.g., block 27). This is converted into a physical track and block number (e.g., track 17, block 3) using the file directory entry for this file.

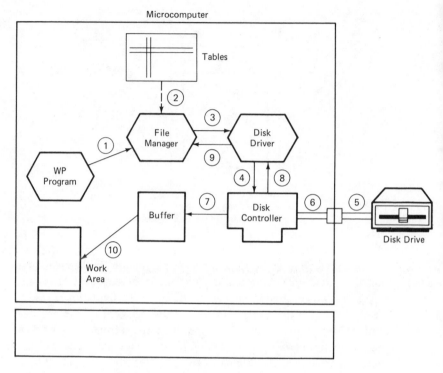

Figure 5.3.3. Flow of control in a WP system.

3. The disk driver accepts a request for the track and block number and con-verts this into one or more physical requests to the disk drive. First the sector number in the track after skewing is found (see Section 4.2). Then a group of computer commands are passed over to the controller to get the disk to the right position. These commands might, for instance, move the head to the track, wait for the proper sector, read data and verify the CRC.

4. The controller accepts one command at a time from the computer for each activity. Each command is converted into one or more electric sig-nals which activate the disk drive.

5. The disk drive carries out the actions, from requests presented as electric signals. It generates a control signal to indicate that it has carried out the action.

6. Data read by the disk drive are sent to the controller.

7. The controller passes the data into computer memory, the buffer.

8. When the controller has filled the buffer, it tells the disk-driver program.

9. The disk driver tells the controller (hardware) what to do next and also notifies the file manager (program) that this block has arrived.

10. The file manager takes the data from the buffer and puts into the work area.
11. The action continues thus until all data needed by the WP program has arrived.

## 5.4 RANDOM FILES

A **random file** is so-called because you can request any area at *random* and the system will go to it directly. It is unfortunate that this term has become popular for both word processers and personal computers. Data processing people reserve the term "random" for use with random access memory (RAM): No matter which byte you address in RAM, access takes the same time. They call the disk drive (and similar devices) **direct access devices**: this conveys that the drive can go *directly* anywhere on the medium without passing through intervening data. However, it should be kept in mind that the time to access an area depends upon the *physical motion of the head*. This time is longest when the head travels from the outside track to the inside track on the disk, or vice versa. The time to position is much shorter in going from one track to an adjacent one. To go from one block to another within the same track takes the shortest time.

I use the term "random file" reluctantly to be consistent with terms used in the WP field. (I'd prefer to call this a direct file.) You can get to any portion of a random file after it is put into use. It takes longer for the hardware to get to remote portions of the random file than to nearby areas. The difference is imperceptible to you—50 milliseconds as opposed to 500 milliseconds is not apparent. (A **millisecond** is 1/1000 second.)

### Need

In the preceding section we have seen how serial files may be used for text processing. So long as the files are relatively short, one or two pages, or if enough memory is provided in the computer, no difficulty arises because all the text is immediately available. Larger electronic documents can not be stored totally in memory and complications may arise.

The random file offers an alternative almost universally adopted in word processing. Each word processor vendor establishes a unit, which I will call the **record**, the quantity of text moved back and forth between computer memory and the disk. A piece of text is read from the disk as a record; text is written onto disk as a record. Often the record is equivalent to a document page. Sometimes it is a little more than a page. This amount is useful when the document is edited, to provide room for small insertions. Pages can later be allocated to records (pagination) to be printed.

*Accessibility*

With random access files we have immediate accessibility to any part of the text. With a 40 page document, you may want to look at text on page 5 (which is certainly not in memory) while editing page 26. The random access facility gets the page in a reasonable length of time, in two operations:

- The first stores text now on memory onto disk at the position assigned to page 26 to clear the work area.
- The second retrieves page 5.

These actions take only a second or so. The system looks in a table to locate pages 26 and 5 on the disk. Then the head positions and the disk rotates to write the old page; another set of operations moves the head to read in the new page.

Some WP systems mask the time required for random access of the disk by "entertaining the operator": as information is being written out to the disk, some systems scroll the text slowly off the screen. Then, as new text arrives it is slowly delivered, line by line, onto the screen. Since the text on the screen is moving, you get the impression that "something is being done." Other WPs put up a message, such as "System Working."

## Data Organization

As data and text are moved about within the system, they are handled in chunks of different sizes by the user, the program and the physical components of the system. Table 5.4 shows data quantities for five different purposes.

**Table 5.4. Units of Data.**

| Geometry | Context | User Defined |
|---|---|---|
| character | character | block |
| line | word | phrase |
| screen | sentence | subdocument |
| document | paragraph | document |
| | page | |
| | document | |

| File | Disk |
|---|---|
| block | byte |
| record | sector |
| file | track |
| | cylinder |
| | surface |
| | volume |

*Text Division*

Table 5.4 shows that the two kinds of quantities used by the operator during editing are oriented to geometry and context. These get considerable attention in Chapter 6. For the moment we turn our attention to another division of the text which is important for file manipulation. This is the record and its relation to the file, as shown in Figure 5.4.1.

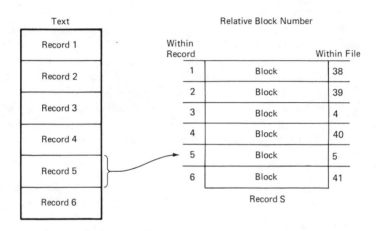

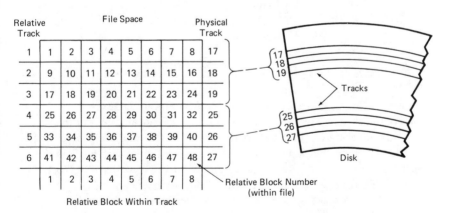

Figure 5.4.1. How the record relates to the file.

As you create a document, it is convenient to think of it as a continuous stream of text, as shown at the left of the figure. Some WPs actually let you work with text in just this fashion. You see it as a continuous stream even without page breaks, if you choose. Such WPs are prevalent in journalism and publishing.

A human editor, especially in the newspaper field, is not restricted to put text into equal sized pages, as is the case in the office. The newspaper page is much larger than the conventional letter. Text is set in columns and winds around photographs and advertisements. Hence it is preferable to consider text as a *stream* of words rather than as a page.

Many office WPs are page oriented. It is thus often satisfactory to consider text in terms of records (size of data unit on disk or in memory) which are approximately page size (as printed on the document). This poses a restriction if you want to go from one page to the next continuously. Some WPs jump from one page to the next without continuity, as in the IBM Display Writer.

In the ensuing discussion we consider only editing where reformatting between records is unnecessary. That is, we consider only small changes in a page which do not cause text to move back and forth from one record to another. The text on the left of the figure consists of six records. These are not usually im memory at the same time.

*Record Makeup*

Figure 5.4.1 shows a record comprised of six blocks. A block here refers to a piece data of sector size on the disk, a fixed size unit. The number of blocks which comprise a record is a function of the WP system.

*The File*

A file consists of blocks numbered according to their relative position within the file. When the file is created, the file manager provides an allocation of a fixed number of blocks, usually a track or a block group, to the text editor. As creation continues, new areas of additional blocks are allocated by full track to the file. New blocks are numbered consecutively to follow the old blocks within the file. A relative block number describes the position of each block in the file, calculated relative to the beginning of the file at the time that this block is put into use. This number is called its **relative block number**.

Blocks which make up a record need not be consecutively numbered relative blocks of the file. The blocks are usually assigned consecutively to a record (as text is created). But during editing, alterations in the text cause alterations in the record structure. Pieces of text are deleted and new ones inserted. The system is free to reassign blocks to a record in any order, thus accounting for records consisting of relative blocks whose numbering is not consecutive. The figure shows that record 5 consists of relative block numbers 38, 39, 4, 40, 5 and 41.

*Physical File*

At the physical level, space is assigned to the file as needed in tracks or groups of blocks. When the text editor uses up one allocation, it asks the file manager for another. The file manager tries to assign the next consecutive track (or group of blocks). This may not be possible if another file is assigned to adjacent space on the disk. Contiguous areas within a file are called **extents**. A file consists of two (or more) extents when the area between is assigned to another user.

The **logical file** consists of a number of consecutive *relative* blocks; each relative block is associated with a physical track and sector. Figure 5.4.1 shows the file as a number of tracks, where each track consists of consecutive block positions. A track has:

- a relative track number—its position within the file to which it is allocated,
- a physical track number—its position on the disk, counting from the outside track, numbered 0.

The device driver uses a table to convert a relative block number to a physical track and sector number (for the skewing).

### Philosophy

The aim of the WP system using random access files is to make the text appear to you as one continuous manuscript. The text is updated during editing, but it maintains its continuity. The changes that you make cause the text to expand and contract in spots. The size of the record is chosen so as to absorb some shrinkage and expansion. However, when you insert a couple of paragraphs onto a page or record, it is pretty certain that some text of the page will overflow to the next page or record.

The system has extra "buckets" when an overflow occurs. It is up to the system designer to determine whether it uses "buckets" for overflow or only large "cups" or "glasses." That is, another full size record may be inserted to receive a few lines of overflow text. Another technique is simply to use additional blocks to hold the overflow.

The WP file management system not only should make editing smooth, providing extra space as needed, it should allow for printing out the document as pages of uniform physical size. Separation of the text into units corresponding to a printed page and numbering each is often done on a separate run, called **pagination**, discussed in Chapter 9.

## Interaction

The three basic software components shown in Figure 5.3.3 manage a random file. For direct access the components are designed differently to interact and serve the requestor more directly. A WP program can ask for text from any part of the electronic document, and these three cooperate to locate the material and bring it forth. The five tables used to do this are shown in Figure 5.4.2.

Record Directory

| Record Number | Relative Block Number | | | | | |
|---|---|---|---|---|---|---|
| 1 | 1 | 2 | 3 | 6 | 7 | 8 |
| 3 | 25 | 26 | 27 | 28 | 29 | 30 |
| 4 | 31 | 32 | 33 | 34 | 35 | 36 |
| 5 | 38 | 39 | 4 | 40 | 5 | 41 |
| 6 | 45 | 43 | 44 | | | |

File Control Block

| Name | Tracks Assigned | | | | | | |
|---|---|---|---|---|---|---|---|
| MYTEXT | 17 | 18 | 19 | 25 | 26 | 27 | 0 |

Bit Allocation Map

| Track | 1 | 2 | 3 | 4 | 5 | 6 | 7 | 8 | 9 | 10 | 11 |
|---|---|---|---|---|---|---|---|---|---|---|---|
| Use | 1 | 1 | 1 | 1 | 1 | 1 | 1 | 0 | 0 | 1 | 1 |

Skew Table

| Track | 1 | 2 | 3 | 4 | 5 | 6 | 7 | 8 |
|---|---|---|---|---|---|---|---|---|
| Sector | 0 | 3 | 6 | 1 | 4 | 7 | 2 | 5 |

Available Block Directory

| x | x | x | x | 45 | 46 | 47 | 48 |
|---|---|---|---|---|---|---|---|

Figure 5.4.2. Tables needed to keep track of text.

The word processing programs use a table such as the Record Directory at the top. Each record of text consists of a fixed number of blocks (six here); each block has a relative block number, its position relative to the beginning of the file, regardless of its physical location on the disk. A record generally consists of relative blocks which are adjacent, but as a record contracts, blocks which are no longer needed for one record can serve for another record. New records for inserted text are added between existing records and consist of one or more relative blocks assigned from the end of the file. The word processing system, the text editor and the print formatter, use a table such as the Record Directory, which associates text with relative block numbers within each track, to locate and put together records of text. Each of these components converts the user's text request into a request for relative block and track number.

The file manager receives requests from the WP program to read data (or to write them out) by relative block number. It maintains a table, the File Control Block, such as the second table in Figure 5.4.2. This is the entry for the file acquired from the File Directory. It is an ordered list of the physical tracks (or block groups) assigned to this file. Since the number of blocks per track ( or per block group) is fixed (eight here), and they are listed in order relative to the beginning of the file, it is simple to calculate the physical track and block number from the relative block number.

The file manager also has a copy of the bit allocation map (the third from the top in the figure) to use when the application program needs more space. When more space is needed, the file manager finds a track adjacent to, or close by, the tracks in use. This track number is added to the file allocation entry and new relative blocks are assigned to the text from this new track.

The disk driver receives a request from the file manager by track and block number; the Skew Table (next to the last in the figure) converts a block number to a sector number. The driver constructs commands to acquire and pass along the blocks requested.

*Next Page*

What is the action required to get the next page (or record) at the operator's request. Suppose you have finished editing page 4 and you ask your WP for the next page. The text editor gets your request and looks at the Record Directory of Figure 5.4.2. He puts away that page (in the same way that he gets a new one, so we omit that explanation). He needs record 5 to display for you to work on.

The Record Directory shows the relative block numbers for the six blocks which make up the next record. You may note that relative blocks 4 and 5 have sneaked into this page. Chunks of earlier text were deleted, freeing these blocks, which were later pressed into service for page 5.

To fill up the work area with the next page of text, the text editor should ask for relative blocks 38, 39, 4, etc. These requests are sent sequentially to the file manager, who converts them into track and block numbers.

The file manager uses the File Control Block of the figure to make the conversion. Let us suppose that there are eight blocks per track. Then blocks 1 through 8 are on the first relative track of the file. The File Control Block lists the tracks assigned to the file in absolute order. The first relative track of the file is that which has physical track number 17. Hence, to get relative block 38, a simple conversion is done. That is the sixth block of the fourth relative track, since $8 \times 4 + 6 = 38$.

To request the blocks which make up the page, the file manager asks for the physical block numbers, where the first number is the track number and the second the block number:

26/6; 26/7; 17/4; 26/8; 17/5; 27/1

The file manager sends these requests to the disk driver. The disk driver activates the disk controller directly. However, the disk driver has to consider skewing. It addresses the disk not by block but by sector number. Hence, while the track numbers are correct, blocks must be converted into sector numbers. The Skew Table (see the figure) shows the sector number associated with each block number. So the disk driver converts 26/5 into 26/4; then 26/6 becomes 26/7; and so forth.

As each sector is read from the disk, it goes into a temporary data buffer, part of the disk driver, who tells the file manager of its arrival. The file manager puts the block into the work area as requested by the WP program. This continues until the entire record is loaded.

This description applies to the page oriented WP as described in Chapter 8. There is no text continuity provided between one page and the next, which is the main fault of this arrangement. Better alternatives are described in Chapter 8.

### *New Allocation*

What happens when the WP program uses up all the space allocated to your file? This is apparent to the WP program when there are no blocks left in its free block directory. It then asks the file manager for another allocation. The file manager looks at the allocation bit map and uses the nearest available track. He sets that bit to 1 and also enters its number into the File Control Block assigned to your file. The WP program notes the additional eight relative block numbers and puts them into the available block directory (bottom table in the figure) to be doled out as the text grows. He must do this now to ensure space for all text being created.

# II
# WORD PROCESSING

# 6
# Text Editing

## 6.1 INTRODUCTION

Anyone being introduced to a word processing system for the first time should have a guide who thoroughly understands the equipment. I would like to be your guide as we step up to the word processor. Moreover, I would like you to think of an array of ten or fifteen WPs from different vendors, and as we go through each step, I will explain the differences, if any, which exist among these devices.

### Keyboard

First, consider the philosophy of the vendors. They assume that people who will use the WP are already acquainted with the typewriter. Therefore, the equipment should resemble the typewriter in its most important aspects. The extent of this resemblance depends considerably upon the vendor. All have duplicated the typewriter arrangement for the text entry keys. The "standard typewriter keyboard" is so-called because the keys are arranged in the three rows found on most typewriters today.

This is not to say that this is the best design for a keyboard. Years ago experiments were carried out on different keyboard arrangments to see which could be learned most quickly. The researchers were not surprised to find that an arrangement which put the keys most used at the easiest fingers to move provided a keyboard (the Dvorak keyboard) which one could learn most quickly and best type with. A move to make this the standard keyboard did not catch on. It would have required retraining all existing typists to use this optimal configuration. Since then it has dropped out of sight.

Given the standard keyboard, there are still variations one might consider, such as the angle of slope and the distance between each key and whether the key is flat or concave. The keyboard developed by IBM for the Selectric typewriter has become a secondary standard adopted by many manufacturers.

Enough said. When you step up to the machine, you find a familiar keyboard, especially if you can type. You notice a number of additional keys at each side and, perhaps, above the regular keyboard.

As your guide I tell you to ignore the extra keys for the moment. I reach in the desk and take out a square, black form that looks like a piece of cardboard, which you know is the floppy disk. I insert it in a slot in the machine and close the door, if there is one. I find the power switch and turn it on.

The vendor knows that it is important for you to get on this machine fast and start being productive. Also, you are not likely to read a manual beforehand, nor even to take an orientation course. Therefore, the machine should assist you when your human guide is absent, with prompts, menus and help text when you ask for it.

### Menus and Prompts

The WP is designed to satisfy a wide range of users, starting with the uninitiated and continuing to the advanced operator who can do complex tasks. The WP can do very complicated things but must be instructed what to do. The question is where to place the responsibility of instructing this sophisticated servant. After many months of experience the operator can get the WP started on a very complicated task with just a few key strokes. But experience has taught the operator just what these key strokes are. On the other hand, the new operator doesn't know a thing and hopes for some assistance from the machine itself. This assistance takes two forms, the prompt and the menu.

The purpose of both is to get information from you about what you want to do; they differ simply in how they go about doing this.

*Prompt*

A prompt takes two forms. The first is a question. As part of the startup procedure, some WPs ask you to furnish temporal information and identification about the user. The complete prompt is simply a question or a directive, such as: "What is your name?" "What is the date?" "Please give the present date and time."

A question or directive does not tell you the form of the desired reply. Should you say, "December 3, 1980" or "12/3/1980" or . . .? Some prompts give an example or a guideline of how you should enter the information.

Another form of prompt not usually found in the office WP but common in the personal computer and with the EDP system is the nondirective formal prompt. It consists of a special symbol or character that tells the experienced operator that the previous action is finished and that the system can accept a new request. This prompt is usually a fresh line starting with a symbol, a question mark, asterisk, etc., such as,

*

(6.1.1)

The cursor positions right after the symbol and you key in the activity that you want—letters and symbols; you must *know* the right combination for the next action.

*Menu*

The menu is a more popular way of getting you to specify what you want. The menu asks a question and then presents a number of alternative answers—it's multiple choice. These are the only alternatives which are acceptable. There are three ways to reply, which we now examine.

Figure 6.1.1 shows the startup menu provided in the NBI 3000. It gives you five alternatives for operations that you might select for the WP to do. The instructions below the menu tell you how to use it. You hit the alphabetic character corresponding to the operation you want. Further information is requested from you by a prompt.

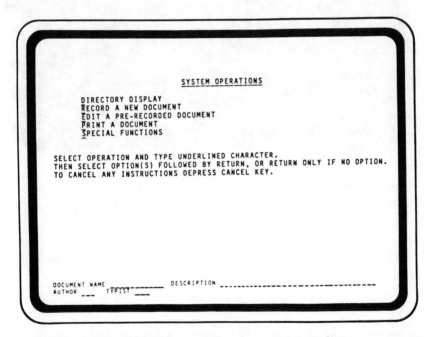

Figure 6.1.1. The NBI startup menu. (Courtesy of NBI).

The second kind of menu is shown in Figure 6.1.2. Again you have a choice of a number of activities. To select an activity, you touch the space bar. This causes the cursor to move down the screen to the next line. When the cursor positions to the line corresponding to the desired activity, touch <u>accept</u> to make your choice.

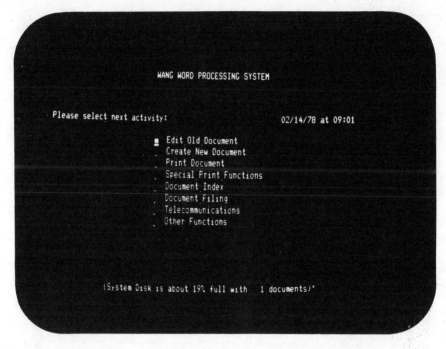

Figure 6.1.2. Wang OIS starting menu. (Courtesy of Wang).

The third way to get information from you is illustrated in Figure 6.1.3. It is closer to a prompt than a menu. The screen wants you to supply the date. It has structured activity so that you supply the date in the exact form needed. The cursor has positioned under the first digit of the two digit month code. If this is September, you must enter "09."

*Objections*

Menus and prompts are indispensable to enable the trainee to produce useful work fast. After a few weeks at the WP, you "know the ropes." You don't need to be prompted. Some WPs let you reply to a question before it is completely displayed on the screen. This saves wasted time, is less tiresome and makes you more

DISC CREATION AND MODIFICATION

LEFT: 5.0 MASTER                                    RIGHT: DISC NAME

DATE FORMAT:                    MM/DD/YY

DATE:                           MM/DD/YY

SYSTEM DISC NAME:               DISC NAME

MACHINE SERIAL NUMBER:          X000-000000

CONFIGURATION:

    DISPLAY                    -   FULL PAGE
    DISC TYPE                  -   SINGLE SIDED
    PRiNTER                    -   STANDARD
    PRINTER ACCESSORY          -   NONE
    SHARED PRINTER INTERFACE   -   NONE
    COMMUNICATIONS MODE        -   NONE

PROCEDURE:

    COPY ENTIRE MASTER DISC TO SYSTEM DISC
    SELECT OPTIONS OR UTILITIES TO BE COPIED

Figure 6.1.3. Xerox 860 date input request. (Courtesy of Xerox).

productive. If you have to wait for three menus to display before you get to work, answering each as it appears, you get bored.

*Help*

Some WPs furnish additional assistance in the form of text presented on the screen any time you need it. When you get stuck and don't know what to do next, press help. A sequence of menus appears to find out what topic you need to know about, and finally, instructions appear about the general procedure for this aspect of operation.

## Starting It Up

As long as there is a system disk in the primary drive, we are ready to start the machine. Don't expect to find the switch in a standard place. On some machines the switch is hidden. If somebody should come by and find an unattended machine on, it might get shut off, thereby destroying an hour's work in memory.

In most cases, turning on the machine elicits the first menu or a prompt. For older machines that have no clock or calendar that is self contained, you are asked the date and time. This can then be associated with each document in the directory so that you will know when it was created or changed. A few machines have battery run clocks which keep track of the date and time without needing to get the information from you.

Next you might select an activity. Some machines give you a choice of four or five activities, such as the menu of Figure 6.1.2. A single key stroke gets you started. The least demanding machine is the CPT 8000. When you turn it on, you get a blank screen and can start typing. The machine assumes that you want to create a document and lets you start work immediately. When you have a page written, it beeps at you to ask you where to put it. You do have to know how to put the page away, because you get no help from the machine.

Some WPs want more information and give you several prompts and menus before you can start, such as the name of the document you are creating and the format of the page. In my opinion, the fewer the preliminaries, the better.

### Entry

Once you have a clear screen, that blank sheet of paper, you can start entering the document. Just operate the keyboard like a typewriter. Key in continuously, disregarding line ends—there is no carriage to return and the WP fills up the lines for you, going on to the next line without bothering you. You need only tell it the end of the paragraph with <u>return.</u>

As you key, you may notice that you have made a mistake—just hit <u>rub</u> to backspace to the letters and type right over them. The "paper" on the screen is altered cleanly. This is the general approach; the differences from on WP to the next are discussed in Section 6.2. The mechanics of the display, differences and similarities are also examined.

### Four Phases

Initially we examine document preparation with word processing by viewing it as four phases. The phases may and do overlap; all four might take place at a single sitting. These phases are:

1. creation,
2. editing,
3. formatting,
4. printing.

In the remainder of this section we introduce each phase. Then each phase is examined more carefully. The sections which follow describe in detail the editing facilities available in even the simplest word processing systems and compare and contrast them. Formatting and printing is left for Chapter 7.

For **creation,** you key in the document initially from scratch. The source of the document may be:

- dictation,
- a rough, handwritten draft or
- thought out and entered at the terminal by the originator.

The intention is to make an electronic document (ED) which conforms exactly to its source. Any mistakes in entry should be corrected as soon as they are detected.

After the electronic document is prepared, you proofread it at the terminal to make sure that it corresponds to the source document. When you find errors, you make immediate changes. Creation always involves editing (unless you are perfect). Hence, full edit facilities must be available. We separate these activities only to simplify explanation.

The second phase of document preparation is **editing** an existing electronic document (ED). You request the document by name. The WP retrieves it from the ED file and makes it available for alterations. These alterations may come from a hand-edited source document. The operator makes the ED conform to these corrections. Or the originator may operate the terminal, correcting the ED during the review.

To **format** the document is to cause it to appear on paper in a physical arrangement which seems suitable to you. This includes a choice of typeface and type size, spacing, margins and so forth. This arrangement is realized (put into effect) when you **print** the document—make a copy of it on paper.

To reiterate, all four phases may be performed at the same sitting.

### Creation

The activities for this phase consist of:

- creating the text in memory by keying in at the keyboard;
- making corrections immediately;
- storing the document onto a diskette when done.

Figure 6.1.4 illustrates the components involved in this phase. This view of memory shows the software components and memory work areas involved. Each device—the keyboard, display and disk drive—has a driver associated with it, a program to operate it. Then there is the operating system, the program which takes care of passing data and directives to the driver; and there is the text editor (TE), the component responsible for constructing and changing the electronic document at your request.

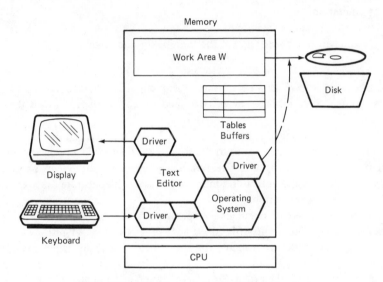

Figure 6.1.4. Components involved in creating text.

You start the action from a menu or prompt and activate the text editor. Most systems provide a **status line**, which displays updated information about the document as it is created: its name, format and where you are (line number, column number, page number, etc.). In any case, there is considerable blank space left on the screen.

As you key in text from a source document or dictated material, an electronic document (ED) is created in memory. The TE keeps it up to date as each keystrike is made. That keystroke is routed to the display for you to verify. During entry, you backspace to correct one or more incorrect keystrokes. (Large deletions are discussed later.)

When the document has been entered, indicate this by a keyboard command. This document is then stored onto a disk where it is safe and preserved for later use.

### Edit

To edit an existing document, start up the system as before, this time replying to the menu or prompt by naming which electronic document is to be edited. The contents of memory at this time are shown in Figure 6.1.4. The text editor accepts the name and requests that the operating system bring the document in from the diskette. In some WPs you may be asked to mount a different diskette or to verify the name of the document. The ED is located and some of it is transferred to memory. You can now work on altering the document. However, the CRT screen cannot display the entire document but only a portion of it, a **screenful**. You determine *which* screenful in the document is presented.

You can review, alter, add or move about portions of the text. Whatever is done, the results are always displayed so that you can verify each action.

When you're done, you tell the text editor through the keyboard. The document is now put away. According to the system design, if you have given it a new name, then you have two slightly different copies of it. With automatic backup (Chapter 7), you always get two copies, one a revised ED.

To edit effectively you must be able to jump around in the document at will and make alterations. Only a portion of the text is visible on the screen at any one time; scrolling lets you select which portion of the document is displayed. Positioning the cursor directs the WP to where you would like to make a change. These subjects get attention in Sections 6.3 and 6.4.

Deletion and insertion are your primary correction activities. Different alternatives for them provided by vendors are discussed in Section 6.5 and 6.6. Another way to find and alter text is *search* and *search and replace,* the topic of Section 6.7. Finally, the need to show all corrections made in the last draft is addressed in Section 6.8.

### Format

It is most natural to decide on the form of the document as you create and/or edit it. The ways and means for instructing the WP about the format of the ED account for much of the additional knowledge required by the WP operator; these differ considerably from one WP to the next. The effectiveness of this operation depends on many factors, the most important of which is the responsiveness of the display. The first four sections of Chapter 7 are devoted to format.

### Print

The last phase of activity prints the document using the components illustrated in Figure 6.1.5. You start the action at the keyboard. The document, which

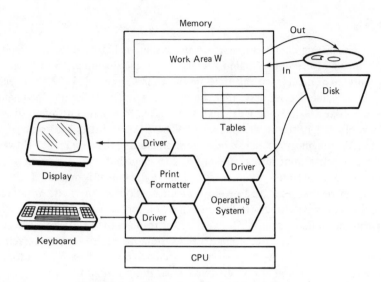

Figure 6.1.5. Components involved in printing text.

is not in memory, is brought in a little at a time. A different program, which I call a **print formatter**, directs the printer using the printer driver program. This program uses the specifications you have made during editing or those that you furnish now, as you initiate printing, to organize the text as it is printed. In most cases, while the document is printed, another may be edited. When printing single sheets, you may have to change the paper for each new page if a sheet feeder is not available. Often an audible tone is produced to alert you.

With some systems you may be allowed to alter the format of the output during printing, overriding the specifications found in the electronic document. Printing is more closely allied to formatting, so the last section of Chapter 7 is devoted to this action, after the intricacies of formatting have been covered.

### Advanced Features

If these edit and print features were the extent of the WP capability, the WP would still be of considerable aid in the office. Other features reduce appreciably the time to prepare, edit and tailor documents to office needs. These advanced features provide valuable WP assistance. The actions which the WP take are complicated to describe; so are the actions you take to instruct the machine what to do. The WP is stupid but capable. Its directions must be accurately phrased and its alternatives understood. Considerable space is therefore devoted here to advanced features, including the "cut and paste" ability and storage and recall of frequently used phrases.

### Subdocuments

Breaking up text into chunks and calling it forth again in whatever order you choose is an important means for reducing the time it takes to put together a complicated document—the subject of Chapter 8.

### Assists

A number of additional programs to assist you in perfecting your documents are examined in Chapter 9. Spelling programs aren't just for bad spellers, although that is their most important function. Heavy editing can introduce spelling errors that nobody catches until it's too late. The spelling checker is really great for this. Hyphenation programs are less useful, especially when justication is used. Various degrees of cooperation between the operator and the WP should be understood, especially when you are selecting a system.

Pagination selects how much text goes on each page. It is a kind of formatting. It is most helpful in constructing a well-balanced final document layout.

Page headings are good for documents which run into many pages; if they may be viewed by several people or gone over at a meeting, it is easy to get the disassembled document back into sequence.

Footnotes, outlines and indexes each get sections in the rest of Chapter 9.

### Automatic Features

Chapters 10, 11 and 12 introduce and discuss in depth many other automatic features and their need.

## 6.2 CREATION AND DISPLAY

**Work Area**

Figure 6.2.1 shows the contents of the memory of interest while creation takes place. The text editor is the most important program. It receives information from the keyboard via the keyboard driver; it sends information to the display

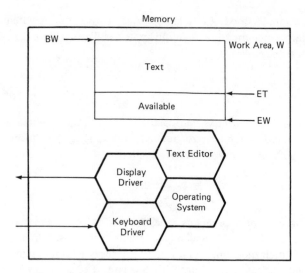

Figure 6.2.1. Memory contents during text creation.

via the display driver; and it updates the work area to modify the electronic form of the document being corrected.

As much space as possible is allocated to the work area which holds the text during creation. Its size is rated in bytes. Each byte holds a character code which in turn represents a character of the text. Numerous counters or markers keep track of different parts of the work area. We name these counters for easy reference by using two boldface capital letters to facilitate the description.

The work area is shown in Figure 6.2.1 as a rectangle. The editor keeps pointers to important areas labeled here with a pair of boldface letters: **BW** indicates the beginning of the work area; **EW** marks the end of the work area; **ET** monitors the end of the text entered so far.

Memory is often presented diagrammatically as a rectangle. It is more accurate to think of memory as a line segment with a beginning and an end. Bytes of memory are laid out along this line, as shown in Figure 6.2.2. The markers for the beginning and end of the work area and the end of the text are also shown there.

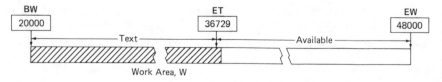

Figure 6.2.2. Text in the work area.

## The Text

As text is entered at the keyboard, it is simultaneously duplicated in the work area and displayed on the CRT.

For the moment, consider that the operator has started the system up and entered the first few characters of the text. The first part of the work area is displayed in Figure 6.2.3. **BW** marks the beginning of the work area and **ET** marks the place where the next character will be entered into this work area.

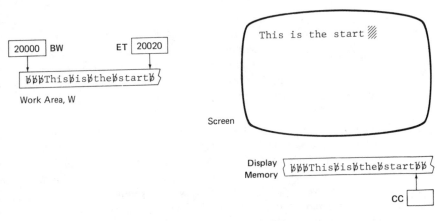

Figure 6.2.3. Display memory is a duplicate of part of the work area.

Note: Although memory seems to hold characters, it is the codes for characters which are actually recorded there. This holds for all the figures in this and succeeding chapters, unless otherwise noted.

Corresponding to the text is a presentation on the CRT at the right of the figure. Note that the information in memory is reproduced on the first line of the screen and that the cursor, indicated by the black rectangle, is positioned where the next character entered at the keyboard should appear.

For the information to be displayed thus, the display memory must contain the corresponding character codes, as shown at the lower right of the figure. The cursor counter contains the number of the byte in display memory corresponding to where the cursor appears on the CRT.

In the figure where blanks should appear in both the work area and display memory, a "b" with a slash through it is shown. This conveys that even a blank has a code.

## Text Entry and Display

Suppose that the text entry has proceeded to the point shown in Figure 6.2.3. Note the first portion of the first line of the text in the working area, which is simultaneously displayed on the screen. The operator keys in a series of characters. As a key is struck, the keyboard generates its code. That code is relayed through the driver to the text editor. The text editor enters the code into the work space at the position pointed to by **ET**.

Immediately thereafter the text editor sends this same character code over to the display. The display receives the code and inserts into the display memory where CC points and the cursor counter is increased by one.

The text editor also updates the work area pointer. ET is increased by one so as to point to the next byte in the work space which will receive a character. Entry, recording and display of characters continues as long as there is room on this line.

### Wraparound

**Wraparound**, or **word wrap**, is a characteristic of most WP text editors. It allows you to type continuously without hitting return except at the end of a paragraph. Characters keyed are placed on the screen at the cursor on the line as keyed until the line fills up. If all of the last word entered does not fit on this line, then the text editor removes that word from the line and puts it at the left of the next line.

To clarify this, imagine typing into an 80-character line: the last word entered there is "position." As you key in the first three letters, "pos," they go into bytes 77, 78 and 79. When the "i" is keyed in, the text editor knows that this word does not properly fit on this line. (The next line should not start with a blank. So even if "i" were the last letter of the word, it should be moved.) Therefore, the text editor removes "posi" from the line, replacing it with four blanks. Then the text editor moves "posi" to start the next line. The remaining letters when keyed in "tion" follow directly on that line.

It is sometimes important to be able to inhibit word wrap. If the line ends with a number of words which should not be separated, a **hard space** can be put between the words. If "Mr. Harris" appears in your text, put a hard space (with the **hard-space** key) to separate "Mr." and "Harris." Should this phrase come at the *end* of the line, Harris will get separated from his title: "Mr. Harris" is either wrapped or left on the line.

*Procedure*

Figure 6.2.4 illustrates wraparound using three pointers:

> **BW** points to the beginning of the work area.
> **NL** points to the beginning of the current line.
> **ET** points to the end of the text.

The difference between **ET** and **NL** is the number of occupied positions on the last line. As long as this difference is less than the specified line length, new characters can be added into the line. In the figure, you are about to key in the last letters which fill up the line. If the next character entered at the keyboard is a blank, then this line is complete so no wraparound is necessary.

In the case described earlier, the next character entered is not a blank, so wraparound occurs and this line is complete. Upon receipt of the "i," it is placed in the work area, as

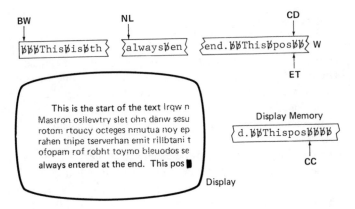

Figure 6.2.4. Memory just before word wrap.

shown in Figure 6.2.5. The text editor fills the positions previously occupied by "pos" on the screen with blanks as soon as the revision is made. To do this the text editor sends the

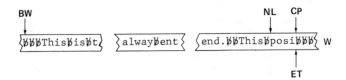

Figure 6.2.5. One more character causes word wrap.

codes for three blanks to replace the displaced letters, "pos" to end the completed line and codes for "posi" to start the new line, to the display memory to update the screen. The display and display memory, as they appear after hitting "i," is shown in Figure 6.2.6.

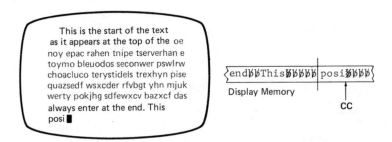

Figure 6.2.6. Display and display memory after word wrap.

**End of Screen**

What happens when the screen fills up? For the page oriented WP with page size screen, often you must put away the page you just made; you may add no more text until you do (see Chapter 8). For most WPs, automatic line scrolling occurs. Suppose that we are typing on the last text line of the screen. The line fills up as illustrated in Figures 6.2.4 through 6.2.6 and completes with a wraparound. However, there seems to be no place to put the new word which overflows from the last screen line.

To make room for the wraparound and new text, the TE moves up the contents of the screen. One line—the top line—is lost. It is lost only in the sense that it is no longer displayed. It is still safe in the work area. The second line moves to the top; the third line moves to replace the second line; and so forth. The old last line also moves up one line position. Momentarily this creates an empty line on the bottom. The wrapped word goes here with the cursor in the next character position. Text entry continues on the last line, as illustrated for the example in Figure 6.2.7.

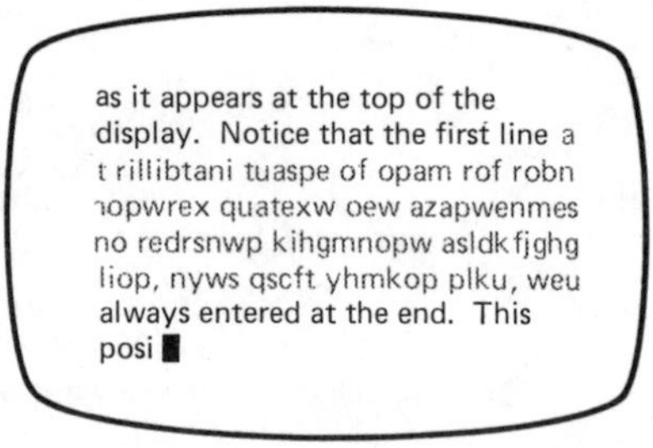

as it appears at the top of the
display. Notice that the first line a
t rillibtani tuaspe of opam rof robn
nopwrex quatexw oew azapwenmes
no redrsnwp kihgmnopw asldk fjghg
liop, nyws qscft yhmkop plku, weu
always entered at the end. This
posi ▮

Figure 6.2.7. Text entry on the text screen line.

When the screen is full, most WPs enter new text at the bottom of the screen. Some users feel that it is tiring to be looking continually at this position. In response, vendors such as CPT, DEC WPS, and AB Dick Magna III use a fixed line a few lines up from the bottom for text entry. Below that you see text which follows this entry point for existing documents.

*Technique*

For automatic end-of-screen scroll, Figure 6.2.8 shows display memory with two pointers:

CC is the cursor counter which monitors the cursor position.
SD is a pointer which indicates the start of the display and is adjustable on command from the computer.

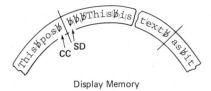

Display Memory

Figure 6.2.8. Automatic end of screen scroll.

The adjustment takes place when the screen is nearly full, as shown in Figure 6.2.8. A single command from the text editor advances **SD** by 80, or one line length, so that the second line is now displayed as the first line, as shown in Figure 6.2.9. Next the text editor transmits characters to the display via the driver: four blanks to terminate the next-to-last line; "posi" to begin the last line.

Figure 6.2.9. Readjusting the start of display within the terminal.

The contents of display memory are shown in Figure 6.2.10 in linear form, before and after the letter "i" is hit.

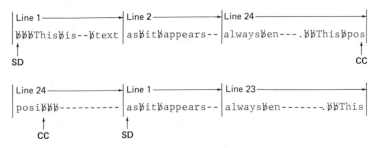

Figure 6.2.10. Display memory after end-of-screen scroll.

## Backspace Correction

Studies show that most errors in entering copy are noted by the operator as soon as copy is keyed in. You merely backspace through the bad characters and enter the proper characters. This is called **backspace correction**. When you note the error, hit backspace or rub the proper number of times. (Usually *both* are not present; when they are, the vendor describes the difference.) As rub is pressed, the cursor moves backward on the display. The position which the cursor occupied is cleared. The character on which the cursor stops may appear in reverse video. The cursor should stand out so you can easily see when it is properly positioned. Now enter the correct characters to replace the old ones.

*Example*

Figure 6.2.11 shows an example and describes the operation of the text editor. Each time rub is pressed, the text editor receives a code. This nonprinting code produced at the keyboard is passed to the keyboard driver. In response to this code, the text editor enters a blank where **CP** points to in the work space and sends a code for blank to the display. The TE decreases the **CP** pointer and signals the display to do likewise for **CC**. The cursor moves backward in response.

In the example, "teh" was entered instead of "the." Hit rub twice so that **CP** points to the letter "e" in "teh." Now when "he" is keyed in, the text appears as shown at the right of Figure 6.2.11.

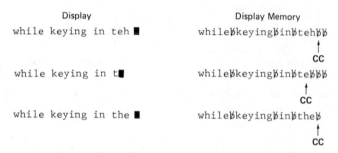

Figure 6.2.11. Backspace correction.

## Line End and Paragraph

*Special Codes*

The text editor needs to keep track of line ending only for the display. As the text editor flits about the text in the work area, it helps to know where lines begin and end. There are several ways to do this. First, assume that **BS** keeps track of the start of the screen with reference to the text in W. Lines can be monitored:

a. by using one marker for each screen line;
b. by recalculating each line with respect to **BS** every time the screen changes materially;
c. by keeping the work space literally—that is, as a total copy of the screen, including all blanks that appear there;
d. by using a special code as a marker at the end of each line.

A special code in this book is placed in brackets. For example, the code for the end of a line is [1e]. When [1e] appears in the text in the work area it directs the text editor to fill the rest of the display line with blanks. (In some cases, display lines are justified, but this topic is postponed to Chapter 7.) Another nonprinting code, [tb], represents a tab request (generated when you hit tab.) Then [tb] means the TE should enter blanks on the screen up to the next tab stop.

**Paragraphs**

During normal text entry, you type continually, completely ignoring the end of a line. The WP wraps words to new lines automatically. Only when you come to the end of a paragraph do you hit <u>return</u> at the keyboard. The text editor detects this signal and places the corresponding code, [cr], in the work space in memory. A unique paragraph end symbol (usually a graphic) appears on the screen. The number of blanks required to fill up the line is sent with the line to the display so that it appears correctly. The cursor moves to the beginning of the next line with an upward scroll if keying into the last screen line.

You may end all your paragraphs in the same way, with perhaps

    a. an additional line following each paragraph,
    b. a standard indent or tab to start the next paragraph.

Some WPs provide a single key to do this. You define the values (a) and (b) for this as part of format specifications (see Section 7.1).

## 6.3 POSITIONING THE CURSOR

**Introduction**

Proper cursor positioning is essential for all edit and create functions because the action takes place at the cursor position. Examples of action which you request at the cursor position are: delete, insert, change, cut and paste and so forth. The exception is the typing line WPs examined on page 00. They do not need nor do they provide for cursor movement.

When positioning the cursor, it is important to keep in mind the following relation:

- The screen holds only a portion of the text—from one-third page to a full normal page.
- A page may be only a fraction of the text.
- For most manuscripts, not all text may fit into memory.

Most office WP systems keep the memory work area small to leave more memory space for a larger edit program, the background print program and buffers for the optional advanced activities. These WPs also provide for background printing. Hence two programs must occupy available memory.

Personal computer WPs and maxicomputer WPs take the simplest way out. They tend to provide large work space and serial file management. But printout cannot be done in the background. It is done separately, not during editing. This will seem wasteful of time until you experience the luxury of moving from the front to the back of a 12 page document in a fraction of a second. Or how about a *search and replace* for the entire 12 page document in that amount of time? The personal computer WP trades off simplicity of the WP program and work space for time.

This section discusses how to move the cursor about the screen to parts of the text in the cursor oriented WP (not the typing line VDT described on page 188). There may be more text in memory and/or on the disk that is important to get to. Getting text from these sources and putting it on the screen is called **scrolling**. Section 6.4 is devoted to that topic.

*Keys*

You enter a request to move the cursor at the keyboard with one of a set of four or more keys. Each key has an arrow or other mark showing the direction of cursor motion. The text editor then moves the cursor as directed. In some personal computing WP systems, cursor motion is requested by a combination of two keys. In either case the keyboard generates a separate control code of one byte for each key (or combination) which the text editor interprets as a request to move the cursor one character in the direction of the arrow. Thus,

- the code we call [cu] means "cursor up";
- when up is pressed, [cu] is produced;
- when the text editor receives [cu], it moves the cursor up by one line;
- when you hold down up, several [cu]'s are produced;
- the cursor moves up once for each [cu] the text editor receives;
- hence the cursor moves up the screen five or six lines per second as you hold down up.

### Geometrical versus Context Positioning

The place where everything happens is where you put the cursor. You want to get the cursor to the right place as soon as possible. It is boring to sit there hitting one key, time after time, just to move the cursor along the line a character at a time. Some WPs let you move along a word at a time. This, combined with the repeat actions of keys on some keyboards, makes the cursor zip along. In fact, you might move right past the spot you want.

Since getting there is so important, we'll look at all the ways you can do so. Positioning methods are classified as:

- geometrical
- express
- contextual

**Geometric positioning** is described with regard to a grid superimposed on the CRT screen: horizontally either to the left or right by single character positions; up or down by lines.

**Express positioning** is a geometric variation. It gets you to specific points quickly. The four corners of the screen are standard express positions. From there you can go on at specific nearby points. Take the Micom 2000 as an example. It has five geometrical positioning cursor keys. Four have arrows pointing, as I name them, left, right, up, down. The fifth has an arrow pointing to the upper left and is called home. It is really a multiplier. Here are the results you get if you hit one or two keys in sequence (not simultaneously, as code or control is used):

- touch right (left, up, down) to move once in that direction;
- hold down right (left, up, down) to move several times in that direction;
- hit home right (home left) to move to the right (left) margin;
- hit home up (home down) to move to the top (bottom) of the screen;
- hit home home to move to the upper left hand corner of the screen.

A different approach is found in the Xerox 860. A small disk in a little box can position the cursor in *any* direction you choose. This is called a **CAT** for "capacitive activated transducer." Direction is determined by the angular position of your finger on the disk: 3 o'clock is to the right; 7:30 o'clock is down and to the left. The harder your press, the faster the cursor moves.

The Xerox STAR has a "mouse," a little box on wheels. Hold it and roll it along the table in the same orientation you want the cursor to move.

**Context positioning** moves the cursor in terms of grammatical units. You can move the cursor a word, sentence or paragraph at a time. The smallest such unit is a character; a blank is a character in this sense, since it occupies one position on the screen or paper. The next context unit is the word. For most WP applications the definition of the word is a set of letters both preceded and followed by a space, a numeral or punctuation. For hyphenated words, each WP has it s own rules; one alternative says that the hyphen comes between two words.

A sentence generally ends with a period, question mark or exclamation point; the next sentence begins after one or two spaces. One might consider two other intermediate units, the phrase and the clause, but these are ignored by WPs.

The next largest contextual unit is the paragraph. With wraparound, the operator enters text continuously, disregarding the end of a line. The paragraph is distinguished by the carriage return [cr] (sometimes called the **paragraph end**) in the work area generated when you hit return. The text editor uses [cr] to position at the next paragraph.

Another textual unit is the page. Where a new page begins depends upon the format parameters, but it is usually off the screen and hence involves scrolling. For the full page screen, requesting the next screen is the same as requesting the next page.

Return to the Micom 2000 for examples of context positioning. It has three keys marked with symbols to convey <u>word</u>, <u>sent</u>(ence), and <u>para</u>(graph). Even if the cursor sits in the middle of a word, press <u>word</u> and the cursor moves to the first character of the next word; press <u>sent</u> and it goes to the first character of the next sentence; press <u>para</u> and it moves to the first character of the next paragraph.

*Others*

Here are other positioning methods which get honorable mention:

1. Some WPs let you use standard outline form. You label each kind of division. You can later use this format to request positioning. This is discussed in Section 9.6.
2. Some WPs let you set up markers at key positions in the text. Then you can request positioning (and scrolling) by naming the marker.

Finally, it is possible to distinguish sections, chapters and other such blocks of text. Their boundaries depend intimately upon the context, but it is generally too difficult to convey that context to the WP, so its use is rare.

**Questions**

Several questions arise. Does the cursor move into the blank areas? This is important when entering text and you try to move the cursor beyond the end of the text. Some WPs won't let you; the cursor keys do not respond if you direct it "out-of-bounds"—to an area where there is neither text nor blanks.

What happens at the end of a line?

A request to move right at the end of one line moves cursor to the beginning of the next line.

A request to move left at the beginning of a line moves the cursor to the end of the previous line.

For WPs where blank area is *out-of-bounds,* the right end of a line means the rightmost nonblank character in the current line, not the right margin.

Is geometrical positioning supplied in a WP where context motion is also provided? Usually both exist and you can take your choice.

What happens when you try to move the cursor up when it is at the top of the screen or down when it is at the bottom of the screen? A request which tries to move the cursor off the screen invokes scrolling and puts new text on the screen, as described in Section 6.4.

### Cursor Motion

Imagine you are at the WP looking at text on the screen; what you see is the current screenful of text. Geometric positioning on this screenful uses one of the four directional keys. Pressing a key once moves the cursor one position in the direction of the engraved arrow; holding a key down produces first a single motion followed by repeated movement at a fixed rate. How does the text editor move the cursor?

When you press a cursor motion key, it produces a nonprinting code. This code is accepted by the keyboard driver and passed along. The text editor response is to augment the contents of the cursor position counter **CP**, which contains the address in the work space corresponding to the character on the screen where the cursor is displayed. To move ahead one position, add 1 to this counter; to move back one position, subtract 1 from the counter.

Suppose that text is maintained in the work area in a one-for-one relation to what is displayed on the screen. Each screen line then contains 80 positions: a downward motion request increases the cursor position counter by 80; an upward motion request decreases the counter by 80.

This is illustrated in Figure 6.3.1. The large rectangle represents the work area. The smaller rectangle is the material currently presented on the screen. There are six counters which define various positions:

**BW** marks the beginning of the work area.
**EW** marks the end of the work area.
**BS** marks the beginning of the screen display.

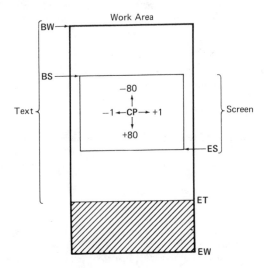

Figure 6.3.1. Cursor positioning.

ES marks the end of the screen display.
ET marks the end of the text recorded in the work area.
CP marks the cursor position.

The cursor is shown in the figure as a small black rectangle. Four arrows point in each of the four directions corresponding to the cursor movement. Next to each arrow is a number. This is a quantity to be added to **CP** to move the cursor as directed.

Once the **CP** is altered to reflect the desired position of the cursor, a similar action must be made to update the display. Recall that **CC** is the cursor counter in display memory. It stores a number corresponding to the cursor position on the screen. Screen positions are viewed as though running along a straight line. Referring to Figure 6.3.1, note that **BS** points to the first position on the screen and **ES** points to the last. The number which should be entered into the cursor counter then can be found by subtracting **BS** from **CP**. This number, which is the difference between the cursor position and the beginning of the display for the text in the work area, corresponds exactly with the character number of the cursor position on the screen.

### Large Motion

According to the WP being used, the operator can move the cursor to other key positions on the screen. Here are some of the possible choices:

- the beginning of the current line,
- the end of the current text presented on the screen,
- the top left corner of the screen,
- the bottom left corner of the screen,
- the other two corners of the screen.

These are simple calculations. For instance, to move the cursor to the upper left hand corner, set CP equal to **BS**. To position to the beginning of the line, find the proper multiple of 80 to add to **BS** so that the result is just less than the current content of **CP**.

## Context Motion

For context cursor motion, you move the cursor according to grammatical divisions within the text. Sometimes you can move backward or forward within the text.

### By Character

Moving the cursor by character is identical to single character motion, left and right, as induced by the geometrical motion keys. Motion left at the beginning of the line takes the cursor to the end of the preceding line; motion right at the end of a line takes it to the beginning of the next line.

### By Word

To scan forward by word, the text editor increments **CP** by 1 and examines the code found at that position. As long as the code is alphanumeric, action continues. A code for a blank signals that a new word is ahead. Intervening blanks or punctuation are passed over. Only when the *next* alphanumeric code is encountered does action stop. The **CP** records this position and the cursor is displayed correspondingly on the screen.

To travel backward, the rule above is also applied, by decreasing **CP** instead. After moving backward over preceding text, past the blank, the **CP** points to the final letter of the preceding word. But that's not where we want it. The text editor continues scanning backward through the work space looking for a blank or punctuation. That blank means that the **CP** points one position to the left of the beginning of the desired word. Finally, the text editor brings us to the beginning of the word, adding 1 to **CP**. Now the cursor is displayed at the first character of the preceding word.

### By Sentence

To move the cursor by sentence, the text editor searches in the work space for terminal punctuation (period, question mark or exclamation point). It continues through null codes to pick up the beginning of the next sentence. To move backward by sentence, decrease **CP** until a period (etc.) is found. Then it moves forward to pick up the first character of the sentence.

### By Paragraph

In a WP which has wraparound, a carriage return [cr] recorded in the work space ends each paragraph. To move forward by paragraph, the text editor checks each code in the work space until [cr] is found and continues past to pick up the first alphanumeric code. To get to the previous paragraph, similar steps are taken.

### Induced Scrolling

Any of the context cursor motions above may move **CP** in either direction past the screen limits as marked by **BS** and **ES**. To present the cursor in its new position requires that a new screenful of text be brought from the work area; this is scrolling.

## 6.4 SCROLLING

### Concept

**Scrolling** changes the screen display by replacing some or all of it with new text. You might scroll:

- by line, forward or backward;
- continually in either direction;
- by adjacent screenful, forward or backward;
- to another position in the text, usually the beginning or the end.

Another kind of scrolling—called **horizontal scrolling**—deals with documents that are wider than the screen. It brings to the screen text that is missing on the right or left (instead of bottom or top). It is discussed in Chapter 11 in the context of wide documents.

**Line scrolling** brings a new line of text to the top (or bottom) of the screen; the text is pushed down (or up), thereby "losing" one line. Line scrolling picks up one or more additional lines without losing the entire current screen.

**Continuous scrolling** is found in some office WPs (such as DEC's WPS) and most journalism and typographic WPs. Hit scroll-up and the text starts to move up the screen. Some WPs let you change the scroll rate (**variable scroll**) by hitting a number key (1 for slow, 9 for fast). The greatest luxury is **incremental scroll**, or **pan scroll**, which requires special CRT logic. This is variable continuous scroll, where the lines glide up the screen.

**Screen scrolling** picks up the *next* screenful of text in either the forward or backward direction. Sometimes this is called **paging**: the text does not move up smoothly on the screen. To maintain continuity, at least one line from the old display should appear on the screen. Thus, in scrolling forward by screen, one (or more) bottom line(s) of the old screen becomes the top line(s) of the *new* display; in reverse screen scrolling, the top line(s) of *this* screen becomes the bottom line(s) of the *new* screen. Screen scrolling is most useful in making sequential corrections while editing text.

Moving to special places in the text can be done by scrolling. Two commonly used scroll objectives are:

- the beginning of the text (as marked by **BW**),
- the end of the text (marked by **ET**).

The first lets you review the text from the beginning after creating or editing for proofreading. The second takes you to the end of the document to add more text there.

Finally, there is scrolling by page, which is either contextual or geometrical, depending on the display size. For the page-size display, page and screen scroll are the same. Some WPs let you scroll to a particular page; for example you can go from page 2 to page 5.

**Activation**

*Continuous*

You induce continuous scrolling with the scroll key. The Xerox 820 and Word-Star for personal computers use a control sequence. For the latter the sequence code Q Z starts the text moving up the screen at a moderate speed. To adjust the speed, hit a number from 1 to 9 (the fastest).

The DEC WPS does not have a single key for this purpose. It extends the cursor controls. Advance and go-back move the cursor forward or backward one character when touched. To start scrolling you need the gold colored key, called gold. Press gold advance; the cursor moves along the typing line to the end. This forces the text up the screen and thus induces scrolling. It continues until you press gold halt.

*By Line*

Sometimes there is no key for line scroll. Remember, it is induced automatically when you move the cursor "off" the top or bottom of the screen. Otherwise a key or control key combination may request it.

Some WPs, such as the Displaywriter do not have line scroll at all. Text management for the Displaywriter is by the screenful. Hence you cannot request the text from the next or previous screenful to be presented with this screenful. You may show the next or previous screen but without textual continuity with the current screen.

Scrolling for the typing line oriented WP is a necessity, but is postponed for a few pages to encompass more detail.

*By Screen*

Frequently you find keys dedicated to screen scroll, such as those marked next-scrn and prev-scrn on partial page of the Wang Office System WPs. Their use is obvious; Wang provides an overlap between screenfuls of several lines.

*By Page*

A lengthy document is broken into pages automatically by the WP without your request by inserting soft or movable page breaks where page separations seem to be. If you alter page allocations by entering a hard page break, because of information to be inserted later, the WP honors your requirement. Now you can ask it to display text with reference to either type of page break.

For the Wang Office Information System (OIS) you use the go-to-page key. To install text starting from the top of the next page as designated by the page break, hit go-to-page next-scrn. The start of the previous page is requested with go-to-page prev-scrn.

You may specify a page by number. This is useful when you have a draft to be corrected and you want to go forward or backward to a particular page to pick up an excerpt for "cut and paste." For the Wang OIS you use a sequence of key strokes: start with go-to-page; key the page number next; then hit up or down to specify the portion of the page you want. Up puts the first character of the page at the top of the screen; down puts the last character of the page at the bottom of the screen. This distinction is necessary because this is a partial page display.

## Line Scroll

What happens in line scroll? When you request line scroll forward, all the material on the screen moves up by one line. The top line disappears and a new bottom line appears. You see the text move up the screen and the new line appear at the bottom.

Computer memory is illustrated in Figure 6.4.1. The long rectangle represents the work area. **BS** points to the beginning of the current screenful of information—a line numbered 1. The counter **ES** points to the last character of the last line, numbered 24. Scrolling forward consists of altering the display to present, in this case, the lines numbered 2 through 25.

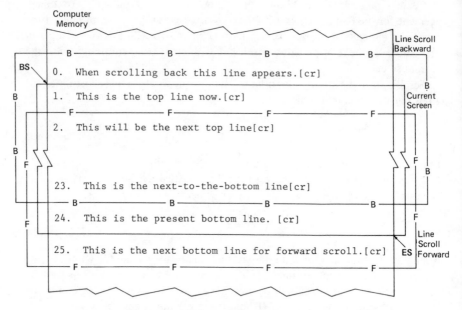

Figure 6.4.1. Line scroll as it effects memory.

The amount of information scrolled depends on the WP rules, the hardware and the present format setting, especially the line length. The case illustrated is for a 24 × 80 CRT with a line length of 80 and the full-screen height used for text. In some WPs, a status line and/or other descriptions are provided at the top or bottom of the display. This information is updated during scrolling, but scroll action is limited to text lines.

Corresponding to the top rectangle in Figure 6.4.1, which shows all the text in the work area, we have the refresh memory shown at the top of Figure 6.4.2. **SD** marks the start of

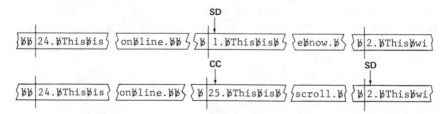

Figure 6.4.2. The start-of-display counter, **SD** is reset during line scroll forward.

the display, the place in display memory where the first screen line begins. The next successive lines are taken sequentially from display memory to its end, then text is taken from the start of display memory for the lower part of the screen until the count in **SD** is reached, the screen bottom. **SD** can be reset to a new first line.

### Forward

You enter a line scroll request. The text editor receives the command code and updates the display. The top line of the display is to be eliminated. The space occupied by the top line is reused. The text editor alters the cursor counter, **CC**, to point to the area occupied formerly by the top line. The text editor transmits the characters for the bottom line to display memory starting at this position pointed to by **CC**. Then TE resets **SD** to position to the second line, as shown at the bottom of Figure 6.4.2. Thereafter it is displayed as the top line. This happens automatically with a single request to the display. It is employed during creation to extend the document.

Subsequent display cycles begin at the place pointed to by **SD**. Thus, the line numbered 2 in the figure is displayed at the top of the screen; the line numbered 25 appears at the bottom.

Line scrolling occurs fast. Since only one new line is transmitted to the display, the new display literally pops up.

### Reverse Line Scroll

It is a simple matter to design a facility in the terminal to reset **SC** one line in the other direction, and to reverse the procedure. Unfortunately, off-the-shelf commercial terminals for WPs and personal computers do not supply this capability; it is found only in tailor-made systems.

Figure 6.4.3 illustrates how rapid backward line scrolling is done. **CC** is moved back to line 24, which is eliminated to be replaced in display memory by line 0 from Figure 6.4.1. This is quickly transmitted. The text editor then alters **SD** to correspond to the start of the display area as it exists in W. Immediately thereafter the display appears correctly.

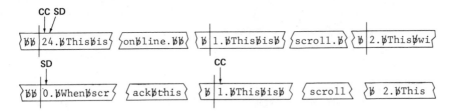

Figure 6.4.3. Rapid backward line scroll by resetting **SD**.

The alternative reverse scroll method is necessary when **SD** cannot be reset externally to move it backward. In Figure 6.4.1, for backward scrolling the text editor resets **BS** so that it points only past two [1e] s and hence at the new first line for the display. After updating **BS** and **ES** correspondingly, the entire screen is retransmitted.

In many WPs, since data transmission for the 24 lines is limited by the serial transmission rate of the display, screen update occurs over many refresh cycles and action is apparent to the operator. The new text seems to tumble from the top of the screen to the bottom over an interval of 3 or 4 seconds. It is amusing to watch several successive reverse-line scrolls. Each time you give a reverse line scroll command, text starts falling from the top again.

There are several ways that WPs get around this. Each requires additional circuitry in the VDT. For many WPs the VDTs are special designs providing such features not available in off-the-shelf VDTs. They provide smooth and/or continuous forward and reverse scrolling.

## Page Scroll

To get to adjacent text not shown, you page when continuous scroll is not provided; you also page to remote text. Let us examine the first alternative.

The entire text on the screen is replaced with new text with the exception of one (or more) lines which may be carried over for continuity. Since even this carryover is in a different position, the new screen presents all new material.

An entire screenful is transmitted to the display. First the TE resets the counters **BS** and **ES** (see Figure 6.3.1) to redefine the screen limits within the work space and to include one old line. The effect on Figure 6.4.1 is shown in Figure 6.4.4.

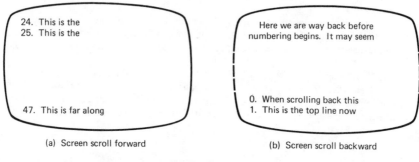

(a) Screen scroll forward                    (b) Screen scroll backward

Figure 6.4.4. The entire screen is transmitted for a scroll by page.

### Forward

To set **BS** altered for forward-screen scrolling, let C be the number of characters positions in the line, N the number of character in the line and T be the number of text lines presented on the screen. Then **BS** is reset as follows:

$$\mathbf{BS} = (\mathbf{BS}) + N(T - 1)$$

(6.4.1)

### Reverse

To scroll backward, the $N(T - 1)$ is subtracted instead of added to the pointer in **BS** thus:

$$\mathbf{BS} = (\mathbf{BS}) - N(T - 1)$$

(6.4.2)

*Display*

In both cases, to update the screen, text transmission starts in the workspace from the point marked by **BS**.

*Go to Page N*

You might enter a page request by hitting the page key, typing the number of the page and then hitting <u>return</u>. The response, regardless of screen size, is to clear the screen and present the requested page. The page begins at the top of the screen following the status lines, etc. The action is as described above.

## Text End

You "scroll to the top" to review the manuscript from its beginning. Then the display coincides with the beginning of the work area. The text editor responds to this command by resetting **BS** to correspond with **BW** and then retransmitting a screenful of text.

The calculation for the end of the text, assuming it is all in memory, is a little more complicated. Certainly the last character of text saved is pointed to by **ET**. But if the text editor were to start there and transmit information backward, the beginnings of paragraphs would appear incorrectly. If [1e] appears in the work space to mark the end of each line, the text editor goes to the end of the text and counts back enough [1e]s to get a full screen to display. If the last line is incomplete and without an [1e], the text editor counts back one less [1e] to make a proper presentation.

If the work space is stored literally, recording all blank codes, then it may be necessary to go to the end of the text and retrace to the next previous paragraph end. It is then possible to retrieve the length of the last line. The new setting for **BS** is then given as:

$$BS = (ET) - LL - C(T - 2) \qquad (6.4.3)$$

## Cursor

After scrolling, what happens to the cursor? This is individual to each system. Some reset the cursor to the beginning of the line or the beginning of the screen. This makes sense, because you may want to review this screenful from its beginning.

Other WPs leave the cursor in exactly the same position on the screen after scrolling, as it was before scrolling. This is useful if you scroll by mistake; when you scroll back to the former screen, you have then not lost your place. This requires that the text editor temporarily save the relative offset of **CP** from **BS**. Then reset **BS** for the new screen or page and transmit the new material to the terminal. Now reposition **CP** by adding the saved offset quantity to **BS**. That new position, which is the same as the old relative position, is passed to the cursor counter in the display.

## Typing Line

Instead of moving the cursor about the screen to find a place in the text to work at, why not move the text to a **typing line?** This is a horizontal line on the screen where you enter or change text. It is just like the typewriter's typing line. The philosophy behind the CPT 8000 and the Magna III is simply that—get the operation as close as possible to what happens on the typewriter. Then any typist will find it easy to learn how to use the WP system.

You *must* do all edit functions on the typing line, which is situated a few lines from the bottom of the screen. This permanent position seems to tire the operator least when looking back and forth between copy and the screen. A ruler appears just below the typing line, marked off in character positions, like the ruler on your typewriter.

A little pointer, like the mechanical pointer on the typewriter carriage, moves along the ruler to tell you where the hypothetical "carriage" is. This serves the function of the cursor. You move the arrow forward by touching space; and move the arrow backward with backspace. Position the arrow at any character and you can overtype that character and those which follow by touching any key(s). You delete or insert in much the same way described in Sections 6.5 and 6.6.

This description applies to the CPT 8000, but the Magna III and the Lexitron 1303 do not differ much in philosophy. Figure 6.4.5 shows how the screen is

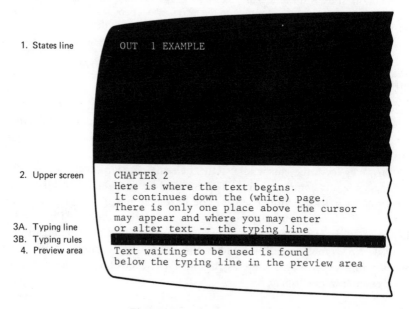

1. States line    OUT 1 EXAMPLE

2. Upper screen

CHAPTER 2
Here is where the text begins.
It continues down the (white) page.
There is only one place above the cursor
may appear and where you may enter

3A. Typing line    or alter text -- the typing line

3B. Typing rules

4. Preview area    Text waiting to be used is found
below the typing line in the preview area

Figure 6.4.5. Typing line display.

divided. All is well when text is now on the typing line. If it is somewhere else on the screen, you *must* move it to the typing line to alter it. This line divides the text into two parts, each of which may, in turn, consist of two parts. We have:

A.  Above the typing line,
1.  there is visible text on the screen, including the typing line—this is the **upper screen**;
2.  there is invisible text above that is an **upper buffer**.
B.  Below the line,
1.  There are a few lines showing on the screen, the **preview area**.
2.  There may be more text in memory, invisible yet available in the **lower buffer**. This can be brought forth by scrolling.

Text may be moved in both geometric and context quantities. There is a key for each: character, word, line, sent(ence), para(graph). The direction of motion of the text is determined by the next key you press:

*   it moves up with up
*   and down with down.

So if you press word up (down), one word moves from (to) the preview area to (from) the typing line.

The other keys are valuable to edit text as you move it from the preview area to the typing line:

*   If you press skip after touching a quantity key, that quantity of text is deleted from the beginning of the preview area; for example, press word and then skip three times and the next three words are deleted.
*   If you press adj (for adjust), the WP brings the next piece of text from the preview area; for example, press char and then adj twice and the next two characters go from the preview area into the typing line. Margins for the upper screen are adjusted at the same time.

*Editing*

As you edit, you direct WP text with up to move text up from the preview area and past the typing line; text displayed from the top of the screen goes into the bottom of the upper buffer. With down, text (if any) moves from the upper buffer into the top of the upper screen, down the screen past the typing line and into the preview area and out the bottom and into the lower buffer. Of course, you can stop it at any position along the way.

To reiterate, text *must* be on the typing line to be altered, to insert or to delete. It is neither as fast or as easy to edit thus as when you can skip about the screen and make changes in context.

## 6.5 DELETION

### Introduction

**Deletion** removes information from the text image in **WP** memory *and* from the screen display for you to verify. First the general concept will be examined and then alternatives on implementation described.

*General*

You start a delete sequence by bringing the text onto the screen that contains the unwanted **string** of information—a sequence of letters, numerals, punctuation, etc.—and position the cursor at the beginning of the string. In other words, if the area containing the string is not on the screen, you scroll to it. Then move the cursor to the string's beginning.

Next bracket the characters to be removed from the text. Some WPs highlight the characters of the string for you to verify. Cancel the delete request with halt; or, if you highlight too much, back up and "unhighlight" with rub. Highlighting makes the string dimmer or brighter than the surrounding text or puts it in **reverse video** (black on white if the rest of the text is white on black, or vice versa).

*Alternatives*

Hit delete or execute and the highlighted string disappears, along with its companion-text string in the work area. To decline, press cancel and the string remains on screen but is no longer highlighted. This is **discretionary deletion**, since you can change your mind. Some WPs have only what I call **immediate deletion**: as you hit delete word, the next word disappears.

How do you tell the text editor what to delete? We know how to scroll and to move the cursor to one end of the deletion string. Next mark it off. WPs give one or more options to do so. The deletion string is usually described rightward from the current cursor position. Some WPs permit you to define the string leftward.

There are three points to consider in deleting:

- The direction to go from the initial cursor position to reach the *other end* of the delete string,
- The length of the string,
- The ability to cancel.

Additionally most WPs fall into two classes:

**action oriented**: you state first what you want to do and then which object you want acted on; the sequence is <u>delete</u> <u>unit</u> (<u>accept</u> or <u>cancel</u>).
**object oriented**: you distinguish the text on which action is to be made before you say what is to be done; the sequence is <u>mark</u> <u>unit</u> <u>delete</u>.

Here <u>unit</u> is some quantity key such as <u>word</u>. It matters little, technically, which orientation you have. They seem equally easy to me. For object orientation, the marking procedure is consistent, whether the object is to be deleted, moved, altered, etc.

## String Determination

Once the cursor is positioned, you mark the string in one of three ways, comparable to cursor movement:

- screen oriented,
- context oriented,
- a combination of the two.

Let us examine the object oriented method, which uses two kinds of keys:

<u>mark</u> is pressed to start the mark sequence.
<u>unit</u> is a set of keys, one for each possible unit which might be set forth as described below. To mark one word starting at the cursor, press <u>mark</u>, then <u>word</u>.

### Screen Oriented

Marking here is geometric. The smallest unit is the character. To mark a character, press <u>mark</u> then <u>char</u>. To mark three characters, press <u>char</u> twice more.

Other geometrical units work almost the same way. They present the question of where to start the marking. If you are in the middle of a line (or screen or page) and you press <u>mark</u> <u>line</u>, different WPs construe this in two ways and would accordingly mark:

- *from here* to the end of the line (page, etc.),
- *the whole unit,* the entire line (page, etc.) that the cursor is sitting on.

To mark a string backward is sometimes an aid to quick editing. Some WPs have a <u>reverse</u> key to indicate this. To mark two lines going backward, press <u>mark reverse line line</u>.

*Context*

It makes more sense to edit in terms of context units. Most WPs provide most or all of these units: <u>word</u>, <u>sentence</u>, <u>paragraph</u>, <u>page</u>, <u>document</u>. A unit usually includes blanks at one end so that units can be combined easily. Thus word includes the blank at the end of the designated word. To mark three words, use <u>word word word</u>.

Marking *may* have the options:

- forward/backward from the cursor,
- from here/all the unit which includes the cursor,
- multiple (words, etc.).

*Combination*

Most frequently the block of interest is not of unit length. It might, for example, consist of two sentences—three words of the third sentence and one character of the next word. Mark this block with <u>mark sent sent word word word char</u>.

*Character Specification*

Some WPs provide another convenient way to mark strings. Tell the WP to mark up to the next keyed character. The Dictaphone Dual Display has a <u>delete-thru</u> key. Move the cursor to the start of the delete string. Then specify a character, such as "d" or ";" or ".". The text editor searches from the current cursor position to find the first occurrence of the designated character. This character marks the other end of the delete string.

Thus, to delete three words where the last word ends in "d", simply use "d" as the terminal designator: press <u>delete-thru d</u>. If none of the intervening words contains "d," then the string you want is displayed highlighted on the screen. If "d" appears within the string, type "d" enough times to get to the "d" at the end of the third word. When the period is designator, the delete string includes all characters up to and including the end of the sentence. By designating a period twice, two sentences are set up for deletion, and so forth.

Reverse character marking, when supplied, marks backward from the present cursor position.

## Immediate Deletion

Some WPs do immediate deletion and do not wait for confirmation of deletion. Once you ask to delete a string, *it's gone!* Others ask for confirmation only for long strings. In this mode, <u>move</u> the cursor to the start of the string. Now make your request: press <u>delete</u> and then the quantity—a character, word, line, etc. The text editor immediately accepts the request. It finds the end of the string and sets **DM**. It moves the text bracketed by **DM** and **ET** backward up to **CP**, reformatting lines for wraparound as it goes. Then the display is updated before your eyes.

To delete three words, use <u>delete</u> <u>word</u> <u>word</u> <u>word</u>. As each <u>word</u> is received, the text editor removes the next word and revises the display accordingly. Sometimes a line, sentence, paragraph or large string requires confirmation. Often this is treated like a block action (Section 8.1); and even though missing from the screen, the deleted string can be reinstated (like a crumpled note from the wastebasket). Syntrex calls this "undo."

*Form of the Request*

As a review, let us examine alternative ways in different WPs to specify deletion. Here <u>unit</u> is the generic quantity key, which might be <u>word</u>, <u>line</u>, etc. For object oriented forward, we have,

$$\underline{mark} \; \underline{unit} \; \underline{unit} \ldots \underline{unit} \; \underline{delete} \qquad (6.5.1)$$

For object oriented reverse,

$$\underline{reverse} \; \underline{mark} \; \underline{unit} \; \underline{unit} \ldots \underline{delete} \qquad (6.5.2)$$

For action oriented forward,

$$\underline{delete} \; \underline{unit} \; \underline{unit} \ldots \underline{unit} \; \underline{execute} \qquad (6.5.3)$$

For action oriented reverse,

$$\underline{delete} \; \underline{reverse} \; \underline{unit} \; \underline{unit} \ldots \underline{unit} \; \underline{execute} \qquad (6.5.4)$$

For action oriented character specified forward,

$$\underline{delete\text{-}thru} \; \{letter\} \ldots \{letter\} \; \underline{execute} \qquad (6.5.5)$$

For character specified reverse,

$$\underline{delete\text{-}thru} \; \underline{reverse} \; \{letter\} \ldots \{letter\} \; \underline{execute} \qquad (6.5.6)$$

Replace <u>execute</u> with <u>cancel</u> to change your mind.

### Implementation, Action Oriented

First examine the sequence of action for object oriented delete:

1) Place the cursor at the beginning of the string.
2) Enter commands to mark the string.
3) Verify and request deletion.
4) The string disappears.

*Finding the Limits*

Figure 6.5.1 spreads out the work area from left to right, showing the markers discussed so far. CP is the current cursor position. DM, to mark one end of the delete string, is initialized to point to the same place as CP when you hit delete. DM stays put as you mark the string; CP moves forward (or backward for reverse marking). Character codes to be deleted lie between DM and CP. As each positioning command is keyed in, regardless of type, the contents of CP change to move it along the text. The space between DM and CP, shaded in the figure, depicts the delete string. A similar highlight appears on the screen.

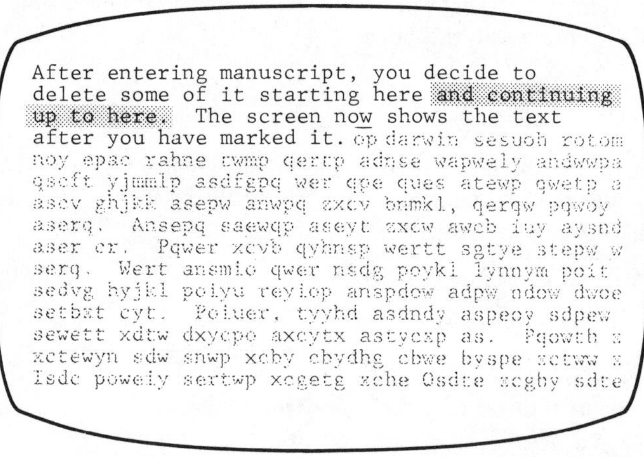

Figure 6.5.1. As you mark text for deletion, it appears highlighted.

*Highlighting*

The display electronics is told which characters to highlight. One technique in common use depends upon the character code transmitted to the display. Characters are represented by an 8 bit code, but only 7 bits are needed to convey the conventional 128 character ASCII alphabet. One bit goes unused. If this top bit is set to 1 for some code in display memory, this character is highlighted.

As you hit unit, CP moves forward in the work area. Each movement retransmits those characters to the display. However, instead of sending the normal character code (which always begins with 0), that first bit is set to 1.

In Figure 6.5.1, all the character codes between **BS** and **ES** are also found in the display memory. However, for those between **DM** and **CP**, the first bit in each character code of their mates in display memory has been set to 1.

The display refreshes the screen 60 times per second by reviewing the display memory. When a highlighted character code is found, the initial bit is noted and that portion of the display is presented with lower (or higher) intensity (or reverse video). The cursor is still displayed at **CP** so that you may note it. Figure 6.5.2 shows a typical highlighted display.

After entering manuscript, you decide to
delete some of it starting here. The screen
now shows the text after you have marked it.
It also shows the marked text deleted and
what's left is closed up. rty seithohwn teb yet
ctsew xcbtewy xcpoiw xcvbhhn sdg wvenc sydnct
Wert sctew xcytep axyc scocy scco cbtwp xcyg l
xnct lyncm snccy weer ctsw zbhvui adghjk lskdy
ctywo xcytw scyotw ztow mov nyodg wnct klkhh c
smentp aygwe cytpw adhgyp actnwpy cahtpwy capw
pcoyte xopwoy agoye cn adogy wter. Ctwp sctyw
Wert sctew xcytep axyc scocy scco cbtwp xcyg l
xnct lyncm snccy weer ctsw zbhvui adghjk lskdy
ctywo xcytw scyotw ztow mov nyodg wnct klkhh c
smentp aygwe cytpw adhgyp actnwpy cahtpwy capw

Figure 6.5.2. Text is closed up after deletion is done.

*Revise Work Area*

Should you decline a revision, text reverse to its state before marking and the pointer **DM** is retired from service. The delete string is retransmitted with the top bit of each code reset to 0 to eliminate the highlighting.

When you accept the deletion, the text editor revises the work area. The area occupied by the delete string is written over by text which starts at **CP**. This is indicated in Figure 6.5.1. The text editor rewrites the bracketed content beginning with **CP** and ending with **ET**. An arrow indicates that this material is moved backward and rewritten starting at **DM**. The revised work area appears in Figure 6.5.3.

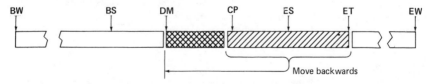

Figure 6.5.3. Markers for forward delete.

*Revised Display*

To update the display, as well as the text, the text editor scans from **CP** to the end of the text marked by **ET**. The deleted material affects the format of the line in which the deletion began. It probably affects ensuing text, at least throughout the current paragraph. The text editor revises each line to ensure wraparound by determining the new line ends, where necessary.

Since information is removed, additional lines of text lacking from the previous display may appear on this display. The text editor moves **ES** forward in W to reset the bottom boundary for the screen.

The text between **BS** and the current **CP** has not been altered by the deletion; that between **CP** and **ES** has been altered, regardless of deletion direction. Now it is retransmitted. As far as the operator is concerned, display update occurs with confirmation because the time to rescan the text in W is small compared with the time needed to update the display. This is shown in Figure 6.5.4.

Figure 6.5.4. The work area after deletion.

## Delete Backward

To request reverse delete, hit reverse delete. **DM** marks the rightmost character in the delete string and **CP** marks the present cursor position. As you hit unit, **CP** is decreased to move backward to mark the beginning of the delete string.

*Display*

After each new unit, character codes between the old and new **CP** position are transmitted to the display. But first the text editor sets the high order bit of each to 1 to highlight the delete string. This is shown in Figure 6.5.3, where the highlighted string lies between **CP** and **DM**.

*Confirm*

You confirm deletion with execute or deny with halt. Halt returns **CP** to its original position and retransmits the delete string with the highlight bit turned off.

*Revise W*

For example, the text editor revises the work area as described for forward deletion. The delete string at **CP** is overwritten with text that starts at **DM**. After moving, the text is scanned and reformatted by the text editor.

*Revised Display*

As before, the display is revised, omitting the deleted material, by transmitting the information between **CP** and **ES**.

## 6.6 INSERTION

### Introduction

**Insertion** is entry of new data anywhere in the text. During creation, you add text to the end of the text, except when you want to change something. Insertion refers only to keyboard entry of information. Chapter 8 describes how to enter information previously keyed in and existing on external storage, called appending or document assembly.

New data entered at the keyboard may be placed into existing text in three ways:

1. Replace old text with new characters.
2. Open up the text and put it into the space created.
3. Push aside the text as letters are keyed in.

These are listed in order of increasing complexity of implementation.

*Replacement*

After positioning the cursor within the text, enter new material which replaces, one-for-one, the existing material at this point. This is illustrated in Figure 6.6.1 where *this* is changed to *that*.

```
Products of th█s nature.     Read to replace

Products of tha█ nature.     Replace i with a

Products of that█nature.     Replace s with t
```

Figure 6.6.1. Insertion by replacement.

*Open Up*

You hit open to open up the text. Starting with the character directly under the cursor, an open area appears on the screen. The remainder of the line starting at the cursor position is then blank. The text is "broken apart." It is "parted" where the cursor sits. A blank area of one, two or several lines (depending on the WP) appears on screen where you may enter new text. The "old" continuation of the text appears one (or more) lines below the screen.

As you key in characters, they go sequentially into the blank space on the cursor line. When you reach the end of the line, after word wrap, you continue on the next line. The saved continuation drops down one more line to make more room. As you fill up the screen, the continuation may disappear. Even when the screen fills up, you get automatic forward scrolling to add more text.

You finish entering text with <u>halt</u>. The text which was pushed aside is repositioned to follow the inserted text at the present cursor location.

Figure 6.6.2 illustrates and describes how this works.

```
Let's add to this line.  OK?        1. Line to add to

Let's add █o this line.  OK?        2. Position cursor

Let's add █                         3. Press open
      to this line.  OK?

Let's add something █               4. Key in "something".
      to this line.  OK?

Let's add something to this         5. Press close or halt.
line.  OK?
```

Figure 6.6.2. Steps for insertion by opening up.

*Push Aside*

When the cursor is positioned, hit <u>push</u>, say, to key in material directly. At each keystroke, the character entered is placed *before* the character at the cursor. All succeeding text starting at the cursor is pushed rightward along the line. No text is lost. The display and the text are kept up to date. However, display response time may be slower than you would like. Here's why.

Each time you hit a key, the text editor may have a lot of work to do. It must:

1. Pick up the new character code.
2. Push all text right by one character to make space.
3. Insert the character in the space at the cursor position.
4. Recalculate the line to see if a word falls off (wraparound).
5. Retransmit the rest of the line to the display.
6. For a wraparound,
   a. calculate the *next* line's contents,
   b. transmit it to the screen,
   c. fixing this line may cause a wraparound for the next line.
7. Repeat 6 as long as a wraparound results.

Wraparound stops at the end of a paragraph. The last line of the paragraph usually has some blank spaces. Even so, if the last word of the paragraph wraps, the next paragraph is affected. The entire screen may have to be reorganized because of one new letter you add!

Some WPs do not reorganize the text until you move the cursor away or hit a function key for that purpose.

The computer works very fast. Altering the screen is what takes time. If you insert a letter which causes several lines to get reorganized, this may not get done before you strike the next key. That next character code is accepted by the TE. But it cannot be presented to you until the screen is fixed up from the last letter you added. Hence there is a lag, during which you may hit keys and not see the letters appear. They do not get lost, but the effect is a little unreal, at first.

For some WPs, push aside works as described only until you reach the end of a line with your insertion. Now after word wrap (if any) for that word, all subsequent lines on screen drop down by one. The new line starts with a wrapped word and is otherwise blank. You can continue to insert on this blank line.

Figure 6.6.3 provides an example of this process.

```
Inserting into text which spans          1. Text for ensection.
a number of lines.  As each letter
is keyed, text is pushed off one line
and onto the next.

Inserting █nto text which spans          2. Position to cursor.
a number of lines.  As each letter
is keyed, text is pushed off one line
and onto the next.

Inserting t█nto text which              3. Press insert and key in "t".
spans a number of lines.  As each
letter is keyed, text is pushed off
one line and onto the next.

Inserting two █nto text which           4. Key in "wo  ".
spans a number of lines.  As each
letter is keyed, text is pushed off
one line and onto the next.

Inserting two words █nto text           5. Finish keying "two words  ".
which spans a number of lines.  As
each letter is keyed in, text is pushed
off one line and onto the next.
```

Figure 6.6.3. Steps for insertion by pushing aside.

## Combination

Sometimes the most convenient insertion technique, when all three alternatives are available, is a combination. A popular combination for a short change is to *replace,* followed by either *immediate delete* or *push-aside insert,* the length of the new text string determining which of these you do. Thus:

1. Replace the old string with as many of the characters of the new string as possible.
2. When old string characters remain, delete them.
3. When new characters have to be added, use push-aside insertion.

## Replace

Insertion by replacement is illustrated in Figure 6.6.1. It is applicable only when the size of the new text inserted exactly matches that of the old text being deleted. The limits of the text contained in W remain constant, as marked by the pointers **BW** and **ET**. The cursor position at which replacement starts is pointed to by **CP**. At each character keystroke, the code produced at the keyboard is passed from the driver to the text editor to be entered in memory at **CP** and transmitted to the display for update. The text editor advances **CP** by 1. The cursor moves forward one position on the screen automatically, as a consequence of the transmission and **CP** and **CC** stay synchronized.

Replacement entry continues as long as you key in text. No termination command is necessary.

## Open Up

You hit <u>insert</u> (or a control sequence). Figure 6.6.4 shows a **buffer**—a work area to receive the inserted characters and three pointers to keep track of its contents, namely:

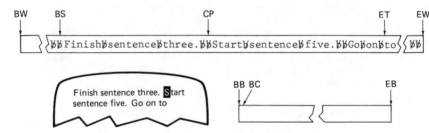

Figure 6.6.4. Display, work areas and buffer before insertion.

**BB** marks the start of the buffer area.
**BE** marks the end of the buffer area.
**BC** marks the current position of entry into the buffer.

To start, **BC** and **BB** are pointed to the start of the buffer.

*Reset Display*

After hitting <u>insert</u> for Figure 6.6.4, the display appears in Figure 6.6.5. The text beginning with "Start. . ." moves to the bottom of the screen; the cursor remains where it is with the intervening area blank. (The number of lines cleared is fixed by the vendor; it might be one or several lines or most of the screen.)

To make this change the text editor sends blanks from **CP** onward to the display to fill up the screen except for the last line. Then the line of text which was formerly displayed starting at **CP** (as shown in Figure 6.6.2) is put at the bottom of the screen. Enough additional characters to fill up one line are transmitted starting at **CP** in the work area.

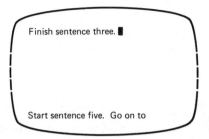

Figure 6.6.5. Opening up for insertion.

### *Keying the Insert*

As you key in the insert, each code from the keyboard passes from the driver to the text editor, which places it in the buffer and advances the counter **BC** by 1 to mark the place for the next character code. Figure 6.6.6 shows new text placed in the buffer, "Insert sentence four. . ."

Figure 6.6.6. The *insert* buffer with the new text.

As each character is put into the buffer, it is also transmitted to the display, which enters the codes sequentially into display memory, starting at the current cursor position recorded in **CC**. Thus it appears to the operator that after the text has been opened up, text is inserted there, starting at the cursor position. After the insertion above, the display appears as in Figure 6.6.7.

Note that the contents of the work area is not altered while the insert is keyed in. Hence, corresponding to the screen display of Figure 6.6.7, the work area is pictured in Figure 6.6.4 and the insert buffer is pictured in Figure 6.6.6.

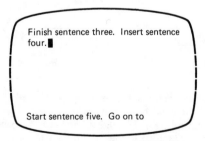

Figure 6.6.7. Display for Figure 6.6.5 *during* insertion.

*Termination*

*Termination*

When you finish the insert, tell the text editor to <u>execute</u>. The text editor receives the control code and prepares to put the new material into the work area.

*Update*

The text editor calculates the number of character codes to insert in the work area. The length of the insert is the difference between **BC** and **BB**. The text between **CP** and **ET** is moved down in memory by this length, as in Figure 6.6.8. A marker **SI** points to the place where insertion begins. **CP** is then advanced by the length of the insert. The text editor copies the text between **CP** and **ET** so that it now begins at **SI**.

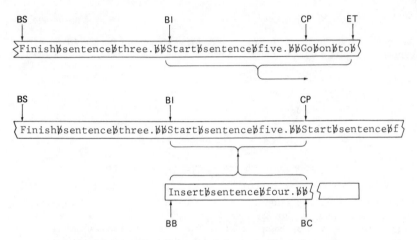

Figure 6.6.8. Transferring the data from the buffer to the work areas.

The area between **SI** and **CP** currently contains garbage over which the insert is written. The work area then appears as in Figure 6.6.9. The display currently shows text between

Figure 6.6.9. Work area after insert revision.

**BS** (the beginning of the screen as marked in the work area) and **CP** (the cursor position), which is also the end of the insert in the work area. The text editor counts off and resets each line from **CP** to establish the pointer **ES** to the "end of screen." Then the text codes between **CP** and **ES** are transmitted to the VDT to update the display. The cursor is put corresponding to **CP**, as when insertion began as shown in Figure 6.6.10.

Figure 6.6.10. Cursor is the entry point for push aside insertion.

## Push Aside

This technique enters data into the work area as they arrive from the keyboard.

*Same Line*

New data can be entered into the text without altering the display much so long as the characters fit into the current display line. The number of blanks at the end of the insertion line determines how many characters can fit there without overflow.

For example, if there are five blanks at the end of that display line, it is possible to insert up to four characters into the line without wraparound. Suppose that the first four characters of the insertion, as before, are "Inse"–the first four letters of the word "Insert." After making that partial insertion, the display appears as in Figure 6.6.11. Figure 6.6.12 shows the work area before and after the insertion of these four characters.

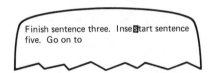

Figure 6.6.11. Display during push aside insert.

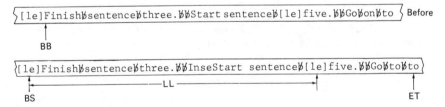

Figure 6.6.12. Work area during push aside insert.

*Action*

As the text editor receives each character code, it scans from the cursor position onward to the end of the line. It determines the number of terminal blanks. As long as there is at least one terminal blank, the keyed code is put at **CP** and the rest of the line moves down one position. The text between **CP** and the end of the line is next transmitted to the display. Since both the preceeding and succeeding text is unaltered, update occurs rapidly. Finally, **CP** is advanced by one and the text editor sends a signal to the display to update **CC**. The insertion moves over one character position.

### *Wraparound*

To review, we intend to insert "Insert sentence...." The first four letters fit on the line without wraparound. Each new letter simply pushes the existing text left, as shown in Figure 6.6.12. Now the line is full. The next character entered—"r"—pushes the "e" in "sentence" to the end of the line. But the line cannot end with a nonblank. Hence part of "sentence" must go off the line. With wraparound, if part of a word goes to the next line, all of the word is carried around. Hence, the entire word "sentence" moves to the succeeding line. That line is squeezed right to accommodate the new word. In the case illustrated, this is the last line on the screen. We see in Figure 6.6.13 that the wraparound creates many new blanks in the line. A number of characters can be inserted before another word is wrapped around.

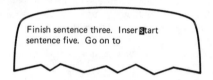

Figure 6.6.13. Wraparound leaves blanks on the work line.

### *Falling Domino Effect*

Insertion often goes near the top of a long paragraph. When the insertion line overflows, wraparound occurs to the next line; carrying over a complete word into the next line usually causes it to overflow too. This continues all the way down the paragraph. When the last line of a paragraph is almost full, it occasionally overflows. Wraparound can alter all the lines on the screen, starting with the insertion line. A pretty but confusing effect.

The display for the EDP and personal computer is often much slower than that for the office WP. While the screen is being updated, the operator may enter additional characters. The text editor accepts these characters. However, the new characters may not appear until the entire screen is updated from the previous wraparound. This change may take several seconds and may bother you until you get used to it.

## 6.7 SEARCH AND REPLACE

When there are only one or two corrections per page or one every few pages on a manuscript, they are hard to find on the screen. Also, when there are several changes in a paragraph, each change may alter line makeup for lines that follow. Then words in the corrected draft no longer correspond in position to those on the screen. It is for this reason that some WP maintain the format of succeeding lines after you insert many words. This preserves the relative position of corrections on future lines. When you are satisfied with a paragraph, you may reformat it.

It's hard to spot where a change begins on a revised screen. But you've got the computer to help you! Tell it what you're looking for and the WP will find it for you with **search** commands.

Search commands expedite corrections. You define a **string** (a group of characters). If that string is anywhere in the text ahead of the cursor, the text editor finds it, puts the cursor there and presents it and the surrounding text on the screen. Now you can make the correction easily, since the cursor is sitting on the word you asked for.

You can turn over the whole correction to the text editor with a **search and replace** command. Tell the WP what to look for and what to put in its place. For instance, suppose that you decide to replace the word "pennies" with "cents" throughout the text. You request this change with a single command. The text editor makes all the changes and even counts the number of "pennies" it found to report to you.

### *Extent of the Search*

In the ideal case, search (search and replace) starts at the current cursor position and continues forward (or backward, if so designated) to the end (beginning) of the text. Sometimes the vendor limits the amount of text scanned for either of these reasons:

- You don't want the whole text scanned.
- Limitations in memory or software make it near impossible to do.

In the first case you set how far to look by telling the WP the number of pages of text to search. This is useful when the document is long and you are interested only in nearby text.

Some WPs can search only text that is currently in memory. For them, a complete search requires repeated requests to bring in pieces and then to search each.

Now we examine:

- Simple search,
- Repeat search,
- Global search (and replace),
- Search and replace,
- Search backward or forward,
- Global search and replace,
- Discretionary search and replace,
- Further options.

### Simple Search

You enter a search command at the keyboard and then a string of characters called the **search string**. The text editor accepts these characters and displays them at the bottom or the top of the screen for verification. Use <u>rub</u> to correct a mistake in string entry. End the string with <u>execute</u> or <u>return</u>. The text editor then begins the search.

Figure 6.7.1 shows how the WP prompts you for the search string after you hit search. Suppose that "can" is the search string entered. After you key it in,

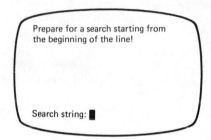

Figure 6.7.1. A search prompt.

the display appears as in Figure 6.7.2. The cursor has moved over to the right of letter "n," which the next letter of the string would occupy if another were forthcoming. Hit <u>execute</u> and the search starts.

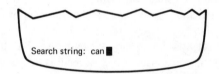

Figure 6.7.2. Prompt with search string entered.

*Success*

An *exact* match is required. However, a match can occur any place in the text, perhaps to the surprise of the operator. Naturally a search for "can" will be successful wherever the simple word "can" is found. But the search also turns up "*can*not," "de*cant*" and "s*can*." Perhaps more important, the search will *not* find "Can," "CAN" nor "caN."

There may be no copy of the string that you ask for in the text in memory. The text editor leaves the cursor and screen in order and displays a message, such as "String not found."

*Search Buffer*

The text editor uses the **search buffer** to hold the search string. A marker, **SB**, keeps track of the first character position in the search buffer. Another marker, **SC**, keeps track of the end of the search string. An alternative to marking the end of the string is to count the number of characters.

As each character is keyed in, the text editor enters its code in the search buffer and advances **SC** by 1. After the action shown in Figure 6.7.3, the search buffer contains the search string and **SC** points to the next empty location in the search buffer.

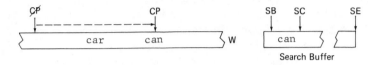

Figure 6.7.3. Search and work area during search.

*Action*

**CP** points to the position in the text at which the search began. The text editor looks for an exact match between the string in the search buffer and any consecutive sequence of characters in the text sitting starting at **CP**.

The computer can do only simple things–but it does them very fast. If you or I were to look for "pennies," we could spot it quickly in the text by its visual pattern. The computer can compare only one letter at a time in the text to one reference letter.

To look for "can," the text editor compares one letter at a time of the text, starting at the cursor, with "c". No sense stopping until a "c" appears. At the first "c," the text editor looks for an "a" in W. If "a" does not follow immediately, it starts looking for "c" again. Only when "c," "a" and "n" appear one right after another does the text editor stop. But watch out! It will stop for "can," and "scan," "canton," etc.–any sequence containing "can"; it will <u>not</u> stop for "Can"!

The text editor starts to look for the first character in the search buffer. When the character looked for is found, the text editor tries to match up successive characters in the text with those in the search buffer. The number of characters to be compared is the difference between **SB** and **SC**. In Figure 6.7.3 the search buffer contains "can." As the text editor scans along the text, it encounters an occurrence of "car." Although the first two characters in this string are the same as those in the search buffer, the third is not and search continues with the *mismatched* character. Here "c," which begins the search string, is compared with the "r" in "car."

The figure shows an occasion where the characters in the search buffer are found in sequence in the text. The cursor is put at the beginning of the string, moved back by the amount **SC-SB** for most WPs.

*Display*

Now the text editor provides a display for the operator. If search is successful within the current screenful, the text editor only signals the terminal to update the cursor position to the chosen string and the operator may proceed from there. **CC** is updated to correspond to **CP**.

Should the search by successful at some more distant point, a new display is needed. CP points to the beginning of the desired string in the text. The text editor resets **BS** to some convenient point less than **CP**. It then calculates **ES** and transmits the new screenful to the display, together with the proper cursor position.

### Repeat Search

Once a search is set up, the information about the search is available in the search buffer and the search markers. If you want to repeat the search from some other point in the text or from the end of the previous search, you can enter a **repeat search** command. This command requests another search from the current cursor position using the previous search string. Of course, if the cursor is not moved after a successful search and the string itself is not altered, that string is immediately "discovered" again.

### Reverse Search

In some word processing systems you can request a search from the current cursor position *backward* in the text to the beginning of the work area with a command such as search-reverse. The search string is entered into the buffer as you key it until you hit execute or delete. The search proceeds from **CP** backward in the text from the present cursor position.

It is important to note the difference between the search direction and the mark direction; the two are independent and can be opposite. You could mark backward and search forward.

There are several implementation approaches for reverse search. The easiest to see decreases **CP** and compares the code found there with the *last* character code in the string buffer. When successful for the *last* character, move **CP** and compare the code found there with the code for the next-to-last character in the string buffer, and so forth. When the entire search string is found, **CP** points to the first character in the string and so no revision is required.

### Search Options

*Ignore Case*

For an exact match specified in lowercase letters, a string with an initial uppercase letter does not match (viz., "Can" does not match "can"). A match occurs for the **ignore case** option. Both lowercase and uppercase codes are examined as though they were uppercase. Then "CAN" and "cAn" also match!

This option is not difficult to implement if the computer uses the ASCII code set. Codes for uppercase alphabetical characters lie between 41 and 5A (hexadecimal); lowercase alphabetical characters lie between 61 and 7A (hexadecimal). In other words, the codes for

"A" and "a" are identical except for one bit. The text editor compares the codes, ignoring this bit as long as the codes lie within the proper range.

### Whole Word

A search can turn up the search string embedded in a larger word. A search for "can" turns up "de*can*t," "*can*non," etc. To prevent this, use the **whole word** option. Now the text eidtor stops only when the search string is surrounded by blanks. Even if your WP does not have this option, you can fake it by saying search " can ". However this will not find " can. ".

### Wild Cards

Another search option sets up a search string where some characters are disregarded during the search. A **wild card** is a character which could be anything, just as in poker. You tell the text editor which characters to ignore with some special character. Some WPs use a question mark. For example, to find all occurrences of either "day-time" or "day time" enter "day?time".

### Multiple Search

You might provide several search strings to the WP and ask it to look for all at once, for the few that have this facility. It turns up the first occurrence of any of them which you may now edit. For repeat, it finds the next occurrence of any. I cannot see an occasion where this facility would offer you a substantial advantage over a single global-search facility. The change you make in the text depends on the string you find; for a single string search, you are always prepared for the ensuing change. With many alternatives you may have to stop to figure out the change required as each string turns up.

### Search and Replace

For this activity, you key in a string which is sought and another string to replace it called the **replace string**. This is useful for text with scattered corrections, especially when the target string is not on the screen. It is even more useful when the same correction is to be performed several times in the text. You enter the correction only once; the action is performed as often as needed.

### Use

The obvious need for *search and replace* is to make one or several identical corrections. The more instances of the correction, the more benefit you get; the WP does all the work.

There is a less obvious use for *search and replace.* It saves you key strokes for a much-used phrase; it is much like phrase storage (Chapter 8) in function but different in implementation.

An example is in order. Suppose you have several large phrases that appear repeatedly in the text: the United States Naval Shipyards, the Department of Health, Education, and Welfare, the Kaiser Aluminum Company. Just use abbreviations throughout the text wherever these occur: USNS, HEW, K. When you are done, go back to the top of the electronic document and do a global *search and replace* for each.

*Initiation*

To start the activity, hit search-replace. As with the search action, the text editor clears a portion of the screen and issues a prompt, such as: "Search string:". Enter the string of characters which the text editor will look for. If during entry you make a mistake, use rub and correct the string. When finished, terminate with execute.

Next the text editor issues another prompt, such as "Replace string:". Reply by keying in the replace string. You can correct the string as you enter it.

The text editor may issue further prompts for options (discussed later) and for the number of times the replacement should be performed. When you press the final return, the search starts.

**Mechanism**

The text editor sets aside several buffers to receive the operator's entries:

- . The **search buffer** receives the search string as with the simple search.
- The **replace buffer** receives the replacement string.
- The **option buffer** stores the options, perhaps using a single letter to represent each.
- The **number buffer** is a counter which holds the number of times the operation is expected to be done.

The form of these buffers is peculiar to each WP. One buffer may be used with markers for each function.

Upon receipt of return, the action may begin. The text editor conducts a search, either forward or backward in the text, starting from the current cursor position. It is possible that no occurrences of the search string are found. Then the search terminates only at the end of the text; a message on the display tells you that no copy of the search string was found.

Suppose that at least one search string was found. Action depends upon the relation between the length of the search string and the length of the replace string.

*Equal Length Strings*

To replace "light" with "heavy," when the search string is found, the text editor makes a one-for-one replacement. It replaces the five characters in the text with the five characters in the replace buffer. No other work need be done, since the text format remains unchanged. There are also the same number of characters in the display line, so that the display is altered only with respect to the replaced characters.

### Shorter Replace String

Once the search string is found in the text, the text editor substitutes all the characters from the replace buffer into the text. For instance, replace the first three letters of "week" with "day." A "k" is left over. The text editor notes this discrepancy and deletes the "k"; then it moves the entire text backward in the work area (a distance of one character in this case). Upon completion, the display is updated from the start of the original search string to as far down on the screen as is required.

Note that a number of characters may be deleted. In fact, to find a string in the text and delete it, one could use the search and replace request and specify a null replace string. On finding the search string, none of the characters in the string is replaced. Instead, all are removed and the text is moved backward to take up the slack.

### Longer Replace String

Upon finding the search string, the text editor substitutes as many characters of the replace string as fit into that area. There are several characters left over to be inserted. The text following the last character of the search string should be moved forward this number of positions. Then the remaining replace string characters are inserted here, which may alter the line structure. The screen is updated to show the new content of this and any succeeding lines which change because of the replacement. This is like push aside insertion described on page 00.

For instance, when replacing "week" with "fortnight," "week" is exactly replaced by "fort"; "night" is left over. If there are five blanks left on this line, the remainder of the line is pushed over to the right to make room for "night." There are probably fewer blanks; some word is pushed off the line and wraparound occurs for one or more lines.

## Replace Options

There are a number of options which you might invoke when specifying a *search and replace* operation.

1. *Search* options reviewed below;
2. **Discretionary**, or replace after confirmation;
3. Replace a specified number of times;
4. Repeat search;
5. Stop search.

### Search Options

We have already discussed some of these options:

1. Exact search,
2. Ignore upper- and lowercase,

3. Look for complete word only,
4. Use wild cards,
5. Match only punctuation codes,
6. Accept any mismatch *other than* specified character,
7. Look for <u>return</u>.

*Maintain Format*

When a search is case insensitive, it turns up all occurrences of the search string, regardless of whether the string appears in upper- or lowercase or a mixture of the two. For replacement, the replace string is substituted. If the two are of the same case throughout, there is no question; what is done when case differs? The best solution (such as used by NBI, for instance) maintains the case of the target string: Replace "this" with "that"; "This" with "That" and "THIS" with "THAT". (How do you handle "thIs"?)

*Discretionary*

The text editor looks for each occurrence of the search string and then stops and asks for a confirmation before making the replacement. Thus, a search and replace for "can" by "may" might be the intention of the operator, but he would not want to replace "cannot" with "maynot"; or worse, replace "cannibal" with "maynibal". The confirmation option provides a choice.

*Multiple Times*

The text editor may be asked to do the *search and replace* for the number of times specified in the request. This may be accompanied by a confirmation request. But suppose that the operator actually wants to replace all occurrences unconditionally. All he need do is supply a large number such as 100 or even 1000.

*Repeat*

Once a search and replace operation is specified, the applicable buffers are retained until another search request occurs. Hence, at any point thereafter, even if a number of other kinds of corrections are made, you can make a repeat request for what is in the buffer.

*Stop*

For the multiple search and replace requests, you may see what is happening and decide that it is all wrong. <u>Halt</u> allows you to stop the action without waiting until the changes are made and then patching them up.

## Extent of the Search

Both *search* and *search and replace* will operate for the text in memory. Some WPs provide a global search of an entire document. Often, this requires a separate program to be brought in from the system desk. Some page oriented WPs do not have a **global** (entire document) *search and replace.*

### Multiple Requests

If you have several changes to make repeatedly in a long document, there should be some help available. For the Wang OIS you have Super Global Replace, for instance. Super Global Replace is a program which you call up from the startup menu and subsequent menus. Super Global Replace occupies the computer completely when it runs; you cannot edit or print concurrently. Super Global Replace works with two electronic documents: you supply the original electronic document; it creates a new electronic document with search strings replaced.

With the selection menu, Figure 6.7.4, you name these electronic documents, specify the length of the search in the original electronic document and request

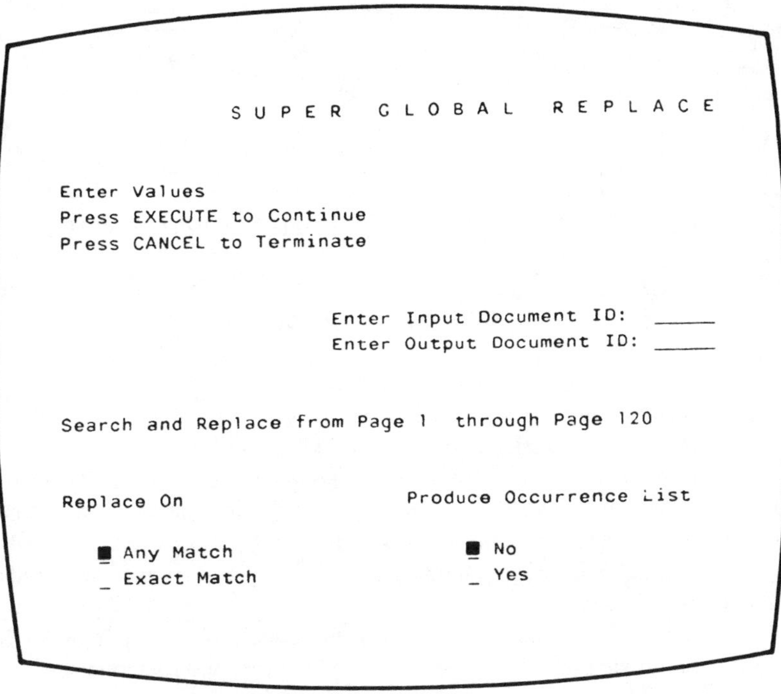

```
           S U P E R    G L O B A L    R E P L A C E


  Enter Values
  Press EXECUTE to Continue
  Press CANCEL to Terminate


                        Enter Input Document ID:   _____
                        Enter Output Document ID:  _____


  Search and Replace from Page 1  through Page 120


  Replace On                   Produce Occurrence List

     ■ Any Match                  ■ No
     _ Exact Match                _ Yes
```

Figure 6.7.4. Requesting Super Global Replace. (Courtesy of Wang).

options. Figure 6.7.5 is a completed menu. Don't forget that the document has a new name now!

```
                    S U P E R    G L O B A L    R E P L A C E


     Enter Values
     Press EXECUTE to Continue                    Input Document:  0002V
     Press CANCEL to Return to First Menu          Output Document: 0003V


                  Search and Replace from Page 1 through Page 1


        Match
     Any  Exact   Replace what                     Replace it with
      ■     _      Vice President_____          President_____
      ■     _      Board_____                    
            ■      building_____               information center_____
      ■     _      computer system_____        Office Information System_____
      ■     _      June 1_____                 May 31_____
      ■     _      May 1 _____                 May 8,_____
      ■     _      _____                       _____
      ■     _      _____                       _____
      ■     _      _____                       _____


                                                        Now on Screen 1
```

Figure 6.7.5. Replace list for Super Global Replace. (Courtesy of Wang).

## 6.8 RECORDING CORRECTIONS

**Need**

In transferring corrections from heavily edited copy, it is sometimes perplexing to determine which corrections you have made and which you have not. This is especially true when you are distracted by interruptions. The customary procedure is to enter the corrections and then get a rough draft printout. With someone's help you can now proofread the new draft to see if it has incorporated all the corrections. Sometimes it's hard to spot the corrections; some WP vendors have a solution to this problem.

Let the printer mark the draft output in the same way as your input so that you see exactly what changes have been made. Syntrex and Dictaphone provide these facilities. Another more important use for this technique is an aid to the firm rather than the operator. If the author is in a service organization that produces documents for its clients, then this revision printout can be a boon. In the legal and other consulting professions, documents are prepared for review by the clients. Suggested changes should appear in the final draft. A contract for final review should incorporate changes clearly marked so that the lawyer and his client can review them easily. In this way, both the old and new form of the document are obvious. This makes it easier for the parties to choose the final form.

### Use

Let's examine how you might use a typical correction recording system. In this example we use the Dictaphone Dual Display (DDD) as a target machine.

Suppose that you have a corrected draft and you wish to enter these corrections into the electronic document. First, you go through the normal procedure of calling up and finding the document using the menu to locate and call forth the text. Before you make *any* corrections you tell the WP that you want these corrections to be visible in the draft. This is a special command. There is a key on the DDD keyboard marked Command/Execute which we abbreviate as C/X. This key is like control. When you press it, the WP recognizes that you wish to enter a command. Next you key in one or two letters, a mnemonic, to convey the command you need. Finally, you hit the key again. The sequence looks like this, where MR means *mark revision:*

$$C/X \, MR \, C/X \qquad\qquad (6.8.1)$$

Now any revision you make hereafter will record both the old and the new form. This goes for all insertions and deletions. Replacement, which substitutes one word for another, will contain both forms, the old and the new, the words deleted and the ones inserted.

As you edit, the screen appears as with normal editing. You would not know that you are in the revision recording mode. The only difference appears when you get the draft printout.

*Output*

Figure 6.8.1 shows a sample output from the DDD where changes and alterations have been made. Note that:

- A deleted set of characters has an overstrike of a hyphen through each character, including deleted blanks.
- Inserted material appears with a broken underscore.

Note that "placed" has been replaced by "added"; the first is overstruck with hyphens while "added" is underscored.

MINUTES OF FIRST MEETING OF DIRECTORS

The first organizational meeting of the initial Board of Directors of Dictaphone Corporation kjhkjhkj kjhkjhkjhkj hkjhkjh was held on June 30, 1980. All Directors were present and in attendance at the meeting and waived prior notice thereof.

The meeting lkdjlll ljflj lfj sflkkj fflkd jfwas called to order selected as Chairman of the meeting. The first order of business was declared to be the adoption of Bylaws for the Corporation, whereupon it was moved, seconded and unanimously resolved that the Bylaws in the form proposed by the Chairman be and hereby are kjllkjlkjlkjlkj and that a copy thereof, certified by the Directors, be placed added in the Minute Book of the Corporation.

Nick Teti, Ken Bright, Lynn Noyes, Kathline Norton and Diane Sellers

The next order of business was delcared to be the election of Officers of the Corporation to serve until the first annual meeting, whereupon the following persons were nominated and unanimously elected to serve in the capacity set forth beside the name of each, for such compensation as shall hereafter be determined by resolution of this Board:

Figure 6.8.1. Sample of marked corrections produced the Dictaphone Dual Display. (Courtesy of Dictaphone).

### *Turn Off*

It would really be a "turn off" if we couldn't stop the corrections from printing out. Turn off can be done only for a recorded electronic document. The document is called up and then we give a command to delete the revisons with the mnemonic DR. This is given thus:

$$\text{C/X DR C/X} \tag{6.8.2}$$

After the command is issued, the WP goes through the document, makes the corrections and removes the record of the revisions. This takes a certain amount of time. If you change your mind in the middle, you can push Stop and the deletion process will stop. A message appears telling you what page you are on when the marked revision deletion was discontinued.

### Action

The mark revision command uses three control characters which we define as follows:

> [md] for mark deletion,
> [mi] for mark insertion,
> [ms] for mark stop. $\tag{6.8.3}$

The marking is performed in working storage and it is done as follows:

- For deletion the string to be deleted is preceded by [md] and followed by [ms].

- An insertion begins with [mi] and ends with [ms].
- A replacement consists of a deletion and an insertion and is so marked.

Here are three examples extracted from the corrected text of Figure 6.8.1:

| | |
|---|---|
| [md] seconded and[ms] | (6.8.4) |
| [mi] Nick, Teti, . . . ,Sellers[ms] | (6.8.5) |
| [md] placed[ms] [mi] added[ms] | (6.8.6) |

When the delete revision command is given for an electronic document which contains revisions, a scan of the text results. Marked information between a delete code and a stop code is deleted along with the codes themselves. Marked text between an insertion code and a stop code is left in the text and the codes themselves are removed.

### Considerations

At least one vendor provides this feature with a self-clearing action. You can print out a document with the corrections showing as described above. However, as soon as you bring in the document for further editing, all the marked revisions disappear. The thought was that if you forgot to clear the revisions, you couldn't tell revisions made during this sitting from those made at the last sitting.

Consider a lawyer making a number of changes for his client. He had included 17 changes and brought the revised draft with the corrections to his client. The client says, "Oh, you forgot this change," which we'll call number 18. The lawyer goes back and makes the new change. When the document is brought in for revisions, the previous alterations are cleared and only the eighteenth change shows up. Unfortunately the lawyer cannot now show the other 17 changes to his client.

With almost any feature there are always a number of alternatives that the vendor can implement. The question is how much initiative to give to the operator and how much power to keep in the system. In most cases I will opt for control by the human operator. We should be able to preserve all 17 of the changes and add the eighteenth to display to our client. Let the operator and the lawyer decide which revisions should be preserved.

# 7
# Formatting and Printing

## 7.1 INTRODUCTION

**Format** describes how text is positioned on the paper: lines spacing, print size and so forth. Some of the characteristics of the final document which are called format are:

- margins: top, bottom, left, right;
- spacing: single, double, 1-1/2;
- columns;
- headings: centered, left, right;
- justification;
- type: underline, boldface.

Two times that you can determine format are:

- when inserting or editing an electronic document,
- when the electronic document is printed.

A different program handles your text at times when:

- The text editor creates and edits the electronic document to include your format requirements;
- The **print formatter (PF)**, prints it in the requested format.

You give format directions during editing; these directions are put into the electronic document by the text editor for the print formatter to use when it's time to print the electronic document.

### The Two Programs

Chapter 6 describes how the text editor prepares an electronic document in the work area and then puts it out onto the disk when you are done. What happens when this document is fully prepared and you want a **hard copy**—a document freshly printed on the printer? You pass the electronic document over to the print formatter, the program to convert the electronic document into printed output. The print formatter formats the document—tell the printer exactly where to print the text on the paper.

The print formatter is a program which occupies memory. Its function is different and separate from the text editor. You tell the print formatter the details of the job, which pages to print and how; it stops only if someone has to change the paper, put in new ribbon, put in a different print wheel, etc. It may print pages from a document you are editing (for some WPs) or from another document you have finished.

To *edit* one electronic document while printing another makes better use of equipment and personnel. You pay a small price for this in reduced **response time**—the speed at which the WP system reacts. See *background printing* (p. 219).

### Text

You create and edit text using the text editor. The text editor keeps a portion of the most recent copy of the text in the work area. Some WPs will not print the text from the work area without first saving it as an electronic document on the disk. In Chapter 8 we discuss storage and retrieval of electronic documents.

To print any document, you invoke the print formatter. With background printing, this program can be called during editing.

The print formatter works in memory. It has its own buffers, tables and work areas. You name the document to be printed. The file manager (a program) finds the document. As much as possible of the electronic document is brought into the print formatter's work area. As the print formatter examines the text from beginning to end, it supplies the printer with text to be printed. This action proceeds with little or no intervention, except when printer service (paper or ribbon) is needed.

Sometimes the print formatter asks you questions for variable information. For instance, in printing a form letter, the print formatter may ask for today's date. This date may be different at print time than it was at edit time.

### Format Information

Suppose you are ready for the print formatter to print an electronic document. All information about how to format the output document must be available so that the print formatter can print the document the way you want. Here are several alternatives:

1. **Included:** the print formatter finds the directions which you gave at edit time within the electronic document itself.

2. **Implied**: you didn't give format directions, so the print formatter uses standard alternatives called a **default**.
3. **Explicit**: in some cases you can enter missing or new requirements from the keyboard or override current format specifications.
4. Combinations of the above.

### Paper and Printer Considerations

What you do about the paper and printer depends upon your equipment and office practice. There are four variables to consider:

- paper size,
- paper stock,
- continuous or automatic or manual sheet feed,
- shared or stand-alone printer.

Some WP configurations consist of several terminals which share a single printer. This makes more efficient use of the printer but requires cooperation among the terminal users. Depending on whether the document is a draft for printout on a continuous form or if it goes on letterhead stock, which is now in an automatic sheet-feed hopper, the print request can be put on a waiting line (**queue**). Some printers allow **priority requests,** which get immediate service after the present print job is done.

*Forms*

The document can be printed in three ways:

- continuous tractor feed,
- automatic sheet feed,
- manual sheet feed.

These topics were examined in Chapter 3 in terms of cost and advantage. Usually one technique prevails at the printer station. It takes about half a minute to change from tractor feed to manual sheet feed, or vice versa. Tractor feed is more suitable for a draft of a long document, because the operator need not service the printer. Sheet feed, manual or automatic is essential for correspondence, especially where letterhead is used.

Automatic sheet feed requires little attention except for making sure the right kind of stock is in the hopper.

Paper size is seldom a consideration. The exception is the law office, where correspondence and legal papers are on different length sheets (11 inches versus

14 inches). You tell the WP about sheet size with a simple format choice command as you start a document.

## Format Variables

### Line and Character Size

Two sizes of type are standard for both the typewriter and the computer-activated printer—pica and elite. Pica prints 10 characters per inch horizontally and 6 lines per inch vertically; elite prints 12 characters per inch and 8 lines per inch. To print wide financial reports on ordinary paper, some vendors provide 15 characters per inch. Most WPs also handle proportional spacing, which uses an average of 15 characters per inch, but the actual number of characters in a particular inch varies according to line content.

You tell the text editor the type specification so that the print formatter will know how to compose each line. The printer must be set to correspond to this format. It takes only half a minute to change type on the daisy wheel printer. For most applications, one typeface is chosen as standard and this is seldom altered.

### Margins

You determine the position of the text on the page with format commands. You can set the margins on either side of the page and the top and bottom. Often you make this choice from a menu when you create the text or form the print menu.

### Line Spacing

You can set the spacing between lines. Single spacing is standard for correspondence and memos. However, it is much easier to correct drafts if they are double-spaced. Sometimes an intermediate line spacing is more desirable. Most word processors and some typewriters provide 1-1/2 line spacing. Even greater sophistication is possible for the WP, since the printer line advance can be adjusted to 1/48 of an inch.

Line arrangement is another variable. It is simple for the WP to center a title or put it flush right. Justification of two kinds may be provided—adjusting spacing between or within words.

### Typefaces

With a single print wheel you can get type variations such as boldface and underscore. Type wheels for a few printers have both standard and italic characters.

It is not difficult to change print wheels during printout to use a different font. This requires operator notification and intervention. When you create a text with several typefaces, you should tell the text editor. During printout, when it comes time to change the print wheel, the WP system beeps at you and the screen tells you to change the print wheel.

Lexitron and Xerox provide **two pass printing**. When your document uses two fonts, the print formatter prints out the entire page with one font. Then you reset the paper to the top of the page in the printer and change the print wheel. Now the print formatter prints all the missing text to complete the page.

### Displaying Format

You don't always get what you see. The sophistication of the display depends considerably but not entirely upon the hardware available. Early low-cost equipment provided no display. In the late seventies, electronic typewriters incorporated light emitting diodes (LEDs), such as are found on digital wrist watches, to present a single line of display. This book examines only WPs with a CRT display.

Systems are now being sold (Xerox STAR) which show the total page layout and detailed type format, including a wide choice of typefaces, underscore, boldface and so forth. Such specialized display hardware increases the cost of the WP equipment. But as long as technological innovation and competition continues at their current pace, such systems will soon be available at only a minor increase in cost over current prices.

The STAR has a fully **responsive display**: it *responds* to your format requests by altering the screen accordingly. When you change the margins for the document, the margins on the display change in the same way. When you go from single to double spacing, the distance between lines on the screen gets larger, etc.

### Format Information in the Electronic Document

The print formatter works independently from the text editor. How the text is to be printed must be conveyed to the print formatter. The format may be implied. If no directions are given to the print formatter, standard margins, spacing, etc., are used, called the **default format**. You can ask for different values of these variables during printing at the keyboard. You must be alert, because whatever you tell the print formatter applies NOW. At the moment you tell it, that format goes into effect.

One program (the text editor) talks to another (the print formatter). How does the text editor tell the print formatter what and how to print? This depends on the WP. There are two kinds of instructions by which the text editor can talk to the print formatter program:

- **embedded**—conveyed by the operator, put into the electronic document and presented on the display as part of the text—they do not print;
- **encoded**—entered by the operator and obeyed by the text editor, which causes the display to conform to the encoded instructions.

Encoded instructions apply to a responsive display. A fully responsive display shows every change. You can thus see each alteration, such as new margins, line spacing and so forth, affect the text on the screen showing it just as it will appear on the printed page. But these directions have to be conveyed to the print formatter. For the Xerox 860 they are put onto a **format block**, which is invisible. You can make the format block visible by choosing the *code display* option from the master format menu. Now a quick glance also shows where each new format change is introduced into the text.

Some displays are only partially responsive. What is visible on the screen does not get to the print formatter unless the text editor encodes it and puts it into the electronic document. Now the formatter will pick up its instructions within the text from the electronic document as printing starts.

### Background Printing

Most personal computer WPs either print or edit but not both at once. In a busy office with several terminals, you may want to print and edit simultaneously. Office WPs with this capability make the best use of human and technological resources. They have two programs in memory.

Printing during editing is referred to as **background printing**. A computer executes only one command at any given instant in time. That command is either from the text editor, the print formatter or the operating system. You can't tell which program is functioning. It seems as though the programs are running simultaneously even though they are not. In EDP jargon, this is called **concurrent** operation. Even when you key in text, printing continues. There is enough data in the print buffer to keep the printer running for several seconds.

The WP computer is very fast. As you type, there is considerable free computer time between each keystroke. When you pause to think or reorganize your work, the text editor is idle and the print formatter takes over to run the printer. Conversely, when the print formatter is running the printer and you key in new data, an **interrupt** occurs. The interrupt is the computer action that gives the text editor control to service the keyboard and the display needs.

**Multiprogramming** is when several programs, the text editor, print formatter and the operating system, run together concurrently.

## 7.2 PAPER AND MARGINS

I divide the discussion of formatting into two kinds of requests:

1. long term,
2. short term.

Long term requests often last for the printing of the whole document. You don't expect the paper size to change. Only in certain instances would you change the typeface. Margins sometimes change during printout, but this is the exception, not the rule.

Short term format applies to a paragraph or more, or as little as a single character. You may indent a whole paragraph for emphasis. You may change to single space to deemphasize a paragraph. But you ask for *overstrike* for just one character to put in an accent mark, for example. Short term format gets attention in Section 7.3.

### Choosing the Format

There are several ways to tell the text editor the form of the output document. The ones which are available to you depend on the WP system that you have. Here are some alternatives:

1. standard format choosen from a menu,
2. default values choosen by making *no* choice,
3. visually derived values,
4. single key specified values,
5. multiple key specified values.

Since long term parameters are seldom changed during a session, you set up the values as you start work on a document.

This section considers three ways that you convey format to the text editor during document preparation. We discuss in order:

1) how the system is started up and a default (standard format) is displayed;
2) encoded commands;
3) embedded commands.

### Startup

You start some WP systems by flipping on the power switch. Many WPs then issue a **prompt**—a request for you to type in what you want to do. You have a fixed set of responses to choose from, such as "edit," "copy a disk," "print." More commonly, the system offers you a choice of activities in a **menu**—a list of alternatives from which you choose one by pressing a single key, a number or a letter.

The first menu you get (in a menu system) might offer a choice between creating or editing; you select "create." Some WPs call this editing a *new* document. You provide a document name so that the text editor will be able to file the electronic document.

The next menu might present document alternatives, or standard formats for the different kinds of documents in your office. Eventually a format menu is shown with the current margin choices, line spacing, etc. By hitting the proper key you may:

a. accept this set of options;
b. alter one of the options presented.

For the menu of Figure 7.2.1 hit "3" to alter the left margin and you get a prompt to enter a new value for it. Enter "15" and a carriage return to set the left margin 15 characters in from the edge of the paper. When you are satisfied with the choices, indicate this and the menu disappears. Format values may now be shown at the top of the screen if the WP has a status line.

```
               FORMAT SETTINGS

           Format:                  Setting:

        1. Page length                 66
        2. Text length                 54
        3. Left margin                 10
        4. Right margin                10
        5. Top margin                   5
        6. Bottom margin                5
        7. Line spacing                 1
        8. Pitch                       10
        9. Proportional spacing         0
       10. Justification                0
       11. Paragraph indent             5
       12. Paragraph spacing            1
```

Figure 7.2.1. A format menu.

*Old Documents*

Suppose that you elect to edit a document. The text editor requests a document name. For an old document, you must **mount** (put in a disk drive) the disk containing the named electronic document. Then the system can locate the electronic document.

The (old) document is found on the disk and the text editor puts part of it into the work area. The text editor displays current format the top (or bottom) of the screen for you to inspect in the **status line.**

The composition of the status line depends on the **WP**. A typical sample is presented in Figure 7.2.2. In the figure, the top line shows the page format de-

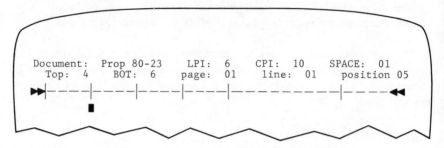

Figure 7.2.2. A status display and format ruler.

fault for the new document (or the initial format for an existing document). In Figure 7.2.3 the outer rectangle represents the paper with the text length and width that you asked for.

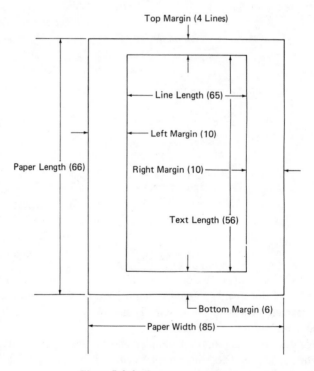

Figure 7.2.3. Format parameters.

The inner rectangle is where text might appear. You set these margins up for the new text; for old text the margin specs come in with the electronic document:

- The **top margin** is the number of lines from the top of the page to where the text begins.
- The **bottom margin** is the number of blank lines after the last line of text.
- The **left margin** is the number of blank characters on the left.
- The **right margin** is the number of blank characters after the maximum length line is printed.

Word wrap affects the right margin. The number of characters in each line differs from one line to the next. Unjustified printing results in a jagged right margin. For justification, spaces are entered to align each line and provide a fixed right margin.

*Display*

The meaning of the first line of the display presented in Figure 7.2.2 should now be clear. Part of the display (the second line in the figure) keeps track of the line and column number where the cursor appears. This was vital with the typewriter. It was *the* way to center titles or put data right flush on the margin. Today the WP does these things for you. Cursor position is given mostly for consistency with the typewriter; occasionally it comes in handy for estimating page length or the like.

The third line in the figure represents the tab and margin settings. In this display, the tabs are set at positions corresponding to the verticals along this line; where dashes are shown, no tab stops are set.

*Alternative Format Parameters*

When you begin a session, you may change the default parameters. How you do this depends upon the WP. Sometimes a separate format screen is presented at the start of editing (as in Figure 7.2.4). The actions for this WP might be:

1. You accept or reject the entire format by entering Y(es) or N(o).
2. The cursor moves to the first parameter value for N(o).
3. You press return to accept it or enter a new value, then return.
4. You accept or alter other parameters in the same way.

```
Format

    Type Spacing    10 Lines per inch
    Line Spacing     6 Lines per inch
    Paper Size       8.5 Wide
                    11.0 Long
    Margins
        Top          4
        Bottom       6
        Left        10
        Right       10
    Line Advance     1
```

Figure 7.2.4. Format display.

*Tabs*

The **tab key** on the typewriter is a fast way to get to the next **tab stop**—an adjustable finger that stops the carriage advance rightward. The **tab clear** key removes all tab stops. You set them by moving the carriage to a position where you want a tab stop. Then hit the **tab set** key.

Tabs on the **WP** usually work the same:

- tab-clear clears the tabs, either one at a time or all at once;
- tab-set sets a tab stop at the current cursor position;
- tab moves the cursor to the next tab stop.

For the standard tab, pressing tab during editing brings the cursor to the next tab stop on the line. Other kinds of tabs are discussed in Section 11.1. That tab stop position is fixed by one of three means:

1. the default value;
2. a value you set when you begin editing;
3. a value entered after editing starts.

The setup display tells you the default values of the tab stops and also, in some cases, the margins. A neat way shows a **format line,** with a symbol at each end, the margin limits in true relation to the screen; symbols along the line show the tab stops. This line appears continuously throughout editing to guide you as in Figure 7.2.2.

To change a tab stop or margin,

a. move the cursor to a symbol or nonsymbol,
b. press a key to remove or enter a marker,
c. the result is immediate.

Typical symbols are L for left margin, R for right margin, T or a vertical for tabs and D for decimal tabs (explained in Chapter 11).

*Choice of Defaults*

Sometimes the WP provides several different sets of default format values when you begin to create a document. A menu appears that lets you choose, for instance, between:

1. rought draft,
2. contract,
3. proposal,
4. letter.

By striking a selection key, you get the preassigned default values for this class of document.

**Altering Margins during Edit**

Several ways to *change* the margins while editing are:

1. with a *format menu* key,
2. with a *margin* key,
3. by a sequence of key strokes.

*Menu*

Some WPs have a key labeled format to get back the format *menu*. You can hit format at any time and the screen clears, to be replaced by the format names followed by the current values (e.g., left margin, 10.) To change any format value, go to that format line and enter the new value (e.g., change 10 to 15 to rest the left margin). You may repeat this for other parameters. Signal when done, (e.g., hit accept) and the text you were editing returns to the screen.

*Margin Keys*

Some WPs have separate keys for each format function. They differ in how you name the settings:

a. cursor position,
b. numerical entry.

For the first, position the cursor to where you want the left margin, press the left-margin key and it's set. To validate your choice, the *format line* (see page 00) shows a symbol, perhaps L, at the left margin position.

For the second method (a different WP), press the left-margin to start the alteration. A prompt asks, "Left margin column?" Entering "15" changes the left margin to 15.

Needless to say, any format change goes into effect immediately.

*Control Sequence*

Some WPs use terminals connected to large computers or commercial terminals connected to personal computers. These terminal keyboards may have no format keys—there is no margin key. Instead, a sequence of keys conveys a margin change. This sequence may start with control or an infrequently used symbol recognized by the text editor.

*Action*

Regardless of how the change was entered, the text editor accepts the request and reacts by:

1. altering the displayed text (responsive display),
2. changing the format parameters displayed:
   a. the format line,
   b. the parameter readout line.

The new format values *must* be put into the electronic document so that the print formatter can print the document as you want it. Format parameters are put into the electronic document in two similar ways:

A. encoded commands for the responsive display,
B. embeded commands.

The former is more common in the office system. In the less sophisticated system for the personal computer or mainframe, the display does not respond. You confirm the action by examining the embedded commands which are themselves displayed, as we see shortly.

### Encoded Commands

For most office WPs the display is responsive to many format requests. Enter a command changing the left margin and the display presents succeeding lines on the screen moved in the number of spaces requested. The command immediately takes effect, so there is no need to display the request itself. Two questions then arise:

- How does the operator convey the request?
- How does the text editor record the request so that it is forwarded to the print formatter?

## Command Entry

Three ways that the WP designer can choose from for you to enter format commands are:

1. a menu,
2. format function keys,
3. a key sequence.

*Menu*

A <u>format</u> key gets a menu display. You alter format parameters from the menu just as described for starting an edit sequence.

*Function Keys*

The keyboard has keys engraved for each function such as tab-set, left-margin, etc. Hit a key and *usually* (not in all WPs) you get a prompt. Hit <u>left-margin</u> and get, for instance, "Enter left margin column number or return to set margin at cursor." For the Magna SL, put the cursor where you want the left margin and you can set it *there* when you hit <u>left-margin</u>.

*Key Sequence*

This method is used where the keyboard does not have special keys—with personal computers and remote EDP terminals. A sequence of keys, beginning with <u>control</u>, transmits the format request.

## Encoding the Command

When the text editor receives the format request it has two tasks:

1. to present the altered format on the display,
2. to put the request in the text for the print formatter.

To distinguish the text from the request for (2), there are two choices:

a. use a string of nonprinting codes,
b. enter a combination of printing and nonprinting codes.

Both alternatives work. The WP designer chooses how to **encode** the format request, that is, enter it into the text so that print formatter can tell the request from text.

*Format Code*

The designer *might* assign one control code to signal a format message encoded within the electronic document. Let us call this the **format code** and indicate it with [fo]. A **format string** is a set of codes beginning with [fo] and ending with another distinctive code such as [cr] (return), [1e] (line end) or [fo]. Let us choose [cr] for the example. Now let us put the **format message** between [fo] and [cr] in the format string using printing codes. For instance "lm" could stand for "left margin." A request to change the left margin from whatever it is to a value of 15 is thus encoded by entering

$$[fo]lm15[cr] \qquad (7.2.1)$$

This goes right into the text at the point where it is to take effect.

The format command entered into the text may additionally be presented at the bottom of the screen or at another convenient place for you to see as you enter it. When terminated, the command itself is obliterated. The format line, when present, is updated to record the new value of, say, the left margin. Subsequent text entered by the operator is formatted according to the new parameters and displayed accordingly. To view all format changes anywhere in the text, return to the format menu in the Xerox 860, for example, and choose *code display*.

As the text editor processes the character codes for the format string, it also enters them into the work area. The work area becomes part of the electronic document which is later passed to the print formatter. While the electronic document is reviewed by the print formatter, it extracts these format statements to update its own tables. The characters between [fo] and [cr] do not print.

**Embedded Commands**

Embedded commands are another way to direct the print formatter about how to print the document. These commands are used when the WP does not have a responsive display or when the display is not responsive to this particular directive. You find them in Jacquard's Type-Rite and in many personal computers.

If you want a format change, move the cursor to where you want it to take effect. Enter a format command at the keyboard. The text editor accepts and displays the command on the CRT as part of the text. The display shows where in the text the format is supposed to change.

To summarize: the format command on the CRT is put into the electronic document. When it is found by the print formatter, the command is not printed but is recognized as a command. It consists of printable characters. Therefore, the WP designer organizes the command structure to be unique, recognizable and unlikely to occur in a normal text. Two common ways are:

- dot commands;
- backslash commands.

*The Dot Command*

There are several rules for writing the dot command:

1. The command always begins at the left margin;
2. The first character of the command is always a period ( . );
3. Two letters and perhaps two or three digits follow the dot;
4. <u>Return</u> terminates the command.

Paragraphs don't begin with a period, so this sequence is not likely to occur in the normal document.

Figure 7.2.5 shows a display after the operator has issued a dot format command ".lm15" at the left-hand margin. The operator changes the left margin to 15.

```
        For positioning the cursor on the screen, it is important
to note the following relationship:
.lm 15
        * The screen holds only a small portion of the text -- from
```

Figure 7.2.5. Dot format command.

The text editor alters the work area, as shown in Figure 7.2.6: the format statement is nested between two carriage returns. (One sets the period to the left margin, the second ends the command.) Now the print formatter can distinguish it from the text to be printed. Hence, this sequence is interpreted as a format command, accepted by the print formatter and obeyed while printing the lines which follow and until otherwise directed.

```
-----toƀnoteƀtheƀfollowingƀrelationships:[le].lm15[le]*ƀThescreen
```

Figure 7.2.6. Dot commands in the work area.

### *Backslash Commands*

These commands look the same, except that the backslash replaces the dot for some WPs for two reasons:

- It appears on many keyboards.
- It is not commonly found within text.

Its use is typically the same as the dot command. Figure 7.2.7 shows a screen display where the left margin is changed to 15 using a backslash command. The

```
meaning.  The choice is, of course, unique to the WP but these

are typical:

.lm 15

      * Page Layout
```

Figure 7.2.7. Backslash format command.

corresponding contents of the work area is shown in Figure 7.2.8. The formatter notes the format command because the carriage return is followed by the backslash in the text string.

```
----ave̸btypical:[le]\lml5[le]*̸bPage̸blayout[le]
```

Figure 7.2.8. Backslash commands in the work area.

### *Mnemonics*

In the format command following the dot or back slash is a pair of letters called a **mnemonic** (Greek for "memory"). The letters are chosen to remind you of their meaning, such as LM for left margin. The choice is, of course, unique to the WP, but these are typical:

- Page layout:
  **pl** for page length,
  **pw** for page width.
- Printer spacing:
  **v** for vertical lines per inch,
  **h** for horizontal characters per inch.
- Margins:
  **tm** for top margin,
  **bm** for bottom margin,

**lm** for left margin,
**rm** for right margin.
• Line advance:
**sp** for line advance between lines.

### Combinations

In some cases, the **WP** display is responsive to some commands and not to others. Some format commands can be embedded while others are encoded. When the display responds to a format command, the command itself need not be displayed, since the results are evident. However, the print formatter must be notified, so the information is encoded and entered into the work area.

For requests to which the display does not respond, the format command is embedded in the text, displayed in this form to the operator and placed in the electronic document text at the proper position.

## 7.3 SHORT TERM FORMAT REQUESTS

**Short term requests** which change format or print parameters during editing are divided into two classes:

• spacing,
• type style.

### Spacing

*Tabs*

Suppose that the tabs are set. Each time you tab, the keyboard sends the tab-control code [tb] to the text editor. The text editor usually enters [tb] into the electronic document. (Later the print formatter sends [tb] to the printer, which tabs to the same position while the document is printed.) To make the screen conform, the text editor sends enough blanks to the display to move the cursor to the next tab column.

To change the tab settings you reset the tabs, as described on page 228.

*Command Entry*

As with format requests, there are several ways that a **WP** system can be designed to accept your commands:

1. format function keys,
2. a menu,
3. a key sequence.

The choice is up to the designer. In the office WP system, at least in theory, the keyboard is designed to suit your needs with a separate key for each function. In the discussion below, we assume a WP with separate function keys. Keep in mind that the action is the same when the keyboard is limited and command entry requires (2) or (3) above.

*Indent*

To **indent** is to move in the left margin a number of characters for the next few lines. You could reset the left margin. But then you might forget the previous margin setting. An alternative is an **indent command**. Hit indent 10 to request that the left margin move in 10 positions from its current reading. A later command, indent 0, restores the left margin.

Another way to indent as you create text is to use tab stops or alternate margins. For the Burroughs Redactor you can enter several Ls or Rs on the format line. The outer (leftmost) L and (rightmost) R set the main document margins. To indent left one level, press SET LM; repeat SET LM to go to the second level (third L). Indent right with SET RM the proper number of times. To return outward use CLEAR LM (or RM) as many times as required.

*Paragraph Indent*

For indented paragraphs, finish the paragraph with return (or two returns) and start the next with tab. One key stroke is saved when the text editor tabs automatically at the end of every paragraph. To use this facility, you inform the WP of the indent value, either by entering commands directly at the keyboard along with values or from the format menu. Typing within a paragraph proceeds with word wrap. When you hit return, the WP ends the paragraph, puts in another line space if you ask and indents for you.

*Margin Release*

You are entering text and you approach the right margin. You want the entire next word kept on this line, even if it extends into the margin (if you're not justifying). You can ask the text editor to release the margin for a particular line. For the left margin the margin release works when backspacing.

*Center*

A time consuming task for the typist is centering titles on a page. The text editor does this for you with a single command. Press center and equal numbers of spaces are placed on either side of the text you enter on this line. You can call for centering before, during or after you enter the text. The responsive display shows the material being centered as you enter it. For a WP which has a center tab instead, <u>tab</u> takes you to a position in the line and text entered thereafter is centered about this position until you <u>tab</u> again (see Section 11.1).

*Right Flush*

Some writers use titles on the right side of the page. Or the cover to a report can have information set up so that lines are aligned on the right margin only (with jagged margins on the left)—a simple task for the text editor. Some WPs provide a right flush tab which can be used for this (see Section 11.1).

*Justification*

In some cases, it is desirable to turn justification on and off. Format commands do this anywhere in the text.

### Emphasis

You can ask for a change in printing the next few characters in the text. Boldface and underscore add emphasis to words. Superscripts and subscripts help with footnotes and are needed for formulas in scientific documents.

*Command*

You can direct the text editor to alter printing for one or more words in the text according to your WP system. There are several ways used by different WPs to do this:

1. Use a different special key for each variation. The Dictaphone Dual Display has a <u>bold</u> and an <u>underscore</u> key which lights when pressed; characters you key in now display in boldface (or underscore). The action and display stop and the light turns off when <u>bold</u> (or <u>underscore</u>) is pressed again.
2. Use a function key (<u>bold</u>, <u>under</u>, etc.) and a graphic appears on the screen when you hit it.
3. Start and end the request with a special printing character.
4. Submit a control string.

You have to say when to *start* and when to *stop* the action. Usually the *same* command turns on *and* off the emphasis. It's like quotes: one pair starts the quotation, another pair ends it.

If you do not have a responsive display where you *see* the words themselves underlined, beware. Be sure you have a matched set. If you start underlining and forget to stop, the rest of the text gets underlined. Of course, if you under-line another word properly later, you get a strange result: <u>all</u> <u>the</u> <u>text</u> <u>is</u> <u>under-lined</u> except <u>the</u> <u>phrase</u> <u>intended</u>.

To alleviate this irritation some WPs *automatically* terminate a short term change at some preset point:

- the end of the current line,
- the end of the present paragraph.

This may also be an annoyance. You have to *restart* underlining (or whatever) to override this feature for each line, paragraph, etc. However, I find this pre-ferable to occasionally getting a full page or more of underlining.

### Graphic

To request emphasis (bold, underscore, etc.), hit the emphasis key. The graphic appears on the screen. After entering (creation) or moving over (for existing text) the string to be emphasized, hit the key again and another graphic appears. The text editor enters the string with the graphic codes in the memory work area. The boldface type or the underscore (and no graphic) actually shows for the responsive display.

### Underscore

Based on the WP system and the printer used, up to three different kinds of un-derscoring may be produced.

a. total underscoring from the beginning to the end of the string,
b. word underscoring but none for spaces or punctuation between words,
c. double underscoring of either type.

### Simple Horizontals

Underscore is a horizontal line under a phrase for emphasis. There are other uses for horizontal lines such as:

- text separators,
- signature lines.

Vendors must provide for them. One way is a separate key to request a line segment of character position length at line level (where the descender starts). This cannot be used to underline; the key may occupy that familar position on the keyboard. You may also get a horizontal line by using the unbroken underscore key: put the mark at the beginning and end of the intended line to print a line in the otherwise blank area.

*Boldface*

Unresponsive displays do not show boldface characters on the screen. An alternative is to highlight characters to appear in the document in boldface. This might confuse you at first, where strings for deletion or search objectives are highlighted. Two special symbols used by some vendors are # and @. These appear on the screen to tell you the limits for which the boldface action applies. Hit bold to start emboldening and bold again to stop; if you forget the second bold, boldface continues indefinitely on the printout unless the WP system is designed to turn it off at paragraph end.

*Subscript and Superscript*

A subscript (or superscript) prints below (or above) the current line. Unresponsive displays use printing characters which are rarely used otherwise. Two common symbol pairs are:

- Up-arrow moves material up and down-arrow moves it down;
- Less-than moves the paper up and greater-than moves it down.

With the first symbol, a superscript starts with up-arrow and ends with down-arrow; a subscript starts with down-arrow and ends with up-arrow.

*Color and Fonts*

Considerable emphasis results when some text appears printed in red instead of black. Unless you have a color CRT, there is no good way to present a color change request except with a nonprinting character. To print in two colors requires a two color ribbon installed in the printer when the document is being printed or color change does not take place.

Change the color with a color key (hit color once for red and again for black). It tells the text editor with a control code. A graphic appears on the screen to show that the material that follows (until the next graphic) is printed in red.

*New Font*

A different typeface also provides emphasis. A change from roman to gothic is immediately evident. Use the same procedure to change fonts. For example:

    a. hit <u>font</u> for the change
    b. a graphic displays
    c. hit <u>font</u> again to return to old font.

This requires operator intervention to change the print wheel on most printers. That is why it has limited application in the present office environment. High quality matrix printers may change this. The computer can request a different font for such printers made by Sanders and Malibu.

*Character Count*

If your WP is not responsive and hence displays an extra graphic whenever you add emphasis, then there are more symbols on the screen line than on the print line. Your character count is off. If you tab on a line which contains emphasis symbols, it probably prints differently.

CPT presents an emphasis symbol for a second after you key it in; then it disappears. This symbol thus does not mess up the character count. But the symbols do not show in the text either. You cannot tell a subscript from regular text. However, if you press <u>code</u> V, the emphasis symbols reappear momentarily for you to check. (You can hold down <u>code</u> V for sustained viewing.)

### 7.4 RESPONSIVE DISPLAYS

**Responsiveness** of a display is the fidelity with which it shows how the final document will look with respect to your format commands. WP systems differ considerably in their responsiveness. At one end of the scale is the Xerox STAR whose display presents a page exactly at it will print. As you edit it further, the display changes. At the other end of the scale is the WP system, such as the personal computer, with a small screen which displays only a partial page, where neither new margins nor any other of the formatting changes show when made. Display size is not nearly as important as responsiveness.

In this section we discuss the most responsive display. WP systems have some but rarely all response features described. Assume the most advanced display available that provides a large character matrix, perhaps $9 \times 14$ dots or larger. Beam positioning is accurate and many formats display. The CRT highlights by dimming, brightening, reversing video or blinking. The display uses a wide range of graphics. Different typefaces display through multiple character generators. The CRT is actual page size.

## Page Layout

The text editor keeps one or more format tables in buffers which specify the format for different parts of the page. This information relative to the cursor position, along with a margin and tab marker, is presented at the top (or bottom) of the screen or not at all, at your option.

To make a change in page layout, enter directions through the keyboard. It applies beginning with the current page or starts at the current cursor position. For instance, a change in the top margin applies to the whole page. When the text editor receives a **global** change which applies henceforth, it:

1. revises the format table in the work area;
2. enters the encoded information in the work area just ahead of the beginning of the page;
3. alters the format line to conform.

## Short Term Parameters

You can indent to change the margins for a paragraph (or block) without altering the margins for the page. This is a **short term** change. Different WPs let you make short term changes in two ways:

- You state the request and the WP keeps it in force as material is entered until the end of the paragraph.
- You move the cursor to each end of the area and mark it; the change applies only to this area.

In both cases, the text editor notes the beginning and end of the change. It encodes one format block or command in the text at the beginning and one at the end of the area.

During later editing, the text editor notes when you move the cursor into one end of the block. As the cursor moves past the boundary, the text editor picks up the encoded format statement and updates its format table. Everything in this area is sent to the display by the text editor in this new format.

A format statement *always* applies to text which follows. As you scroll *forward* through the text, the text editor keeps pace, advancing through the electronic document. As each new format statement is encountered, the format table is updated. The text which follows is displayed according to these revised specifications.

Scrolling backward is a different matter. The text editor scans backward to a format statement which indicates a change, but for subsequent not preceding text. The format in force for the preceding text is governed by the next previous format statement. The text editor scoots backward in the text to find that format statement, install it in the format table and apply it to text it is now beginning to display at the top of the screen.

This is shown in Figure 7.4.1. Format information is contained in the work area as a string marked by two distinctive nonprinting character codes. The choice of the codes depends upon the WP. A typical string is preceeded by [fo], the format character, and terminates with [cr], the code for return. The figure shows cursor movement from **CP** (marking the first cursor position) to **CP'** which marks the new cursor position; the format statement encountered on the way back shows that the cursor was in a block with different format parameters. Once at the new position, **CP'**, a further backward scan is necessary to get the new format information. The next previous format statement updates the format table and the presentation.

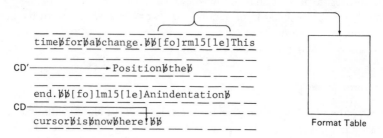

time♭for♭a♭change.♭♭[fo]rm15[le]This

CD'————————→Position♭the♭

end.♭♭[fo]lm15[le]Anindentation♭

CD—————————————

cursor♭is♭now♭here!♭♭                  Format Table

Figure 7.4.1. Format information about the display goes into a format table.

*Incremental Format*

As each change in format is encountered, some WPs put a complete format statement in the text. Only values which change need be noted. The text editor keeps a format table with current format values. As you scroll into an area with new values, the text editor needs to know only the parameters that change.

Figure 7.4.2 illustrates this. At the top we see a page formatted with a 10 character margin on both the left and right. The operator changes both margins to 15 for a block of information to add emphasis. The result appears in the middle of the figure with the indented margins as requested. At the bottom, note a format statement as it might appear in the work area. One format statement starts the indentation and another terminates it. The text editor encodes them into the work area text.

Actually it is the text editor which is responsive; it retransmits the indented material, sending five additional blanks for the first and last characters of the indented block. The second format statement alerts the text editor of the old margin requirements. The remaining text is sent to the display unindented. It is pushed down because the indentation provided less characters per line. **ES,** which marks the end of screen in the work area, moves backward. Text is pushed down the screen. The text dropped off the bottom of the screen is not lost, of course; it is carried over to the next page when you scroll to it.

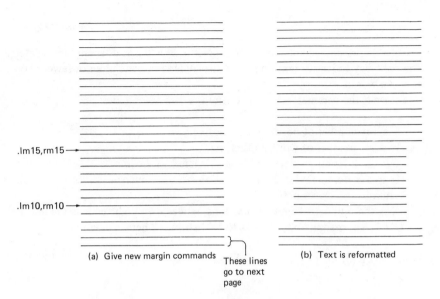

.lm15,rm15 →

.lm10,rm10 →

(a) Give new margin commands

}These lines
go to next
page

(b) Text is reformatted

Figure 7.4.2. An incremental format change.

*Redisplay*

When an old document is edited, its text is brought from external storage into the memory work area. The text editor scans it from the beginning. The text editor starts with default values in its format table. As text is displayed, the current format setting is used to put the text on the screen until a new format statement is encountered. Since format is incremental, only the parameters which change are altered in the format table and presented on the format line.

The text editor uses the format table to compare each line it sends to the display.

**Justify**

The responsive display justifies text on the screen, showing even margins on both sides. Even the conventional display can be programmed for **word justification**—entering extra spaces between *words* (not between *characters*)—to make all lines the same length (see section 3.3).

*Word Justifying*

Most CRTs presents characters in fixed positions (cells), as do many line printers. The only way to justify text on such a display is to provide more or fewer blanks between words.

Consider the parameters which control the display of a line:

**N** is the number of positions on this line.

**W** is the number of words in this line.

**C** is the total number of nonblank characters in the line.

**O** is the number of occupied positions—the number of characters plus the number of spaces between words.

**X** is the number of unused positions between the right end of the line and the right margin, extra blanks to be distributed between words.

From the definition of O and X we have,

$$X = N - O \qquad\qquad (7.4.1)$$

X—extra blanks needed to make even lines—is the critical quantity.

For instance, consider a 50 position line with eight words containing a total of 38 characters, as shown in Figure 7.4.3. One blank is required between each word, a total of seven more blanks. The number of occupied positions, O, is 38 + 8 - 1 = 45. There are five unoccupied positions to be filled with blanks: X = 50 - 45. Distribute these extra blanks between each of the first six words. Except for the last three, the text editor puts two blanks between each word of this line on the display; it puts a single blank between the sixth and seventh and between the seventh and eighth words on the line. The justified string at the bottom of the figure is transmitted to the display.

```
A line constructed as specified in the example.
AØØlineØØconstructedØØasØØspecifiedØØinØtheØexample.
```

Figure 7.4.3. Display justification between words.

When each screen line is justified in this way, neat margins appear on both the left and right, regardless of how print justification is done.

### Typefaces

You would like the display to show all the typefaces and emphasis that the printer can print. Chapter 2 explains how a 5 X 7 dot matrix character generator creates a character at each position on the screen corresponding to the code in the refresh buffer at the corresponding position. A larger dot matrix provides more detail for each character constructed on the screen by having several character generators. Any one of them can be called up by the computer. STAR provides several typefaces. By doubling the thickness of the vertical and horizontal strokes of each character, boldface is shown. Another character generator has tilted verticals to present italics. Pedestals are placed at the top and bottom of the verticals, called **serifs**, by the roman character generator.

There is room for either a single or double underscore below each character. When so directed by the text editor with a control code, the VDT adds underscore for the designated string.

As you create or edit text, indicate with a typeface key or with control codes how you want each group of characters to appear. The text editor responds by embedding or encoding a message into the text of the electronic document. At the same time, the text editor sends codes to the display to tell it which character generator to use to present the forthcoming set of characters on the screen. The display reacts as directed. You can immediately see results—roman, gothic, boldface, italics, etc.

## 7.5 PRINTING

**The Text**

The data in the electronic document consists of a stream of bytes which contains both printing and nonprinting character codes. As the print formatter scans this stream from its beginning, it easily separates commands from data. The commands, whether encoded or embedded, tell the formatter what the page should look like.

The print formatter starts at the beginning of the electronic document and examines it continuously from start to finish. The print formatter never has to go backward within the electronic document. (This is not like the text editor which skips around within the text at your command.)

As the print formatter rolls along, reviewing the data stream, it sends a similar stream of character codes, but with additional control codes, to the printer to print out the text sequentially on the paper at the printer.

Sometimes the print formatter runs into situations which require it to talk to you. For instance, when printing single sheet stock without an automatic feeder, the print formatter tells you when the printer needs a new sheet of paper. You get a message on the screen. You do not have to pay attention to the printer except at this moment. The printer or the display also "beeps" to attract attention.

**Action**

There are other occasions when the print formatter talks to you or asks questions. When you start up the WP system, you get a menu (or are asked questions). If you choose to print a document, this invokes a format menu (or further questions). The format menu lets you change the static or overall format parameters, such as pitch or margins. Dynamic requests in the electronic document, such as indents or emphasis requests, are not affected.

You name a document. The print formatter sends the name to the file manager to find the electronic document on the disk. If absent, the print formatter prompts you to supply and mount a disk containing the electronic document.

### Static Format

The print formatter now has control. It brings in the first part of the text to be printed. At the beginning of the text stream there is a static format statement. (Some WPs mark it with a special code to convey that.) When you call up the print formatter, your format parameters, if any, are substituted instead of this statement. Otherwise those in the format statement in the electronic document are entered into the format table if you declined to provide a new format.

### Format Change

As text is scanned the print formatter comes across format statements, encoded or embedded in the electronic document. As each is encountered, the print formatter revises the format table. Each is then enforced by adjusting tab stops on the printer (see below) or whatever is required.

This format table is a constant reference for the print formatter, while it constructs the data stream to the printer. The table provides the current setting for line advance, margins, tab stops, etc. It also keeps track of the line number and other output print page information (page number, etc.). The table tells the print formatter when to advance to the next page, what the page number should be and so forth. The print formatter uses this table to construct control codes to put in the data stream to the printer, accordingly. For instance, at the end of the page, it sends enough line feeds to position to the top print area on the next page (for continuous forms).

### Print Control

The printer contains one or more **hardware buffers,** a storage area which holds the text to be printed. The text formatter reviews the electronic document. It sends the text and control codes to the printer to produce each line of text. These data go into the print buffer. Commands to control the printer are mixed with data in this buffer.

Each printer manufacturer provides its own set of command codes; there is no industry standard. The print formatter converts format blocks in the text stream into control codes designed for *this* printer. If the same print formatter is associated with a number of different printers (multiple shared resource), then a different driver is needed to control each printer.

### Tabs

The printer has tabs which are set by the computer. The print formatter starts its work by sending over a command to clear all the tabs left over from the last print job. The format table that the print formatter has created tells where tabs should be set. The print formatter sends over control codes to set the printer tabs to agree with the table.

When you tab while editing at the WP, the text editor picks up the tab control code, [tb], and enters it in the text in the work area. The screen reflects this action because the text editor sends enough blanks to the display to position the cursor to the tab column.

When the print formatter finds [tb] in the text, it sends this tab control code to the printer, which then advances the carriage to the next tab stop (set earlier). If you clear and/or reset tab stops, this puts a new format block in the electronic document. When the print formatter arrives at this format block, the print formatter changes the format table. For new tab settings, the print formatter puts control codes into the data stream to the printer to reset the printer tab stops. Now subsequent tabs that you put in your document are sent as control codes to the printer, which moves to the new setting.

### Express Tabs

The printer has another tab action. The manufacturer sometimes calls this the **direct tab function**, or **express tab**. The print formatter can ask the printer to move the carriage to a specific column. To see how useful this function is, especially for bidirectional printing, consider that the printer has just finished printing the next-to-last line of a paragraph with the carriage traveling to the right. The carriage is now at the right margin; after spacing up one line, it has to move left many positions without printing to get to the right end of the last line of the paragraph. By sending an express tab control code to the printer, the carriage moves at high speed to the position for the last character of the sentence. Non-printing motion is faster than the carriage speed when printing.

### Printer Driver

The printer driver coordinates the print formatter and the printer hardware. The driver determines when the printer has consumed the information in its buffer and needs more. The driver tells the print formatter to send over a new bufferful. Since the printer is slower than the computer, you can edit another electronic document while the printer goes about printing this line of text.

*Review*

The print formatter acquires a portion of the stream of text and format information. As it scans this portion, it extracts the format information, keeping its print format table up to date. To construct the output stream for the printer, the print formatter references the format table. It chooses control codes for the printer and intersperses the data stream with them to make the printer produce text in the right format.

## Justification

Justification to provide even margins is neat and subtle when spaces are put between each character instead of between words. The print formatter controls every movement of the carriage from one character to the next. The text formatter calculates character advance for each group of characters on the line. Carriage advance on daisy wheel printers is standard at 1/120th of an inch—one *unit*, The first part of the line usually requires character advance of one width, whereas the second group of characters requires a different width.

The print formatter sends a simple nonprinting code or multiple codes to the printer to control the number of units for the carriage to move after *each* of the forthcoming character codes. The text formatter intersperses carriage advance length requests with text in the data stream to the printer.

Table 7.5.1 shows the printer motion directives for the NEC Spinwriter which

**Table 7.5.1. Escape Key Printer Control Codes.**

| | |
|---|---|
| ESC 1 | Set Horizontal Tab |
| ESC 2 | Reset Horizontal Tab (Individual) |
| ESC 3 | Print in Red |
| ESC 4 | Print in Black |
| ESC 5 | Set Vertical Tab |
| ESC 6 | Reset Vertical Tab (Individual) |
| *ESC 7 | Clear all Tabs and FF Length |
| ESC 9 | Reverse Line Feed |
| ESC | Reverse Print (Right-to-Left) On |
| ESC = | Read and Store Operator Control Switches |
| ESC | Forward Print (Left-to-Right) On |
| *ESC ? | Set Format Mode |
| *ESC @ CR | Reset Format Mode |
| ESC J or j | Set Right Margin |
| ESC K or k | Reset Right Margin |
| *ESC L or l | Set FF Length |
| ESC M or m | Set Left Margin |
| ESC O or o | Reset Left Margin |

start with the control code called **escape,** designated here as [es]. A single print
character code follows [es]. Horizontal and vertical express tab functions and
line advance requests consist of three codes, as shown in Tables 7.5.2 and 7.5.3:

**Table 7.5.2. Horizontal Escape Codes.**

| | | | Spacing | Form Advance | |
|---|---|---|---|---|---|
| 1st | 2nd | 3rd | (inches) | 3rd | (inches) |
| ESC | ] | @ | 0 | P | 1/48 |
| | | A | 1/120 | Q | 2/48 |
| | | B | 2/120 | R | 3/48 |
| | | C | 3/120 | S | 4/48 |
| | | D | 4/120 | T | 5/48 |
| | | E | 5/120 | U | 6/48 (1/8) |
| | | F | 6/120 | V | 7/48 |
| | | G | 7/120 | W | 8/48 (1/6) |
| | | H | 8/120 | X | 9/48 |
| | | I | 9/120 | Y | 10/48 |
| | | J | 10/120 (1/12) | Z | 11/48 |
| | | K | 11/120 | [ | 12/48 |
| | | L | 12/120 (1/10) | \ | 13/48 |
| | | M | 13/120 | ] | 14/48 |
| | | N | 14/120 | ^ | 15/48 |
| | | O | 15/120 | − | 16/48 |
| | | | | | |

the first is [es]; the second is a group character; the third conveys the exact column or line advance quantity. Carrier-advance and form-advance codes once
set remain in effect until altered. There are given in Table 7.5.4.

When the printer detects [es], it expects to find one or two more character
codes. These *are not* to be printed; they are part of a command. The next code
tells whether another (print) code is forthcoming. This completes the control
sequence. If a printing character code follows, it will print; another control sequence, which starts with [es] or a control code, may follow.

Note the sequence for horizontal and vertical motion as we examine two examples. They include bidirectional horizontal motion, which speeds printing.

## Table 7.5.3. Vertical Express Codes.

| | Reverse | | | | Forward | | | |
|---|---|---|---|---|---|---|---|---|
| 1st | ESC | | | | ESC | | | |
| 2nd | X | | Y | | Z | | [ | |
| 3rd | @ 0 | P 16 | @ 32 | P 48 | @ 0 | P 16 | @ 32 | P 48 |
| | A 1 | Q 17 | A 33 | Q 49 | A 1 | Q 17 | A 33 | Q 49 |
| | B 2 | R 18 | B 34 | R 50 | B 2 | R 18 | B 34 | R 50 |
| | C 3 | S 19 | C 35 | S 51 | C 3 | S 19 | C 35 | S 51 |
| | D 4 | T 20 | D 36 | T 52 | D 4 | T 20 | D 36 | T 52 |
| | E 5 | U 21 | E 37 | U 53 | E 5 | U 21 | E 37 | U 53 |
| | F 6 | V 22 | F 38 | V 54 | F 6 | V 22 | F 38 | V 54 |
| | G 7 | W 23 | G 39 | W 55 | G 7 | W 23 | G 39 | W 55 |
| | H 8 | X 24 | H 40 | X 56 | H 8 | X 24 | H 40 | X 56 |
| | I 9 | Y 25 | I 41 | Y 57 | I 9 | Y 25 | I 41 | Y 57 |
| | J 10 | Z 26 | J 42 | Z 58 | J 10 | Z 26 | J 42 | Z 58 |
| | K 11 | [ 27 | K 43 | [ 59 | K 11 | [ 27 | K 43 | [ 59 |
| | L 12 | \ 28 | L 44 | \ 60 | L 12 | \ 28 | L 44 | \ 60 |
| | M 13 | ] 29 | M 45 | ] 61 | M 13 | ] 29 | M 45 | ] 61 |
| | N 14 | ^ 30 | N 46 | ^ 62 | N 14 | ^ 30 | N 46 | ^ 62 |
| | O 15 | - 31 | O 47 | - 63 | O 15 | - 31 | O 47 | - 63 |

CHARACTER KEY ───────▶◀─────── TAB POSITION

Example:

To tab to a vertical position 26 lines before the preset line (reverse), press the following keys in this order:

    1st key ESC
    2nd key X (or x)
    3rd key Z (or z)

## Table 7.5.4. Carrier Advance Codes.

| 1st |  |  |  |  | ESC |  |  |  |  |  |  |
|---|---|---|---|---|---|---|---|---|---|---|---|
| **2nd** | P |  | Q |  | R |  | S |  | T |  | U |
| **3rd** | @ 1 | P 17 | @ 33 | P 49 | @ 65 | P 81 | @ 97 | P 113 | @ 129 | P 145 | @ 161 |
|  | A 2 | Q 18 | A 34 | Q 50 | A 66 | Q 82 | A 98 | Q 114 | A 130 | Q 146 | A 162 |
|  | B 3 | R 19 | B 35 | R 51 | B 67 | R 83 | B 99 | R 115 | B 131 | R 147 | B 163 |
|  | C 4 | S 20 | C 36 | S 52 | C 68 | S 84 | C 100 | S 116 | C 132 | S 148 |  |
|  | D 5 | T 21 | D 37 | T 53 | D 69 | T 85 | D 101 | T 117 | D 133 | T 149 |  |
|  | E 6 | U 22 | E 38 | U 54 | E 70 | U 86 | E 102 | U 118 | E 134 | U 150 |  |
|  | F 7 | V 23 | F 39 | V 55 | F 71 | V 87 | F 103 | V 119 | F 135 | V 151 |  |
|  | G 8 | W 24 | G 40 | W 56 | G 72 | W 88 | G 104 | W 120 | G 136 | W 152 |  |
|  | H 9 | X 25 | H 41 | X 57 | H 73 | X 89 | H 105 | X 121 | H 137 | X 153 |  |
|  | I 10 | Y 26 | I 42 | Y 58 | I 74 | Y 90 | I 106 | Y 122 | I 138 | Y 154 |  |
|  | J 11 | Z 27 | J 43 | Z 59 | J 75 | Z 91 | J 107 | Z 123 | J 139 | Z 155 |  |
|  | K 12 | [ 28 | K 44 | [ 60 | K 76 | [ 92 | K 108 | [ 124 | K 140 | [ 156 |  |
|  | L 13 | \ 29 | L 45 | \ 61 | L 77 | \ 93 | L 109 | \ 125 | L 141 | \ 157 |  |
|  | M 14 | ] 30 | M 46 | ] 62 | M 78 | ] 94 | M 110 | ] 126 | M 142 | ] 158 |  |
|  | N 15 | ^ 31 | N 47 | ^ 63 | N 79 | ^ 95 | N 111 | ^ 127 | N 143 | ^ 159 |  |
|  | O 16 | − 32 | O 48 | − 64 | O 80 | − 96 | O 112 | − 128 | O 144 | − 160 |  |

CHARACTER KEY ─────── TAB POSITION

Example:

To tab directly to horizontal position 59, press the following keys in this order:
1st key ESC
2nd key Q (or q)
3rd key Z (or z)

## Examples

*Short Paragraph*

Figure 7.5.1 shows a two line paragraph. The explanation to you at the top, given in English, describes the meaning to the printer and points to where each should appear in the data

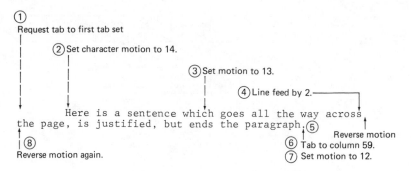

Figure 7.5.1. A justified two line paragraph.

stream to the printer. Figure 7.5.2 shows data found by the print formatter in the electronic document. Note that control codes appear only for tab [tb], line end [le] and carriage return [cr].

```
[tb]Hereɓisɓaɓsentenceɓwhichɓgoesɓallɓtheɓwayɓacrosstheɓpage,ɓisɓjustified
,ɓbutɓendsɓtheɓparagraph.[cr]
```

Figure 7.5.2. Text stream to print formatter for Figure 7.5.1.

Figure 7.5.3 shows the data stream sent to the printer. The additional control codes were entered there by the print formatter. The numbers found in the Figures 7.5.1 and 7.5.3. correspond to these actions:

Figure 7.5.3. Data and control stream for print formatter for Figure 7.5.1.

1. The tab code moves the carriage to the first tab position.
2. These three codes set character advance to 14 units.
3. The next three codes change the character advance to 13.
4. A line feed of two produces double spacing.
5. Reverse printer direction.
6. Express tab to column 59.
7. Change carriage advance to 12.
8. Reverse direction for the next line.

When the carriage moves backward, the data in the print buffer must be in reverse order from how it reads on the line. It is the print formatter that notes when the printer should reverse. The print formatter finds the right end of the line in the electronic document and transmits the character codes backward from there, putting in the printer control codes as needed during reverse motion.

*A Second Example*

Figure 7.5.4 includes underlining and column tabbing. Tabs were preset by a string of directives to the printer. The figure shows what is transmitted to get the printer to perform actions in this order. The column headings are written from left to right; they are underlined from right to left; the first item in each column is then printed from left to right.

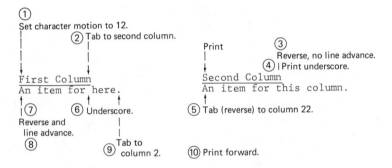

Figure 7.5.4. A columnar tabbing example.

Figure 7.5.5 shows what the print formatter starts with. Figure 7.5.6 shows what the print formatter sends to the printer, numbered according to the explanation below:

1. Set character motion for 12 units.
2. Tab to the second column.
3. Reverse the printing.
4. Print a number of underline characters.
5. Move directly to the end of the first column.
6. Continue to underline.
7. Reverse direction.

```
-First¢Column-[tb]-Second¢Column-[cr]An¢item¢for¢here.[tb]An¢item¢for¢t
is¢column.[cr]
```

Figure 7.5.5. Text stream to the print formatter for Figure 7.5.4.

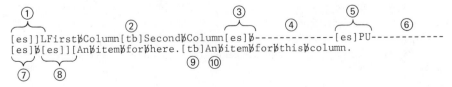

Figure 7.5.6. Data and control stream to print formatter for Figure 7.5.4.

# 8
# Electronic Documents and Subdocuments

## 8.0 INTRODUCTION

**Why?**

There are several reasons why you create separate electronic documents and later combine them. First, several people can work on a large report. Whether the document is being written by one or several people, it is still possible to break up the dictation and transcription for several operators to key in. Each operator then edits the pieces which are printed out as separate drafts.

After final editing, a new document is required. Without the WP, the pieces of text are assembled and a final document is typed. It is difficult to have several people work on the final document for three reasons:

- Typewriters differ and portions typed on different machines do not look the same.
- You cannot put numbers on the pages until all the parts are back together.
- A last minute change is next to impossible.

With word processing, it is sheer simplicity to prepare a large document. Several operators key and edit the pieces. One person assembles the multiple electronic documents into the final electronic document. The WP system prints it out continuously at a page a minute (or even faster, when a laser printer is available). And the pages are numbered properly at the same time!

*Phrase Recall*

Recurring phrases, sentences or paragraphs appear in many of the documents produced in the office. For instance, the lawyer writes wills, contracts and papers for service which use almost identical paragraphs from one document to the next. A "library" of paragraphs can be collected on one or more disks, each a separate document.

To prepare a paper, the lawyer indicates which paragraphs should be pasted together and enters some new material and then a legal secretary or assistant can use the WP system to "paste up" the desired legal document.

Libraries of standard paragraphs on disk are sold by computer legal services, so they are on file like paper forms. Clearly, much more flexibility results. After the first draft is created, substitutions are easy as pie: a block is deleted; a new paragraph is brought from the electronic file; and so forth.

An engineering firm or scientific research organization often submits proposals which include vitas of the principal investigators. Proposals also include background information on the organization. This text is sometimes called "boilerplate." How easy it is to assemble with the aid of the WP system!

*Selection*

The word processor can find an electronic document or subdocument by name from a disk and enter it into the text during editing. Often a portion rather than all of a document is selected to be entered into the text. For some WPs you review the subdocument on the screen to pick the sections you want.

Some print formatters select names and addresses to merge into a letter or document as it is printed. Discussion of automatic document inclusion is postponed to Chapter 10. Another alternative which is postponed to that chapter is automatic document assembly, which proceeds without operator intervention.

Electronic documents (EDs) and subdocuments (ESDs) are complete sections of text which you compose in memory and put away onto disks to keep them safely and securely. EDs can be small (a short business letter of a page or so) or very long (a report or a chapter of a book). Unwieldly large documents can be broken into smaller parts called **subdocuments,** a portion of a document. *You* define the subdocument.

*Subdocument File*

A convenient way to store ESDs is to create one file (or preferably several files divided according to application) containing only ESDs. This file, a collection of ESDs, has a name. Each ESD has a name or an identifier too. For the WP to find an ESD it should be able to locate first the file and then the ESD within the file. Each vendor provides rules to simplify access to the ESD. Rules consist of:

- conventions for constructing names,
- prefix tags,
- graphics in the names or prefixing them.

The ability to break documents up into smaller parts (subdocuments) and then put the pieces together (**document assembly**) is an aspect of the WP system. The WP system may make it easy, inconvenient, difficult or impossible to perform these document functions. Then again, your office may not need document functions (but I doubt it).

The ease of handling electronic documents is tied up with whether the WP:

1. is page or document oriented,
2. provides automatic or manual text advance,
3. has random or serial file management.

All WP systems handle small documents with much greater ease than does the typewriter. When it comes to large documents, there is even further improvement. Regardless of size, the automatic features of the WP:

1. facilitate training (especially if you use temps);
2. help you to combine smaller documents into large ones;
3. speed up work flow.

**Plan**

The thrust of this chapter is the many ways to deal with electronic documents, all of which should be understood. Section 8.1 examines manual page oriented systems, where the operator manages and keeps track of the pages which comprise the document. Section 8.2 looks at automatic page oriented systems where the WP system does much of the work but keeps the document in separate, recognizable chunks. Section 8.3 describes WP systems which handle complete documents automatically without viewing them as separate pieces and without any substantial limit in size. Section 8.4 looks at the use of serial files for documents, restricted mostly to WPs for personal computers and large computer systems.

The smallest subdocument that we examine is called a **block**. It is defined by you when you need it, as you create or edit a document. It is often a temporary subdivision of text, useful only during editing. Section 8.5 describes how to define and manipulate the block, to move it to any place in the text with a single command.

It is easiest to define and work with small documents or parts of documents. The subdocuments are combined later to compose the final report. Section 8.6 examines how to break up documents and then put them together from subdocuments.

Much more space is available on the disk than in memory to hold one or more electronic documents. Even so, disks become full. What happens to documents in process when space becomes exhausted? Utilities copy documents from one disk to another, make indexes and directories and keep track of what is going on, the subject of Section 8.7.

**Terms**

The most confusing aspect of dealing with this topic is the lack of good terminology and conventions. Vendors don't want to use anything except "page" to describe chunks of text. They seem to think that this keeps the WP closer to the typewriter than to the computer, which many operators seem to be afraid of. Most vendors do not provide a definition of the page, so you can never tell what a salesperson means when the term is used. It usually does *not* mean what the next vendor means!

Data processing has good terms which are used consistently, even though they may not correspond to what the WP vendors use. We define these terms below and later relate them to different vendor concepts for page.

A **track** is a circular area on the disk defined by the position of the head in the drive; it represents a *fixed* quantity for a vendor's disk system.

A **sector** is a *fixed* radial fraction of a track and applies within a specific track.

A **block** (for the disk) is a *fixed* quantity of text identical to the sector but numbered differently and referenced to a track.

A **block** (user defined) is defined in Section 8.5.

A **record** is the chunk of text moved in (and out) of memory from (or to) the disk and corresponds most closely to the *page* as used by the vendor.

The **work area** is the place in memory where editing takes place and text is assembled and dealt with.

The **file** is the text associated with a manual document—a collection of records; it may be a set of subdocuments.

## 8.1 MANUAL PAGE MANAGEMENT

For **manual page management**, reading and writing an electronic document is totally under the control of the operator. Data is brought in and out in records of about three or four thousand characters in the typical system. The operator decides when to read this chunk, usually called a page by the vendor; writing a record from internal memory to disk is also under the control of the operator. Typical manual page systems are those produced by Vydec, the 1200, 1400 and 1800.

For the rest of this section the term "record" designates a fixed size chunk of data, regardless of whether it prints as a single document page or as either more or less. Since the Vydec machine is typical of manual page machines, particulars are discussed with reference to it, although they may not apply to all manual page oriented machines.

## Approach

The manual page oriented machine leaves the organization and manipulation of text to the operator. This has the advantage of giving you the feeling that you are totally in control of data flow and manipulation. It gives the designer and the vendors the advantage of simplifying the software. Since the operator controls most file management activities, it is possible to reduce these software functions, if not to eliminate them entirely. Further, since only one record is in process in memory at any one time, the amount of memory needed to store text is substantially reduced. There was a need for economy in older machines before memory prices came down. With simpler software and less internal storage, hardware memory is kept small.

The disadvantage to this approach is that activities that other WP systems now handle automatically are left for the operator to take care of:

- assign text to disk tracks;
- keep a directory of these assignments;
- work with one page at a time even for a multipage document;
- move pages in and out of memory (to and from the disk) according to the earlier assignment;
- make specific requests to read and write each page;
- and so forth.

## The Vydec System

The original Vydec 1200 WP system was released in about 1975. The 1400 and 1800 provided improvements in capacity and technology. The overall concept and configuration shown in Figure 8.1.1 is the same for all of them. At the right is the operator's terminal containing the computer with the screen at the left and a control console at its right. At the left is the printer. Below the table holding the terminal are the disk drives.

The full page screen provides 64 lines, each of 96 characters. Depending on the model, one or two disk drives are supplied. Each accommodates an eight inch, soft sectored, floppy disk. After overhead allocation, there are 30 tracks left to store text.

Figure 8.1.1. Vydec configuration. (Courtesy of Exxon Office Systems).

*The Disk*

Even though this is a single sided disk, the user sees it as consisting of two sections of 30 "tracks." Each section is called a "side." Side A contains 30 tracks and side B contains 30 tracks. It is unimportant that a "track," is physically a half track.

*Reading and Writing*

The console is part of the terminal. The portion controlling disk activity is shown at the right of the screen in Figure 8.1.2. More detail is provided in Figure 8.1.3.

Figure 8.1.2. Operating the Vydec console. (Courtesy of Exxon Office Systems).

Buttons labeled "1" and "2" select one of the disks. To select one of the "sides," you press A or B; the window lights up to show whether A or B is being addressed. Below this is a track window showing a track number between 1 and 30. You advance this number by 1 by pressing the up-arrow button; decrease the track number by pressing down-arrow. Each disk is addressed separately.

To perform a disk function, use the bottom two buttons. To read a track into memory, overwriting the current memory contents, first move the cursor to

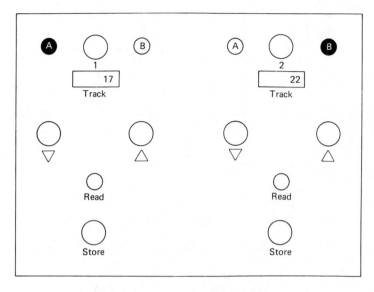

Figure 8.1.3. Detail of the disk function panel.

the home position at the upper left hand corner of the screen (1) as shown in Figure 8.1.4. Then press <u>read</u> and the indicated track is brought (2) into the work area (3) in memory to replace any existing contents (4).

Suppose that there is text in memory and the cursor is not in the home position. Text in memory (and on the screen) from the home position downward to the cursor is preserved. Text is read in from the track starting at the cursor position and continuing for the remainder of the screen. If the amount of text on the track exceeds the available space in the work area in memory (and on the screen), then the remaining text from the track is entered into the buffer provided for that purpose, called the **spill area** (5). Using this spill area is described later.

<u>Store</u> writes information from memory to the disk. All the information between the current cursor position and the end of the screen is written to the designated track of the disk drive for which <u>store</u> is pressed. If the track has data on it, store must be pressed twice. To store the entire screen page, the cursor is put at the home position in the upper left hand corner (press <u>home</u> first).

To store only the top portion of a page, move the cursor just past the last character to be stored. Press the <u>end-page</u> key and an *end page* code is entered into memory (and displayed). Then <u>home</u> the cursor and press <u>store</u> for the disk (twice if there is data on the track). Text between the top of the screen and *end page* mark goes to the selected disk and track.

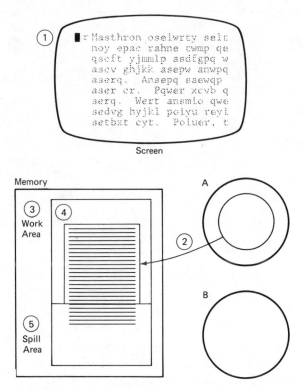

Figure 8.1.4. Reading a track into memory for Vydec.

## Creating a Document

When you turn on the power, the system initializes. File A shows in the display windows for both disks and the file windows read 01. You usually keep the file index on track 01. Remember, everything is managed manually. To know what is on each disk, bring the index from track 1 to the screen.

When you start, estimate how many tracks you need for this document and find a free group of (preferably continuously numbered) tracks for the new document. As you store a page, the "file number" (track) is automatically increased by 1. You don't really have to keep track of pages if you have chosen a consecutive set of tracks. For instance, suppose that you find tracks 5 through 8 free when you get the index. Type into the index page that tracks 5 through 8 are assigned to "WP report" (or whatever). Store the index back on track 1 and you are ready to start. Then set the file number to 5.

Set up tabs, margins and format functions. Start typing to fill up the page. Proofread and edit on the screen. When it is satisfactory, store it onto the disk at the assigned track, print it or both. For Vydec you may print a page at a time from the same memory buffer you edit. Press <u>roll</u> and continue entering the next page on the blank screen; edit it and <u>store</u>.

Be sure to advance the file number to the next track allocated when using nonconsecutive tracks. When that track number appears in the window, <u>store</u> the document from memory onto the disk track. The text remains on the screen—press <u>roll</u> and the stored text is cleared from both memory and the screen.

### Editing an Existing Document

Editing an existing document which entails neither growth nor contraction is easy. Bring in a page at a time, alter it and return it to the track from whence it came. The procedure becomes a little more complicated when:

1. You insert text onto a page so that it grows beyond the length of a single page and overflows into the next page.
2. You delete so much text from one page that there is a large hole which requires text from the next page to fill this one up.

*A Growing Page*

You have a page where much additional text will go. Move the cursor there. Estimate the number of additional lines to add. Press <u>line-enter</u> and the WP puts blank lines into the text at the cursor position (enough to fill up the screen, if need be). As you add blank lines, the text following moves down the screen. Some of it may be pushed off the bottom of the screen into the spill area. Don't worry! This buffer holds overflow text and is of comparable size to the main area.

Enter the new text. As you do, it moves into the blank lines on the screen (and goes into the work area in memory). If you stop typing in the middle of a line, you should reorganize the text: press <u>adjust</u> to move text from the next lower line into the incomplete line. This realigns the entire paragraph.

Text overflow beyond your present vertical position may exist at the bottom of the screen and even be (invisibly) in the spill area. When you see enough text on the screen to make up your page, move the cursor to where you want the page to end. Enter a *page end* mark by pressing <u>page-end</u>. <u>Home</u> the cursor.

To store the page, select the track and disk number, if you have not already done so. Hit <u>store</u> once (or twice, if there is old material on that track). The system stores all the text in memory up to *page end* onto the track.

To remove the stored text from the screen, press <u>rollup</u>. All the text up to the *page end* mark disappears. The text below this mark (and from <u>spill</u>) moves up to the top of the screen.

A special case arises when your insert is at the bottom on an existing page. As before, you enter a few empty lines and push down the text into the spill area.

But you hit line-enter only for enough empty lines to fill up the screen page, even though the insert may be larger. Now fill the empty lines with the new text, hit a page-end and store the page. Press rollup to bring up the bottom of the page from spill.

There is still more text to insert. Add additional blank lines at the top of the screen for the insertion with line-enter. Type in the rest of the insertion and continue from there.

### Partial Page

When you are done, you may be left with a partial page. If this is the last page of the manuscript, it can be put away. For a leftover chunk of text in the middle of the manuscript it is necessary to bring in more text from the next page of the electronic document. Press rollup to bring in the leftover text. Then be sure to move the cursor to the bottom of the text. This is where you add the material from the next disk page. The last store operation has advanced the file counter to the next page. Be sure to check that you are bringing in the proper page. Then press read.

Text from the specified track is placed at the cursor on the screen. The text fills the screen (and the work area); if there is more text left over, it goes to the spill area.

Continue editing as described. Write out pages as you compose them. Text left at the bottom of the screen and/or in the spill area is brought to the top of the screen with roll as memory is flushed of stored text.

### Text Contraction

Suppose you delete considerable material from a page. What you have left is a **partial page**. There is no text in spill. It may not seem enough to store and it is not the end of the document. (Automatic pagination clears that up on the Vydec 1800.) You want more text to fill up this page. Set the cursor to the end of the text on the screen. Set the file number to the next track to bring in the next page. The text goes into the work area and the screen starting at the cursor position. Extra material goes into spill.

Edit the page on the screen, setting *end page* for the page length you wish. Then store the page onto the previous track. Roll the remaining material out of the screen and up from the spill area.

Alternate

A short page in the middle of an electronic document *is* acceptable and you can put it on its own track. But you don't want your *printed* document to have a short page! Several procedures make up pages of about equal size (except the last).

1. Use a pagination run (Section 9.3) to make up the final page format. (There is one for the Vydec 1800 but not the 1400 or 1200).
2. Take care of hyphenation and pagination at the same time, that is, reorganize the document with a combined run.
3. Use the print formatter program to collect text into pages of a length you prescribe.

## 8.2 AUTOMATIC PAGE MANAGEMENT

### Introduction

For this method your electronic document is also divided into sections, usually called pages by the vendor, which we go along with here. You may have to help divide your document. However, you are relieved of two requirements of the previous system:

- The system allocates tracks or areas of some other size to each page.
- The system manages the index for you; it keeps track of each document and the pages which belong to it.

*The Page*

To maintain a parallelism with the written document, the vendor calls this unit of information the page. This is equivalent to the record defined in Chapter 5. However, this scheme is usable even for CRTs, which have screens which display less than a page (perhaps 24 lines). Hence a page of text is usually several screens of text.

For instance, the page for the CPT 8000 is a maximum of 8,000 characters long. Even though a full page screen is provided, this amounts to more than can be displayed at one time there. Frequently the "page" of the electronic document you create and edit may produce several pages of printed document. A larger electronic document may require several (vendor) pages (records) and many more screenfuls.

*Index*

There is considerable variation in the unit of text kept by different WP systems. At the very minimum the automatic system allocates records (calling them pages) and determines which tracks and blocks are assigned to each. The user has no concern about which areas on the disk are associated with pages of the document. All systems keep track of the number and position of pages allocated to a document. Some WPs (CPT 8000) allow you to name each page so that you can reference it directly by this name if you have some idea of its contents when you begin to edit a particular document and can call it up directly.

*Page Management*

There are two approaches to managing disk space.

1. Pages are a fixed size. Allocations are made by the full page regardless of how much text goes on each.
2. Pages are of variable size. They are put together from fixed size blocks. As many of these blocks are allocated to a page as are needed to store the page text. Hence, the number of blocks allocated to a page changes as the text assigned to the page is edited.

Both these methods are described below.

### Fixed Page Size

The Micom 2000 is an example of a WP system which provides automatic fixed page size management. Its CRT displays 31 lines of text, each a maximum of 80 characters. Three status and control lines at the top leave 28 lines for text. The internal work area provides for about 7,500 characters; this quantity of text is called a "page." It corresponds roughly to one track of the disk, about 94 lines of text. The rest of this section applies to the Micom 2000.

*Creating Documents*

You may set the format as you start to edit. However, for some WPs you can turn on the system and start typing, using the default format. As you key in, the cursor follows along the line and wraps around the screen. Text scrolls when the cursor reaches the screen bottom. You can type continuously through three screens of information. Then you will get a warning as you approach the last line of the work area.

At this point, or perhaps earlier, you should store the page. When you get the page end prompt, press open; name a document using up to 12 characters; press return. All the text in working storage, a page, is sent to the track assigned *by the system.* Now continue typing until you have enough for the second page. Again, you can decide when you have enough or you can wait for a prompt. To put the page away, you press open and then return. The system knows that this is the next page of the same document.

To review text (on previous pages), simply hit previous and the last page that you entered is put on the screen. Text in the work area is automatically stored on the page assigned to it. When you finish creating the document, put it all away by pressing stop.

*Revision*

To revise a file, press recall. You get a prompt asking for the file name. You start editing from the first page or a page number you choose. The page is brought into memory and the first part is presented on the screen. You can scroll forward and backward through the page with scroll (but not past page boundaries). At any time you may add or delete text with simple edit commands. When you are finished with the screen page, return it to the disk page it came from by pressing update. You can continue to review pages of the text, calling for the next page with update, then editing, updating and returning pages to their places in the file with recall.

To facilitate editing, it is wise to keep pages to 50 lines or so. During revision, these pages can then expand to the maximum size of 94 if need be. For further expansion you must revert to a different procedure.

*Expanding Pages*

To revise and expand a file, start as before. Since you know that your file is expanding, you may use a second file as the destination for the revised copy. In this way you also have a backup copy. Begin with the first page and edit it. Then open a new file by pressing open and provide another name for the second file. When you press return, the revised page goes to the new file.

Suppose that the second page is expanding. Get this page with recall. As you insert new copy, the entry point reaches the bottom of an optimum size page; issue open again. The second page, which is in memory, goes to the new file. But you are not finished entering the insert. You continue to add material to whatever remains in the buffer. When you have another page, press open again and this third page goes to the new file.

You proceed thus with your revision. As you need new pages from the old file, press recall; when you have assembled a new page in memory, press open. When you are finished with both files, press stop and you are done. If you choose, you may now delete the original file and release the disk space being left with only the revised version.

*One File*

You can do the job with a single file that you update. While editing and placing an insert on page 3, suppose that it overflows. That is, while editing you get a prompt warning you that you are near the end of the memory page. Place the cursor to divide the memory page into two parts: the top part is written out; the bottom you keep to work on further.

You get this result by hitting open space space. You then get a prompt asking if you want to store the top (a for above the cursor) or bottom (b for below). Type a return; text up to the cursor is stored back onto page 3. Continue the insert. When finished, the text in memory and on the screen belongs between pages 3 and 4 on the disk.

To store the page, press open 3 for the page number *after which* it goes. The text editor notes that there is no page which you *recalled* and did not then *open*. A prompt follows, asking for the page number after which to enter it; you reply after page 3 instead of over it. Micom lets you answer the prompt before it displays. The page stored is assigned the number 3.1 automatically.

**Variable Page Size**

Variable disk page size is the most popular text file organization. It is flexible and puts most of the burden of document organization on the WP system instead of the operator. This type of file is also broken up into pages, but each page may be a different size. Space for a page is allocated on the basis of its size and in multiples of fixed size blocks. Block size varies from one WP system to another but is fixed for a given WP. Common block sizes are 256 and 516 characters. You may put a small amount of text on a page; it occupies only one or two blocks. A page corresponding to a document page might use 10 to 20 blocks. You might have a page of 40 to 50 blocks. Remember, the page for an electronic document might be considerably larger than a printed page. The maximum size a page may be depends upon the particular WP system.

Although a number of blocks are allocated to each page, this number depends on the individual text size and varies from one page to the next. Space on the disk is used more efficiently with a variable than with a fixed allocation, since small pages require fewer blocks than larger ones. Wasted space is space left over in a *block* not a *page*.

*Philosophy*

Let us examine the philosophy of variable page size space allocation. This is the generalized philosphy; the details may not be accurate for any particular system.

When you create a document, you name it and the text editor is invoked to manage it. The text editor opens a file with that name. The file manager provides an initial allocation for the electronic document of, perhaps, a track. This is called the first **relative track** of the file. The text editor notes the assignment and also that none of the track has been used so far. He keeps an assignment directory for this file which logs the allocation of each block on every track of the file. It is returned with the file when that file is written onto the disk.

After you create the first page and are satisfied with it, you indicate this to the system and you request that the page be stored. The text editor examines the amount of text to store by measuring its length in the work area. He determines the minimum number of (fixed size) blocks that are required. He selects consecutive (if available) blocks from the assignment directory. He associates this page number with the relative block numbers in the order used and writes this in the assignment directory. Then he sends the text to the file manager, requesting that the text be stored sequentially into these relative block numbers. The final bookkeeping step notes in the free space directory that the relative blocks assigned to this page are no longer free. Only the remaining blocks on this track are free.

You create more pages of text. As each page is stored, it is handled as described. Eventually the blocks for the current track are used up. The text editor asks the file manager for another track; the file manager obliges, making note of the new track assigned to this file. The tracks allocated need not be consecutive on the disk.

Relative block numbering continues for the second and forthcoming tracks assigned to the file. The text editor assigns consecutive relative block numbers to consecutive pages which you put away. Then the text editor sends over the text along with the relative block assignments for the file manager to write on to the disk. The file manager converts these relative block numbers to physical track and block numbers for this file and passes this to the disk driver. (The driver converts them into track and sector numbers.)

When you finish the document, the text editor has two directories. The first shows the assignment of several relative blocks (in the file) to each page (of the document). The second indicates the remaining empty relative blocks of the file (free for future assignment). The text editor includes these directories with the file when it is closed. As the text editor closes the file, the file manager notes the physical tracks assigned to the file and their order, so that the text editor need not bother with this detail (of converting relative block numbers to physical track and block numbers).

## Revision

To revise a document you go through the call up procedure for your WP system, naming the document (and the page number if you wish to start somewhere in the middle). Suppose you wish to revise the document from the beginning. The text editor asks the file manager for the first relative track which contains the directories and the first page or so of text. This text is presented on your display where you can begin editing. As you ask for additional pages, they are brought in by the text editor. He looks in the table for the relative block numbers associated with each page and requests these of the file manager. As the file is presently organized, he simply asks for consecutive file blocks.

*Growth*

Suppose you get the third page on your screen and you decide to make a large insert. When you are finished with your revision, this page has grown by several hundred characters. This does not concern you. You tell the text editor to store this page.

The text editor examines his directory and finds that the current page length is greater than the previous page length by three blocks. No problem. The original blocks assigned to this page are recorded in that order. Three additional blocks are needed. The text editor examines the available space directory and selects the closest three blocks. These he removes from the available block directory and lists them in order in the assignment directory.

The text editor invokes the file manager and sends him all the text, indicating the relative blocks into which they are written, according to the new assignment. When a file is closed the assignment directory is *always* written back at the beginning of the file. It notes in sequence the relative track and block number of *every* block which makes up the ED. Even when huge inserts are made, the location of all blocks is properly recorded here.

*Shrinkage*

The other alternative is that your revision reduces the current page size. When you are done with your revision, you tell the text editor. He compares the current page length to the previous page length occupied on disk. Since the new page is shorter, several blocks are released. These blocks are removed from the assignment directory and noted, instead, in the available space directory. Then the text from memory and the shortened list of blocks into which it goes are sent over to the file manager, who writes the page into those blocks.

When block assignments are made for expanding pages, they are chosen so as to be close to the existing relative blocks. This means that there is less head movement required to get to blocks that are for the same page.

## CPT 8000

The CPT 8000 uses the variable page principle. Unlike some WPs, it provides a fixed typing line. The screen as shown in Figure 8.2.1 is divided into four parts:

1. At the top is the status line.
2. The upper screen comes next and contains most of the visible text for the current page.
3. A single ruler near the bottom of the screen shows margins and tab stops; above this is the line onto which the operator types.
4. The lowest part of the screen at the bottom is a preview area. Text here may be passed up to the typing line to be altered or past to the upper screen to be viewed in context.

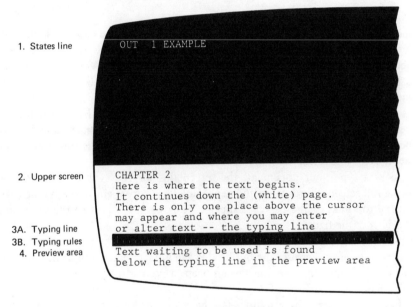

1. States line

OUT   1 EXAMPLE

2. Upper screen

CHAPTER 2
Here is where the text begins.
It continues down the (white) page.
There is only one place above the cursor
may appear and where you may enter

3A. Typing line      or alter text -- the typing line
3B. Typing rules
4. Preview area      Text waiting to be used is found
below the typing line in the preview area

Figure 8.2.1. The CPT display is divided into four parts.

The work area of 12,000 characters provided, as shown on the left of Figure 8.2.2, is divided into four parts. These partitions are movable. The area labeled B corresponds to the upper screen; C is for the lower screen. Above B is an area labeled A to store text which has been rolled off the top of the screen (which is not displayed). D in the figure holds text which has not been brought into the preview area as yet.

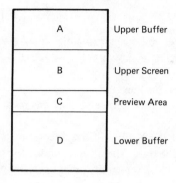

Figure 8.2.2. The CPT work area in memory has four parts.

*Creation*

Once you turn on the machine you can immediately start to create a document. You may set margins and tab stops by a simple procedure. The screen below the typing ruler is white and the screen above it is black. You move "paper" past the ruler and into the typing area by pressing advance. The "paper" appears white and moves into the upper screen just as a sheet of paper would pass by the platen in a typewriter. When the "paper" appears at the height for the desired top margin, you start typing. All typing must be done on the line directly above the ruler, the **typing line**. As you continue to type past the end of the line, the last word wraps and the "paper" moves up.

As you type your document, the screen fills up. You can continue typing with a full screen. Words wrap and new blank lines appear above the typing ruler and the top lines of the paper disappear. They go into a part of the work area labeled A in the figure.

When you have a full memory page, you may put it away. But you don't have to stay alert, because the buffer area can hold at least a couple of pages. If you should forget entirely, the system beeps at you when you get near the end of the work area.

For initial editing you can move text back and forth across the typing line, but all entry must be done on this typing line.

You press out when your page is complete. Remember, this page may be more than what appears on the screen; it includes text in upper overflow; the text editor writes out both A and B and leaves C and D. The system prompts you for a document name and a page name. The latter may be omitted.

Now the text editor takes over and assigns relative block positions to the page you have created. These are then sent to the file manager as described earlier.

There may be text left in the work area below the typing line in the preview area or invisible below that. This text, now in C and D, is combined. With roll you bring it up onto the upper screen and even out the top. Compose the next page and when you are done, press out. This is for the same document; you may ignore the prompt for the page name and simply press return.

When you are finished creating your document, press stop and the rest of the document is put away for you.

*Revision*

To revise a document you press in, enter the document name and press return. The text editor tells the file manager the document name. The file manager brings back the first relative track of the document which contains the directories. The text editor puts the directories aside, finds the first page and puts it into the preview area (and the invisible area D below). Now you press up to move text from the preview area onto the upper screen. To make a minor change, stop pressing up when the entry point appears on the typing line. Enter, delete or alter text on that line. Continue this through the first page.

If these changes do not alter materially the size of the page, then the text editor notes the relative blocks assigned to this page. When you press out, the page is returned to overwrite those same blocks.

Suppose you insert text so that the page grows. Perhaps part of it is moved past the upper screen into the work area marked A. Press out and the page is accepted by the text editor. He uses the previous block assignment, but may require additional blocks as explained earlier. He gets these from the "empty list." If there are not enough empty blocks available, he makes a new request of the file manager for the next track assignment. He obtains empty blocks from the new track, marks them according to their relative number and assigns them to this page. Then he sends the text to the file manager, together with the relative block assignments, and the page is stored on the disk.

## 8.3 AUTOMATIC DOCUMENT MANAGEMENT

**Principles**

**Automatic document management** means that the WP system maintains each document as a whole. The document need not be divided into pages. You see it as a continuous stream of text.

*What Does This Mean To You?*

You compose and edit the text as a continuous stream. While composing and editing your document, you don't ever *have* to think of where one page ends and the next one begins. You don't *have* to consider when to put away text and when to bring new text out. This is done automatically.

Remember that under automatic *page* management, some WP systems free you from watching for the end of a record. If you forgot to watch, the system beeps at you to tell you to give some thought to how much text should be put away in this record.

Some systems make it difficult to edit across record boundaries. That is, if you want to alter text that flows from one record to another, you cannot see simultaneously the end of one page and beginning of the next page (The Displaywriter, for example). Automatic page management brings together on the screen the bottom of one record and the top of a succeeding record.

With automatic *document* management you set up your document format and the system tells you where each **page break** (the temporary boundary between document pages) occurs for the format you have requested. But this page break can appear any place on your screen and you can move material from one side of the break to the other without any problem. If you want to reserve the page contents, even after later editing, you can insert a hard page break.

*Requirements*

To make this technique possible, the system must incorporate certain features. The first of these is random access file management. The second is a fairly small block size, so that movement of information back and forth between the computer and the disk is hardly noticed. The third is a more complex directory system for the management of blocks. The directory has to be large enough to keep track of all the blocks which compose the document and, preferably, to keep track of which blocks are associated with each record.

**Document Creation**

To start a document, merely turn on the system and provide a document name. After that, you can simply keep typing indefinitely until all the text is entered. You don't have to watch the screen nor use the return key, except at the end of a paragraph, since you have word wrap. It's like typing on an endless sheet of paper. You just keep entering text and the system moves out old text, replacing it with blank paper for you to continue typing on.

When you start a document, you may provide format parameters for page length, margins and so forth. If you omit them, default parameters are provided with standard page lengths, widths and margins. Whether the format parameters are implied or explicitly entered by you, they are the basis for the WP system to determine the beginning and end of each page (page breaks).

When you have entered enough text to fill a page, according to the applicable format, the WP system determines this and presents a marker, the page break, to tell you that you are starting a new (document) page. Often this marker is a dashed line which extends from left to right on the screen. As you continue to enter text, the text scrolls upward, taking the marker along with it. The top of the page moves up the screen.

*Scroll Backward*

At any time during text entry, if you wish to see previous text which has passed out the top of the screen, merely scroll backward. Press <u>down</u> and earlier text moves in at the top and down the screen, showing continuously the preceding pages with page breaks separating them.

There is an alternate method. Since your format statement (or the default) has established a page length and set up page breaks, pages are clearly marked within the document. You can direct the WP system to scroll backward to a preceding page by giving that page number. The WP system finds the corresponding page break and presents it at the top of the screen, together with the text which follows.

Once you have moved backward in the text you will naturally want to move forward again, if you are going to continue to add text or edit. You may do so with any of these actions:

1. scroll continuously forward,
2. page forward by page number,
3. go to the bottom (or top) of the document.

### Directories

Directories keep track of allocations and the available space. WP systems which provide automatic document management differ, from one to the next, with respect to how they manage and keep their directories. We discuss a typical system, although it may not be exactly like any existing system. We propose two directories:

1. The **space directory** keeps track of all blocks unassigned to pages but which have been assigned to this file.
2. The **allocation directory** keeps track of all blocks which contain text. It shows their order, which page they are assigned to and where they belong in the text.

As document creation starts, the text editor gets an initial allocation, probably a track, from the file manager. This track is doled out in blocks by the text editor to store segments of text. The text editor divides the empty track into blocks, gives each block a number, its position in the track, and places these numbers in the space directory. They are the relative block numbers.

*Example*

Let us examine a fictitious example. Assume a work area in memory which corresponds to about two screens of information. It is divided into a number of block size areas which I will call **slots,** each of which can hold one **segment,** as shown in Figure 8.3.1. This example work area uses ten segments, of which the screen can show up to five. As you start to enter text, the screen displays as many as five segments. The figure shows segments 1 and 2 in their slots and being displayed.

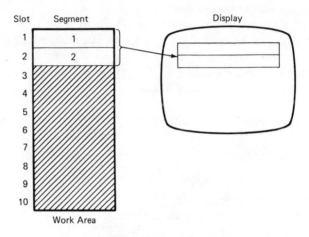

Figure 8.3.1. Start of creation and the display for partial text.

As the screen fills up, the text editor scrolls the text upward on the screen and shows the most recent five segments. Figure 8.3.2 shows how segment 6 is entered into slot 6 and is being displayed at the bottom of the screen as segment 1 scrolls off. In Figure 8.3.3, the screen displays segments 3 through 7 as you key in part of segment 8 into slot 8 and the bottom of the display.

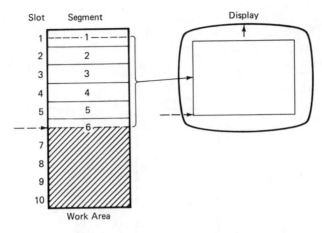

Figure 8.3.2. End of screen scroll begins.

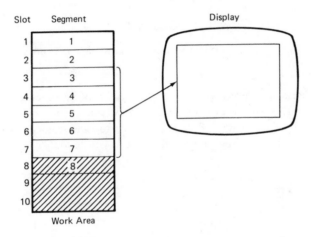

Figure 8.3.3. The work area is not full yet.

As you continue to enter text, the work area fills up; soon there is no room left there. As the tenth work area segment begins to fill in Figure 8.3.4, the text editor releases the first segment, sending it to the file manager to write out as the first block of the file. Slot 1 of the work area is now free to receive text.

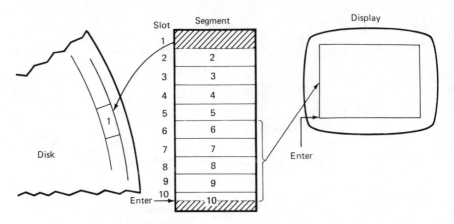

Figure 8.3.4. Part of the text is stored on disk to make room in the work area for what you key in next.

As you finish typing segment 10, new text you type becomes segment 11 and goes into slot 1, as shown in Figure 8.3.5. Now the screen displays part of segment 6 and all of segments 7, 8, 9 and 10 at its top and segment 11 from slot 1 at the bottom. In this way you see the text as continuous, when actually the

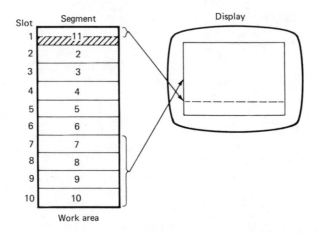

Figure 8.3.5. Memory wraparound displays text continuously.

text wraps around, both in memory and on the screen. This is **memory wrap-around**. Figure 8.3.6 shows text of segment 13 going into slot 3. Segments 1, 2 and 3 are safe on the disk. The screen shows part of segment 8, all of segments 9, 10, 11 and 12 from slots 9, 10, 1 and 2, and part of segment 13 from slot 3.

As you create more text, more segments are written into blocks until the track is filled. The text editor asks the file manager for another track and you continue thus.

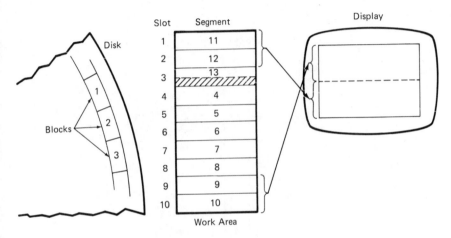

Figure 8.3.6. More text goes onto disk.

### Revision

The random access feature makes simple revision possible. Revision causes text to expand in some spots and contract in others. Expansion requires extra blocks to hold additional text. Free blocks are always available until the disk runs out of space. They are numbered according to their physical position in the file. But they need not be used in that sequence. Since this a random access file, it is easy to acquire or write blocks in any sequence. Thus the sequence in which the text is presented is smooth, although the sequence of the blocks from which the text is fetched is irregular.

When text is deleted, fewer blocks are necessary to store the text. A block which is freed no longer appears in the assignment list for any page. It is instead listed in the free block directory. In obtaining text for the work area, the file manager sequences from one block to another, ignoring the empty blocks in between.

*Diagram*

The action is more difficult to describe in words than to convey visually. Figure 8.3.7 shows a document to be revised, consisting of blocks on the disk represented by a set of squares filled with letters. Each number is the relative block number assigned to this segment of text. The numbers are consecutive from 1 to 13 because the document was created continuously. Blocks were assigned consecutively by the text editor.

Three numbered arrowheads convey three editing activitiess; I (1) is a large insert; D (2) is a deletion; I (3) is another large insert. The arrows point into the blocks where the activity will take place.

The following discussion is general and is not meant to describe the specifics of any one WP.

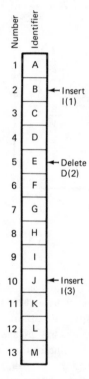

Figure 8.3.7. Blocks of an electronic document to be edited.

*First Insert*

You start editing, with your automatic document management word processing system, by first giving it the name of your document (and directing it to a library if you divide your documents that way). The document request is relayed via the text editor to the file manager. The file manager looks up the name of the document in the file directory, finds the physical track assignments for it and makes a request for the first physical track.

The first track of the file is brought in; it contains the allocation and space directories. The text editor fills up part of the work area by bringing in (eight) blocks in the order they are listed in the allocation directory. You make small changes which do not affect the size of the first segment. Figure 8.3.8 outlines the contents of the work area and the display.

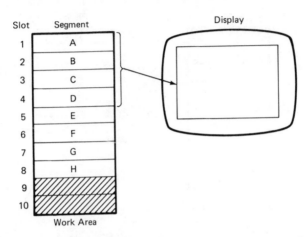

Figure 8.3.8. Part of the electronic document is brought into the work area.

You make an insertion in segment B which requires the space of two more slots. Since only two segments of space are required, the insertion is handled in working storage by the text editor. Now segment B becomes B1, B2 and B3 in slots 2, 3 and 4, as shown in Figure 8.3.9.

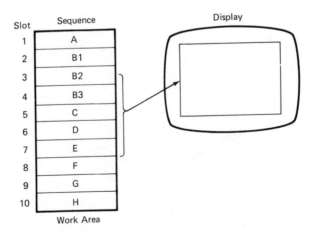

Figure 8.3.9. The first big insert is made.

*Delete Text*

Text deleted from block E (and its neighbors) releases a complete slot in the work area as shown in Figure 8.3.10.

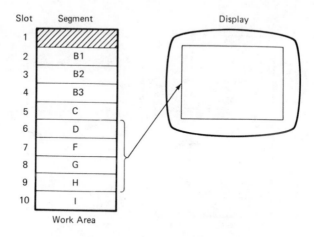

Figure 8.3.10. About a block is deleted.

*Scroll Ahead*

As you scroll ahead, there is no longer room in the work area. The top of the work area is not in view on the display and can be written back to the disk. It is put into blocks vacated earlier when text was first put into the work area. This is illustrated in Figure 8.3.11.

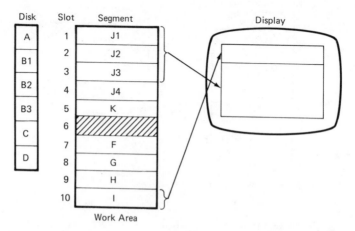

Figure 8.3.11. Some of the new text is put back on the disk as corrections proceed.

*A Second Insertion*

Figure 8.3.11 shows further material added during the editing of the segment J. Text added is enough to fill three additional slots. The expanded segments, J1, J2, J3 and J4, occupy slots 1 through 4. As you add text at the terminal, the text editor makes assignment for the disposessed segments, using vacated blocks on the disk.

*Completion*

As you finish editing, more segments are left over in slots than there are empty blocks assigned to the text on the disk. The text editor simply uses blocks listed in the space directory. When this is depleted, he asks the file manager for another track to continue assignments from. Figure 8.3.12 shows the disk assignments for the labeled blocks after the changes indicated in Figure 8.3.7 have been made.

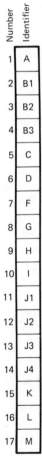

Figure 8.3.12. The disk stores the edited document.

**Summary**

The text editor, the random access file organization and the allocation and space directories make it possible for the text to appear to the operator as one continuous document. The process is easy to achieve when the document is created. Later, when extensive revisions take place, with large insertions and deletions, the task becomes more complex. The mechanisms built into the text editor and random access file manager programs make the activity transparent to the operator. The computer works so fast that the user is unaware of how complex the actions are.

## 8.4 SERIAL FILES

Serial files are not popular among word processor manufacturers. However, they are in considerable use in personal computers and large computing systems. The users of these computers generally have little need to print the documents at the same time that they edit. Serial file management has these advantages: it is simple to implement; its file manager requires very little space. This frees up considerable memory, if no background printing is taking place, so that much text is immediately on hand without access to the disk.

**Restriction**

The serial file described in Chapter 5 must be accessed from beginning to end without the capability to go back to review material. Further, a file that is used for reading cannot be written into; conversely, one which is being written cannot be read from.

As you create a file, you can edit and alter any material now in memory. But as you write the file out from memory to disk, the part which is written cannot be reviewed or altered until all writing is completed. As a consequence, to revise a file, two files are open:

1. The original file to be revised is read from.
2. The altered text is written out to a new file.

**Creation**

The ease with which creation and editing processes are performed depends upon the size of the document and the amount of memory provided in the word processor. Word processing software for personal computers is designed to work with fairly small memories of 32K ($32 \times 1{,}024$) or sometimes less. You can provide your computer with up to 64K and sometimes more. All the additional memory is available to hold text. With maximum memory (64K), you can expect to store internally text of up to 40K. Thirty thousand characters represent about ten single-spaced pages or twenty double-spaced pages. Any part of it is instantaneously accessible without any disk operations.

To create a document up to the maximum size of working storage, no file operations are necessary until you are done. The document is always in memory during its preparation and totally accessible. Upon completion of creation, simply tell the WP system that you are done and that the document is written onto the disk.

Revision of this small document is also done totally in memory, requiring only that the file manager bring it in and move it out.

### Larger Documents

When a document does not fit entirely in memory, it must then be handled piecemeal. Once the memory is full, it is necessary to remove some of the old text before new text can be brought in. There are several techniques to invoke file management:

- manual, when memory is full;
- manual, at your descretion;
- automatic, by the full memory;
- automatic, by piece.

#### *Manual by Full Memory*

When editing starts, part of your large document is brought into memory to fill it almost completely. If all available memory were used up initially, then there would be no room for even a small insertion. During editing you skip around rapidly within the text, backward and forward as you chose. However, when you reach the bottom of the text in memory, it seems to end. Any attempt to scroll further fails.

When you are done with your editing of this portion of text, issue a command to the text editor to being in more text. With this simplistic system, all the text in memory is written out to a second file and a new memoryfull from the electronic document is brought in from disk. Now you have a restriction: you cannot reach earlier edited text which has been stored away. This restriction is not hard to live with once you are familiar with it. You prepare all your editing and do it piece by piece. (A piece may be five or ten pages.) Also, if there are changes remaining after you have finished editing, you can take the new electronic document and edit it in the same manner.

*Manual by Discretion*

As editing begins, the text editor fills memory with text. Whenever you wish, you can bring in more material as long as you make room by storing some edited text. However, you can chose *how much* of the text will be written out and re-placed by new text. One scheme lets you place the cursor at a dividing point in the text. Then tell the text editor that you want to write out edited text up to the cursor and bring in more text. The text editor sends the edited text to the file manager to write at the beginning (or continuation) of the second file. The text editor calculates the size of the freed space and requests this new text be from the file manager. Note that:

a. The "written" text is now inaccessible.
b. The text seems to start at the position where the cursor was at the time command was given.
c. The text continues smoothly with the new text brought in.

Although some new text might precede old text in physical memory, the text editor keeps track of it, using memory wraparound, and presents it in the proper order. When you want more text, you continue in the same way. When you are done, any text in memory is written to the second file. Also (and importantly), if there is text unread (and consequently unedited), it is read into memory from the first file and written immediately to the second file (sight unseen).

*Automatic by Full Memory*

This scheme differs little from the first one. However, when you try to scroll past the end of the text in memory, the text editor automatically takes over. The text editor removes *all* the old text and writes it to the second file. The text editor then fills memory with text from the first file. Since the old text is then un-available, this scheme is less useful because you are prone to forget that scrolling will induce storing all of the preceding text. Overlap of a few lines from the old memoryfull provides context.

*Automatic By Piece*

As you start editing, the memory buffer is filled. This can be done a little at a time or all at once, depending on the system. As you scroll ahead, new text is read from the first file in *memory* until the buffer is almost full. Thereafter, some of the oldest text in memory is automatically written to the second file each time you scroll ahead, so that equivalent text can be brought in to replace it.

This goes to the bottom and appears on the screen immediately. Only one or two blocks are stored and replaced; most of the preceding text is still available. Thus you can edit continuously from one end of the document to the other, hardly being aware of any discontinuity. As you get into the latter part of the text, scrolling requires the text editor to both write a block from memory and read a block from the first file to replace it, and hence may take a little longer. This is the only noticeable difference.

The problem arises when you wish to return to an earlier portion of the text. Since scrolling and writing of the text to the disk are done in terms of blocks or block multiples, much of the preceding text is still in memory. At any point you may scroll backward to review your corrections. However, the size of the work area limits your review capability. You have available only what is in memory. The second file *cannot* be used to read. If you have a 30K work area, it stores the most recent 10 pages of text—a good quantity.

The activity is as smooth and imperceptible as is that for automatic document management. You can always move forward and backward within the text. The limitation and frustration is only apparent when you:

a. deal with a long document,
b. get near the end,
c. and realize that you forgot something in the beginning.

You can always finish up, close your files and start all over. This method is not found in office WPs, but some personal computer WPs such as Autoscribe$^{TM}$ have it.

### Summary

Serial file management allows you to edit both large and small documents. If that is what you have, you should buy as much memory as you can afford. For smaller documents it is the fastest way of moving about in the text. For larger documents it presents an obstacle, because earlier text becomes unavailable when you are editing the end of the document. This obstacle can be easily overcome if you are circumspect. Even if editing has left mistakes in the revised copy, you can reedit this copy as a separate operation.

### 8.5 BLOCKS

There are many times during the day when you come upon a chunk of text which you expect to be using extensively at some time later on. A chunk may be big or small; it may be for long term or short term use. In all cases, for this section, we call the chunk a block.

WPs provide different facilities according to the size and/or term of use. Short term small blocks are called phrases and are often kept in memory only while you edit one document. But some WPs keep these on disk too, so there is no hard and fast rule.

### Definition and Need

The **block** (as used now) is a chunk of text defined by you. It may be a sentence, a paragraph or simply a group of words. You define a block to ask the WP to take an action with it, such as:

- *Delete* removes the block from the text and destroys it.
- *Move* removes the block from its current position and puts it some place else in the text.
- *Save* makes an interim copy of the block for later use.
- *Copy* leaves the block where it is but makes one or more copies of it in other parts of the text as directed by you.
- *Write out* copies it onto the disk under a specified name.
- *Cancel* ignores the block and leaves the text intact.

**Block move** is by far the most powerful block feature. It gives you the "cut-and-paste" capability that is so important for extensive revision. Before the WP, the (human) editor would revise a document by cutting it into pieces. Some pieces would be thrown away; others would be pasted together in a different order, adding handwritten insertions to make up a new document. This document would then be retyped.

With the WP, only new material need be keyed in. The cut-and-paste operation is specified by the originator on the latest printout. Portions to be moved around or deleted are defined as blocks. The WP can reposition a block any place you want it. No retyping is necessary. After editing, a new printout employs all the advanced features, such as centering, justification and so forth that make for ease of reading.

*Action*

You perform the following actions when working with blocks:

1. Define the block.
2. Select an action.
3. Find the site of the action, if any.
4. Initiate the action.

### Define the Block

You mark both the beginning and end of the block. You move the cursor to one end of the string (for some WPs, either end). Then you press <u>mark-block</u> (or simply <u>mark</u>). This transmits a control code to the text editor, which sets a marker to note this end of the block. Now you move the cursor to the other end of the block and press the <u>mark</u>. The text editor points another marker at this end of the block. In Figure 8.5.1 the Block Beginning and Block End markers, **BB** and **BE**, mark the beginning and end of the block, respectively, in the work area. Other methods for marking areas as blocks were described in Section 6.4.

*Display*

The best way for the screen to display the designated block is to highlight it by dimming it or presenting it in reverse video. Other WPs place a symbol or graphic (such as a triangle) on either side of the block. WP on personal computers and text editors for mainframes may employ less frequently used symbols as __ or @.

### Choose the Action and Site

You tell the WP what to do with the block in one of several ways:

  a. There may be a key for each action, <u>move</u>, <u>copy</u>, etc..
  b. The WP presents a choice via a menu.
  c. A prompt requests you to choose by touching a key.

For *move* and *copy*, you specify a destination, a **site**, where the block will go. Select the site by moving the cursor there. Place the cursor on the character *before which* the block will go.

### Store The Block

If the marked block is to move about in the text or to disk, a copy is required. The block cannot simply "push aside" existing data. It is stored temporarily while the text in the work area is opened up to make room. Temporary storage is provided in one of two ways:

  • A separate area in memory called the **move buffer** is set aside for this purpose.
  • The block is written out to disk as a subdocument and then written back at the cursor.

*Choice*

The choice made by the WP designer between a memory buffer or a disk area depends on the file management method and the memory available. With automatic document management, small block size and random access, the use of disk is more common. NBI's WP puts all blocks on disk.

It makes little difference to you *how* the block is taken care of; what concerns you is the extent of your involvement. This may be identical for either case, as described below. For some WPs which use disk, you may need to name or identify the block.

## Move Backward

The most complicated block action is the *block move;* if you understand it, the other actions are easy. You may move the block *backward*—toward the beginning of the text—or *forward*—toward the end of the text. The backward move consists of several steps that differ from one WP to another. For one technique the text editor:

1. copies the block into a buffer;
2. moves the text between the cursor and the beginning of the block to make room;
3. inserts the block.

Here are the technical details, using an internal memory buffer.

*Copy the Block*

The text editor cannot simply move the block from one place to another without obliterating useful text. Instead, the text editor copies it into a **move buffer,** shown at the right of Figure 8.5.1. Markers point to the Beginning, Current position and End of the Move buffer area, labeled respectively **BM, CM** and **EM.** The text editor copies the block from the work area into this buffer. The length, M, of the block is the difference between the Beginning and End block markers, **BB** and **EB.** After copying the block, **CM** records the next free position in the buffer; this is the byte *after* the last character recorded.

*Make Room*

The text editor does less movement of text in the work area with the method illustrated in Figure 8.5.1. It shows four areas:

**A** between the cursor and the block that has to move;
**B** the block itself;
**C** after the block that stays put;
**D** before the cursor that does not move.

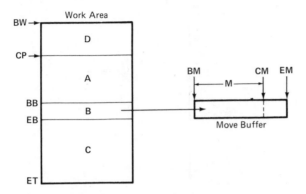

Figure 8.5.1. Parts of the work area in preparation for a block move.

Action consists of:

1. saving the block in the move buffer, Figure 8.8.1;
2. moving **A** forward M bytes to cover **B**, Figure 8.5.2;
3. putting the block now in the *move* buffer into the area vacated by **A**, Figure 8.5.3.

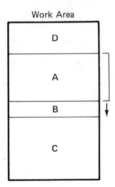

Figure 8.5.2. First move **A** down.

The result is shown in Figure 8.5.3. **C** and **D** do not change; **A** moves down over **B** to make room. **B**, the contents of the contents of the move buffer, overwrites the work area starting at **CP.**

## Move Forward

Figure 8.5.4 demonstrates how to move a block forward. Consider these four areas:

**B** the block (M bytes) to be moved (between **BB** and **EB**);
**A** the area between the end of the block and going on for M bytes beyond the cursor (between **EB** and **CP**);

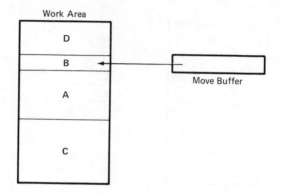

Figure 8.5.3. Then put the block in the vacated area.

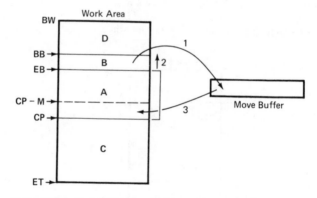

Figure 8.5.4. Redefining the work area for a forward block move.

**C** the area after M bytes past the cursor up to the end of the text (from **CP** to **ET**) which stays put;

**D** text from the top of the work up to **B**.

Moving the block consists of interchanging **A** and **B**. **B** was copied into the move buffer (1). The text editor copies **A** backward by M bytes over **B**. **A** then starts at **BB** (2). This leaves a "hole." (Memory always contains something—this is an old copy of part of **A**). This "hole" is M bytes into which the text editor moves the block from the *move* buffer. The last area **C** is not affected. The result appears as Figure 8.5.5. Note that the hole lies between **CP-M** and **CP.**

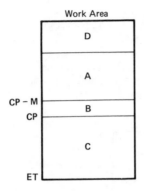

Figure 8.5.5. After the block move.

## Large Block

Consider a block, called **B** in Figure 8.5.6, that is larger than the move buffer. It consists of three parts, **B1, B2** and **B3**, where both **B1** and **B2** are F bytes, the size of the *move* buffer, but **B3** may be smaller. Parts **D** and **C** remain fixed. The movable part is **A** with a lower boundary **M** bytes past the cursor position, **CP**.

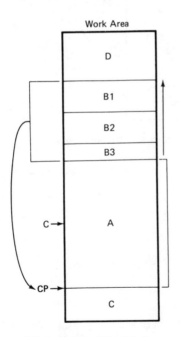

Figure 8.5.6. Before a large block move.

But the text editor cannot put the whole block into the memory move buffer. (A disk buffer is not limited in this way.) It does the next best thing; it moves the block by filling and emptying the move buffer three times. Start by filling the buffer with F bytes of text from **B1**, beginning at **BB**, where F is the buffer size.

Three moves are needed; the first is shown in Figure 8.5.7. **E1** consists of the rest of **B** that was not saved, **B2** and **B3** and **A**. This is moved up by F bytes to make room for **B1** just above **C**.

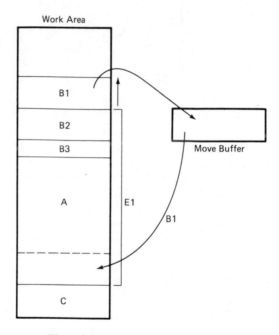

Figure 8.5.7. The first chunk is moved.

Now the situation is shown in Figure 8.5.8. Save **B2** in the buffer and move **E2** backward to make room for **B2**.

Finally, all that is left is **B3**, in Figure 8.5.9. Save it; move **E3** up; place **B3** in the space.

**Other Actions**

Several other block actions could be chosen.

*Copy*

To copy a block, a duplicate of the block is put into the *move buffer*. The original block is left in the text in the work area. Move the cursor to where you want to make a copy. Hit copy. The text editor inserts the text from the move buffer at the cursor. The block is still in the *move* buffer and now appears twice in

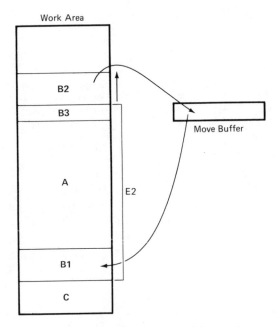

Figure 8.5.8. The second chunk is moved.

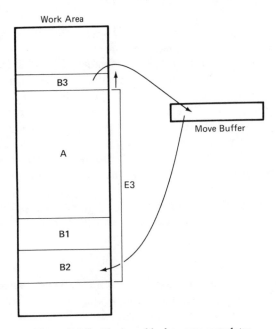

Figure 8.5.9. The large block moves completes.

the work area. It may be copied as many times as you want, provided there is space in the work area.

Instead of being entered into the work area, the text copied into the move buffer is written onto disk as a new electronic document or as an addition to an existing ED. You may eliminate the original block after you make the disk copy.

After you mark a block, you may remove it from the text. The text editor closes up the text by moving backward all the text which follows the deleted block to overwrite it. Since it takes little extra effort, some WPs move the block into the buffer before it is eliminated. Since the block is saved, you can always restore the deleted block ("undo" as Syntrex calls it), as long as no other block action intervenes.

## Multiple Blocks

Some WPs provide memory space for a number of small blocks. You can stash many phrases which recur throughout the document. You enter phrases as you encounter them. The text editor puts them away in a memory buffer, using a name you supply. When you want to put a stored phrase into the text, request it by name and it is placed at the current cursor position.

One mechanism for **phrase storage** is a number of fixed size **phrase buffers**. Another technique provides a single buffer with a number of markers to distinguish where one phrase ends and the next one begins immediately.

To see the advantage of the phrase buffer (or register), consider 10 phrase registers of 100 characters each and one phrase buffer of 1000 characters with markers for 10 phrases. For multiple registers, no phrase can exceed 100 characters; for the phrase buffer, the space left over from a number of small phrases can be used for larger phrases, so long as the total does not exceed 1000 characters.

A phrase buffer in *memory* is not different in principle to the user from phrase storage on disk (explained in Section 8.6.); only the implementation is different.

Here is a typical sequence for using phrase storage. While creating a document, you notice a recurring phrase. Instead of keying the first occurrence into the text, request phrase storage by hitting phrase-store. Designate a name by typing

P3, for instance. Now key in the phrase, which appears on the screen as you do. It is not yet part of the text. For instance, the cursor may jump to the bottom of the screen with a message "Enter P3:". While keying in the phrase, a back-space correction lets you fix mistakes. When done, hit <u>enter</u> and the phrase is stored.

Whenever this phrase is needed in the text, hit <u>phrase-recall</u>, followed by "P3"; then <u>return</u>. The text editor recovers the phrase from the phrase register; enters it at the cursor and displays it on the screen. You can insert a phrase any place in the text, just like a block move.

*Keeping Track*

Which phrase is at P3? You might remember. Or you might make a list. Some WPs provide a **show phrase** function by which you may call up P3 before using it. The TE gets the text and presents it at the bottom of the screen. Alternatively, the WP might put P3 into the text with the option to cancel without the trouble of marking and deleting a block.

## 8.6 COMBINING ELECTRONIC DOCUMENTS

**Inclusion**

Suppose you want to edit an ED called X. At specific points in X, you wish to incorporate paragraphs or pieces called Y1, Y2, etc., from a disk as shown in Figure 8.6.1. You have the names of these subdocuments. Install the disk which contains them. What is the process by which you get the text editor to include the subdocuments?

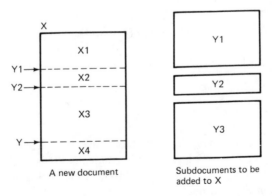

A new document          Subdocuments to be
                        added to X

Figure 8.6.1. A document and subdocuments to be appended.

1. Bring to the screen the portion of the text, X, where the first insertion goes.
2. Move the cursor to the character just before which the subdocument should be inserted.
3. Tell the text editor that you want to *append*.
4. The text editor may issue a prompt asking you for the document name.
5. Enter the name of the subdocument.
6. You may see part of the text of the subdocument for verification (see below for more details).
7. Accept (or reject) the displayed subdocument.
8. The subdocument text is inserted into the working area.
9. The screen is updated to display the old document up to the cursor and the subdocument thereafter.

What the text editor does to process your request depends on whether the file manager accesses the file serially or directly.

### Subdocument Capability

WPs handle subdocuments in different ways. Most of them have some facility for appending part or all of a subdocument. Some can pass variable values into the subdocument (examined in Chapter 11). However, the ESD capability varies considerably. Here are some of the variations starting from the simplest. You may:

1. Choose the subdocument and it is inserted *without* you seeing it first.
2. Choose, examine and accept (or reject) a subdocument.
3. Choose and view a document and then accept or reject sections, as each section is presented on the screen.
4. Select a section without seeing it.
5. Select a section, view and accept (or reject).

In all cases which follow, you name the subdocument and the WP system finds it for you.

*Choose only*

After you name a document, it is inserted in the text wherever the cursor sits. Only then do you get to look at the subdocument. Using normal editing commands you can delete part or all of it. Now you may delete the undesired portions as shown in Figure 8.6.2.

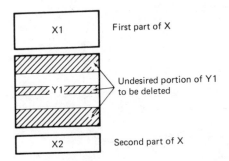

Figure 8.6.2. After a document is appended undesired material may be deleted.

*Examine*

After naming the document the WP displays it. There are then two alternatives again:

1. The WP replaces the present display with the subdocument.
2. With a split screen the WP can show you part of the document you are editing on one side of the screen and part of the subdocument which you chose to append on the other side of the screen. In some cases, such as Syntrex, you can move text from one side of the split screen to the other. We say more about the split screen in Chapter 9.

After seeing the beginning of the subdocument, you usually know enough about it to determine if you want it or not and can accept or reject it. In Figure 8.6.3 we see the split screen employed to help you append. In the top panel you have requested Y1; the text editor has acquired it and displays it at the bottom of the split screen. You see it as five parts, only two of which you need. You want B and D; A, C and D are to be discarded.

Select the block B by marking it as a block; move the cursor to its beginning and hit <u>mark</u>; then mark the end. Now move the cursor to the top half of the screen to the end of X1 and request a *block move*. Y1B moves from the bottom of split screen to the top and is pushed in between X1 and X2 as shown in the middle panel.

Now mark D and move it similarly as presented in the third panel.

*Sections*

Some WPs let you break a subdocument into sections as it is recorded on disk. You can group a number of phrases or paragraphs into one subdocument. Then

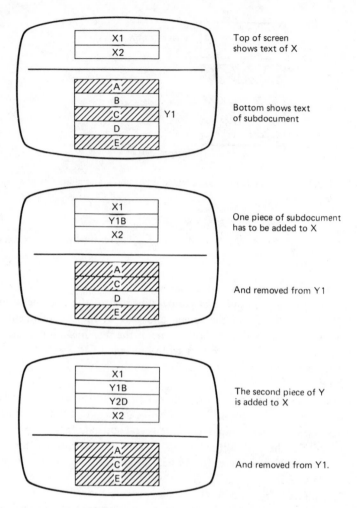

Figure 8.6.3. The split screen can help in editing a subdocument as you append it.

you can call up any section or paragraph from disk to add to the text you are editing.

The alternatives for selection and review mentioned above apply to sections. For one system you may choose a subdocument and section which is brought in without viewing it. Another vendor's WP not only lets you select a section but also presents it on the screen for you to decide if that's really the section you want.

The way you bring in a subdocument depends largely upon the file management function provided in the WP system. The three kinds of file managers are examined separately:

- manual by page,
- serial,
- automatic by page (random files).

### Manual by Page

In this approach, the disk is just one mass of text divided into tracks, each about equivalent to a single-spaced page or slightly more. You can think of the track as:

- a subdocument,
- a form letter (see Chapter 10),
- several subdocuments.

Let's see how to use a track for storing and accessing a number of frequently used paragraphs as would be useful in preparing a legal document. Use as an example the Vydec 1200 or 1400. Suppose your contract is on tracks 16 through 19 and the subdocuments are on tracks 23 and 24 as paragraphs. You want to take paragraph number 6 from track 23 and put it on the page which is now on track 17:

1. Bring in all inserts on track 23.
2. Delete all but paragraph 6.
3. Count its number of lines, say 5.
4. Put it alone on an empty track, say track 30.
5. Bring in the text from track 17.
6. Find the insertion point with the cursor.
7. Insert enough lines for the new paragraph.
8. Read that paragraph from track 30.

These steps are easy to perform as you assemble a document from several subdocuments. You add or **append** each section at the *end* of the page. When the addition is too large to put on the page, then it overflows into the lower buffer. That buffer can hold a full page; none of the text is lost.

However, you may have more than a full page in the combination of the screen and the buffer. Put away the page on track 17 and then take out the overflow text. Move it up from the buffer with <u>roll</u> (for the Vydec). Move the cursor to the end of the page. Then get the next page from track 18. It goes after the text on the screen. Any excess goes into the buffer. Compose this page and put it back on track 18. Handle any excess in the same way.

## Serial Files

Serial files are broken up onto records. The break is determined by the file management system. Often this break is the carriage return which separates paragraphs from each other.

Assume that you are now going to look at material from the subdocument, either to accept or reject it. The text editor needs some place to put this material—another buffer. Call this the append buffer. Figure 8.6.4 shows an append buffer called AB with three markers: **AB** marks the beginning of the append buffer; **AC** marks the current end of the subdocument; **AE** marks the end of the buffer as supplied in memory.

Let us now see what happens as you append a subdocument.

1. Position the cursor to the place where the subdocument should go.
2. Hit <u>append</u> or use a control sequence.
3. The text editor receives a control code indicating that you want to append a document.
4. The text editor issues a prompt asking for the subdocument name.
5. You key in the name and hit <u>return.</u>

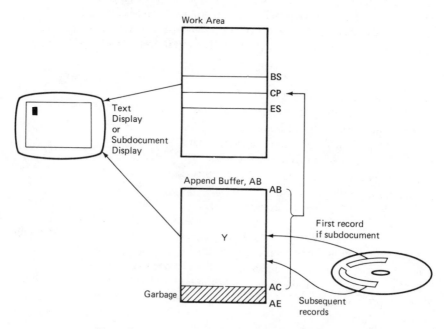

Figure 8.6.4. Appending with serial file management.

6. The text editor looks for the document on the disk. If it is not found, you get a message and you have to start all over again.
7. When the text editor locates the document, it requests the file manager to fill the append buffer with as much of the subdocument as it will hold.
8. The file manager brings the text, shown in Figure 8.6.4 as Y, into the append buffer, leaving some garbage in the bottom if the document doesn't completely fill the buffer.
9. The text editor now displays the document on the screen. For the full screen technique the markers **SE** and **SB** keep track of the beginning and end of the screen display in the work area. The text editor transmits this part of the append buffer to the display.
10. If you have this option in your WP system, you are given a choice to accept or reject the subdocument by pressing a prompt key.
11. If you reject the subdocument, you may have to start all over again.
12. In either case, some WPs allow you to continue to select records from the subdocument to append in your text.

*Insertion*

If you elect to append the subdocument, the text editor takes over. **CP** points to the place where the subdocument goes. The record in the buffer is moved into the text, as described in Section 8.5.

After appending, the WP system generally returns to edit mode to edit the subdocument as part of your text.

If you want another record from this subdocument, some WPs allow you to request it. The subdocument file is already open and if the record lies ahead of this one, the file manager can sequence through the file to find it. If the subdocument you want next is earlier in the file, the file must be closed and reopened, since that portion of the file is no longer accessible to the serial file manager.

## Random Files

The random file is composed of a number of records, each fairly small. Insertion of more than one or two sentences into one record may cause many other records in the file to change. Hence, we expect restructuring of the file to take place when a subdocument is incorporated. A subdocument of several pages may require considerable accounting, all transparent and rapid to the user.

## Creating Subdocuments

Where does the subdocument come from? There are four general sources. It is:

- an existing document,
- the product of a block write from another document,
- a phrase written to disk,
- a special document for this purpose.

*An Original Document*

Any electronic document created or edited as described in Chapter 6 is eligible as a subdocument. This provides the mechanism to assemble a large report or text. Different operators may create and edit original documents. Then each of these is pasted together by starting with the first and appending each subsequent document onto it.

An ED may contain an important paragraph or section. As you create a new document you may recall that a paragraph you need is in something else that you created. Use that document as a subdocument. Find the place in the new document where you would like the paragraph. Put the cursor there. Then request the document with that paragraph. "Thumb through" the second document visually to find the desired paragraph. Append that area. When done, delete extraneous material, if any, to leave just the paragraph that you want. This action is made easier with a split screen.

If your **WP** permits you to have more than one file open for editing, you have another alternative:

1. Open the file containing the old document.
2. Scroll through it to find the excerpt.
3. Block the excerpt.
4. Save it on disk as a named subdocument.
5. Close the old file.
6. Return to the new document.
7. Move the cursor to where the excerpt should go.
8. Insert the subdocument.
9. The excerpt is available for future use with less fuss.

*Block Write*

When creating a document, you may decide that a paragraph or section that you are writing will be useful in the future. Treat this block of text as described in Section 8.5. Mark it and request a *block write*. Furnish a name for the block. The text editor writes the block onto disk. If you want to remove it from the text, you can do a *block delete*. The named and written block is now available on the disk to be incorporated into another document.

*Write A Phrase*

This action is like the *block write* just described and yet it is different. When you request *phrase write*, the text editor prompts you to name and write the phrase. It is stored on the disk under that name but not in the text. You can use the phrase by calling it by name into the text. You can put it into the text you are making right now. As long as you don't destroy the phrase, it remains on the disk and can be requested for any future document.

*Special Construction*

When you construct a subdocument which consists of several records, this is the technique you use. The way that the records are named and separated within the document depends upon the particular word processor you are using. This technique is used in creating form letters discussed at length in Chapter 10.

## 8.7 DIRECTORIES AND UTILITIES

Directories should give you lots of information about existing documents. Utilities allow you to move electronic documents around in various ways.

### Directories

A WP directory is a list of electronic documents on a disk mounted on one of the drives. The file manager also needs a directory of files in machine readable form. We have seen in Chapters 4 and 5 how the file manager keeps track of documents, brings forth old ones and stores newly created ones. The file manager serves the text editor, the print formatter and the overall word processing system. The file directory is used by the file manager to look up the file name and find its physical location on the disk. Then the file manager, through the disk driver, activates the disk and gets part or all of the file.

The document directory is available to the WP user. It lists all the documents on a given disk and gives information about them. Here is a list, in no particular order, of what you *might* find in a typical document directory:

1. Name: the name which the creator assigned to the document and which is usually different from the title of the document; a short name may be preferable to a long title.
2. Description: a written description of the document, which can be anything from a couple of words to a paragraph.
3. Size: the approximate number of characters, lines and/or pages which make up the ED and is usually determined and entered by the WP system.
4. Author: name, initials or other identification of the document originator.
5. Operator: identifications for who keyed in the ED.
6. Creation date: the date when you first started to create the document even if you didn't get it finished then.

7. Revision number: in some WPs the number of times the document was revised or altered is recorded.
8. Revision date of the latest copy of the document.
9. Protection status.

The system keeps the directory up to date: when you delete an old file or create a new one, its description is dropped from or added to the directory.

*Organization*

When you ask to see this directory, it can be presented to you in different ways, such as:

1. alphabetically by document name,
2. by creation date,
3. by revision date,
4. in the order in which they appear on the disk.

Perhaps the most useful is alphabetical order. This allows you to look up the name of the document and find its description and other particulars. However, if you don't remember the name of the document, perhaps it would be better to have a list in order of revision date. Then the most recently used documents appear at the beginning of the list. You're probably looking for one that you used fairly recently, and you may be able to get its name from the description you provided. It is easier for the WP system to keep track of the documents by creation date.

For manual page management (such as the Vydec 1400), *you* create and maintain the directory. If you are negligent and forget to enter a document name, it is likely that the electronic document will get lost. It is a good policy to indicate your track allocations *before* you create a document; you can always release tracks that you have assigned but have not used.

*Directory Maintenance*

Most WPs have a directory maintenance program. When you are done creating or editing a document, the file manager is notified when the file is closed and it updates the file directory. Then the directory maintenance program is passed the relevant information about the ED to create a new entry for the new document and put it into the directory. For an existing file, the revision date and number changes. After updating the document directory, the maintenance program returns it to the disk.

The directory is kept in one of the organizations described above. It may also have the extent, track and block number information which you don't see. Each vendor chooses whether the WP keeps separate or integrated directories. Some WP systems allow you a choice of several organizations for display. If the directory is kept by revision date, for instance, then the maintenance program will sort the directory for alphabetical presentation, on request. Most WP systems are more restrictive however and just provide a single directory format.

## Protection

Document protection is important if not essential. The small stand alone system with a single user may make do without it; but a shared logic WP is vulnerable on several counts unless good system protection is provided to deal with:

**privacy**: Some users cannot permit their products to be exposed to the eyes of others.

**negligence**: The careless or inexperienced operator can inadvertently destroy EDs.

**dishonesty**: The willful user could gain access to important information for profit or self gain.

*Levels*

Your WP *might* provide security at any or all of five levels of protection:

**open**  No protection; you are free to alter or destroy any ED at this level.

**write**  You may not alter this version of the document but you can read it, print it or make a copy of it.

**copy**  You can look at the ED but you cannot copy it.

**read**  The ED is listed in the directory but you cannot look at it.

**list**  The ED is not listed in the directory; you cannot find its name unless you have authority.

**Encryption** uses a secret code to record text. Then, even if a villain breaks through the protection system, the text still looks like garbage. This additional security is mandatory when WP is used in highly classified governmental work.

*Enforcement*

The system can prevent unauthorized access in several ways:

**work station**  In a shared system, document availability can be limited according to the work station which is accessing the hard disk.

**log on** The operator keys in an identification which defines what documents are available and under what restrictions.

**password** A document (or directory) is available only if the user supplies the right password. There may be passwords for each level or for just one.

The last system is easiest to implement and most universal. It works on stand alone systems.

### Utilities

Utilities are programs which manipulate files, disks and subdocuments.

#### Disk Copy

A simple but important utility makes an exact copy of a disk for you. A disk may have a number of important documents. You can put them away for safe keeping by copying them onto another disk, which is then called an **archive**.

#### Copy File

There are may times when you might copy a single electronic document. For instance, you may have a report to which you expect to add a number of pages. The disk it is on doesn't have much room for expansion. Copy it onto a fresh disk. You can now add considerable material without any worry.

You may have a disk with several documents containing frequently used paragraphs, salutations, phrases and other subdocuments. These might be useful to other people. Why not make a copy of one or more of these files, put them on another disk and give them to a coworker?

#### Destroy a File

Some offices keep documents indefinitely; they are less bulky on floppy disks than on paper. However, some intermediate documents are like scrap paper; throw them away or destroy them to free up room on a disk.

For instance, when making a large report, several people may create portions of it. When these portions are assembled into the first draft of the report, the electronic subdocuments may be disposed of. Further, as other revisions of the report are created, the old ones may be destroyed.

#### Format a Disk

When you've filled up one disk and you want to store more electronic documents on another disk, you cannot simply take a new disk from the supplier and use it immediately. Most WP systems require that the disk be formatted. The format utility does many things. First, it checks out the disk to see if all of it can be written on and read back successfully. Some WP systems need part or all of the operating system on every disk; this utility may write them there. Next, a file directory is created for the file manager. A document directory is then set up for your use (if the two are not the same). Finally, programs which have to be immediately available, such as the text editor and text formatter, may be written on the disk if you have a single disk drive system.

*Directory Printout*

It is nice to have a printed directory to keep with each disk. Then you don't have to go to the trouble of putting the disk into the drive and reading the directory on the screen to check what's on the disk. You know immediately if the document you want is there by checking the printed directory. Naturally, you must have an up-to-date printout.

Good practice demands that every time you alter a disk, you should print out a new copy of the directory to put in its envelope.

*Rename*

Sometimes you want to keep several different versions of a document. When you edit one version, you want to give the second version another name. There are other instances when the name for an existing file ought to be changed.

*Sort*

A sort utility is really a data processing function (see Chapter 12). Some WP systems provide a sort. It can be useful when you deal with lists of your clients and creditors and many mail lists. The sort utility arranges these lists:

- alphabetically by name,
- by zip code number,
- by a utility code which classifies them.

For instance, this utility code can be used to separate vendors according to the product that they sell—hardware, stationary, soft goods, etc.

**Overall Document Directory**

A complete document directory shows which document is on which disk. With a hard disk and centralized EDs, it is easy to keep such a list automatically. No one has come up with an automatic method to do this for a large collection of floppy disks. It seems like quite a feat.

# 9
# More Edit Features

## 9.1 HYPHENS AND HARD SPACES

We are all acquainted with the hyphen, a small dash that connects two words or parts of words. Actually the hyphen has two separate and distinct uses:

- It makes a compound word out of two separate words.
- It associates two parts of a single word which are physically separated.

The most common occurrence of the hyphen is when a word begins at the end of one line but does not fit totally on that line. You break the word properly into two parts: the first part stays on the line with a hyphen added; the rest of the word starts the next line. The problem is breaking up that word properly. The rules for breaking up the word are complex and there are many exceptions.

### WP Assistance

The word processing system gives you assistance at various levels for finding the right place to break a word. At one extreme it does the whole job of hyphenation for you. At the other extreme it lets you do the job yourself in whatever way you wish, assisting only in suppressing the printing of soft hyphens when they would appear within the line.

Most WPs provide at least two kinds of hyphens:

- The **hard hyphen**, once in your text cannot be removed by the text editor unless you ask it to and will always print, regardless of the position of the word on the line. But the word may be divided when the hyphen properly goes at the right margin.
- The **soft hyphen** is always omitted by the text editor except when the word occurs at the end of the line and is split into two parts.

The need and provision for a third kind, the "very hard" hyphen is examined shortly. The WP system provides three levels of assistance:

**310**

1. None.
2. **System assisted hyphenation,** where you work together with the WP system to find out the best hyphenation.
3. **Automatic hyphenation,** where the WP system does it all.

Some systems provide all three alternatives; you choose which level you want. In all systems, compound words (like father-in-law) are totally under your control and you must enter hyphens for them manually.

## Manual Hyphenation

**Manual hyphenation** means that you determine where the hyphens go and you key them in. There are two reasons why you might employ manual hyphenation:

1. You are hyphenating a compound word.
2. The word processor does not provide any hyphenation assistance.

*No Assistance*

This sounds like a dire alternative. Why doesn't the WP system do the work for you? Well actually it's hardly necessary. Let us consider both unjustified and justified text.

For unjustified text, paragraphs have lines of different lengths. When a large word is wrapped, this leaves a particularly short line. Since a high percentage of words are short, this eventuality arises only infrequently. Simply hyphenate as explained below.

For justified text, all lines print out to the same length. However, when a large word is wrapped, there are fewer characters in that particular line. The result, depending upon the justification method, is either larger spaces between words of more space between characters. The effect of providing no hyphenation at all depends entirely on the width of the page or the column which is being entered. As a rule of thumb we have:

- For narrow columns of 30 or so character positions, the lack of hyphenation is marked.
- For the average correspondence and report width of 60 to 80 positions, the effect is noticeable but not distressing.
- For very wide pages, 80 columns or more, the effect is hardly detectable.

*The Action*

When a word has been wrapped because it is too long, you can observe this on the screen. You will usually need to hyphenate only if there is a large blank at the end of the previous line. You find the wrapped word at the beginning of the next line and decide how to split it. You insert a soft hyphen before the first character which should appear on the lower line. The soft hyphen is insurance against future editing. If editing causes this hyphenated word to move to the middle of some line, the soft hyphen does not print but the hard hyphen will.

For most WPs, the line that you alter remains displayed on the screen after the change. When you move the cursor away from that line, the text editor is alterted and reorganizes that portion of the text. Some WPs leave the altered text and reformat the screen only on command.

An example of the first action is shown in Figure 9.1.1. At the top, the word "typewriter" has been wrapped, leaving a large space on the previous line. In Figure 9.1.1b you split the word by inserting a soft hyphen to get "type-writer." Move the cursor to the "w"; hit <u>insert</u> then <u>soft-hyphen</u>. The lines remain displayed thus until the cursor is moved. At that point "type-" is removed from the lower line and placed in the upper line, as shown in Figure 9.1.1c.

```
Because most of the space on the line is used up,
typewriter ▉
```
a. during entry

```
Because most of the space on the line is used up,
type-▉riter
```
b. you hyphenate

```
Because most of the space on the line is used up, type-
writer is wrapped for you.  You enter a soft hyphen and
the first part of the split word is moved back later
```
c. the first half is unwrapped

Figure 9.1.1. Manual hyphenation.

## Compound Words

Some large words are made up of small words pasted together with hyphens in between each. Here are some examples:

mother-in-law
well-trained
ex-president
ten-year-old boy

Personally I prefer to use as few hyphens as possible. This is a matter of taste. Others feel that when in doubt, hyphenate. In any case, the WP must make some provision for hard hyphens. The standard hyphen key usually produces a hard hyphen. The hyphen always appears regardless of where the compound word appears on the page.

What does the WP do when it finds a hyphen in a word eligible for word wrap? This depends on the WP. Most break the word at the hyphen. The hyphen remains on the upper line.

A problem occurs when a hyphenated string should not be wrapped. For instance, if a hyphen appears in a part number or other identifier, such as "ABC-123" it is preferable to wrap the entire string. (Not like what just happened!)

Some WPs even provide three kinds of hyphens:

- the soft hyphen disappears when the word occurs totally within a line;
- the hard hyphen always appears but allows for breaking the word and wrapping the second half;
- the **very hard hyphen** always appears *and* the word may *not* be wrapped.

As far as I know, no WP automatically finds compound words and sets up their hyphenation. This is mostly because it is a personal opinion which compound words should be hyphenated.

## Soft Hyphens

A soft hyphen conveys to the WP an acceptable way to break a long word during word wrap. If you had to insert soft hyphens in all words which might be hyphenated, it would make your entry job twice as lengthy. Usually, the only time that you enter a soft hyphen, is when you encounter a large word which has been wrapped that you would like to break up.

Why do you need a *soft* hyphen if you are going to break up the word? The reason is that subsequent editing might reposition this word. If the hyphen is hard and goes along with the word and the word appears in the middle of the line, you are stuck with a hyphen that should then be deleted. The soft hyphen is removed by the print formatter when printing the document, except when the word is split and partially wrapped.

When the soft hyphen appears at the end of a line, it is displayed. But what happens if the soft hyphenated word gets pushed inward along the line during editing?

How will you know it's there? Do you really need to know if it's there? WPs handle this in different ways:

1. Display the soft hyphen with a graphic or special nonprinting character.
2. Do not display it.
3. Do not display it but make it possible to view.

When soft hyphens are displayed, you always know where they are. The problem is that the display character adds a character position to the line. It really does not exist within the line. This makes it difficult to tab and align columns properly. But if they are not displayed, you don't know they are present. The third alternative lets you ask the WP to find the soft hyphens and display them momentarily or for as long as you want.

### Hot Zone

The **hot zone** is an area just to the left of the right margin where hyphenation might occur. It is very much like the bell zone on the typewriter. When *typing*, you need to be alert for when the margin is coming up because you do not have word wrap. Otherwise, you might type right up to the margin. In that case, you must use the margin release and then hyphenate properly.

Some few WPs work the same way. As you approach the right margin the WP notifies you at a specified distance (the hot zone) by beeping or otherwise getting your attention. A standard default distance, usually six positions, is furnished without request. Should you wish to change the hot zone width, making it larger or smaller, most WPs let you do so.

One form of computer aided hyphenation works during entry. As you approach the end of the line and enter the hot zone, the WP beeps at you. If you are just finishing a word in a WP with word wrap, you need pay no attention to the beep. The word after the one which ends in the hot zone will be wrapped properly and you can continue typing. Should you be typing a long word, you can slow down to decide where a hyphen should go. You enter a soft hyphen in this position and continue typing. The word is broken at the hyphen and wrapped.

### Hyphenation Scan Program

Reports, proposals and important letters may be revised several times before the final document is acceptable. Hyphenation which appears correct on creation may have to be adjusted several times during editing. An alternative is to omit hyphenation entirely until you seem to have a final document. At this time, you request a **hyphenation program** to review your text from the beginning.

A hyphenation program, such as that for the NBI 3000, has the same kind of hot zone as described above. It has a default value of 6, which you can change. As the program operates, you see the results on the screen. A word which straddles the hot zone causes the program to stop. The word is highlighted, the cursor appears on the questionable line at the beginning of the hot zone. You move the cursor to where you want the hyphen and hit <u>soft-hyphen</u>. A hyphen is inserted, the word is broken and the second part is wrapped to the next line. The scan program then continues, stopping for each word which extends over the margin.

Other hyphenation programs lead you to the targeted word which has been wrapped on the left of the lower line. You move the cursor along this word to the point where it may be broken—the first letter of the second half. Then press <u>accept</u> or the like. The hyphen is entered and the first half unwrapped as you watch.

The scan program cannot present its results all at once, because each hyphenation decision that you make affects subsequent text. Your decision may cause a word on one of the following lines to be pushed out of the hot zone or a new word to be pushed in.

*Reject*

Some words—proper names, part numbers, etc.—are not amenable to hyphenation. When the program turns one up, you reject hyphenation and accept the word unsplit on the lower line.

**Automatic Hyphenation**

Two kinds of automatic hyphenation are presently available:

- algorithmic,
- dictionary.

Some WPs, such as the CPT 8000, provide automatic hyphenation. When you start creating a document, you default to automatic hyphenation. You can turn it off, if you wish. There is a hot zone for the automatic hyphenation too. When your typing enters the hot zone, the hyphenation program is entered. If you start a new word within the zone by entering a space, the new word is wrapped. If you continue typing to the margin, the hyphenation program takes over. It breaks the word and hyphenates it for you. You are not informed; you continue typing with wraparound of the second half of the broken word. It's all automatic.

The hyphenation program works on a probability basis. It tries to find the syllables which comprise the word. It uses some of the features of the spelling program, described later in this chapter, to distinguish prefixes and suffixes. Words can usually be broken where a prefix or suffix is distinguished (an exception is the word "pregnant").

Another hyphenation technique depends on letter combinations. Certain combinations of vowels or consonants or both signal the existence or nonexistence of syllables within a word.

*Accuracy*

The accuracy of algorithm hyphenation programs can be as high as 90 percent. This leaves you with 10 percent of the hyphenations incorrect. What do you do about them? Whatever hyphenation has been supplied automatically can be overridden by you. To check these decisions, you review the text, examining only the right hand margin. Check wherever a hyphen appears. If you see that the hyphen is improperly placed, you can change its position with normal editing. These are soft hyphens. Delete an incorrect hyphen and insert a soft hyphen elsewhere if you choose. The line is adjusted by the WP system. If subsequent lines are disrupted, the WP alters their hyphenation, dropping the soft hyphens where need be and closing up the word.

*Dictionary*

An alternative to the algorithm is an extensive dictionary containing the break between each pair of syllables for each word. Only a few words—the ones which are in the hot zone—need be looked up on each page. As the ED is scanned, each hot zone word is picked up. An index or directory will expedite lookup in the dictionary resident on disk. It is easy to find the optimum break in this word to provide an attractive line. This method may gain popularity as hard disks become more economical.

**Hard Spaces**

Some words and phrases should be kept together. When these phrases occur at the end of the line or get pushed there during editing, you do not want them to get wrapped. You decide if it is preferable to have a hole in the line rather than to separate the words. To make this clear, some examples are in order:

> January 23, 1950
> Mr. Hacker
> Part Number DEF 456.

It is preferable *not* to separate any part of the date. Similarly, it is undesirable to separate a person from his or her title. Finally, a part number consisting of a number of alphabetic characters, whether separated by a space or a hyphen, should be preserved as a unit.

Each WP has its own way to show a **hard space**, which guarantees that the two words it separates are on the same line. A hard-space key (or key sequence) enters it. The hard space may show as a unique character on the display.

For instance, CPT calls this the "code-space" because you hold down code and depress space. The text editor accepts the control code generated and enters a control code in the work area instead of a blank. You see a hard space on the screen as a dot above the line instead of a blank.

Should you enter a regular space instead of a hard space in the text, this is easily corrected. You will get word wrap during editing which, hopefully, you will notice. You replace the soft space by a hard space by simply overtyping code-space.

## 9.2 SPELLING

Spelling programs are relatively new in the word processing field. IBM provides such a program with its Displaywriter. Deliveries of this unit are in progress at this writing, so it is not yet possible to gauge users' response to this feature. Spelling programs have been around for several years to run on large computers with text processors; spelling software for personal computers is now emerging.

In a technical book there is much jargon. A spelling program flags jargon as well as misspelled words. You can copy these words to a supplementary dictionary. Then when you use it later, the spelling program can recognize words which you have previously checked.

### Need

I see a pressing need for a spelling program for three situations:

1. The intelligent and capable executive may be a poor speller. Fear of the terminal may also include the worry that the document produced may have misspelled words in it. If we can convince the executive that the spelling checker finds and corrects almost all these errors, this may be reassuring.
2. Many secretarial employees are poorly trained because of weaknesses in the educational system. Some graduates come out without much confidence in their ability to spell (or with confidence in their inability to spell). Still others truly lack this ability and try to spell all words as they sound. Most offices do not supply spelling training for their new employees who come from the employment pool in that geographical area. A good spelling checker program can supplement the typist's knowledge to provide documents with few, if any, mistakes. This improves the typist's sense of

self worth. It also lightens the load of the manager, who does not have to send back material constantly for correction.

3. Many of us who spell well are either poor or careless typists (or both). Besides, you can type much faster if you ignore your errors. If there is a spelling program to point out errors (due to any cause), typing goes much faster. The motivation for the first spelling program was to detect keyboard errors made by programmers.

I have used MicroSpell for checking most of this manuscript. At one time my terminal produced double character codes due to contact bounce in the keyboard. It was hard to catch all these errors manually, but hopefully MicroSpell found all the ones which I did not.

### Overview

The spelling program reviews the text. It pulls out each word and checks it. A word is defined by the program as a number of characters surrounded on each end by a blank or punctuation. A hyphen separates simple words in a compound word; thus it ends (or begins) a simple word for which spelling is to be checked. This may cause problems when a hyphen appears at the end of a line to break up one word into two parts. Hence, if there is a separate hyphenation routine, it is usually better to check spelling first.

One technique for checking words is to use an extensive dictionary. Except for large computers with large memories, the text and the dictionary cannot be in computer memory at the same time. A choice must be made about which is kept on disk and which is put in memory, the text or the dictionary.

*Errors*

The spelling program can make three kinds of errors:

1. accept a misspelled word,
2. reject a correctly spelled word,
3. accept a correctly spelled word which is not properly used.

The first kind of error is deadly. The whole purpose of this program is to come up with misspelled words. The second item is acceptable as long as the user can override the misspelled word and accept it. (Since Microspell automatically changes "teh" to "the," it constantly corrected one of my backspace correction examples.) It is standard practice for a spelling program to reject a specialized word. The question about what to do with this misspelling is tackled later. Finally, accepting an improperly used but correctly spelled word is something that we must all live with. The words "to," "too" and "two" are homophones. They sound alike and can easily be interchanged by someone typing from dictation. A secretary's intelligence in proof reading cannot be replaced by the computer without a long and expensive program.

**Design Choices**

The spelling program designer makes a number of choices about how the program works and what options to present to the user.

*Interactive*

All spelling programs are interactive in the sense that the user makes the final choice for spelling words flagged by the program. It might be a better to call some **real time** programs. This pinpoints when a choice is provided to the operator. We have:

1. The entire text is processed as a batch. When an error is encountered, it is flagged but *not* presented. The text is played back only after it is completely reviewed. All misspelled words appear highlighted on the screen for the operator to review.
2. For the real time program, as the spelling program reviews the text and finds a bad word, it is sent to you. You make a decision about this word and the program continues.

Both methods are described subsequently, when I examine the IBM Displaywriter and the MicroSpell program for personal computers.

*Replacement Suggestions*

When the program finds a word, it may have suggestions for alternative spelling. In other words, it is a *spelling corrector.* It is your final choice: you pick one of the suggestions, keep the old spelling or reject all the program's suggestions and supply a new one.

*Supplementary Dictionary*

If the program flags a word which is unfamiliar to it but is correct (perhaps it's jargon), there are two remedies:

1. Ask the program to put it in an immediately available **local dictionary** containing all unfamiliar words so far encountered. Should this word appear

in the remainder of the text, the program will not flag it, because you have told it not to. This temporary expedient lasts for the duration of this scan of the text. The new words are gone.

2. On request, the program makes a copy of this word in a **supplementary dictionary**. This dictionary can be used on subsequent runs of the program against the same or different text to supplement its own dictionary so that these new words will not be flagged.

The two methods are often combined. In this way, a specialized word does not get flagged if it occurs again during the present run, nor will it be flagged in subsequent runs against other text, when the supplementary dictionary is provided.

### Existing Spelling Programs

There are several different existing spelling programs for large computer systems and their text editors. One example is DEC-10; another is UNIX TYPO. Several programs are being marketed for microcomputers. If you use a word processor program on your personal computer, such as Word Master, Magic Wand or Electric Pencil, then you now have the ability to check the text produced by it. Three such programs are Microspell and Spell Guard and SpellStar for WordStar.

### Approach

There are many approaches to spelling programs. A few of these are considered below.

#### Total Dictionary

A dictionary containing all the words which anyone might be expected to use is prepared by the program designer. Such a dictionary might have 40,000 to 50,000 words. This approach is used in spell programs which run on large computers and have lots of disk space and internal memory to spare. The program contains some technique for moving around within the dictionary and looking words up quickly.

#### Multilevel Dictionary

An analysis of many typical documents shows the following breakdown:

- 200 common words comprise 50 percent of the words used in most documents.
- 1,000 to 5,000 words specific to a particular class of documents make up 45 percent of the words in the document.

- 20,000 words make up the remaining 5 percent of those which might be used in the typical document.

Thus, if only dictionary lookup is used, a better approach uses three levels:

1. The first level comparison is very fast, because each word is checked against only 200 common words which can be stored within the program. This eliminates 50 percent of the text.
2. Next, each unaccounted-for word is looked up at the second level in a dictionary compiled for this particular office or discipline within the office. The size of the dictionary depends on the extent of jargon found in the environment. Checking is slower, since each text word is looked up in a dictionary of 1000 to 2000 words. This still leaves a few words in the text unaccounted for.
3. The remaining 5 percent of the text words may be either judged by the operator or looked up in a larger (and much slower to access) dictionary.

*Digram Analysis*

A **digram** is a pair of adjacent letters; a **trigram** is a triplet of adjacent letters. Information theorists have done research and examined most words in the English language to find the frequency of occurrence of all possible digrams and trigrams among all these words. Tables of these frequencies can be incorporated in a spelling program. Each word that the program encounters is broken up into pairs and triplets of letters. Each pair and triplet is used to enter the digram and trigram table. If several infrequent and improbable combinations are encountered in a single word, the word is flagged. This is the approach used by TYPO.

*Affix Analysis*

A **prefix** is a set of letters with a specific meaning which is frequently added at the beginning of many roots; a **suffix** is a combination of letters often found as the ending of a word. An **affix** is either a prefix or a suffix. There are relatively few affixes in the English language. The same word may contain one (or more) prefix and/or suffix.

All the common affixes can be combined into one (or two) table(s) and used to analyze every word encountered. Prefixes are stripped from the beginning of a word and suffixes stripped from its end. The result is the pure root. A dictionary which holds only roots is considerably smaller than one that records all words.

The rules for stripping affixes may be complicated. For instance, a word that ends in "ies" can be stripped of this suffix as long as we remember to add the "y" to replace it.

Here are some examples of how compound words are analyzed:

wanted = want + ed    present = pre + sent

wants = want + s    applies = apply - y + ies

misappropriation = mis + a + p + pro + priate - e + ion

One problem is that a root and an affix associated in the text may not be properly placed together. Here are two examples of words which are improperly composed:

prefane = pre + fane    disfound = dis + found

**Displaywriter**

After you have edited a document on the Displaywriter, you may verify the spelling by pressing the spell key. The system then closes your document file. A menu appears and the system automatically sequences to the spelling task. If the system disk is available, the spelling program is automatically loaded into memory. Then you get a prompt asking for the document name. You supply the name and the spelling program asks the system to find it.

Now the program and a dictionary are obtained from the system disk and put in memory. The document is found and scanned. It is brought into memory a page at a time. Each word on the page is checked against the dictionary. Any word which does not check is flagged. Then the page is rewritten into its file on the disk. Each page takes several seconds to check.

When the entire document has been checked, the task selection menu is displayed again with the typing task highlighted showing the "revised document" subtask. If you simply press enter, the system defaults to the document just checked. You acknowledge the default and the first page appears on the screen.

Any word which the program found questionable appears highlighted on the screen. Some of them are correctly spelled words which are not in the dictionary; others are actually mistakes. (When demonstrated, both "IBM" and "Displaywriter" were highlighted.) You press find/spell and the cursor goes to the first highlighted word. Once there, you may change the word, if you agree that it is incorrectly spelled. Whether you change it or not, press cancel next. This removes the highlight. You must repeat this sequence for every highlighted word on the page.

Once the page has been checked and all the *highlights* cancelled, you can sequence to the next page and repeat the operation until the whole document has been reviewed. Thereafter, you can feel reasonably secure that all the words are spelled correctly.

There may be many words that your office uses that are not in the vendor's dictionary. You can prepare a list of up to 500 of these words and place them into a supplementary dictionary. (It's not done automatically for you.) You have several of these dictionaries. When you run the spelling program, you may request one or more of these dictionaries and they will be loaded along with the standard dictionary. The total word count of the combined supplementary dictionaries used on any run may not exceed 500.

## Microspell

This system consists of a spelling program, a dictionary divided into four parts (each small enough to fit into memory with the program) and a number of utilities. To run this program, you request the operating system to load it, along with the first dictionary, and give it control. The program brings in a block of text and scans through it, looking up each word in the dictionary. Words which are accepted after affix analysis are presented on the screen on the fly. They are split into affixes and a root for you to verify.

When a word is found by the program which does not check, it is displayed along with a number of words on each side to provide context, and processing stops. You may interact with the program immediately. There are a number of action choices, some of which are:

1. Accept the (so-called misspelled) word.
2. Accept the word *and* insert this spelling into the local dictionary in memory. Any future occurrences in *this* document will not be flagged.
3. Accept one of the guesses provided: one or more numbered alternatives are presented; you type the number of the desired alternative.
4. You reject the current word spelling and all the suggestions made by the program. Then you receive a prompt, to which you reply by keying a *new* spelling for the targeted word. (If you make a mistake *now*, it persists.)
5. Request that the word be placed into a supplementary dictionary which the program creates for you. This alternative also requires that you make one of the other choices.

Action then continues with the program stopping at each unfamiliar spelling that it detects. When the scan is complete, the program stops and replaces the first dictionary with a second. It now starts a new scan from the beginning of the document. There are four dictionaries, one for each of four portions of the alphabet. When the last of the four scans is complete, the program signs off, leaving two files: one has the text with the flagged words replaced as you requested; the other contains the original text without corrections.

A third file, the supplementary dictionary, may be useful in the future when you run the program against the next document you create. Each run produces a new dictionary. A utility can merge them so that you have only one supplementary dictionary which keeps growing. The size of the supplementary dictionary that you may specify for a run is limited only by the amount of memory that your hardware has. Another utility makes a single dictionary out of the reference dictionary and the supplementary dictionary. This is sorted so that access is faster.

Scan of 10 double spaced pages takes about a minute. This does not include interaction time. Each questionable word requires a few seconds of your time while the computer waits.

## 9.3 PAGING AND PAGINATION

**Introduction**

**Pagination** is breaking up the text into units, each of which will print as a page. **Paging** is putting a page number onto a page. The document you create may be part of a larger document. Hence the page numbering may not begin from 1.

Several considerations for page make up are:

a. the size of the electronic document;
b. who separates the document into pages;
c. when the document is separated into pages;
d. the kind of file manager provided.

*Size of the Document*

If you are writing a one page letter, pagination is hardly a consideration. The format of the page, the margins and how the text is placed on it are of course of importance.

We consider pagination for multipage documents. A document may consist of subdocuments. For a moderate sized document of a few pages, say ten or so, it is usual to assemble the entire document before pagination takes place. However, for a book, chapters begin with new pages, so pagination of each chapter is likely to be done separately. You might consider each chapter to be a document. Now you can direct that paging of this document begins from 36, perhaps.

*Who*

**Manual pagination** means that *you* do the page make up. **Automatic pagination** means that the computer does all the page make up without your assistance. For

**computer aided pagination** you and the computer work together to set up a good page organization.

There are three points in time when pagination might be done:

- during editing, perhaps not when you create the document, but when you edit it for the last time;
- as a separate pagination run between editing and printing;
- during printing, if pagination is totally automatic.

The alternatives that you have depend on the WP system and its file organization. For the Vydec 1200 and 1400, file management is manual by page; you must do the pagination yourself. The Vydec 1800 also has manual page management but provides a separate automatic pagination program. If the system provides automatic text handling, either by page or by document, you may expect all or some of the pagination to be done by the system.

WP systems borrow these terms from typography. A **widow** is the first line of a new paragraph which prints as the last line of a page. An **orphan** is the last line of a paragraph which prints as the first line on a page. WP systems with automatic pagination will often find and remove widows and orphans, either on a separate run or as part of the pagination run. They move the widow ahead or add a line from the previous page to keep the "orphan" company. Perhaps these situations are annoying to perfectionists, but I don't find them particularly disconcerting. I would rather leave them than sacrifice useful space on a page.

What I find annoying is when a section title, such as those used in this very book, is separated from the section which it describes. I don't like to see a section title on one page and the text belonging to it on the next. It is hard to instruct the pagination program to distinguish an isolated title from an isolated line. Moreover, how should a pagination routine handle a list of items, each of which is a partial line ending with a return? Should it break up such a list in the middle or carry all of it over to the next page? Most WPs leave the list as is.

**Manual Pagination**

With manual pagination and a manual file management system you are in complete control. That's another way of saying that you don't get any help from the system. You may prepare your document in any way you choose while you edit it. When you are ready for final pagination, you start from the beginning of the document.

For a system such as the Vydec 1200 or 1400, it's a good idea to have your document on one disk and prepare your final output on a second disk (or half of a disk). As you paginate, you may also reformat the document. Creating and initial editing may thus use single spacing to cram more of the document into each page and to require less disk activity while your edit. You can change this to double spacing as you paginate.

To prepare each page of your final document, bring in a page from the original document. Reformat it and choose exactly what will be on this page. Push unused material down into the spill area. When you are done, put a page number at the top. This page can be printed out immediately from the screen, as a final draft copy for Vydec. It is also transferred to the other disk as the first page of your new document.

To prepare the second page, bring up any text in spill to the main screen and continue to edit it as described in Chapter 8.

**Automatic Pagination**

For automatic pagination the system does it all. Just set it and forget it. Create your document in any format that you choose. Edit it often or not at all. When you are done you have an electronic document on disk. To print it out, call up the main menu and select the print function. This may include pagination or it may be done on a separate run.

Most systems now provide you with a format menu. Regardless of the format under which you created and edited the document, you may now change the format parameters for printing. These static parameters (page length; top, bottom, and side margins; line spacing and so forth) are set up by this menu and remain constant throughout the printing process. The dynamic or short term parameters which you edited into your document, such as indentation and paragraph indent, remain as initially set. This is efficient for standard documents. Defaults for the standards may appear on the menu.

Once you have set the format information, print activity begins and continues under the control of the print formatter program without any intervention from you, except to enter paper or change print wheels as per instructions sent to the screen. You may get widows or orphans if your WP does not remove them on this run; you will get uniform, neatly printed sheets of paper.

Most text and simple letters yield to automatic pagination. Some automatic pagination programs will even take care of widows and orphans if you desire. The program inserts page numbers at the top or bottom as you indicate. Paging begins with whatever number you enter.

## Combination

Many WP systems allow for a separate pagination run before printing. It presents each page to you to review its makeup and alter it if you choose. Most systems provide two kinds of **page breaks**, indication of where the page ends:

1. The **soft page break** is set by the WP to show where it has calculated that the page should end.
2. A **hard page break** can be entered by you to indicate where the text for this page *must* end; afterward, the system advances to a new page. It overrides the soft page break.

During the pagination run you may set the overall format parameters to the values they should have during printing. For the interactive run, the text appears on the screen exactly as it will print for the full page responsive display.

For partial page displays, a page occupies two or three screens. A symbol, such as a horizontal dashed line, appears to tell you where one page ends and the next begins. As you review the text, you will notice the soft page breaks at various points in the text.

There are several reasons why you might want to alter the soft page break.

A. You notice a widow or orphan.
B. The text contains a diagram or figure created on your word processor by using horizontal and vertical lines and labels. If it is split between two pages, it will not be readable.
C. You have left space on the page because a diagram, chart or picture will be pasted into this space; if the space is at the end of the page, it may be broken up.

If you are dissatisfied with the current page makeup, you can delete the current page break and insert either a hard or soft page break in a new position in the text. The latitude that you have depends on the word processing system. All permit you to move the page break back up the page so that you have fewer lines on the page. Some permit you to lower the page break so that there are more lines on this particular page. Others will not lower the bottom margin, a precaution that prevents the printer from printing on the platen after the paper in a single sheet operation has been removed or from printing along the perforation of a continuous form.

*Hard Blocks*

A figure with a caption, a space for a figure, a table or something with a caption should not be split between two pages. There should be some way to assure that splitting does not happen, if you inform the WP of what you want.

I call a set of text lines that should not be broken a **hard block**. The Dictaphone Dual Display has this facility: mark the beginning and end of the block with commands that have mnemonics, BB and EB. Then this block will not be split during automatic pagination. A short page may result when the block is moved to the next page, because there was not enough space on this page. But that's what you asked for.

After reviewing the entire document for pagination, you store it. Now you can send it to the printer, which prints it using the format and pagination information found in the document.

## Page Control

The print format program monitors the page being printed and associates a number with it in logical order. The first page is 1; the second is 2; etc. You may want this number placed on the corresponding page.

*Head and Foot*

The WP provides a convention by which you specify in the head (foot) where the current value of the page number should go (see page 00). The print formatter notes this when it creates the head (foot) and replaces the symbol it finds there with the correct page number; e.g., on the thirtieth page it enters 30.

You may want to print out only part of a document for hard copy editing. You request this from the menu or when your WP requires it before printing starts.

*Starting Page*

Some mechanism is also provided in each WP to alter the first (and succeeding) page number by a constant. Thus, if Chapter 2 is a separate electronic document, its number should begin after that for Chapter 1 ends. If Chapter 2 ends with page 30, you can tell the WP to start the page numbers with 31. Then all numbers that it comes up with it offsets by 30; e.g., the third page bears the number 33.

*Skip*

NBI has a nice feature which allows you to put a head (foot) on a blank page (of paper) along with its number. You can paste figures or photos on these pages and still the head (foot) has the proper number.

*Roman*

In books and manuals, the front matter (preface, title page, table of contents, etc.) is sometimes numbered separately in roman upper- or lowercase numerals. The rest of the text starts from page 1. Some WPs (NBI, for example) let you choose the number style and starting place to achieve this format.

## 9.4 HEADINGS AND FOOTINGS

**Definition**

Heads and feet are lumped together because both are printed outside the text boundaries defined by the margin statements of the format. We have:

- a **head** (sometimes **header**) is text entered at the top of each page;
- a **footing** (sometimes a **foot, footer** or **trailer**) is text placed beneath the text and within the bottom margin of the page.

A footnote is one (or more) line(s) which appear(s) above the bottom margin but below the other text on the page. Section 9.5 is devoted to footnotes.

*Page Number*

It is important to number each page of a multipage document. Numbering can be invoked regardless of whether you use headers or footers. When a header, footer or both is used, one of them generally includes provision for a page number. The placement of page numbers can add a slight complication, which is discussed at the end of this section.

*Document Management*

The handling of headers and footers is intimately associated with the document (or file) management system provided in the WP.

*Time of Incorporation*

Head and foot blocks can be both fabricated and incorporated at different times from the document editing. These blocks may be stored internally in the computer memory during page makeup or they may be brought in from disk each time they are needed. Hence we have the following incorporation times:

1. Put into ED at edit time.
2. Put into document at print time.
   a. Store the head and foot block once in the ED, then hold in a memory buffer during printing.
   b. Store blocks on external storage (disk) and merge with text as needed for each document page.

**Manual**

Take Vydec 1200 and 1400 as an example of a manual page oriented WP system. Suppose that you want headers and/or footers on your multipage document. Prepare a separate page for them, labeling it as such in the index. Then create an edited document on several pages of this disk. When you are satisfied with hyphenation, spelling and so forth, simply edit the header and the footer into each page of this document.

To edit a head (or foot) into each page is simple. Bring in the page. Place the cursor at the top (or bottom) of the page; enter as many blank lines as are required to build the head (or foot). Then position the cursor to the start of the header (footer) and read in the head. Text from that head (foot) page goes to the top (bottom) of the screen. Insert the page number where it belongs within the head (foot).

When both a header and a footer are necessary, you can put them on separate pages and do separate actions for each, as described above. Another possibility is to put them on the same page and separate them, sending one to the top and the other to the bottom. This uses editing procedures which are easy to master.

**Edit Time**

**Edit time header insertion** conveys that headers and footers are added to the electronic document during editing or pagination, not during printing. Then each page appears with the header and/or footer during your editing for you to verify.

As an example of edit time entry we examine the Xerox 860 WP. At any time while you create or edit a document you may decide to put headers and/or footers into the final printout. To do this, start at the beginning of the document and touch format. This brings forth the format display of Figure 9.4.1. For the Xerox system you find a line on the menu by pressing line several times. Each touch moves the highlight down by one line. The section on the screen titled "Page Labels" is where to store information about headers and footers.

Move the cursor to the header line. To enter a header, touch accpt; this moves the highlighted area down below "Header." Now type the header. You can center

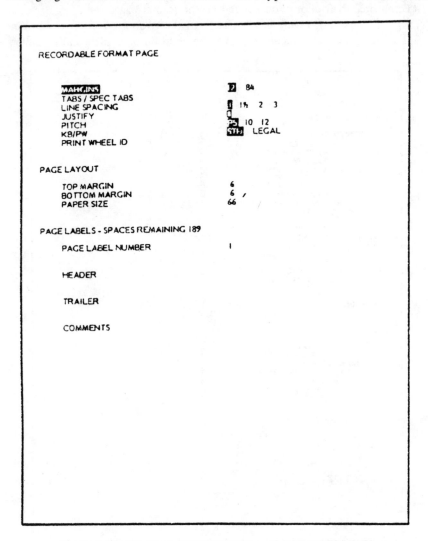

RECORDABLE FORMAT PAGE

MARGINS
TABS / SPEC TABS
LINE SPACING
JUSTIFY
PITCH
KB/PW
PRINT WHEEL ID

PAGE LAYOUT

TOP MARGIN
BOTTOM MARGIN
PAPER SIZE

PAGE LABELS - SPACES REMAINING 189

PAGE LABEL NUMBER

HEADER

TRAILER

COMMENTS

Figure 9.4.1. The Xerox 860 format menu. (Courtesy of Xerox).

or align parts of it with function keys. The header as it displays on the screen now is entered on each page.

To get an advancing page number, first type a label for it such as PAGE. Then enter a system page control symbol. For Xerox, this is <u>code 2</u>. When you touch these two keys in sequence, a number sign within a box replaces the cursor. Now the top of the fifth page is headed by "PAGE 5" when it displays after pagination.

To enforce the options you entered on the format page, press <u>format</u> again. You get the menu of Figure 9.4.2; check off the two pagination options. You want to repaginate the document, since the addition of headers and/or trailers

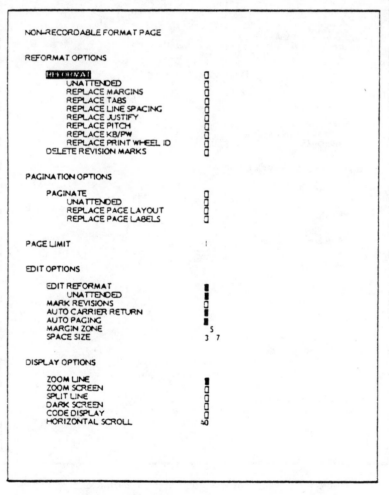

Figure 9.4.2. The Xerox 860 non-recordable format page. (Courtesy of Xerox).

may cause a reorganization of each page. The second request is to "replace page labels." This enters the trailer and header onto the page. Then press accpt. The system goes to work to repaginate and reorganize the pages of your document, entering trailers and headers. When it is done, you can review the document by bringing it back to the screen. If you are confident that the action will take place properly, you can simply store away the document without looking.

**Edit Time Specification; Print Time Inclusion**

For this method, the header (footer) is specified and included in the electronic document at edit time. The header (footer) must be specified only once, if it does not change throughout the document. However, it may be altered during editing as desired (except for the page number). This is explained below. The header (footer) is stored only once in the ED but is entered at print time at the top of *each* page, of course.

The actions needed for this technique are the following:

1. You define the header (footer) and enter it into your document once.
2. As the document is examined for printing, the header (footer) is found and placed into a buffer.
3. Each time the top (bottom) of the page is noted by the print format routine, it obtains the information from the buffer and enters it at the top (bottom) of the page.

*Example*

This example uses the Digital Equipment Corporation's word processing system (WPS). The keyboard has a control key which is not labeled but is colored gold, so, it is called gold in this description.

To activate the print control to enter a header or other request, you press two keys. First touch gold and then the key called CMND. In response, where the cursor was positioned, the screen shows a horizontal line of dashes with the words START PRINT CONTROL in the middle. Anything that you type now becomes part of the command. You specify a header by typing TOP; a footer is preceded by typing BOTTOM.

For a header, for instance, type TOP and press return. Follow this with the text to be used as a header. When finished, touch gold CMND. The screen displays the starting Print Control Marker, the header, and after you have pressed the other two keys, it produces a horizontal dashed line in which is included END PRINT CONTROL.

A footer works in essentially the same way, except that you type BOTTOM first. Both a header and a footer may be specified in the same document.

You may request that a page number appear anywhere in the header or footer. To do this you type a backslash followed by "p." Wherever the print formatter sees this combination, it is replaced by the page number assigned to this page. WPS also allows you to request the date similarly.

At any time while you are creating or editing the document you may see fit to alter the header or the footer for succeeding text. Go through the preceding steps at this point. The new formulation does not apply until the print formatter arrives at the next header (footer). Then it refers to the new information which it takes from the electronic document to put in the buffer.

For WPS, you request that a document be printed from a menu. You set the starting page number for the document. The print format program gets control. It retrieves the document to be printed. It stores the TOP and BOTTOM statements from the ED in buffers. If there is no header or footer information at the beginning of the document, neither are printed. When the print format program encounters the next print control statement in the electronic document, that statement is placed in its buffer to replace the previous occupant, if any.

When the print program comes to the end of an allocated page, it examines the footer buffer and procures the information from there to be printed as the footer. It then gets the header from the header buffer to print at the top of the next page.

**Print Time Inclusion; Separate Document**

Here you create a header and/or a footer page as a separate document. Each of these pages has all the information that should be printed at the top and/or bottom of each page of your final printed document. Directions about how to print your document are included in a control page, which also gives the name designated for the header.

The CPT 8000 is an automatic page oriented WP system. After you prepare and edit your electronic document, you cannot print it out properly unless you make up a **control page**. This control page contains a number of items, including the page length, margins, justification, pagination and so forth.

If you want a header and/or footer, then you create one on a separate page and give it a name. The header (footer) page contains title information formatted as you chose. If you want a page number which changes from one page to the next, you can enter it using what CPT calls a "hat code." This is a key with a symbol that looks a little like a hat. You press this key and then another key with a special shape on it. This goes into the position where you want a changing page number.

Now make up a control page. An example of one is found in Figure 9.4.3. The line starting with TOP: then indicates the disk drive on which the header is found and the header page name follows. The line starting with BOTTOM: contains the drive and name for a footer. Also in the figure you see a line that starts with STARTING PAGE NUMBER:. Following it is the number which will be used on the *first* page of your document.

```
TEXT:    1 SAMPL-2.1 SAMPL-2.5
PAGE LENGTHS:  54, 66
MARGINS:  1, 60
ADJUSTED
JUSTIFIED
TOP:  1 SAMPLHD
BOTTOM:  1 SAMPLFT
STARTING PAGE NUMBER:  12
```

Figure 9.4.3. Format page for the CPT 8000.

## Alternating Header and Footer

At the top of most books, the header on the left hand page is different from that on the right hand page. The page number for the left page is in the upper left and that for the right page is in the upper right hand corner. The page numbered 1 is on the right side.

Also, the content of the header may be different on odd and even pages, which is true for this book, for instance.

However, in most installations we do not print on both sides of the sheet of paper. This would require after printing on one side that the sheet be reinserted to print and align properly on the second side. This action could not be done without intervention..

Such being the case, you might ask why would we wish odd and even pages to have different headers (or footers)? When a WP installation is used to prepare technical manuals or other information to be printed by photo offset composition, then we might expect to see such a need. That is, the copy prepared on the word processor is photographed onto an offset lithography plate and then a hundred to a few thousand can be printed by an offset press on both sides of each page. Later the sheets are bound or holepunched for a ring binder.

When you read this manual or report, you see two pages at once and it is nice to have the header and/or footer positioned differently on each side.

*Methods*

The alternating header (footer) could be entered into your final document:

- manually,
- during pagination time,
- at print time.

*Manual*

If you are performing the action yourself, you can set aside one page each for the odd and even header (or footer). You compose your text and later on, when you are satisfied that it is paginated properly, you provide the proper head (foot) for the page, choosing it according to whether the page number is odd or even.

*Pagination Time*

Many WPs allow you to specify what your heading or footing will be as you prepare your document, either through the format page or in the text. Sometimes both methods apply because at some point in your text, you may want to change the heading. If you insert the new heading in the text, the WP recognizes that hereafter the new heading applies.

The technique used by the Dictaphone Dual Display is described. To employ it you enter a command in the text. Recall that the DDD uses <u>command</u> to start and terminate a command. To request a heading to appear on *all* pages, you hit <u>command</u> followed by the letters HD, then the heading and finally <u>command</u> thus,

$$\underline{\text{command}} \text{ HD } [\text{heading}] \text{ } \underline{\text{command}} \qquad (9.4.1)$$

Instead of HD you can use OH or EH (odd or even headings), FT (footings on all pages) or OF or EF (odd or even footings).

*Print Time*

Many WPs enter headers and footers only at print time. You set up the head and the foot when you compose and format the document. The purpose of the pagination run is to provide room on each page for the required additional matter. The information is not incorporated at that time. Instead, when the print formatter program is run to create the hard-copy document, the information is obtained from its source and placed at the head and the foot of the document.

This is a technique used in the Micom 2001. To create a header page, you clear the screen and set format for the header page. Then you position the cursor at the left edge of the first line and press <u>code u</u>. An up arrow appears, indicating that you can now enter the heading. If you want automatic numbering of pages to appear within the header, you move the cursor to the position where the number should appear and enter <u>code 1</u>.

The next few things that you do open the document for which the header belongs and indicate the page number within the document for the header page. This is not a page which will print by itself; it is used only for providing headers and footers for the text pages to be printed eventually.

Micom allows you to have as many as four alternatives: one or two headers and one or two footers. When there are two heads (foots), the first one goes on the odd page and the second on the even page.

During pagination, space is *allocated* to each text page for the header, footer, footnotes and pages numbers. These are *incorporated* in the text only when the document is printed and not before.

## 9.5 FOOTNOTES

**Handling Footnotes**

Footnotes are required in specialized environments. Many offices can get along nicely without ever using them. On the other hand, some enterprises use footnotes all the time. When the lawyer prepares a brief, many cases are quoted. In fact, the validity of the case is founded on precedents, actions taken in similar cases which must be quoted—hence the footnotes. Also technical and scientific writings often refer to the work of others by footnotes citing ongoing work in the field.

The point of the footnote is to allow the casual reader to read the text without stopping. The reader who wants further information can look down at the bottom of the page to find it.

*Needs*

In working with footnotes there are several capabilities we would like to have:

1. An indication in the text where a citation is made. A superscript which calls attention to each footnote is usually a numeral, but it may also be an asterisk, a dagger or some other symbol. Another alternative puts a number or symbol within parentheses or brackets at the point of citation.
2. The footnote itself goes at the bottom of the page, between the text and the footer, if any. Sometimes footnotes go at the end of a chapter or document, however.
3. You should be able to edit any part of a text and the footnote is no exception.

4. When altering the main text the citation points may move from one page to another as the text grows or contracts. The footnote must move to the page where it is cited.

5. A thorough editing capacity allows us to delete undesirable footnotes and add new ones at will. This may affect the numbering of the footnotes in the document. Some WPs renumber them for you.

*Alternatives*

There are several alternatives to what the vendor furnishes to assist in handling footnotes:

A. Manual (no automatic assistance),
B. Automatic print time insertion,
C. Automatic pagination time insertion.

**Manual**

If you are preparing a document on a WP system for eventual conversion to a typeset document, the page size and format may not correspond. The typographer requests that footnotes be included in the text right after the reference to the footnote. After typing the line with the superscript referring to the footnote, a horizontal line is written with dashes and the footnote is put beneath it, followed by another horizontal line to establish the end of the footnote and the resumption of the text. This is shown in Figure 9.5.1.

A footnote is required here.[1]  However, the text continues
[1] This is the footnote on its own line
and winds around the footnote.

Figure 9.5.1. Preparing a footnote for the typographer.

Putting footnotes at the bottom of a report is often best handled in WP systems by manual intervention after final page formatting. Use the same technique the typographer requires, as shown in Figure 9.5.1. Then the footnote can be moved during the pagination run.

*Moving A Footnote*

Suppose that you have typed your document and put a footnote in the middle of the text, as shown in Figure 9.5.1. Conduct a computer aided repagination run. As each page is formatted by the WP system, it is presented on the screen.

You can observe the placement of the footnote, even on a partial page display. Find the footnote, mark it as a block, move the cursor to the bottom of the page and move the block there. Delete both horizontal lines. The page reforms automatically with the footnote at the bottom where you need it. If there is more than one footnote, move each similarly.

*Editing the Footnotes*

With the typographer's method, the document can be edited extensively without problem. Add and delete text as you choose. When done, repaginate. Footnotes go along with the text to pages in which they belong. Now move them to the bottom as described.

Editing the footnotes is okay; only deleting or adding footnotes makes trouble. The numbering is thrown off. But, you can do a search and replace for the superscript to find and alter it.

*Command Program*

If your WP provides command programs, as discussed in Chapter 10, you can set up a program of key strokes to search the text and move the footnote automatically for you.

**Print Time Insertion**

For this technique you specify and create the footnotes in the text and hand them over to the system. It keeps track of them and the space needed for them on each page, moving them around internally as you continue your editing. You do not usually see the footnotes within the text unless you call for them, as will become clear later. The only time the footnotes and the text are actually put together is at print time. The NBI 3000 system typifies this activity; we use it as an example.

*Create*

Let us look at an example where citations are made using superscripted numbers. As you type along in the text, you come across the third citation. After the point where the author is named, you type a superscript 3 thus:

super 3 sub $\hspace{8cm}$ (9.5.1)

The superscript appears on the screen but the system is not yet aware of a footnote.

To enter the footnote mode, you press the footnote key, foot. This causes the screen to clear; you may now type your footnote. You are told that you are in footnote mode by the message line at the bottom of the screen. When you have finished typing the footnote, you press foot again. The action is done thus:

$$\text{foot } \{\text{footnote text}\} \text{ foot} \qquad (9.5.2)$$

When you press foot the second time, the footnote disappears and the text reappears. The result of the activity is that a footnote pointer is embedded in the text. The footnote itself becomes a separate subdocument. It is invisible and so is the pointer. The only way that you know that there is a footnote in the text is that there is a superscript on the screen and following the superscript there is a white blob indicating that a command has been stored with the text.

*Editing Text*

If you add or delete text, exclusive of the footnote itself, the system still keeps the footnote associated with its citation point in the text because of the pointer and the enclosed length of the footnote which is carried along. Hence any page on which the footnote appears has an allowance for text the size of the footnote.

*Print*

Repagination is automatically performed by the NBI 3000 during printout unless the user specifically suppresses it. Text is allocated to pages dynamically except where you have specified a hard page break during editing. The basis for page allocation is the format block embedded in the text of the electronic document. As text is read from the electronic document it is sent to the printer until the page is used up as specified in the format block(s), or unless a footnote is encountered. The footnote usurps part of the space at the bottom of the page and reduces the amount of text that can be put on the page thereafter. The WP keeps track of the space allocation for each page as it is sent to the printer.

If a footnote is encountered near the bottom of the page, there may not be enough space for the entire footnote; the footnote is hence continued on the next page. For a very large footnote, the space occupied might be greater than a page and it may flow over to subsequent pages. NBI's WP guarantees that each page of the document contains at least one or two lines of text.

If a footnote occurs in the last line of text, there will be no room for the footnote at the bottom of the page. In this case, the last line of text is placed on the next page, guaranteeing that there is room for the footnote. You can tolerate a page which is one line short.

*Editing a Footnote*

Before you can edit the footnote you must find it. The footnote command registers on the screen as a white blob following a superscript. You may have a superscript in the text without a footnote, as perhaps in a mathematical equation. But no white blob follows.

Once you have found a blob following a superscript and you position your cursor there, you are now ready to view the footnote. As you press <u>foot</u> the screen clears and the footnote magically appears. Now, using editing commands, you can alter the footnote to suit your purposes. When you are satisfied, simply press <u>foot</u> again and the text and the blob reappear to replace the footnote.

*Add or Drop a Footnote*

To delete a footnote entirely, proceed as before to find the footnote. Place the cursor on the white blob, verify that you have the right footnote and then delete the blob. After you do so, the footnote is no longer attached to the text. It is parted from the text and deleted. It no longer exists and you cannot retrieve it. Now delete the superscript.

To add a footnote, you proceed as discussed under creation. This often arises when you add new text in which you cite a reference. When the citation point comes up, insert a superscript or special symbol and then, using <u>foot</u>, call for the footnote screen and key it in.

If you add or delete footnotes, beware! If you have footnotes numbered 1 through 8 and you delete the third footnote, then a number in the sequence is missing. The footnotes numbered 4 to 8 should now be renumbered 3 to 7. To renumber footnotes, simply move the cursor to the superscripted number and overstrike it with the new number, being sure that you catch all the citations. The same applies if you add a new citation; however, it is clear that you are adding a duplicate number. Another alternative uses an asterisk instead of a number; later go through and enter numbers for all the superscripts; do a *search* for * and replace it with the number.

## Pagination Time

The approach here, as before, is to create and edit the document and the footnotes before they are incorporated into the text. But now on a separate run—the pagination run—the footnotes are incorporated. During this run, or immediately thereafter, you can look at the electronic document on the screen and judge whether the footnotes need alteration. After you have seen the document, it can then be sent to the printer without hesitancy.

The Dictaphone Dual Display (DDD) uses this approach and we describe in detail how the various features are activated. To summarize some of its advantages:

- Because the WP monitors and assigns the number to each citation and footnote, you need not concern yourself about renumbering when you add or delete a footnote.
- You can review the document *before* it is printed.
- You can format the footnote in a variety of ways.
- When a footnote spreads over several pages, it bears a label on each.

*Creation*

When you come to the place in your text where you wish to cite a reference, you now command the WP to record the reference at this point. DDD uses a command key after which a mnemonic is entered. The mnemonic for the footnote is, logically, FN. Thus, when you reach the point where the footnote is required, hit command; then enter FN, followed by the text which comprises the footnote. When all the text has been entered, hit the command key again. This is summarized as:

$$\text{command FN } \{\text{text}\} \text{ command} \qquad (9.5.3)$$

An interesting feature is that you can make several citations at exactly the same point in the text. To do this, you perform the operation of (9.5.3) several times, once for each citation that you wish to make. To summarize this we have:

$$\text{command FN } \{\text{text1}\} \text{ command command FN } \{\text{text2}\} \text{ command}$$
$$(9.5.4)$$

Whenever you enter the footnote information as described above, the same information appears in boldface on the screen, such as:

$$\textbf{(FN,Here is footnote text)} \qquad (9.5.5)$$

The one line display (remember, DDD has a light emitting diode display just above the keyboard) repeats this information.

*Editing an Unpaginated Document*

Whenever you call up an unpaginated document with footnotes in it, each footnote appears as in (9.5.5). As you add or delete information within the electronic document, the footnote moves forward or backward within the text. Since its place on a page of the hardcopy document has not yet been decided, there is no problem about its position in the electronic document.

If you wish to edit the footnote itself, you move the cursor into the text area of the footnote and add and delete text.

To delete a footnote, you perform a delete operation which stretches from the left parenthesis to the right parenthesis. The entire footnote disappears. To add a footnote you go through the procedure of (9.5.3) and the footnote is inserted in the text just as though you were creating it originally.

*Pagination*

In Section 9.3 we discussed how the pagination run divides a document into pages using: (1) the format requirements that you declared at the beginning of the document; (2) the changes in format that you have noted as the document progressed. For the DDD, the pagination run also takes care of the footnotes.

For footnotes, the DDD, during pagination, performs these important operations:

1. The WP assigns numbers to footnotes in ascending order as it encounters them.
2. The number assigned to the footnote is placed as a superscript at the citation point.
3. The WP keeps track of the space required for the footnote.
4. The WP continues to place text on the page as long as there is space after the allocation for the header, footer and footnote.
5. The footnote is placed at the bottom of the page, properly formatted.
6. The number assigned to the citation starts the footnote at the bottom.
7. Mulitple citation numbers may be assigned to the same place in the text when multiple footnotes requests were made.

When you request pagination, you may create a separate paginated document and keep the unpaginated one, or you may put the paginated document back to replace the unpaginated one.

Once the paginated document is available, you can alter the format with editing commands.

*Editing a Paginated Document*

If you want to append or delete information to a paginated document, you may do so. Recall that DDD has two displays. The VDT shows the text exactly as it will print. The LED shows a line at a time of the text. As you move the cursor through the text, a partial line also appears on the LED. The LED displays the footnote just as it did in the unpaginated document. Editing of the text or the footnote can therefore be performed upon the paginated document using the LED display.

As you edit the paginated document, the results may look strange. Thus, if you insert material on a page, you cause some of the material from that page to overflow to the next page. But this would be hard to display dynamically. Hence, a new page which is only partially full may be created. The effect may be disturbing.

It seems preferable to do all your editing on the unpaginated copy and then paginate it when you are done. For additional changes, go back to the unpaginated document, make the changes there and repaginate.

If you do decide to edit a paginated document, it must be repaginated before it is printed or you will get a mess.

**Footnote Format**

For WPs which provide automatic footnote handling, they may provide the following features automatically. (If these are not provded automatically, you may wish to do them manually.)

1. Footnote numbering might be on a per page or a per document basis. On a per page basis, numbering of footnotes starts from 1 for each new page.
2. You may not want to start numbering the footnotes from 1 (initial number) if this is a partial document—a chapter of a book, for instance.
3. In some cases you may wish to collect all the footnotes and put them at the end of the document like a bibliography. Little WP footnote management is required for this.
4. The margins for the footnote may be different from those for the rest of the document, or different from the text which is just above the footnote.
5. You might want a horizontal line to separate the footnote from the rest of the document.
6. You could start the footnote itself with the citation number on the line, with or without parentheses, with the footnote number as a superscript; you might want to indent the footnote.
7. When the footnote is continued on the next page, you might want to prefix it with "cont.," or perhaps something else.
8. The spacing of the footnote might be different from that of the rest of the text, especially if the text is doublespaced.

All these alternatives give you a wide range of choices, which you need if your work uses footnotes extensively.

## 9.6 OUTLINE FORM

**Definition**

We find outlines of many forms in many places. When I write an article or a chapter of a book, I always prepare an outline first. Many people prepare outlines for talks. Conferences and meetings have agendas and they are often in outline form. There is no single standard for the outline, but there are several standards, some of which people adhere to very closely, such as the Harvard outline form. Having a standard allows you to look at your outline and pick out where you are; the outline dictates that the more refined the level of detail, the more indented the title of the topic will be on the page.

In outline form, titles of the broadest topics appear near the left margin. Details about any one topic appear indented. As many as six levels are defined in some outlines. There is a system of numbering (or using letters) to designate each level by the kind of label that prefixes the sentence on that level.

The Harvard Outline Form works thus:

- The first or outermost level uses uppercase roman numerals.
- The second level uses uppercase letters.
- The third level uses arabic numbers.
- The fourth level uses lowercase letters.
- The fifth level uses arabic numbers within parentheses.
- The sixth level uses lowercase letters within parentheses.

*Section Numbering*

Another important application for the outline form is in section numbering. Government agencies, especially the Department of Defense, use this format in writing proposals, request for quotations, reports and other documents. In this format, each principal section has a number associated with it. Subsections have a double number separated by a decimal point; section 3 has a subsection, 3.4, which has a subsubsection, 3.4.5, and so forth. Each level is indented one more place than the proceeding level. The situation is thus very much like the outline form and the same mechanism which prepares the outline form can be used here.

*Automatic Management*

The first advantage of automatic outline management is that the operator need not recall what the numbering is for a given level. By keying, the operator requests a level; the next number is automatically assigned by the WP. But the advantage really comes into play when an outline is edited. A single deletion or insertion early in an outline can throw off the numbering of the remainder of the outline. For a manual system, the operator has to alter each number. However, with automatic outline management, the renumbering is performed by the WP, as we will examine.

**Example**

Although there are several WPs that provde automatic outline maintenance, the system provided by NBI seems to have the most features. It is therefore used as an example.

*Set Up*

To put the system into operation, you set it to recognize the outline form. The first action is to set tabs for each level in the outline (for NBI; other WPs specify level in other ways). During use, the first or highest level of title produces a number at the left margin and text goes in at the first tab stop. The second level produces a number or letter at the first tab stop and text goes in at the second tab stop. The third level produces a number at the second tab stop and text goes at the third tab stop. This continues all the way down. Hence, for six levels of outline, six tab stops are set.

The classification of the outline, the numbers and letters used at each level, can be set up by you. However, if you use the standard Harvard outline form, it is the default option furnished by NBI at setup. We discuss that method of entry next, before we describe alterations.

*Enter*

The NBI 3000 has a key, called <u>outln</u>, devoted entirely to the outline form. To enter a statement at some level, you press <u>outln</u> the corresponding number of times. For the third level, press <u>outln</u> three times. The next number for this position in the outline is entered by the WP at that level tab stop; the cursor then goes to the next tab stop for you to enter the text for this level. If the text is more than one line, as much as a paragraph, word wrap occurs and the word which is wrapped appears indented to the text tab stop for this level.

When you have finished entering the text for this topic, press <u>return</u>. You get no extra line spacing unless you press <u>return</u> again. The WP cannot know at what level to put the next topic; accordingly, you press <u>outln</u> as many times as you need for the next topic or item and start typing.

*Edit*

It is no big deal to get into the outline and alter the sentences or phrases found there. But when changes affect the outline form itself, such as changing a topic from one level to another, deleting an item or adding an entirely new item, then the automatic system really pays off.

To change the level of an item to a higher numbered level, place the cursor at the left margin of the line in question. Depress <u>outln</u> once and the level moves up by one; the item moves rightward to the next tab stop and the kind of numbering is altered; the item number is changed to be proper for this level.

To lower the level of an item, that is, to bring it rightward, again position the cursor at the left margin of the line. You want to delete one of the <u>outln</u> symbols. You have to press three keys at once as indicated by:

$$\underline{\text{alt-}\underline{\text{shift}}} + \underline{\text{shift}} + \underline{\text{del}} \qquad (9.6.1)$$

Repeat this for each level that the item is to be lowered.

To delete an item consisting of one line, place the cursor anywhere on the line containing the item and then press <u>alt-shift</u> and <u>del</u> at the same time. If the item consists of more than one line, repeat this procedure for each line of the item. When done, the item is removed, but more remarkably, all the succeeding items in the outline are renumbered to accommodate the deleted item.

To insert a new item any place in the outline, move the cursor to the left margin at the line position before which the new item is to be inserted. Press <u>insert</u> and then enter the item preceded by as many <u>outln</u>'s as required for the item to be placed on the desired level. Again, after entering each item, the numbering of succeeding items is changed, if need be, automatically by the system.

*Reset Numbering*

If you are creating a document that has several outlines sprinkled through it, then you will need to reset the numbering as you begin each. Each outline should begin its numbering from scratch. When you get to the second outline, press <u>outln</u> <u>return</u> just once to reset the numbering. This tells the WP to reset all levels. Now the outline uses the same format but starts from the very beginning.

**Choices For Numbering**

You have a wide variety of choices for numbering each level. You get the default option, the Harvard outline form, if you do not make a choice as described below. To choose a different outline form, you press <u>mode</u> and get a menu for format activities, as shown in Figure 9.6.1. Next you type "O" to choose the

I.  FIRST DIVISION
    A. First Subdivision of First Division
       1. This level describes a subsection
          a.  more detail
              (1)  still more detail
                   (b)  the lowest level of detail
              (2)  again more detail
          b.  subsection
    B. Second Subdivision
II. SECOND DIVISION
    A. First Subdivision of Second Division
       1. No level should appear if it's predessor level is missing
       2. Long items wrap around and the text is continued immediately below the start
          of the item text as demonstrated.
    B. Second Subdivision

Figure 9.6.1. Outline form menu. (Courtesy of NBI).

outline form. In the bottom line of the display, a number of choices is immediately presented to you.

Figure 9.6.2 displays the choices which you might make; the figure is also in outline form. At the first level five choices show under I in the figure. For D and E there are no further choices. For the others the choices are indicated.

I.  MAKE OPTION CHOICE FOR FIRST LEVEL
    A. Letters
       1. Upper case
          a.  no punctuation
          b.  period
          c.  parentheses
       2. Lower case
          a.  no punctuation
          b.  period
          c.  parentheses
    B. Roman Numbers
       1. No Punctuation
       2. Period
       3. Parentheses
    C. Arabic Numbers
       1. Same alternatives
    D. No Numbering – No Choices
    E. Multilevel – Again No Choices
II. CONTINUE OPTION CHOICE FOR OTHER LEVELS
    A. Choices Are Only A–D Above
    B. For (IB) All Level Are Determined Already

Figure 9.6.2. How to use the automatic outline feature to get automatic numbering (in outline form). (Courtesy of NBI).

After making first level choices, go on to the next level and make choices here too, unless you have chosen "no numbering" or multilevel numbering (each level gets an additional number separated from the previous one by a period).

### Paragraph Numbering

You can get the WP to keep track of the numbers without indenting or tabbing. Thus you place a number at the desired level any place you want in your manuscript. To activate this feature, you move the cursor to the place where the number is desired. Then you press <u>shift</u> + <u>outln</u> a number of times corresponding to the level which you need.

The WP program keeps six counters, one for each level you might use. When the next item is at a level lower than the previous item, all higher level counters are reset to 1. Each time that you repeat a given level the counter for that level is incremented.

Figure 9.6.3 shows ways that you can use the numbering feature for different

I.

A. LEFT FLUSH NUMBERING–To type the "A.", position the cursor at the left margin and depress SHIFT + OUTLN twice. Then TAB and type the text.

1. To type the number 1, position the cursor at the left margin and depress SHIFT + OUTLN three times. Then TAB and type the text.

2. Each time you depress SHIFT + OUTLN, the Automatic Numbering advances to the next Outline Level, but the cursor does not move.

B. LEFT FLUSH NUMBERING & INDENTED TEXT

1. To type the number 1, position the cursor at the left margin and depress SHIFT + OUTLN 3 times. Depress INDENT and type the text.

2. You may position the Number at many locations. You may depress center, tab or indent to position the Number, or depress the PARA key as in the paragraphs below.

II.

PARAGRAPHS: Depress PARA to create the blank lines and position the Automatic Numbering in the text below.

A. After depressing the PARA key, depress SHIFT + OUTLN twice to type the letter A. Then TAB and type.

B. In text which is typed with an Automatic Return, you must depress TAB or INDENT after typing the Automatic Numbers.

III.

A. To type the "A.", first TAB, then depress SHIFT + OUTLN twice. Then depress INDENT and type the text.

B. How many other formats can you think of?

Figure 9.6.3. Using outline form for numbering. (Courtesy of NBI).

document formats. To get centered roman numerals, you request that the text which follows be centered by pressing center and then press shift + outln only once. The next roman numeral (from the last one produced) appears.

## 9.7 INDEXES, INVERTED FILES AND DIRECTORIES

There are a number of services which some WPs supply to help you deal with documents. These services are not classified as utilities. They are of use to some specialized installations.

### Indexes

An **index** is a list of words with page numbers indicating where these words appear in the manuscript. You choose the words listed in the index as important words. (The WP program is not intelligent and thus cannot judge the importance of words.) There are three ways to tell the program which words are important:

- You *tell* the program which words are important to you by making a list.
- You indicate in the manuscript which words are important by marking them.
- The WP program scans the manuscript and determines important words by their frequency of occurrence. The program can discard common words such as "the," "a," "for," "in," etc.

I do not know of WP program that extract important words. Such programs do exist on large computers to classify and categorize documents for information retrieval applications. These programs tend to be large, too large for WPs, because they have discretionary powers to distinguish between frequently used common words and infrequently used important words.

*Index Generator*

You submit a list of important words to the **index generator**. The program then reviews the document, finds the occurrences of each list word in the text and makes a note of the line and page where it finds each word. One such program is a command program or glossary program developed by Wang for its OIS system. It is now described.

To use the index generator, you first access the document through the WP menu and then press go-to-page W. The system then displays a work page on the screen. This page is probably blank. You create a list of terms, each on its own line and ending with a carriage return. The words appear in any order on the page; the output will appear in the same order unless you sort the list. This is easy to do by simply sending the list to the sort utility. However, in sorting a list, upper- and lowercase letters are treated differently, as described in Chapter 12. Hence it is best to keep the list in all lowercase characters. The index program is case-insensitive (ignores case).

To invoke the index generator on the Wang OIS, return to the word processing menu and select *advanced functions*. When that menu appears, select *index generator*. The initial program display is presented with a prompt to enter the document ID. You identify the document and provide the password if the document is protected. Now the program acquires the work page (W) from the document and displays the key words, a group at a time. You check to see if the list is correct and complete. When you are satisfied, press <u>execute</u>.

As the program does its work, it may present a display on the screen, showing its progress, the number of key words it is currently looking for, and the page it is currently scanning. When the program is terminated, it displays results in one of the two forms shown in Figure 9.7.1. The work which the program has

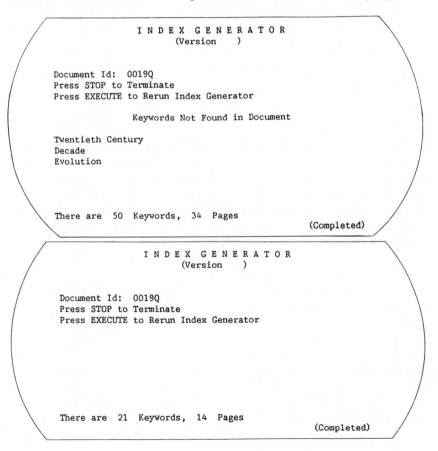

Figure 9.7.1. When the index generator is done, it is in one of the forms shown above. (Courtesy of Wang).

done is placed in your document following the last page written by you. You may now go back to your document, display this page and print it, if you desire. A typical page is shown as Figure 9.7.2.

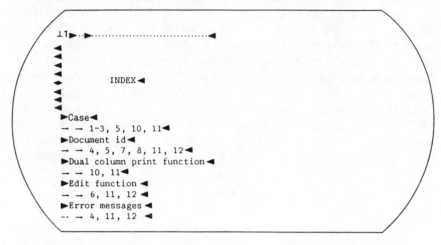

Figure 9.7.2. An index created by the index generator. (Courtesy of Wang).

*Marked Manuscript*

Another way to select words is to mark each one in the manuscript. The problem is that the marking itself may print out with the manuscript, which may not be desirable.

My WP precedes each occurrence of a boldface phrase with an "at" sign. The term is followed by the same sign. When the print formatter encounters this symbol, the phrase between the two signs is printed in boldface. By now you have noticed that when important terms are first introduced, they appear in boldface to alert you to the definition which follows. This comprises a satisfactory search marking in the electronic document.

I have written a simple BASIC program which searches any electronic document for the prefix symbol indicating boldface. The program then extracts the term and calculates an approximate page number (because my electronic document does not have the page breaks marked and accessible to BASIC). Then the program prints out a list of the words it has discovered, along with the approximate page number and entry number on the page. I have used this list to help prepare the glossary which you will find in the back of the book.

You may ask how this will help you. Most office WPs provide a BASIC program capability as an option at a modest cost. Many users are writing programs in BASIC. Microcomputer user groups exist which exchange programs at only nominal costs. WP users are also forming similar groups. Chapter 12 has more about programs.

### Document Directories

We have examined the document directory in Section 8.7. The need for a good system for file and disk management cannot be overstressed. If you cannot locate a document, whether it is paper or electronic, a search may slow down the office procedure considerably as well as cause frustration.

I have not encountered a good way to manage floppy disks and the documents which they contain. The best procedure is to print out the directory of a disk each time you finish using it and keep the printed directory in the envelope with the disk.

When your system has a large external memory, 5 or more megabytes of storage, there is usually a composite directory of all the files on this medium. Some hard disks provide several hundred million characters of storage. This amounts to thousands of documents, so an adequate system is needed to catalog them. An example of such a system is the NBI Office Automation 64. Its options include up to four hard disks, providing a total of up to 132 million bytes of storage. A directory keeps track of all the documents stored in the system. In addition to a list of documents according to author, operator, date of revision and the title, each document is associated with a user directory. Each user directory additionally provides password security to safeguard the item from unauthorized users.

Convenience results because the operator can call up a directory compiled at the moment upon a particular characteristic such as:

- the user directory name,
- the author,
- the last date revised,
- wild card search.

The last item is particularly powerful. It allows the operator to request the document by providing only part of the title. Any title which contains the words supplied in the order mentioned is recovered and presented on the screen.

### Library Contents Search

The ideal situation might be to ask the system for all documents which contain specified key words or groups of words. Such a system is not totally available.

Burroughs furnishes a product which seems to do this. It is named OFISfile. Its purpose is to keep track of every document that you create as a file and later to enable you to call forth all documents which contain a list of key words.

The system presumably creates an immense inverted file, which is a dictionary of all the words encountered in all the documents. As a new document is stored, the inverted file is updated. It keeps track of where, and in which document, a particular word appears. Common words such as "the" are not included.

When you present your query, the system looks in the inverted file for the words which you have distinguished. It comes up with an index.

A single word may not pinpoint your choice. If you have a number of descriptors you may localize the document fairly well. Once a number of documents has turned up, you can narrow down your search further by applying additional key words to this set of documents.

The system works only when large external storage is available to hold all your documents. We are talking about something in the $50,000 to $100,000 range.

# 10
# Variables and Document Assembly

This chapter is about the repetition which the WP handles for us:

- Preprinted forms, where the WP tells you what to write and you just fill in the blanks; all the positioning and aligning is done for you (Section 10.2 and 10.4).
- Form letters, where each is the same except for the name and address and some other personal information. You write only one copy of the letter; the WP produces each personalized copy (Section 10.3).
- Document assembly, where all the paragraphs of a typical contract are stored on disk; instead of typing each one over for each contract, call them forth as you need them and they are assembled by the WP (Section 10.5).
- Command programs, where you assign one key to do the work of many key strokes (Section 10.6).

We start by studying variables which arise because they pinpoint the places in the text which change; all other text stays the same. The WP makes copies and substitutes the right words to replace the variables.

## 10.1 VARIABLES, THEIR NEED AND USE

Variables enable you to create multiple copies of the same document, which differ only in a few places. If the documents were totally identical, duplication would be no feat. When they differ in only a few ways, mark them and the WP will fill them in from a list you supply.

The documents are the same except in a few places. At these places, you put a distinguishing symbol, usually accompanied by a name. This is the variable.

The document becomes a form with "holes" in it, a stencil. The holes are filled in automatically, semiautomatically or manually from a variable list. After the holes are filled in, each electronic document produced becomes one copy of the output document.

**Definitions**

A **variable** is the special symbol, which may be accompanied by a name, that appears in your form. A string of characters or symbols, called the **variable value**, is to be substituted here. These values are kept in a list, the **variable list**. The copy of the text into which the substitution is made to replace the variables is the **stencil**. A document assembled and printed from the stencil with the variable values plugged in is the **copy document**.

The substitution is like what happens for an equation or formula in mathematics. Here a single letter is used as a variable; when values are substituted for all but one, the equation may then be solved. A calculation uses the values substituted instead of the symbolic names. An example is in order.

*Example*

The formula to convert temperature from Centigrade to Fahrenheit is:

$$F = 9C/5 + 32 \tag{10.1.1}$$

If we substitute a value for the temperature, in Centigrade degrees, for C and then make the calculation, the result is the temperature in Fahrenheit. For instance, when C is 20 degrees Centigrade (or Celsius), substitute 20 for C and we have:

$$F = (9 \times 20)/5 + 32 \tag{10.1.2}$$

By doing the arithmetic we find the Fahrenheit temperature is 68:

$$F = 9 \times 4 + 32 = 36 + 32 = 68 \tag{10.1.3}$$

**How To Use**

Regardless of the facilities provided in the WP system, the sequence of events is standard:

1. Create and edit a stencil.
2. Where there are holes to be filled in, place a variable name which is tagged to be evident.
3. Make a list with one set of variable values for each copy document to be produced.
4. Make copies of the stencil, substituting values from the variable value set where there are variables in the stencil.

The difference in the kind and method of using variables depends upon two things: the need which you are fulfilling and the facilities available in the WP system. You may have up to three choices in your WP for the ways that values are substituted to replace a variable:

A.  totally manually—you find the variable names in the stencil and replace each with the desired value;
B.  semiautomatically—you and the system cooperate;
C.  automatically—after you direct the system what stencil and list to use, the WP makes all the substitutions and prints the document without further intervention.

*Kinds of Values*

As described above, you determine the value that goes into each "hole." This is true for the most part, but you can get some assistance from the system. This depends on the kind of variable that you are using. Obviously, the system can't know to whom you are sending a letter, but it can provide information on other things:

- the number of the page that is being typed;
- the number of the line being typed;
- and, in some cases, even the date and time.

This information may be useful in assembling your document.

## 10.2 MANUAL FORM LETTERS

**Principles**

This method works on any WP system. Some systems such as the Vydec 1200 and 1400 do not provide any computer assistance for document assembly. To prepare form letters on these or similar systems, there is really no alternative to the manual method. However, all the work outside of variable substitution is done only once. Printing the copy *is* automatic.

This technique is fast and useful when there are few copies to make, even when automatic merging is available. That is, if you are making only five identical letters to different people and you don't need to keep a list, this method is still rapid.

As a final incentive, the technique uses edit functions with which you are already familiar. You do not need additional knowledge about your WP system. Hence, if you are on a new system (or telling a new person what to do), it is quicker to use this technique than to learn (or teach) the proper directives for an unfamiliar WP system.

*The Steps*

For all the methods, the steps are about the same:

1. Create a stencil as an electronic document, with variable names in the proper place.
2. Store it away.
3. Make one ED copy for each hard copy document that you need.
4. Substitute specific values for the name in the stencil.
5. Store the copy onto disk.
6. Print the document during this process or afterward in the background.
7. Repeat (3 to 6) for each copy.

### Creating the Standard Document

Throughout the chapter we refer to a *stencil,* a standard document, which contains variable names to be replaced by variable values. In all cases we start by making the stencil. For both manual and automatic techniques there are different means for setting off the variable name from the rest of the text. It is important to understand what these alternatives are.

A.  Use *no* variable name; use a variable value instead.
B.  Use a variable name which looks like any other word in the document.
C.  Precede the variable name with a special graphic or a printing symbol.
D.  Use no variable name; just use the special symbol or tag.

To make the task more concrete, consider a stencil for a form letter which produces many identical copies except for the name and address. Figure 10.2.1 shows the stencil. The letters produced from it are identical from one to the next, except for what appears between the &'s.

### Variable Value Only

The first alternative is to create a document, the first letter, and use it as a stencil for those that follow. Let us pinpoint the actions. First you type a letter to the first recipient as it will go out. Save the document and start printing if you wish. Recall the document to the screen. Go through the document, looking for all variable values. Position the cursor (or the document, in a line-oriented system) to the variable value. Then replace the present value with the next value.

To find the value you may do a search using the first few letters of the old value. When you get there, do a *delete* and *insert.* Be sure to find all the old variables and change or remove them. The trouble with *search* is that you have to know what to look for; if you see the old word on the screen, it's just as easy to move the cursor there as to enter the search string.

*Store* and *print* the second document. Go through the same process with this document, this time to replace the latest variable values with the third set of values. And so on.

```
                            &date&


&na&
&ad1&
&ad2&
&ad3/o&

Dear &gr&,

        I received your article on &ar&, some time ago.  Unfortun-
ately, I have been so busy finishing up my Word Processing Hand-
book that I did not have any time to look at your article.
Things have cleared up and I note that it is quite acceptable.

        I am sending a copy of this letter to Larry Hager, my editor
at Van Nostrand to inform him that, except for minor editing,
your article is satisfactory.  He will be in touch with you and
will be sending the honorarium of which we spoke.

        Thank you again for your prompt and considered submission.
I hope to be speaking with you soon.

Yours sincerely,



Ivan Flores
```

Figure 10.2.1. Copy of a form letter.

## Named Variables

For this method and subsequent ones you really set up a *stencil,* not a copy document. In each position where text may vary from one copy to the next, a variable name is entered. It is important to choose and display names that stand
out when you use the stencil. One way is to use capital letters for each variable,
such as: NAME, ADDRESS, SALUTATION, PRODUCT, etc. If your screen
displays boldface, use it. After you make your stencil, store it away.

*Copy*

To make each copy, *recall* the stencil to the screen. *Search* to the variable name
(or part of it), or position the cursor manually. Insert the value to replace the
variable name. Continue thus to replace all names by values. For some variables,
you may have empty values: a variable name is removed and no value is entered.
For example, some addresses use two lines; others require three or four lines.
Replace ADDRESS4 by *null* when this last line is not needed. (Delete the line.)
    The new copy of the document is now complete. *Save* it and *print* it, *recall*
the stencil and use it to make each copy document you need.

## Tagged Variables

For this technique, each named variable is prefixed by a special printing symbol or nonprinting graphic called a **tag**. If your WP supports special graphics, they are most useful. Otherwise, symbols which do not appear in the stencil, such as a percentage sign (%), exclamation point (!) or vertical (I) can be prefixes.

Then you can easily do a search for that symbol as described below. After you construct your stencil, *store* it for future use.

*Copy*

To create a copy document from this stencil, first recall it. The stencil appears on the screen with prefixed variable names in positions where values should be inserted. Do a *search* against the single prefix symbol (%, ! or I). The cursor positions to the first occurrence of the tag, which is followed by a variable name. *Delete* both the symbol and the variable name and *insert* the variable value or *replace* both with the value. For an empty variable, *delete* both.

Do a *repeat search* for the next and successive variables. If you perform a *repeat search* after the last variable, you eventually get a message that there are no further occurrences found. This verifies that you have caught all the tagged variables.

## Tag Only

The previous description may suggest that the variable name itself can be omitted. Every place where a value is to be inserted can merely be tagged. No name need be associated with the tag.

To create your stencil simply place the special symbol (%, ! or I) wherever a variable is to be inserted. *Save* the stencil and *recall* it for each copy document. Do a *search* and *repeat search* for each variable value. Of course, there is no hint at any variable position of what should be inserted there, since no variable name exists. However, if you have just set up the document *you* know what goes there.

A problem arises only when you try to use the stencil later and find you have forgotten what variable goes in which position. Also, when some other person tries to use your stencil, the items to be inserted at some tags might be mysterious.

## 10.3 PREPRINTED FORMS

### Forms Are Legion

Most offices abound with forms. There are forms for travel, petty cash, invoices, bills of lading, purchase orders and on and on. To fill in a form on the typewriter, you have to put it in straight, align it vertically so that it is on the proper line and then move the carriage so that you are at the proper horizontal position. You must position horizontally to each field in the form. It gets tiresome!

The WP system has many features which aid you in filling out any form. For some, such as the Lexitron VT 1303, the action is almost entirely automatic. Even a WP which does not have as many automatic features as the VT 1303 can make the action move considerably faster.

The action is akin to that discussed earlier: you create a stencil which is your guide for filling in the form. Fill in the stencil from your keyboard and the WP system prints out the form in the printer with everything in the right place. The only requirement is that you insert the form properly into the printer and align it on the first starting line; the rest then goes smoothly, without fussing with the paper.

### Creating a Form Stencil

You create an exact duplicate of the preprinted form, the **form stencil**. You do not want the preprinted information to print out, since it is already on the form; you want the field that *you* enter to be printed on the form in exactly the right position.

The *form stencil* that you create must be accurate. It drives the printer in all future action. The line spacing in your form should correspond exactly to the line spacing on the preprinted form so that line advance for the two will coincide. Similarly, the horizontal position of a field to be filled in on the line must correspond to its position on the preprinted form.

Before you attempt to create the ED form, you should carefully measure the preprinted form to find the character spacing and the line spacing so that the two correspond. It is probable that the document is printed in either 10 or 12 pitch (elite or pica). Adjust your screen display to correspond. Vendors supply a plastic ruler to help measure pitch, horizontal field position and line spacing. Figure 10.3.1 shows a supply order form with line(s) and character position(s) measured and entered on the form to facilitate setting up the form stencil.

Construct the Stencil

Once you have made the measurements and set up your display, you create your stencil. Duplicate each line by typing in the title of each field from the form. Instructions on the form may be omitted, but they may be useful, should somebody else use your form.

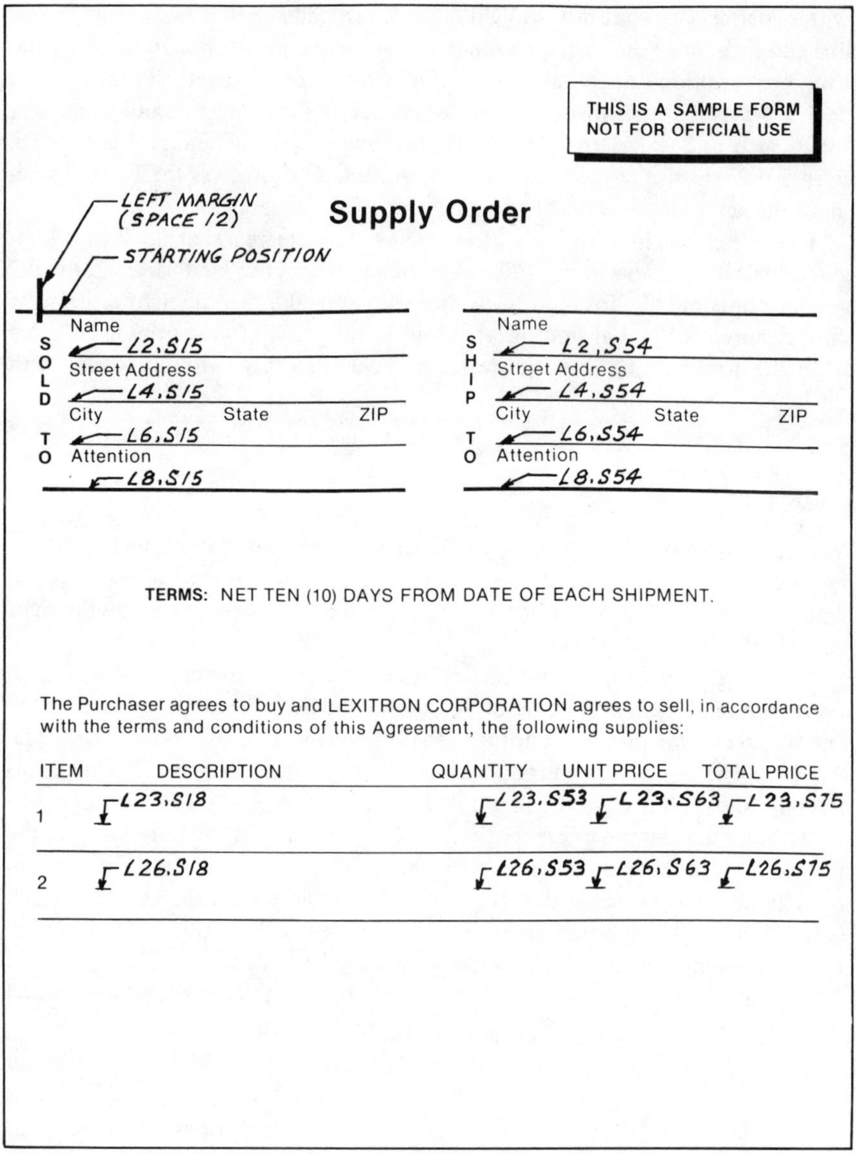

Figure 10.3.1. A form with line and space measurements entered. (Courtesy of Lexitron).

We now examine the VT 1303, which has two features that make stencil preparation and use easier:

1. You insert a graphic, called the **form tab graphic**, and a triangle appears wherever you want a variable value to go.
2. You enter a <u>nonprint</u> character (I) into the text by pressing <u>nonprint</u>. Text included between two <u>nonprint</u>'s does not print.

To create the stencil, type each variable name between two <u>nonprints.</u> Then enter <u>form-tab</u> where the field value should be entered. Figure 10.3.2 shows a sample ED stencil. Each field (where you enter a value) begins with the triangle, the <u>form-tab</u> character.

```
                        |SUPPLY ORDER FORM|



 |SOLD TO                           SHIP TO|

    △                                 △

    △                                 △

    △                                 △

    △                                 △






 |DESCRIPTION                       QTY    UNIT      TOTAL|

    △                                △      △         △


    △                                △      △         △
```

Figure 10.3.2. The ED form stencil for Figure 10.3.1. (Courtesy of Lexitron).

To enter a variable name in the stencil: press nonprint; type the variable name; press nonprint again. Now move the cursor to the position where you will later enter the variable value when you fill in the form. To insert the form tab graphic requires two keys (much like the control code). At the variable value position, press special-shift and immediately thereafter form-tab. A triangle appears to replace the cursor, which moves to the next character position to the right. Repeat this at all data entry positions on the form.

After preparing the form stencil *save* it on disk and in the case of VT 1303, indicate that the form is an *archive*. This protects it against writing over.

Figure 10.3.3 shows another form stencil ED with field labels included.

Petty Cash Voucher

Name: ▲                                        Date: ▲
Department: ▲
Reason: ▲

Authority: ▲

Figure 10.3.3. Another ED stencil.

## Use

To use your stencil, first put the blank form in the printer. Turn the platen and position the form so that the carriage is aligned to print the first line of the form.

Now go to your archive diskette and *recall* the stencil. You probably have handwritten information to copy into the form. Bring the form stencil to the screen. Sequence through the form by pressing form-tab. Each touch brings you to a new blank field. Line advance is automatic; pressing form-tab actually starts a search for the form tab graphic.

The graphic begins the empty field; the variable name directly precedes the cursor. Enter the information from your handwritten copy, typing *over* the form-tab graphic on the screen. Continue to hit form-tab to sequence through the form, filling in variable values.

When the form is finished, press print. Only fields that you have entered print on the form.

### Other Uses

You may want to print a copy of the form stencil without any values entered into it. Recall the stencil from your archive. Then enter one *nonprint* character at the top corner of the stencil. Now issue a *print* command. The additional *nonprint* code causes printing and nonprinting portions of the form to reverse.

Everything which formerly would not print now *prints*. If you had entered any variable values, they would not print.

Perhaps you would like to print your own form, both the fixed and variable text. It would look better if the variable names and variable values were printed in different type. With the automatic features described, you use two print wheels, each with a different typeface as follows. Recall the stencil from your archive. Fill in the values for a particular copy of the form that you want to make. Now print it in two passes.

On the first pass, print out the variables that you have filled, in using one type wheel. When you get done, reposition the paper in the machine to the top line. At the upper left corner of the screen, enter a *nonprint* character. Change the print wheel, putting in the one to print the variable names. Issue another *print* command the the printer produces the variable names in the other typeface.

**Other WP Systems**

Most WPs do not have special provisions for preprinted forms. It is still fairly easy to handle them. Remember that form-tab is merely a *search* to a special symbol. You can provide your own special symbol in your form stencil. When you do a *search* to that symbol, you are then at the proper position to insert an entry on your form.

The *nonprint* function is more troublesome to replace. Many WPs do not have a *nonprint* function. If or when you are ready to print out your form, the screen should contain only things which are to be printed by the printer. To make this possible, your form stencil should contain only special symbols and other characters, all of which will be eliminated. This becomes clear as you read the cookbook stencil preparation recipe.

*Stencil Recipe*

This recipe serves many, if followed to the letter. Have the ingredients ready in advance.

1. Measure the form accurately and determine the size of type and the line spacing.
2. Reproduce the form on your screen as well as possible.
3. Verify that your layout is precise by putting a copy of the form into the printer, advancing it to the first line and overprinting your copy onto this form. The overprinting should be accurate.
4. Find the starting point of the first field by measuring it accurately. Repeat this measurement on the screen; and at the beginning of a blank field, enter a special character (such as I).

5. Follow this symbol with a set of letters which conveys to you what should be placed there. It is necessary that these characters remind you what goes there, since the preprinted legend will be missing. For instance, you might enter lLNAME to remind you that the last name of the new person just hired goes here.
6. Repeat steps 4 and 5 for every field on the form.
7. Your form stencil contains both the preprinted information and the entry point for the value you will supply each time you use it. The preprinted information should not print; it must be removed. DO NOT DELETE IT. (This changes the line makeup.) Instead, write over the "preprinted" information with blanks. This removes what is printed on the form without moving the other information on that line of the form stencil.
8. Reposition your form in the printer at the starting position. Print out this reverse stencil. The names you put in each field (such as lLNAME) should print in the blank areas.
9. Save stencil on disk until ready to serve.

*To Serve*

You now have a stencil safely on the disk. When you want to make out a form, simply <u>recall</u> the stencil. Insert a blank form in the printer. Do the following:

1. Perform a search on the special symbol (l).
2. When you arrive there, the letters following the symbol should tell you what information to fill in. When you reach lLNAME, replace it (type over it) with REAGAN, for instance.
3. Fill in the form completely in this manner. Be sure that an absent entry is overwritten with blanks. For instance, for a single person, the entry for "spouse's name" should be typed over with blanks.
4. Be sure that the form in the printer is aligned to the first line.
5. Press <u>print</u> or whatever is necessary on your WP system.

## 10.4 AUTOMATIC FORM LETTERS

**Introduction**

Form letter capability is a very important feature found in most WP systems. Yet there is considerable variability from one to the next on how this function is implemented.

For *automatic* assembly and printing of form letters, two electronic documents are involved:

1. The **stencil**—the form letter with certain essential variable values missing;
2. The **variable list** which contains names, addresses and/or other pertinent information to go into each copy of the form letter.

A set of information in the list for *one* letter is a **variable record**. One record is merged with the stencil to make one hard copy form letter.

The stencil and the list are prepared before the merge can take place. However, the action can occur in one of two ways:

A. A copy of the stencil and a set of variable values from the list can be merged together to form a *new electronic document*. This document may or may not be presented on the screen. In any case, it is stored separately and used for printing at another time (letter assembly only).
B. Assembly *and* printing occur automatically without operator intervention or display. One set of variable values is entered into the stencil and the resulting letter is printed. This is repeated for each variable record in the variable list. In some WPs, assembly and printing may take place in the background while editing a different document.

The directions about which stencil to merge with which list is given in two ways:

1. As part of the print menu—you enter the stencil and list document name to complete the print menu. For instance, for the Wang WP system, the stencil is called the primary document and the list is the secondary document. You furnish both document names (or numbers, in Wang's case).
2. The stencil itself may contain a reference to a list. Calling for the stencil is then sufficient to activate the WP system to bring in the list and merge it with the named stencil. This has the disadvantage that when you are combining a stencil with a new list, the stencil must be edited to point to this new list.

*Keying in the Values*

It is most important for the WP system to associate values from the list with the right spots in the stencil. Otherwise the letter will come out all wrong. Most of this section is devoted to making this association, to correlating the variable name (in the stencil) to the variable value (in the list). There are three ways to do this:

1. **Ordinality**   The order of the variable value in the record corresponds exactly to the order of a variable name or mark in the stencil.
2. **Name**   Each item in the list is named. This name must correspond to a name in some position in the stencil. This correspondence tells the word processing system where to put the value.
3. Some other strategy or a combination of the above.

**Ordinality**

This method is terse. That is, it saves key strokes in constructing both the stencil and the list. It requires that you mark, in a unique way, the place in the stencil where a value belongs.

Our best recourse for marking is a graphic, a symbol which displays but does not print. Graphics are available only if your WP system provides them. There is no standard for graphics. Wang Office Systems 5, 25, 20 and 30 use a double vertical arrow. Xerox 860 WPS uses a box with an "x" in it.

*Switch Code*

In some WPs the graphic alone is used without any variable name following it. It is then called a **switch code** to convey that this code causes the WP to *switch* from the stencil to the list; it also appears after each variable value in the variable list to force the WP to *switch* back to where it was in the stencil.

*Stencil*

As before, you create a stencil by typing and editing it. Wherever a variable is required, enter the switch code graphic symbol: for Wang, touch merge and the double arrow appears; for Xerox touch code 7 and the box with the "x" appears. The hole in the stencil is marked only by the occurrence of the graphic; no name is assigned. A variable value is identified by its ordinal position in the stencil *and* list. Consider a set of variable values in the list, the record. The *first* value in the record replaces the *first* graphic in the stencil; the *second* value in the record replaces the *second* graphic in the stencil; and so forth.

Imagine a form letter which addresses the recipient by a first name. Perhaps you use this first name several times during the course of the letter. Suppose his name is Billy. Then "Billy" should appear several times in the letter at, say, the sixth, tenth and twelfth occurrences of the graphic. The same graphic identifies *any* insertion. You must be careful to note this and put "Billy" at positions 6, 10 and 12 of this variable record.

*The List*

For each form letter, a set of variable values is necessary, a record. Your list has records for each copy document to be created. Each record consists of a number (the *same* number) of variable values. The variable values are called **fields**. Each field is separated from the next field in the record by a switch code or according to the rules for your word processor.

For the Wang system, each field may contain one or more carriage returns; a field can thus span several lines. Each field in the variable list is separated from the next by the same graphic used in the stencil to mark variables, the double vertical arrow. To create the list, type each field (variable value) exactly as you want it to appear in the letter. After each, press merge. Enter two returns between records. Hit cancel and execute to end the list.

*There must be exactly as many fields in each record as there are entry points in the stencil.* In our letter to Billy, we addressed him by his first name three times. Three occurrences of "Billy" must appear in his variable record.

What about absent fields? Suppose the letter to one of our sendees will not have one of its variables filled in? That is an easy one. Simply place a switch code (a double vertical arrow for Wang) right after the last switch code. Since there is nothing between the two separators, nothing will be printed at this place in the letter.

*Print Request*

The way that you request a form letter printout is independent of the way that the variables are marked in the stencil; it depends only on the requirements of your WP. Wang Office System uses an overall menu to chose an action. On it you specify *merge print* and a second menu appears. Enter the merge and format specifications. For Wang, you furnish the document number for both the stencil and the list. Then the action begins.

### Named Variables

The advantage of using named variables is that the value for each variable need appear only once in the variable list, regardless of how many times the variable is used in the stencil.

The word processor must still distinguish a variable name from other text which surrounds it. Most systems require that a graphic or special symbol prefix a variable name. For the TypeRite of AM Jacquard, you enclose a variable name within square brackets.

*Stencil*

To prepare your stencil using variable names, simply type the text and wherever a variable value goes place a variable name with a tag or put in brackets. The name should remind you or a later user of its purpose. For instance, wherever you need the last name of the sendee, you might actually use !lastname or [lastname]. Some WPs do not allow such large variable names, so use [LN].

*A List*

A list consists entirely of variable values. There is one record of values for each document to be produced. Records are separated by carriage returns or other symbols.

Each record consists of a number of **entries** and each entry consists of two parts:

- The variable name corresponds to some variable name in the stencil.
- A variable value to substitute into the stencil for this copy of the document to replace any occurrence of the named variable.

Since each value is identified by name, there is no need to keep the values in order within the record. One value may be substituted in several places in the stencil: "!FIRSTNAME Billy" is listed only once, but it can be plugged into several positions in the stencil. Keeping the variables in a fixed order for simplicity when typing them is usually helpful. When a value record is long, this helps you make sure that you have not forgotten any values.

*Making the List*

Each record in the list consists of several entries which are pairs: variable names and variable values. Having to type in both to make up the list is double work. But there's a way out: keep a set of names in phrase storage or as a subdocument. As you begin a record, recall this "name" subdocument and half your work is done! Now fill in the values and repeat.

## Incomplete Record

What happens if you leave out one of the values in a record of variable values? If your stencil has six different variable names in it, then six variable values are needed in each record to plug in. A null value is different from a missing value. What the WP system does if you have provided only five depends on the system and how friendly it is.

When the merge program runs, it finds each variable name in the stencil and looks for that name in the list. If a name is missing from a variable record, the record is incomplete. It is not so clear if you are using ordered variables. That is why the vendor requires that you keep variables for the same document together in the form of a record. If you don't, the system will get out of step. For instance, if you were supposed to supply six variables and have supplied only five, then the system will assume that what was actually the first variable of the next group was the last variable of this group and you will be in trouble.

*Remedy*

What if the WP system notes a missing variable value? This depends on whether it happens during printing in the background or during assembly or printing in the foreground.

For background printing you are probably editing another document. The WP has no choice but to stop the printing job and let you figure out what to do next.

If you are assembling documents to be printed later in the foreground, then the WP can be more friendly. When it comes to a missing variable, it can prompt you to fill in that variable.

You can use this feature to fill in variables at assembly time which are perhaps long and that you did not want to include in the list. For instance, suppose you put the variable [PS] at the bottom of your stencil. If [PS] has a value in the value record, it is inserted. Otherwise, when the WP detects that there is no value for this variable, it prompts you to enter one. Now you can put in a "PS" or postscript which is personalized for this letter, if you chose. Otherwise a carriage return provides an empty variable and nothing is entered into this letter.

## Mixing Names with Order

The advantage of using variable names is that values used more than once appear only once in the variable record; the advantage of using order is that items in that variable record are not named, thus saving key strokes. It would be nice to get both advantages without any disadvantages.

There is a way for the vendor to supply this: use names in the stencil; use order in the list. The way to relate order in the list to the names in the stencil is an ordered record of names at the beginning of the value list. This sounds like double talk, but it's really easy.

*Ordered Record of Names*

An additional ordered record of names makes sense of each variable record. The **order record** can be placed in either the two places:

1) the variable value list,
2) the beginning of the stencil.

Let us explain the NBI method, where the order record is in the front of the variable value list. Here is how it works.

Create your stencil; use any variable names; put them at any position in the text. Before putting away the stencil, note the variable names you used.

Now make the list of values. At the beginning of this list, provide a record consisting of names. The order of the *names* in this record dictates the order of the *values* in all the other records. An example appears in Figure 10.4.1.

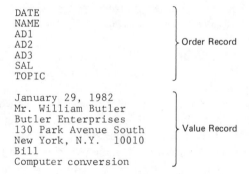

```
DATE
NAME
AD1
AD2          } Order Record
AD3
SAL
TOPIC

January 29, 1982
Mr. William Butler
Butler Enterprises
130 Park Avenue South   } Value Record
New York, N.Y.  10010
Bill
Computer conversion
```

Figure 10.4.1. Variable list using the order record.

**Considerations**

The power of form letters cannot be underestimated. If your office deals with a lot of duplicate letters, a WP system may be worth the investment just to do this chore. There are a few considerations that you should keep in mind when purchasing a WP system for this purpose.

*Interchangability*

We have seen how a stencil and a list are tied together to produce many almost identical letters. You may want to use the same list to send different form letters or you may want to send the same form letter to different lists. The system you select should then provide interchangability between lists and form letters.

*Print Only*

After you are satisfied with your stencil and you list, you want to print out the letters. Some WP systems do not let you print the letters directly. You assemble the letters individually and place them into a file on disk; you can print the letters only *after* you have assembled them as electronic documents.

*Partial List*

You have a stencil and a list, but the list may be dynamic. You may be constantly adding names to it (your new customers). When you have a batch of new names, you may want to send out a (welcome!) letter, but only to the *new* names. You want a letter sent to only part of your list.

Some WPs allow you to select a continuous group of records from your list, say the thirty-fifth through fortieth, or the eightieth up to the end or the first 25. Be sure that the system has this feature if you need it.

*Selective Print*

Your list may have additional variable values in each record only for the purpose of selection. This is a powerful feature. It allows you to keep a large list and make selective mailings. Here are just a few factors (found with each record) by which you might select recipients:

- standing of the company according to its dollar volume,
- geographical area,
- product category of the company,
- favored discount standing.

The VT 1303 allows you to request in your print command characteristics of records for which letters are printed. Other WPs provide record processing to extract a selected list from our existing list (see Chapter 12). This serves equally well.

## 10.5 AUTOMATIC DOCUMENT ASSEMBLY

**Aim**

Each of the three words in the title of this section are important:

- *assembly*   Brings together a number of subdocuments;
- *automatic*   Once started, action continues without intervention unless you see fit;
- *document*   The purpose of the activity is to provide one document put together from a number of subdocuments.

*Components*

Three kinds of electronic documents take part in this activity:

- There is just one **output document** which is *assembled* by the activity and printed out.
- There are a number **subdocuments** chosen from a **subdocument file** and put together to compose the output document.
- There are **assembly directions** which may be in a separate electronic document. They convey which subdocuments are chosen, in what sequence they appear, and what changes to make, if any.

*Need*

Proposals are written by large and small companies alike to secure grants and contracts from city, state and federal governments and from private sources. There is a considerable amount of common text from one proposal to another. For example, there are resumes and vitae of the major contributors and administrators in your firm. Then there are descriptions of the company, its earnings, assets, resources and so forth. If this information could be written once and then duplicated automatically as needed without retyping, a lot of repetitious work would be eliminated.

Automatic document assembly includes only the selected subdocuments that fulfill the needs of this particular proposal or document. A lawyer creates papers, wills, contracts and so forth, composed of paragraphs which differ only slightly from one paper to the next. Automatic document assembly makes it possible to reproduce the paragraphs, altering them where necessary, without the tedium of retyping each paper completely.

*Action*

A file of subdocuments consists of sentences, paragraphs or even pages. Each subdocument may be altered from time to time if, for instance, the experience of a researcher changes. Each subdocument has a simple but unique label to identify it.

The output document is designed by somebody who understands the makeup and construction of the subdocument file. The designer may have a printout of the file showing each subdocument name and text. To choose subdocuments, enter their names into the assembly directions. Subdocuments may be combined with original one time text and varied, as described shortly.

To summarize, the assembly directions contain a list of the subdocuments, the changes necessary in them and the additional text in the proper format for your WP system.

The document is assembled and printed according to the template furnished by the assembly directions. It is sometimes desirable to prepare and save an electronic document at the same time. In this way, if further changes are to be made, the electronic document can be processed instead of repeating the assembly.

*Variations*

A number of variations are available. The first of these places original text in the assembly document without creating a separate subdocument for it.

The second variation provides for variable values to be plugged into subdocuments, similar to form letter creation. Variable values are supplied in the assembly directions and replace variable names in the subdocument. This power is necessary, especially for legal work, where a paragraph describes an action that names the parties concerned. The names are the variable values which appear in the assembly directions, to be plugged into the subdocument.

A fascinating and powerful capability is for one or more of the subdocuments to be assembly directions. Then the output document is determined by one set of assembly directions which in turn refer to other sets of assembly directions which refer directly to subdocuments. This is called **nesting** by programmers. It may be carried along to several levels:

1. directions contain a list of subdocuments, one of which is further directions;
2. the second list of subdocuments *also* refers to one or more set of directions;
3. this may continue for several levels.

## Subdocument File

The file of subdocuments must be available when you are ready to assemble an output document: it is on a disk mounted in a drive. The rules for creating and modifying the subdocument file are a function of the WP system. For instance, a page oriented WP may require that each subdocument be a separate page. In the assembly directions you call forth a subdocument by page name. A document oriented WP system may not have such a requirement. The WP provides a convention for naming a subdocument: the name is not part of the subdocument text; the WP system must distinguish the subdocument name from its text.

## Output Alternatives

Your WP system may be able to produce an assembled electronic document, a hard-copy assembled document or both. A system is most desirable which gives you the choice of either or both.

The TypeRite system from AM Jacquard assembles subdocuments to produce an electronic document to meet your requirements. One additional step prints this out: this is semiautomatic because you participate in the assembly.

## Variables in the Subdocument

Some WPs allow the subdocument to contain variables. A variable is marked by:

- a name prefixed by a symbol;
- a bracketed name or number;
- a graphic or switch code.

The variable value is referenced from the directions either by name or ordinality.

A subdocument, which contains variable names or indicators, needs variable values to plug up the holes. For the form letter, variables values are in a list. However, only one copy of the subdocument occurs in the output document, so only one set of variable values is required. The assembly directions contains one set of variable values for each subdocument it requests which needs values.

## Assembly Directions

The assembly directions comprise an electronic document which is prepared by you to produce the output document. It is desirable to print a copy of the directions to keep on hand. Only what is requested in the directions goes into the output document. Assembly directions may include three kinds of items:

S   The name or number which identifies a *subdocument* to be incorporated at this ordinal position of the output document.

V   A set of *variable values* associated with the subdocument just called, with each value identified by ordinality (a switch code) or a name as required by the WP.

T   *Text,* which is to be inserted in the output document at this position or used as a header, a footer or a title.

Each WP system has its own method for identifying and distinguishing each category of information. To make the discussion more meaningful, we examine the Lexitron VT 1303.

### The VT 1303

Table 10.5.1, which summarizes the assembly instructions available for this WP, refers to a subdocument as a paragraph. Each assembly document must include:

- a title,
- at least one paragraph,
- and an end statement to indicate when the assembled document is finished.

All assembly instructions are enclosed in square brackets. A simple assembly document is illustrated in Figure 10.5.1. The first instruction, a title request, is followed directly by the title to appear at the beginning of the document. Next we find a list of paragraph indicators, followed finally by an end statement.

Table 10.5.1.  Summary of Assembly Instructions.  (Courtesy of Lexitron).

| Instruction Name | Typical Instruction | Description |
|---|---|---|
| Title | [Title] | Must be the first instruction typed on every instruction list. Follow each Title instruction with a document title at space 32 on the next line. |
| Paragraph Number | [P101] | Number of each standard paragraph you want the system to assemble. |
| End of Document | [End] | Must be the last instruction typed on every instruction list. |
| Line Number | [L30] | Start a particular paragraph, page number, header, or footer at the line indicated. |
| Insert | [Insert] | Insert the text typed on the next line(s) during assembly. |
| Paragraph Spacing | [S6] | Insert the additional blank lines indicated after a particular paragraph. |
| Paragraph Range | [P100–104] | Assemble each paragraph in the range indicated. |
| Page Advance | [Advance] | Start the next paragraph at the top of the next page. |
| Page Number | [N1] | Number each page in the document automatically. Appears after the Title instruction but before the Paragraph instructions. Normally preceded by a Line Number instruction. |
| Header Insert | [HI] | Insert the text on the next line above the upper page set markers on every page. Appears after the Title instruction but before the Paragraph instructions. Preceded by a Line Number instruction. |
| Header Insert | [H101] | Assemble the specified paragraph above the upper page set markers on every page. Appears after the Title instruction. Normally preceded by a Line Number instruction. |
| Footer Insert | [FI] | Insert the text on the next line below the lower page set markers on every page. Appears after the Title instruction but before the Paragraph instructions. Preceded by a Line Number instruction. |
| Footer Insert | [F101] | Assemble the specified paragraph below the lower page set markers on every page. Appears after the Title instruction. Preceded by a Line Number instruction. |

```
[Title]                                    {Title Instruction
                    Credit Response Memo
[P101]                                      {
[P203]                                      {Paragraph
[P201]                                      { Instructions
[P202]                                      {
[End]                                       {No more instructions
```

Figure 10.5.1. VT 1301 paragraph assembly instructions.

*Second Example*

Figure 10.5.2 shows another example. After the title, we find a header included in the assembly; spaced six lines down are directions. A footer would be requested similarly. The assembled document includes the first paragraph, numbered 203, after the title and header. Then text from the directions is inserted. Next comes a second paragraph followed by four blank lines and then another insert. A final paragraph ends the assembly.

```
[Title]
                    Sample Assembly Instructions
[L6]
[HI]
                      Lexitron Example
[P203]
[Insert]
        Here are some paragraphs, as requested.
[P198]
[P166]
[Insert]
        And now comes the final paragraph:
[P208]
[End]
```

Figure 10.5.2. Assembly with inserts.

*Another Example*

Perhaps the most interesting example uses the assembly instructions of Figure 10.5.3, which contains ordinal variables. The paragraphs from the subdocument

```
[Title]
                    Credit Investigation Results
[L3]
[Entry]
January 7, 1981
[L3]
[P301]
[1] Ms Mary-Ellen Quintana
[2] 166 Sixth Street
[3] Hoboken, NJ 07030
[P303]
[1] His/her bank account at MHT, Number 303-6635-99765 is
overdrawn.
[2]
```

Figure 10.5.3. Assembly directions with variable inserts.

file are presented in Figure 10.5.4. The output document assembled from the instructions is presented in Figure 10.5.5.

Numbers in the assembly directions within brackets relate a value to its intended position in the subdocument. The value to be inserted follows the bracketed number on each line.

```
[P301]


        The following applicant has been given a credit
examination:

        [1]
        [2]
        [3]



[P302]

        His/her credit has been checked carefully an found to be
satisfactory.  He/she has been issued Gold Credit Card Number
[1];  the date of issue is [2].



[P303]

        His/her credit is unsatisfactory for the following
reason(s): [1] [2].
```

Figure 10.5.4. Sample paragraphs for insertion.

```
                    Credit Investigation Results


January 7, 1981


        The following applicant has been given a credit
examination:

        Ms Mary-Ellen Quintana
        166 Sixth Street
        Hoboken, NJ 07030

        His/her credit is unsatisfactory for the following
reason(s): His/her bank account at MHT, Number 303-6635-99765 is
overdrawn.
```

Figure 10.5.5. Memo produced by the assembly directions of Figure 10.5.3.

The assembly directions tell the WP system what paragraphs to put into the output document and, for a given paragraph, what variable values to plug in to replace variable symbols.

**Advanced Features**

Some automatic assembly systems allow variable length lists to be incorporated into an output document. For example, consider a purchase order. The information for the purchase order may be taken from a list for the headings and shipping information. The parts to be ordered may require one or several lines of descriptions. The list may be set up to include a number of sublists where each sublist represents a particular item to appear on this purchase order.

Instructions to create output documents with a variable number of item entries is complicated and beyond the scope of this book. Suffice it to say that such applications exist.

## 10.6 COMMAND PROGRAMS

**Concept**

In your office you may deal with a number of similar documents. As you create and/or edit similar documents, you may go through the same sequence of steps many times. Wouldn't it be nice if there were some way to record the sequence of steps you make and play them back later by pressing a single key. This recorded sequence is called a **command program**.

When you press one of the keys at your keyboard, such as <u>delete</u>, <u>insert</u> or <u>search</u>, you invoke a program. The signal produced by touching this key causes the computer to go through a set of actions to perform the request you made. The actions the computer performs are uniform. Some vendors allow you to set up your own sequence of actions, a command program in terms of function and data keys on your keyboard.

*Why?*

What can you do with this capability? Well, that is up to you. Any sequential activity which requires 3 to 100 keystrokes for you to perform can be reduced to a single keystroke, if your WP permits.

Handling footnotes is one such activity, if your system does not handle them automatically; few systems do. There is no reason for moving footnotes about until you have a final draft of your document. If you keep each footnote where it was first cited, it is simple to move it to the bottom of its page and reformat the page for the final draft.

If you handle many simple, individual letters in your office, then you have to make out an envelope for each. This means retyping the name and address to print in the center of the envelope. Wouldn't it be nice if you could press a single key and all the action to create the address for the envelope would be done for you. The example at the end of this section shows how you might do that in one WP system.

*What's My Name*

WPs call command programming by different names; there is no standard. CPT calls it **keyboard programming**. Digital Equipment Corporation calls it the **user defined key**. Your WP reference manual describes this capability, if provided.

*Use Me*

To use this facility you go through the following steps:

1. Note that you frequently employ a sequence of operations.
2. Keep track of the keys that you press, including the letters, numbers, symbols and function keys.
3. Set up a command key by using the actions prescribed by the vendor of your WP system.
4. To call forth this sequence of activities, usually all that is necessary is to press one key.

**The Program**

Most command programs are similar in the way that they are recorded, regardless of the vendor. Let us take the Digital Equipment Corporation's WPS as an example. WPS provides up to 10 user-programmed keys. To call forth a user program, you use the gold key, gold, followed by a numeric key from 0 to 9. Of course, if you have not created a program to correspond to this key, nothing happens.

*Write Me*

To create a command program for WPS:

1. Enter the main or the editing menu. If you are editing, press gold menu.
2. Select from the menu by typing in one or two letters at the keyboard. To define a user program key, type DK and then the number of the key. Type DK 3 return to define a function for the key numbered 3.
3. The keys that you touch hereafter form a sequence which *is* the command program.
4. To terminate your program, touch gold.

The program is now recorded. When you press gold 3, the keystroke sequence is played back.

*See Me*

You don't have to type in the dark. As you enter keystrokes, they display. The name corresponding to any function key is presented for you to see. If you press delete-char, this is displayed as "Delete Char." If you press back-up to move text in the reverse direction while your program is running, the screen displays "Back Up." *This applies as you* key in *the command program.*

WPS distinguishes the name of a function key from letters or symbols that you type. If you type several characters together, WPS shows them as characters separated by spaces. Each time you hit the space bar, WPS presents "space." Hence, if you type in "go to" as part of your program, the display presents:

g o space t o                                    (10.6.1)

*Fix Me*

As part of the command program, you may use back-up and return. Hence you cannot use them to correct the program you are entering.

There are two ways to make a correction. If you are defining a function for key 3, then pressing 3 causes the last character that you enter to be deleted. That is the only real editing command you have. Perhaps you would prefer to start from scratch: Press gold and start the definition all over again.

### One Stroke Addresses

To see the power of command programs, let us look at a way to organize your letters so that a single command key can automatically fabricate the address for the envelope. The method requires that you put three additional keystrokes into every letter you write.

The format of a typical letter is shown in Figure 10.6.1. At three points in your letter, you add a special printing symbol to permit a search against it. I use an exclamation point (!) as the symbol; it does not appear elsewhere in the letter. That is an important factor. If your WP system has a graphic which is not otherwise engaged, use it.

```
April 24, 1981


!Mr. George Burns
2334 Easy Avenue
Middletown, OR 97183
!

Dear George,

         I have been approached to consider still another movie
with you.  It seems ................................

Sincerely yours,


John Denver
!
===============================================================

April 24, 1981


!Ms Elizabeth Taylor
The Great Square
Alexandria, Egypt
!
Dear Liz,
```

Figure 10.6.1. Letters using ! as markers.

The symbol appears at three places in your letter:

- before the first character in the sendee's name and address,
- after the last letter in the sendee's name and address,
- at the very end of the letter after everything else.

Figure 10.6.1 shows a letter formatted as described using the exclamation point. After the last ! in the first letter there is a dashed horizontal line, the page break you or the system inserted to separate one page from the next. Following this letter is the next letter to Ms. Elizabeth Taylor.

```
April 24, 1981


Mr. George Burns
2334 Easy Avenue
Middletown, OR 97183

Dear George,
        I have been approached to consider still another movie
with you.  It seems .................................

Sincerely yours,

John Denver

==================================================================
                        Mr. George Burns
                        2334 Easy Avenue
                        Middletown, OR 97183

==================================================================

April 24, 1981

!Ms Elizabeth Taylor
The Great Square
Alexandria, Egypt
!
Dear Liz,
```

Figure 10.6.2. Letters with addresses interspersed by command program of Figure 10.6.3.

*Objective*

Assume that you are using a manual sheet feed printer. When you are finished printing a letter, you remove the letterhead paper and insert an envelope, advancing it to the proper line. When you press <u>print</u> or <u>return</u> to start the printer again, the address produced by your keystroke program for this letter prints on this envelope.

Figure 10.6.2 shows the display after you have used the command program to be described shortly. All graphic symbols or ! have been removed from the first letter. After the page break, the address of the sendee has been inserted and moved to the right to print properly on the envelope. This is followed by another page break which marks the beginning of the second letter.

*The Command Program*

The command program appears in Figure 10.6.3 and on the right are notations. The program is a collection of key strokes. The underlined words represent a single key function. Keystrokes appear on different lines of the figure to provide clarity in describing and reading the program. Actually, they display as one continuous stream of characters.

On the first line the first keystroke, <u>search,</u> initiates a search activity. The next keystroke, !, is the string for which the search is made. <u>Return</u> tells the WP system that this is the end of the <u>search</u> string. When the string is found, we want to delete the ! found there and mark this as the beginning of a block to be moved. The second line searches for ! and when it is found, deletes it and marks the end of the block. The third line searches for a third occurrence of the ! symbol, deletes it and inserts a page break. The fourth line indents the address 40 positions, copies the block, the address, to this area and then resets the left margin by changing the indent to 0.

| Line Strokes | Action |
|---|---|
| 1. <u>search</u> ! <u>return</u> <u>delete</u> <u>char</u> <u>blockbeg</u> | Remove !, mark block |
| 2. <u>search</u> ! <u>return</u> <u>delete</u> <u>char</u> <u>blockend</u> | Remove !, mark block |
| 3. <u>search</u> ! <u>return</u> <u>delete</u> <u>char</u> <u>newpage</u> | Remove !, new page |
| 4. <u>indent</u> 4 0 <u>moveblock</u> <u>indent</u> 0 | Indent, insert address and restore margin. |

Figure 10.6.3. Command program to copy addresses.

*Use*

Before you can use the command program, you record it as described earlier. Then the entire program can be called forth by the touch of two keys, gold and then a numeric. Type your letters following the format of Figure 10.6.1. The command program takes care of one letter each time you touch the two keys.

Once letters are typed, start at the beginning of your electronic document and press the command program key. The address for the first sendee is extracted and the document appears as in Figure 10.6.2. At this point you can add additional information on the envelope, such as the building number or the word "Personal."

The command key affects one letter at a time. If you press the command key after processing all your letters, it is a search against a missing string since there are no more occurrences of your special character (!) in the remaining text. You will get a message, such as "String not found."

# 11
# Tables and Wide Documents

## 11.1 COLUMNS

Tables are a useful way to present information. A **table** is a rectangular arrangement of text and/or numerical information. WP features assist you in setting up and manipulating tables and in doing arithmetic. This chapter is devoted to the setup and manipulation of tables and multicolumn text and the activation of simple arithmetic processes.

Some or all of the features needed to deal with column and numerical data and arithmetic may be combined into a separate program. This program is often supplied as an option, with an additional charge. It is brought into memory only when needed, being called in from the (system) disk. It is variously called a statistical or math package but actually may do neither math (algebra or calculus) nor statistics (averages, correlation, etc.).

### Columns and Rows

The table extends in two directions, horizontally and vertically. A **row** is information on one horizontal line between one margin of the table and the other. A **column** is information which extends vertically, from the upper to the lower limit of the table. Where a row and a column intersect is a **cell** or **entry**, which may contain textual or numeric information.

A factor which limits the effectiveness of a table is the size of the page containing it. This is confusing because vendors use "page" in three different ways:

- the amount of text defined as a page for a page-oriented file management system,
- the amount of text held in the memory buffer,
- the information printed on a sheet of paper.

To make the discussion easier to follow, let us dispense with the first usage.

For the purpose of this discussion, page size is affected by two factors. The printer carriage limits the width of the paper you can use. The length of paper that a printer can handle is set only by practical limitations. You could construct a table 20 inches wide and a mile long, but who could read it? You can purchase a printer with a 26″ carriage and some people do have them.

A WP system often limits table size by the amount of computer memory assigned as work area for your text. If that area is 4K and your table width is 200 characters, you cannot deal with more than 20 rows in your table.

### Establishing Columns

The WP lets you set up columns quickly and enter data there. **Tabulation** is the principle means. **Tab keys** (or simply **tabs**) provide express motion to bring the cursor to the entry point at the next column. Figure 11.1.1 contrasts the four kinds of tabs:

- left flush,
- right flush,
- decimal,
- centering (*see* Column Titles).

```
        Normal tab 32.68   This is centered   Rflush
L.....I............D............C................F..R
 \Format Ruler
```

Figure 11.1.1. Illustrating four kinds of tabs.

*Left Flush*

The **left flush tab** is the standard tab supplied on the typewriter. It brings you to the leftmost character position of a column. Thereafter, as you type, characters are entered from left to right. This tab is most suitable for text.

*Right Flush*

After you establish a **right flush tab** and tab to this position you are at the right extremity of a column. As you type characters, they enter at this position and force characters previously typed at this tab leftward. In the figure you see the letters "ABC" that you typed in that order are aligned so that the "C" is at the tab position. It is useful for putting whole numbers into columns and for putting titles or other text flush against the right margin.

*Decimal*

The **decimal tab** allows you to align numbers on their decimal point. When you tab to a decimal tab position and enter digits, commas and a decimal point, the number displays with the decimal point at the tab stop. It works like this:

1. As you enter digits, commas and other text, these move leftward just as with the right-flush tab.
2. When you enter a period or decimal point, it appears at the tab position. (In Europe the role of the comma and the period are reversed and a WP for that market must suit its needs.)
3. Digits which you enter after the decimal point move to the right as though this were a left flush tab position. A decimal point aligns on the tab. A number entered without a decimal point is aligned flush right at the tab.

WPs differ in what they do with nonnumeric information. Some balk at handling letters or dollar signs at decimal tabs and do strange things when they are encountered. Decimal tabs are indispensable for quick entry and alignment of numbers at their decimal point on the tab stop in the column.

*Setting*

All tabs are set approximately the same way. The options that you have, depend upon your word processor:

A. Recall the format menu and set the tabs from there.
B. Move the cursor horizontally to the tab position and use a tab-set or tab-clear key to set or remove a tab stop. The result may then appear on the format line.
C. Type in a tab mnemonic followed by the numeric character position on the line where a tab should be set or cleared.

These were examined in Chapter 7.

**Column Titles**

Tables present information in two dimensions. One dimension, for instance, may show *how* you spend your money and the other dimension may show *when* you spent it: rows might show the different kinds of expenses—production, materials, personnel and so forth; the columns may show years or months. A table is no good unless it clearly gives the meaning of each row and column. It is easy to put titles in the rows; these are found at the extreme left, simply written along the left of the row. A column title appears at the top, explaining that this is for 1978 or for whatever.

The column title column should explain the meaning of that column of information; it should also be neat and presentable. You could put the title for a column flush left beginning with the start of the column. This is easy to do with the conventional left flush tab.

Some people like centered titles. It is more trouble to set up on the typewriter. Hence WP vendors have provided assistance for you in centering column titles. Two methods are possible:

- tabs,
- column definition.

### Center Tab

Some WPs provide a **center tab**. You set a center tab to the position (for each column) about which you want to center the title using the status line, tab setting keys, or by typing in a command.

To use the center tab, simply tab to that position and enter the title with underlines or boldface, if you wish to add emphasis. These characters appear centered about the tab stop. This is independent of the material which appears in the column below: text, numerals aligned on a decimal point or numerals aligned flush right are entered at a *different* tab stop. Centering is independent of the column size. A large title might exceed the width of the column, but it is centered above the center tab stop.

When you set up a table, you may not know how the numbers will look. That is why some people do not set up center tabs for the titles until the table is laid out. This is particularly recommended for decimal numbers.

### Column Centering

An alternative to center titles is provided in some WPs. First you set up the table so that each column is visible. Then define each column as you would a block, by using column definition keys: place the cursor in the upper left-hand corner of the column; press column-start (or what your WP requires); move the cursor to the lower right-hand corner of the column; press column-end.

To enter the column title, move the cursor to the line where the title should appear and type in the material. Then press the center key and the material is automatically centered within this column.

## 11.2 WIDE DOCUMENTS

**Screen Width versus Document Width**

There is no standard definition for a **wide document**. It could refer to a document larger than the screen size or one larger than standard paper (which is 8-1/2 inches wide). Often these two alternatives converge, since many screens do not accommodate text wider that 8-1/2 inches. Hereafter let us confine our examination of wide documents to those for which the text does not display properly within the screen width provided. When you use 12 or 15 characters per inch, even a conventional document may turn out to be wide.

A line of text for *our* wide document is wider than the screen. How does the vendor make it possible to see all of the text? Three techniques are used by vendors:

- split screen,
- horizontal scroll,
- folded lines.

With the first method, the WP presents the entire text on the page displayed simultaneously in one way or another. For the second method you can move across the page or up and down the page by scrolling.

*Page Size*

The page size is limited in both width and length by two factors:

- ɪ...ᴛen width of the printer,
- the computer memory and program limits for handling pages beyond a given size.

You cannot handle 28″ paper with a 15″ carriage. If you are tied into a automatic sheet feed mechanism, then the length of the page is also limited by the stock which the feeder handles.

While printer limitations are obvious, it may not be clear what the internal limitations of the word processor are until you investigate thoroughly width, length or a combination of the two.

*Limitation*

Limitations in length or width of the page are stated explicitly by the vendor and these are easy to understand. It is the combination limitation which is difficult to cope with. It's a little like the formula that the Post Office has for parcel post packages. I can never figure it out. You add the length and the width and the breadth and double one of them and so forth to find out if the Post Office will accept your package.

The internal WP limitation is generally caused by one of these two factors:

- a work area of limited size for holding text during editing,
- the page size in a page oriented WP.

Page size, rated in number of characters, determines the quantity of text you can handle as a unit. For a 4K page, the text length, line size times number of lines, cannot exceed 4K. The printer program acquires pages to be printed and can handle large documents generally. But it is not equipped to cope with tables that straddle page boundaries.

Work area size limits the amount of text which is immediately available. This restriction is less difficult to deal with; some vendors make it transparent to the user.

## Split Screen

**Split screen** does not imply any defect in the display. It describes a display divided into two (or more) parts to present simultaneously the entire width of wide text you are working on. If the text does not exceed twice the width of the screen, then the screen can be divided into two parts: the top displays the left side of the text; the bottom displays the right side of the text. If the WP divides the screen into more than two parts because of a very wide document, it really becomes difficult to work with. Then each part of the display can contain only 8 or 9 lines for a partial display, or 20 lines for a full screen.

The program to implement a split screen is simple. The text editor sends the left halves of lines to the top of the screen and the right halves of lines to the middle of the screen. Internal accounting keeps track of the half lines.

This is confusing to use and is found only infrequently.

### Folded Lines

This technique, hardly worth mentioning, is employed with some personal computers whose WP programs are not sophisticated, but where the need to handle wider documents may arise. The **folded line** deals with long lines by splitting them into two parts. The left half of the first line appears normally; the right half, the continuation, appears just below it. The second text line appears on the third and fourth screen line, and so forth.

This can be tolerated in wide documents which contain only text that can be read continuously. For tables it is practically impossible to use.

### Scrolling

Scrolling moves the text past the viewing area. **Vertical scrolling** moves text up (or down) the screen to view succeeding (or previous) text. We have seen various ways in which scrolling can be effected:

1. by the screenful or pageful;
2. by line, where the text moves up (or down) by one line for each request;
3. variable, where text keeps moving up (or down) a line at a time at a rate adjustable by you until you stop it;
4. continuous, where text moves up (or down) a fraction of a line at a time and hence seems to move continuously up the screen.

**Horizontal scrolling** moves the text of a wide document horizontally across the screen from right to left (or from left to right). This is *the* most important method for viewing and editing wide documents.

*The Wide Document*

The wide document exhibited in Figure 11.2.1 shows a portion of text restricted both horizontally and vertically. The portion of the figure, labeled I, is the left hand area of one portion of this document. Remaining within this hori-

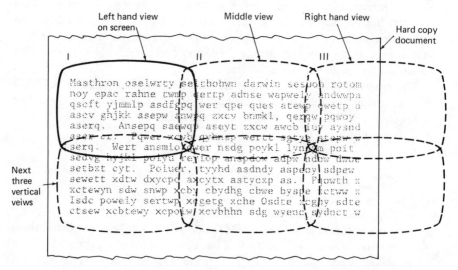

Figure 11.2.1. A wide document broken into screenfuls by the text editor.

zontal strip there is text labeled II and III to the right of the current right hand screen boundary. Text above and below the displayed area can be brought forth by vertical scrolling.

Horizontal scrolling moves text to the left or right to bring into view other portions of the same horizontal strip.

### Kinds of Horizontal Scroll

Horizontal scrolling provided by vendors differs in:

* how you request the scroll,
* the quantity of information moved for each single scroll initiated.

*Initiation*

Horizontal scroll can be initiated manually, automatically, or both. Manual initiation can be achieved in one of two ways:

* a horizontal scroll key or control/key combination,
* a command typed in using a mnemonic, such as "hs."

Automatic horizontal scroll can be initiated as with vertical scrolling. In some WPs, you move the cursor to the bottom of the screen by holding down the down-arrow. If you keep pressing down-arrow after the cursor "bottoms," this causes upward line scrolling. The amount scrolled can be a single line or a screenful, according to the WP. Similarly, if you move the cursor to the top of the screen, you get downward scroll when the cursor hits the top for some WPs.

In creating a document, when you get to the right margin you usually get word wrap. However, for the wide document, the right margin is off the screen. So when the cursor gets to the right hand side of the screen, this is a good time to induce horizontal scrolling leftward. Text moves to the left as you tab or enter new characters at your keyboard. The distance of the motion to the left is discussed below.

The same action may occur automatically during editing:

* as you move the cursor to the right side of the screen, leftward horizontal scrolling takes place if text is hidden;
* similarly when you move the cursor to the left of the screen and there is still text to the left, you induce rightward horizontal scrolling.

*Quantity*

When you induce scrolling, text moves horizontally but:

- how much text moves across the screen?
- at what rate?
- and is this controllable by you?

The most popular quantity is the screenful. When you reach a margin, the screen is altered to show another screenful of the document with a small carryover. Let's take some figures. Assume a 200 character line showing the left hand margin. When you move the cursor past the right side of the screen, a new portion of text comes and old text moves out. If old text were totally removed, there would be no continuity between the old screenful and the new screenful. Usually the first 60 characters are removed; the new screen begins with the sixty-first character of each line and ends at character 140.

The most effective horizontal scrolling moves text continuously, a character at a time horizontally in either direction. This could be done continuously at a constant rate which you could set; or it could be done on request from you each time you hit the vertical-scroll-left (or -right).

The machinery to do this is complicated and it's questionable whether it is worthwhile to invest programming in an area where the profit may be small.

**Horizontal Scroll Implementation**

To put it into perspective we first review vertical scrolling to set forth the important concepts to be broadened for horizontal scrolling.

*Vertical Scrolling*

Recall that the memory of the computer is organized like a straight line and not a rectangle, which is the usual shape of the text. Figure 11.2.2 shows text laid out in memory as a straight line. When the information is displayed on your screen, the section labeled *line 1* goes to the first set of characters in refresh memory. *Line 2* goes to the second area and so forth.

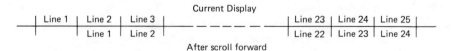

Figure 11.2.2. The work area for a normal document broken into lines for display.

To scroll forward by line, the computer sends the next line which is not included on the display over to the refresh memory to replace the line which is currently first. Then the second line is relabeled as the first display line. This all happens very fast and the text moves up immediately.

To scroll by the screenful or pageful, the new screen content is transmitted and displayed as a unit. The text editor program simply resets the display markers in its buffer and transmits the contents of this newly designated memory area over to the refresh memory to be displayed. This is shown in Figure 11.2.3, where the dashed lines mark the boundaries of the new screenful. The new text area partially overlaps the previous one for editing continuity. When it is transmitted to the display, the present contents are wiped out. The WP often shows some constant information at the top, the status display. This may be altered to reflect the scroll, but its overall format remains constant and it rarely seems to change.

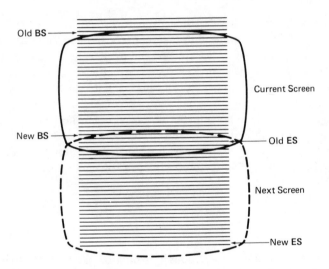

Figure 11.2.3. Vertical scroll of a normal document showing work area and markers.

*Horizontal Scroll*

Figure 11.2.4 again shows memory considered as a long continuous line. The word

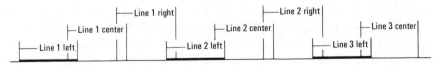

Figure 11.2.4. For a wide document the text editor presents lines for a screenful extracted from the work area according to the scroll position.

played on the first text line of the screen. It is labeled *Line 1 left*. More text immediately following labeled *Line 1 center* and *Line 1 right* belongs to the rest of this line but is not being presented. Text marked *Line 2 left* is displayed on the second line of the screen. Other sections of memory are similarly labeled *Line 3 left, Line 4 left* and so forth to correspond to these current screen display lines.

Let's scroll right by the screenful. The text editor now transmits new text to replace each line of the display:

*Line 1 center* replaces *Line 1 left*,
*Line 2 center* replaces *Line 2 left*,
and so on.

Once the WP program has determined the text to be displayed on the screen, these lines must be retransmitted *in their entirety* to the refresh memory of the display. It takes a fast WP at least one second to alter the display by the screenful. Transmission from the computer to the conventional display occurs only during retrace periods when characters are not being presented. This slows down the alteration of the screen.

Although it is simple to program the movement of text horizontally a character at a time, the problem is the response time of the display. Since it takes one or two seconds for the screen to redisplay, it takes a minute of more to pass over 60 positions. This is too slow for comfort. Hence most vendors settle for horizontal scrolling by the screenful.

*An Alternative*

One or two vendors supply continuous horizontal scroll. How can they do this? The video display terminal (VDT) contains extra hardware, a large memory with a built-in microprocessor. The entire wide page is in the VDT memory. Your keystrokes at the terminal direct the terminal what to display. The internal microprocessor resets refresh memory and the display logic immediately, so as to present a different portion of the text. In a fraction of a second (1/30 or 1/60) the new display appears, since there is no transmission time involved. Now you can scroll horizontally at 10 to 30 positions per second.

You get the benefit of continuous horizontal scroll if the vendor has built it into the terminal. As technology evolves it will be possible to build more and more intelligence into a terminal without appreciably increasing its cost.

## 11.3 COLUMN MOVEMENT

**Need**

When you insert or delete in normal text, the WP program maintains the margins and justification that you specify, adjusting any change in the text to conform. With tabular text, the integrity of each column is of prime importance. Any change in one column should have no affect on the arrangement of other columns, in the headings of the columns nor on the titles for rows. WP vendors are aware of this and give you aids for altering tabular text.

*Types*

Your WP usually provides one of three types of column movement:

A. **Masked**: you set up a mask and move text past it to perform editing and column management.
B. **Save and recall**: you save a column in memory or on disk and move it back into the table where you want it.
C. **Key defined**: you enter a key sequence to move the columns.

**Masked Column Manipulation**

*Principle*

When your WP provides this kind of column capability, you:

1. bring a ruler line to the screen,
2. create a mask by entering characters into the ruler which specify the action,
3. scroll the text past this mask.
4. As the text moves by, the WP alters it according to the directions in the mask.

The AM Jacquard Type Rite WP system is our example of this.

*Set Up*

TR (TypeRite) has a sequence of menus by which you enter the modify mode for editing. During editing, TR prompts you for a command. Imagine text on the screen which includes a table to edit. For convenience, you scroll the text so that the table is near the bottom of the screen. Then you move the cursor above the table and key in the command CM for column mode.

The cursor is on the line just above the table where you create the mask. You now press ruler/print and a ruler appears, a pair of page width horizontal lines with verticals marking off character positions and otherwise blank, as shown in the top of Figure 11.3.1.

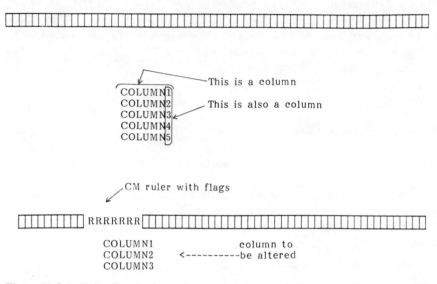

Figure 11.3.1. Ruler line (top); a column (center); a mask (bottom). (Courtesy of AM Jacquard).

*Mask*

The **mask** *is* the ruler line with flags entered in it. A **flag** is a character which you put in the mask to determine what happens to characters at that position in the column as you move them by. A typical mask is shown at the bottom of Figure 11.3.1. To make it, you put the cursor at the first position where an R appears and type in seven R's. The mask is applied to the column. In the middle of the figure we see a column defined just below as a vertical set of one or more characters.

Table 11.3 is a list of TypeRite flag characters and their meaning. Return to the bottom of Figure 11.3.1. The flag R (for right) requests that all columns to the left of the first R be moved rightward; the number of R's in the mask determine *how many* positions the columns to the left move rightward.

*Action*

You have set a mask above the table. You move the text up vertically past the mask; press scroll-up and the columns move up and rightward as you watch. Several examples of other actions are presented and illustrated.

**Table 11.3. Flags and Their Meaning.**
**(Courtesy of AM Jacquard).**

| Flag(s) | Column Movement Performed |
|---|---|
| B | Blank out a column |
| D | Delete (squeeze out) a column |
| D | Delete a column and replace another |
| R | Shift columns right |
| R | Shift columns left |
| P | Paste in/over a column |
| I | Insert a column |
| L | Copy and leave a column |
| S | Swap columns |
| B with I | Blank and reinsert a column |
| B with P | Blank a column and replace another |
| D with I | Delete and reinsert a column |
| D with P | Delete a column and replacing another |
| L with I | Duplicate a column and reinserting a copy |
| L with P | Duplicate a column and replacing another |

**Blanking a column** removes the column without moving the other columns in your table. Use this to revise one column heavily. The flag character B specifies blanking. Figure 11.3.2 shows how you set this up. The mask at the top of the

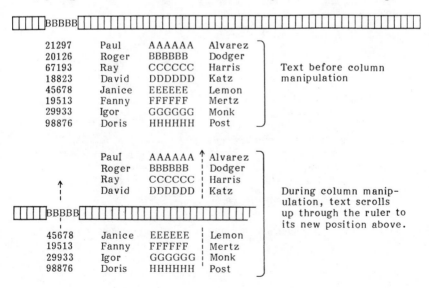

Figure 11.3.2. Blanking out a column.

figure contains B's above all the positions in the column to be blanked. Below this is the table to be altered. In the lower half of the figure we see the screen as the action takes place.

As you scroll the table upward past the mask, the B's "wipe out" text in that column which goes by. There is no effect on the other columns. If you scroll the text back down, the B's make the column reappear!

**Delete and realign** removes text from a designated column and moves left all columns to the right to replace the removed text. The D flag requests this action. At the top left of Figure 11.3.3 a mask with five D's eliminates the numerals in the left hand column. The columns to the right of the D's move leftward to replace the deleted material when you scroll-up, as shown at the bottom of the figure. Notice that the edited table is not flush left as was the original table. Only five D's appear in the mask; hence the other columns move five positions left. There are 10 positions on the first line between 2 and the P in Paul. Put 10 D's in the mask and the rest of the table is aligned flush left. If additional D's were put in the mask, the column would move even farther leftward.

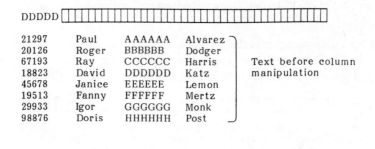

```
21297    Paul    AAAAAA    Alvarez ⎤
20126    Roger   BBBBBB    Dodger  |
67193    Ray     CCCCCC    Harris  |   Text before column
18823    David   DDDDDD    Katz    |   manipulation
45678    Janice  EEEEEE    Lemon   |
19513    Fanny   FFFFFF    Mertz   |
29933    Igor    GGGGGG    Monk    |
98876    Doris   HHHHHH    Post  ⎦
```

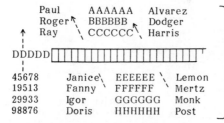

```
         Paul    AAAAAA    Alvarez  ⎤
         Roger   BBBBBB    Dodger   |   During column manip-
         Ray     CCCCCC    Harris   |   ulation, as text
DDDDD                               |   scrolls up through
                                    |   the ruler, the first
45678    Janice  EEEEEE    Lemon    |   column is deleted,
19513    Fanny   FFFFFF    Mertz    |   and the remaining
29933    Igor    GGGGGG    Monk     |   columns shift left.
98876    Doris   HHHHHH    Post   ⎦
```

Figure 11.3.3. Deleting a column and realigning the remaining columns. (Courtesy of AM Jacquard).

Swapping interchanges two columns. Put S flags in the mask above each of the two columns to be swapped, as illustrated in Figure 11.3.4. It is important to define the length of the **flag field** the contiguous set of flags, equally for the columns being interchanged, even if the text part of the columns are not equal. If "Popodopolis" were in the second column of the example, only "Popodop" would be moved in the example since the flag field contains seven S's.

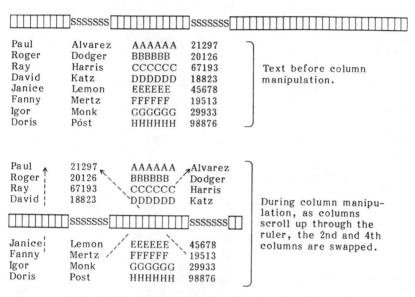

Figure 11.3.4. Swapping columns. (Courtesy of AM Jacquard).

### Reverse

When a table is moved up through the mask, the action specified by the flag field is performed. When you finish, the table is above the mask. If you scroll the text down through the mask you reverse the action just made. THIS IS TRUE FOR ALL ACTIONS DESCRIBED.

Table 11.3 shows that R is used for both a right shift and a left shift. This is possible because a left shift is performed by scrolling text *down* through the mask. A mask of R's is positioned at the *bottom* of the table. Then as you scroll text *downward*, the columns shift left.

A column being removed by blanking with B's can be inserted in another portion of the table where an I flag appears. Figure 11.3.5 is an example: as you scroll-up the table, the second column is blanked by the B's in the mask; the blanked item is put *above* the I in the mask. Columns between the B's and the I's move rightward by the number of B's in the mask; columns to the left of I's are unaffected. The I's could be on the right of the B's; you still move the blanked column into position at the mask of I's. This is shown at the bottom of the figure.

To remove the blank column, move the right columns leftward by the blank column size; change the B's to R's in the mask and scroll the text *down* through the mask.

In this example, as the columns move upward through the ruler, the column containing first names reappears in the field that contained last names, and the last names are shifted right to accommodate them.

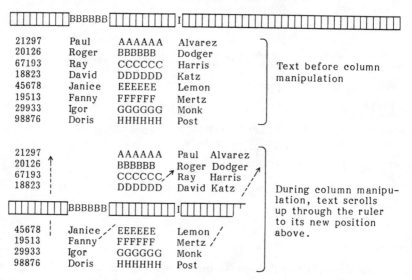

Figure 11.3.5. Blanking and reinserting a column. (Courtesy of AM Jacquard).

Sometimes it is desirable to **copy** a column from one table into another table. This is shown in Figure 11.3.6. The L flag requests that a copy of the desired column be put away in a storage area. The copy is recalled later as shown in the figure, which consists of three panels. In the top panel the mask of L's sits above one

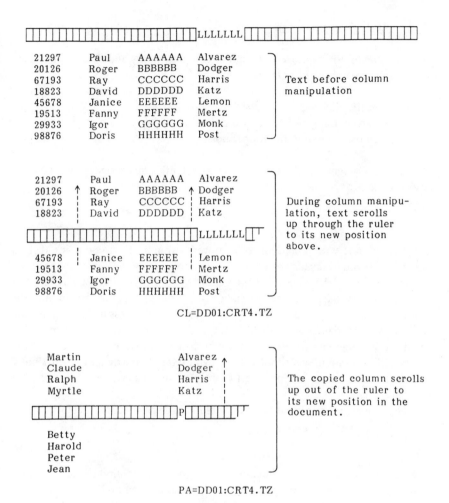

Figure 11.3.6. Duplicating a column and inserting a copy elsewhere in the same document. (Courtesy of AM Jacquard).

table. In the middle panel you scroll-up; the table moves up through the mask and a copy of the selected column is put away.

You create a new mask above another table (bottom panel) with a single P where the saved column is to be deposited (Placed). Scroll-up through the mask; the saved column is deposited with its left edge aligned at the P flag.

**Save and Recall**

For this type of WP, to move any column you put it away and then bring it back
to the table where needed. These actions are:

1. mark the column,
2. save the column and delete it if desired,
3. recall the column in the proper position.

The AB Dick Magna SL (hereafter, the MSL) typifies this design, so we examine
how it works.

*Designate*

You have a table with a column to be moved within it. First you point MSL to
that column; you **designate** the column. Begin by moving the cursor to the upper
left hand corner of the column. Press column to tell MSL that you are designating
a column. Press right to move the cursor to the right margin of the column; the
top line of the column up to the cursor is highlighted. Press down to move the
cursor down the right side of the column; as the cursor moves, each entry in the
column is highlighted. Release down when the cursor reaches the bottom of the
column. If you should overshoot when moving either to the right or down, simply
reverse the cursor direction (press left or up); the cursor moves backward and the
highlight is removed.

When you are satisfied that the exact column is designated, press column again.

*Save*

Press save to save the designated column. A copy of the column is made in a save
area on the disk. Now if you press delete, the column is removed and the columns
to the right move leftward over the deleted space by the column width. If you
press clear, the highlight is removed from the column which remains in position
and intact.

*Move*

You now have a copy of the column in a save area of the disk. Move the cursor
to a position in the table where you want the *upper left hand corner* of the column
to be entered. Then press recall. The column is shoved in between existing columns. Columns to the right of the cursor move right.

**Command Keys**

The action desired is described by entering commands or pressing keys:

1. Define the column at a tab stop with a command key.
2. Specify the operation.
3. Note the location where the action should take place.

As an example we use the Burroughs Redactor III, which is hereafter referred to as the RIII.

*Define*

A column for RIII must be defined at a tab stop. Either press <u>tab</u> or move the cursor to the tab stop for this column. Press <u>insert/delete</u> and then press <u>set</u> <u>C</u> to tell RIII to do a column edit operation. The column is highlighted for you to verify.

Now describe the action to the RIII. For instance, to delete this column, press <u>clear auto</u>; to move the column, press <u>move</u>. In either case the column disappears.

*Action*

To move the saved column, put the cursor for the tab stop at the destination. Press <u>set</u> <u>C</u>; then press <u>move</u> and the column reappears in the new position. The previous column and its right hand neighbors move right one column tab stop.

**Insert a New Column**

To contrast the three techniques, we examine how to insert a new column of figures along with a column head into an existing table between the existing third and fourth columns. Of course, there must be enough room for one more column to the right, within the margins defined for the page. There must also be enough space in memory to hold the added text.

*No Assistance*

Suppose your WP system has no feature which gives assistance in inserting a new column. Here is how you might proceed. Position the cursor at the left of the heading for column 4. Insert enough space for the new column. If it is 10 characters wide, insert ten spaces here. Move the cursor down one position and insert ten spaces there; continue thus for all rows. You have added a new blank column.

Go back to the top of the blank column and fill it in: you overwrite the blanks. In this way you add no additional length to any row.

*Masked*

Create a ruler line just above your table. Over column 4 insert a series of 10 R's. Scroll-up through the mask. All columns starting with the fourth move right by 10 positions. Enter the new information in the blank column.

*Save and Recall*

Position the cursor at the extreme right of the table. Create the new column here. When you are done, designate the *new* column. Save the column. Move the cursor to the beginning of column 4. Recall the column.

*Key Define*

This method is almost identical to *save and recall.* To define the column on the right side of the table, set up a tab stop of the right type. Enter the new column at this tab stop. Move the column at the right and enter it at the fourth column tab stop.

## 11.4 TOTALS

### Introduction

This section discusses addition in tables. Many WPs have this capability and more; *some* have only this capability. But first consider how to signify negative numbers.

### Signed Numbers

There are several ways that negative numbers might *appear* in a table. The method that you chose depends on the purpose of the document and who shall read it:

**Sign prefix** Each number is prefixed with a sign, either plus or minus. A number without sign denotes a positive number. Only negative numbers are prefixed with a minus sign, entered with the hyphen (viz., -36).

**Parentheses** A negative number or credit is indicated by putting the number within parentheses (or sometimes brackets). Positive numbers do not have parentheses about them [viz., (36) for -36].

**Suffixes**  Bankers prefer a suffix such as CR or ** for a credit or negative number (viz., 36.00 CR).

This is how the *reader* distinguishes negative numbers from positive ones. The questions for the vendor are: should the program recognize numbers in *all* these forms above as negative? Can they be intermixed? How does the WP present a negative result? Vendors take one of two approaches:

- You chose one method by signifying this to the program; you must stick with that method throughout the arithmetic.
- The vendor choses his method and you must abide by it.

In the latter case, if you don't like his method, you must still use it. Later you can clean up the table with editing commands.

For instance, the vendor requires negative numbers in parentheses. After doing arithmetic for you, the WP provides an answer with a negative number in parentheses and entering CR after all negative numbers with:

search ( replace  
search ) replace CR  (11.4.1)

where names in italics refer to function keys. Note that a *null* replaces "(."

### Specifying Functions

Tables differ considerably. You may want to take totals of rows or columns or both. Which columns participate? Where do the answers go? These are specified to the WP to get the results:

1. Construct a mask and scroll the table through the mask.
2. Key in a formula, using mnemonics.
3. After giving control to the table arithmetic program, you get prompts to ask for actions.

### Masks

You set up a mask, scroll the text past and totals appear where you request them. TypeRite arithmetic masks use different flags, displayed in Table 11.4.

**Table 11.4. Flags for Arithmetic. (Courtesy of AM Jacquard).**

| | |
|---|---|
| A | Add columns |
| S | Add rows and create a column of sums |
| T | Add rows but do not create a column of sums |
| G | Add rows of Ts and Ss to create a grand total |
| D | Specify number of digits after decimal point |
| + | Add a constant |
| – | Subtract a constant, or append a minus sign to negative quantities |
| * | Multiply by a constant, or fill with asterisks |
| / | Divide by a constant |
| $ | Insert a floating dollar sign |
| , | Insert comma divisions in large numbers |
| < > | Enclose negative quantities in brackets |
| I | Define the action Type-Rite must take when invalid characters are found in a column |

*Simple Column Total*

To add a column, Figure 11.4.1, you put the letter A in the ruler above the decimal point for the column. As you scroll past the mask, the WP takes a total. To deposit this total at the bottom of the column, simply press F5.

Construct a ruler so that an A is located above the decimal point:

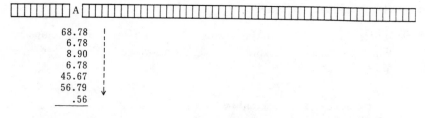

Figure 11.4.1. Add a column of decimals. (Courtesy of AM Jacquard).

Another example, in Figure 11.4.2, uses the A$ flag, positioned in the mask above the decimal point so that the total is prefixed by a dollar sign. The text is scrolled by the mask; the total is taken and may be deposited at the bottom of the column.

*Multiple Columns with a Grand Total*

Figure 11.4.3 shows two columns, each to be added. Above the decimal point of each is the flag A. For a grand total, the sum of the two totals, put T in the mask

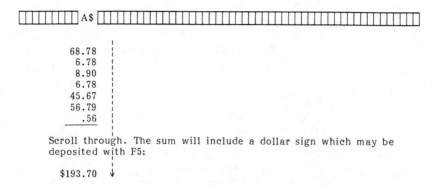

Figure 11.4.2. Add a column of decimals and insert dollar sign ($) in total. (Courtesy of AM Jacquard).

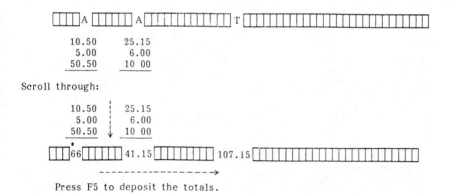

Figure 11.4.3. Sum down and across: one grand total. (Courtesy of AM Jacquard).

at the decimal point of the grand-total column. As text is scrolled past the mask, totals are taken and deposited at the bottom of each column. The grand total is deposited simultaneously, with its decimal point aligned beneath the T and in the same row as the other totals.

### Row Totals

For a row total, an S flag is placed in the mask in an empty column. The sum of cells within a row is taken and placed in this position. If multiple row totals are desired, other S flags are used; the WP takes row totals from the left to the first S, then between each S and the next S.

In Figure 11.4.4 we see two sets of two columns each. The two sets are separated by an empty column for which there is an S flag in the mask. The sum of the right hand pairs of entries in each row is taken and deposited in the third column; the sum of the second pair of entries is put in the right hand column.

The G flag is used in conjunction with the S or T and A flags to sum across columns as you scroll. It acts as if a T flag were inserted and does not deposit the subtotals as it goes. Subtotals will be placed beneath the S; a grand total beneath the G as you scroll.

Construct a flag in the form:

☐ A ☐☐☐☐ A ☐☐☐☐ S ☐☐☐☐ A ☐☐☐☐ A ☐☐☐☐☐☐ S ☐☐☐☐☐ G ☐☐☐☐☐☐☐☐☐☐

| 5.00 | 10.50 | 35.65 | 16.81 |
| 18.15 | 5.00 | 11.22 | 40.00 |
| 20.20 | 51.52 | 60.56 | 30.10 |

Scroll through the columns:

| 5.00 | 10.50 | 15.5 | 35.65 | 16.81 | 52.46 | 67.96 |
| 18.15 | 5.00 | 23.15 | 11.22 | 40.00 | 51.22 | 74.37 |
| 20.20 | 51.52 | 71.72 | 60.56 | 30.10 | 90.66 | 162.38 |

[43.35☐☐ 67.02 ☐☐ 110.37 ☐ 107.43 ☐☐ 86.91 ☐☐☐ 194.34 ☐ 304.71 ☐☐☐☐☐☐☐

Press F5 to deposit the totals.

Figure 11.4.4. Sum with grand totals. (Courtesy of AM Jacquard).

At the extreme right, a G in the mask requests a grand total for every row. As text scrolls by, the WP first takes subtotals for S's and then adds them together to get a row total for the column with the G.

The sums for columns 1 and 2 and for 4 and 5 are taken because of the A in the mask. The sums of the subtotals in columns 3 and 6 are also taken. The grand total appears in the last column. These appear in the last row of the table.

**Formulas**

For some WPs you enter a formula to tell the WP what action to take. For instance, an action to be applied to all the entries in column 4 refers to "C4." The formula consists of the signs of arithmetic, plus, minus, etc., and the equal sign.

The sequence is to:

1. define the table, indicating the columns and rows which comprise it,
2. enter the formula,
3. request the action.

As an example we examine the Micom 2001.

*Define The Table*

With the table displayed on the screen, move the cursor to the decimal point of the upper left entry. Then perform the following sequence:

command D T execute                                      (11.4.2)

Command starts a command. "D T" says that you are Defining a Table; execute says to go ahead and do it. Now move the cursor to the lower right hand table entry at the bottom of the last column. Be careful to verify that this entry is empty; it receives the total. Align the cursor at the intended decimal point, usually the tab setting, and press execute.

As the cursor moves down and right, it highlights the table. When you are in the lower right hand corner, the numerical part of the table is highlighted. If this does not seem correct, you may alter the cursor position which causes the highlighted area to change.

*Entering the Formula*

You begin to enter the formula with command; next, type L (for "let"); an equation follows; the variable on the left is the column to receive totals; an equal sign follows; other variables on the right connected by arithmetic signs indicate the action taken. Finally, hit execute.

*Example*

For the table in Figure 11.4.5, first define it: put the cursor at "." in 1,456.82 and

```
┌─────────────────────────────────────────────────────────────────────┐
│                    Manufacturing Cost Breakdown                       │
│                          First Quarter                                │
│                             1979                                      │
│                                                                       │
│                     JAN          FEB          MAR        TOTAL         │
│                                                                       │
│ Direct Labor                                                          │
│   Costs          1,456.82     1,487.93     1,499.81                    │
│ Time keepers        72.95        72.95        72.95                    │
│ Insurance           89.25        88.12       (6.13)*                   │
│ Rent               460.00       460.00       460.00                    │
│ Electricity        111.11       135.59       189.34                    │
│ Heat                84.88        95.43        82.37                    │
│ Clerical and                                                          │
│   Office           225.59       245.43       230.40                    │
│ Miscellaneous      567.90       321.83       471.50                    │
│                                                                       │
│                  ─────────    ─────────    ─────────    ─────────      │
│                                                                       │
│   TOTAL                                                               │
│                                                                       │
│ *Adjustment in refund                                                 │
└─────────────────────────────────────────────────────────────────────┘
```

Figure 11.4.5. Table without totals. (Courtesy of Micom).

enter "<u>command</u> D T <u>execute</u>"; move the cursor below the line in the "TOTAL" column to where the decimal point should be; press <u>execute</u>. Now enter the formula for the WP. Let's ask for new totals first. For every row ask that the last (fourth) column be the sum of the first three columns. This is simpler to write than to describe:

<u>command</u> L C4 = C1+C2+C3 <u>execute</u>         (11.4.3)

As soon as you press <u>execute</u>, totals appear in the right hand column as in Figure 11.4.6.

```
                        Manufacturing Cost Breakdown
                             First Quarter
                                 1979


                     JAN          FEB          MAR        TOTAL

Direct Labor
   Costs           1,456.82     1,487.93     1,499.81    4,444.56
Time keepers          72.95        72.95        72.95      218.85
Insurance             89.25        88.12       (6.13)*     171.24
Rent                 460.00       460.00       460.00    1,380.00
Electricity          111.11       135.59       189.34      436.04
Heat                  84.88        95.43        82.37      262.68
Clerical and
   Office            225.59       245.43       230.40      701.42
Miscellaneous        567.90       321.83       471.50    1,361.23


   TOTAL


   *Adjustment in refund
```

Figure 11.4.6. Table with row totals. (Courtesy of Micom).

Perhaps you would like the columns totaled. Position the cursor in the bottom line of the table and make the request by formula, thus:

<u>command</u> T C <u>execute</u>         (11.4.4)

Here T C asks for a total for each column. The result appears as Figure 11.4.7.

```
                    Manufacturing Cost Breakdown
                          First Quarter
                             1979

                     JAN          FEB          MAR         TOTAL

Direct Labor
  Costs            1,456.82     1,487.93     1,499.81    1,487.93
Time keepers         72.95        72.95        72.95       72.95
Insurance            89.25        88.12       (6.13)*      88.12
Rent                460.00       460.00       460.00      460.00
Electricity         111.11       135.59       189.34      135.59
Heat                 84.88        95.43        82.37       95.43
Clerical and
  Office            225.59       245.43       230.40      245.43
Miscellaneous       567.90       321.83       471.50      321.83


  TOTAL           3,068.50     2,907.28     3,000.24    2,907.28

*Adjustment in refund
```

Figure 11.4.7. Table with row *and* column totals. (Courtesy of Micom).

The Micom 2001 provides two levels of subtotals: a **subtotal** and an **intermediate total**. These may be programmed only for a column. Figure 11.4.8 shows how to set this up. Wherever you want a subtotal, enter code 1 at the decimal point for that entry. (The figure shows this as 1 inside a square.) For an intermediate total, enter code 2. A grand total needs no entry; the WP detects a bottom line with no entry and puts the grand total there.

When you have set up your table with the two classes of subtotals and the grand total, you ask for all three kinds of totals with the single command, (11.4.4). The result for Figure 11.4.8 is shown in Figure 11.4.9.

### Prompt

With this technique, after you call for the program for numerical processing, it prompts you by asking questions. If your response is accepted, further questions ensue. You continue thus until the program is satisfied that it has all the answers and then it executes your request. The Xerox 860 works in this manner and is the example.

|  | CAPITAL AND LIABILITIES | |
|---|---|---|
|  | 1978 | 1977 |
| SHAREHOLDERS EQUITY INTEREST | | |
| Ordinary share capital | 1,705.80 | 1,704.60 |
| Share premium account | 233.20 | 230.90 |
| Retained profit | 4,232.00 | 3,999.40 |
| Revaluation surplus | 3,206.10 | 2,967.90 |
|  | ☐1 | ☐1 |
| SUNDRY PROVISIONS | | |
| Long-term provisions | 1,829.30 | 1,439.80 |
| Short-term provisions | 232.50 | 237.30 |
|  | ☐1 | ☐1 |
| INTERMEDIATE TOTAL | ☐2 | ☐2 |
| LONG-TERM LIABILITIES | | |
| Convertible debenture loans | 340.30 | 338.10 |
| Other debenture loans | 1,610.20 | 1,638.20 |
| Other long-term liabilities | 834.30 | 928.90 |
|  | ☐1 | ☐1 |
| CURRENT LIABILITIES | | |
| Banks | 120.50 | 240.20 |
| Accounts payable and accrued taxes | 969.60 | 1,000.40 |
| Accrued expenses | 334.30 | 330.70 |
|  | ☐1 | ☐1 |
| INTERMEDIATE TOTAL | ☐2 | ☐2 |
| PROFIT AVAILABLE FOR DISTRIBUTION | 340.30 | 318.70 |
| Interim dividend made payable in December | (102.30) | (102.30) |
|  | ☐1 | ☐1 |
| GRAND TOTAL | | |

Figure 11.4.8. Table where *code* 1 and *code* 2 cause the boxes with "1" and "2" in them respectively to appear. (Courtesy of Micom).

*Setup*

After you create your table, you bracket the numerical portion of the table. For the Xerox 860 the first character of the first entry (upper left) must be code 6, an invisible mark which tells the program where your table starts. The bottom of your table is similarly bracketed. For the Xerox 860 the first character of the first entry (lower right corner) on the last line (where totals go, if any) is set to code 6.

| | CAPITAL AND LIABILITIES | |
|---|---|---|
| | 1978 | 1977 |
| SHAREHOLDERS EQUITY INTEREST | | |
| Ordinary share capital | 1,705.80 | 1,704.60 |
| Share premium account | 233.20 | 230.90 |
| Retained profit | 4,232.00 | 3,999.40 |
| Revaluation surplus | 3,206.10 | 2,967.90 |
| | 9,377.10 | 8,902.80 |
| SUNDRY PROVISIONS | | |
| Long-term provisions | 1,829.30 | 1,439.80 |
| Short-term provisions | 232.50 | 237.30 |
| | 2,061.80 | 1,677.10 |
| INTERMEDIATE TOTAL | 11,438.90 | 10,579.90 |
| LONG-TERM LIABILITIES | | |
| Convertible debenture loans | 340.30 | 338.10 |
| Other debenture loans | 1,610.20 | 1,638.20 |
| Other long-term liabilities | 834.30 | 928.90 |
| | 2,784.80 | 2,905.20 |
| CURRENT LIABILITIES | | |
| Banks | 120.50 | 240.20 |
| Accounts payable and accrued taxes | 969.60 | 1,000.40 |
| Accrued expenses | 334.30 | 330.70 |
| | 1,424.40 | 1,571.30 |
| INTERMEDIATE TOTAL | 4,209.20 | 4,476.50 |
| PROFIT AVAILABLE FOR DISTRIBUTION | 340.30 | 318.70 |
| Interim dividend made payable in December | (102.30) | (102.30) |
| | 238.00 | 216.40 |
| GRAND TOTAL | 15,886.10 | 15,272.80 |

Figure 11.4.9. The WP has filled in all three classes of totals.
(Courtesy of Micom).

*Program*

The 860 has a function key called program. When you touch program, you tell the system that you want one of its so-called generic programs. This one is called "Table Math." So you perform the following sequence: touch program; type in #TABLE MATH; touch accpt.

*Prompts*

A dialogue now occurs between you and the system. Questions appear on the command line at the top of the screen. You enter replies which may be positive or negative: to say "Yes" touch accpt; to say "No" touch stop.

Suppose you have constructed a table such as the one in Figure 11.4.3 for which you need only totals at the bottom of each column. The dialogue takes place as below, where the computer asks the questions (which end with ?) and you supply the answers (which are underlined):

> ADD ACROSS? stop
> ADD DOWN? accpt
> REPLACE VERTICAL TOTALS? stop
> ALTER MATH OPTIONS? stop
> OUTPUT $$$? stop
> DECIMALS? stop
> COMMAS? accpt
> PARENS FOR NEGATIVE NUMBERS? accpt
> OUTPUT PLUS SIGN? stop
> DO NUMERIC COLUMNS BEGIN AT LEFT COLUMN? stop
> . . . . . . . . . . . . . . . . . . . . . . . . . . . . . . . . . . . . . (11.4.5)

When the last question is answered, the program takes over and when done, the status display reads "ADDITION COMPLETE." You press stop to remove the message and to continue editing or to store the document.

## 11.5 MORE ARITHMETIC

Although the tabular arithmetic described so far is simple, it will do for most offices. But if you consider the powerful computer available, these functions are rudimentary.

What kind of capability could you use in the office setting?

1. More complex functions, statistical measures, such as the mean, the variance, the standard deviation.
2. A place to store intermediate results to call up later for more calculation.
3. Selective requests for operations on some of the rows or columns which make up the table.
4. Sequential operations, such as: take the sum of a group of numbers; divide by a constant; then add in some other constant; and so forth.
5. Given a table with the calculations filled in, let's change some of the numbers and have the WP recalculate the values.
6. Specify how many decimal places you want for the result.

7. Do calculations outside of tables.
8. In generating reports from lists and files, calculation would be helpful along the way.

In this section we explore how these requirements are met by some vendors. But first we examine how calculations of a more complex nature can be specified.

### Specifying Calculations

Regardless of how simple or complex calculations are, the WP cannot read your mind. It has to be told exactly what to do and in what sequence. Therefore, we examine and constrast the three ways described in this chapter for specifying arithmetic operations.

*Masks*

Masks work quite well for specifying column and row totals, subtotals and some additional activities involving constants. We can also do selective operations on columns.

When it comes to being selective about rows, to doing sequential activities and for storing intermediate results, masks do not work and must be discarded or supplemented.

*Prompts*

When the alternatives and the choices within an alternative are few, prompts work well. We are familiar with both menus and prompts for specifying format and other parameters involved in processing text. Now we need to select a set of numbers from a large table or array. The more selective we become, the greater the number of prompts and prompts within prompts that are necessary.

*Formulas*

What remains is the tried and true method of describing arithmetic operations, the formula. The trouble is, the operator and the fabricator of the table are less familiar with mathematical notation than the situation demands. The point is, therefore, to make the description as simple as possible so that the operator with minimum training can convert what is needed into this formal notation. NBI uses the letters "c" and "r" to specify columns and rows. A number then calls out a specific column or row; "c5" specifies the fifth column.

This method gets pretty close to programming. When you are at home with singling out rows and columns thus, it is a short step to use BASIC to state what is necessary. Only formulas have the flexibility to express all the operations needed. The terminology can be complicated and the activity itself can scare people away.

### Additional Features

To make more arithmetic functions possible, additional features help immeasurably:

A. Memory cells for temporary results
B. Action on only some rows and/or columns
C. Sequential calculations
D. Recalculation of previous results where some numbers have changed
E. Form of the results
F. Nontabular arithmetic
G. Arithmetic in reports.

### Memory Cells or Registers

The computer has at its disposal a large number of memory cells. Why not make available a few of them to hold the temporary results of arithmetic. Similar cells are furnished in many hand calculators: in doing a long calculation you may come up with an intermediate result: to preserve it for later use assign the result to its own memory cell. Calculators specify temporary cells in different ways. My Texas Instrument calculator has a button called sto. If I press sto followed by a digit, the number in the accumulator is stored at one of nine temporary registers: sto 6 puts the temporary result into cell 6. To bring it back later, press rcl (for recall), followed by the number of the register: press rcl 6 to retrive the result.

In a similar way you can tell some word processors that you want to take the sum of a column and place it into a register or memory cell, let us call it M1. Later, you can recall this result and use it for calculation. This is the very thing to do in taking an average: you find the column sum and save it; then you divide it by the number of rows in the table.

*Selective Action*

A table consists of rows and columns. We have seen how to specify actions which take place on all the rows of a specified column. You may ask to add column 1 and 2 together and put the result in column 3. As the WP scans each row, it adds the cell in column 1 to that in column 2, and puts the result in column 3.

But suppose you want to exclude some of the rows. Your table may include text and some rows to which the calculations do not apply. You want the WP to skip three rows. If only the first four rows are used for calculations, one way to do this is row by row, if your WP permits.

First, let's review how to set up for the NBI stat/math package. The text document is now active:

1. Scroll to the table
2. Move the cursor to a blank line within the table
3. Press <u>mode</u> to alter the mode of entry
4. Type <u>s</u> for statistical
5. The prompt displays: "STAT MODE: <u>E</u>nter new calculation, <u>D</u>isplay old, <u>R</u>emove old. <u>Set</u> display format, <u>C</u>ompute, <u>V</u>erify."
6. Type <u>e</u> because you want to enter a calculation
7. The prompt displays: "Calculation number."
8. Press <u>return</u> and it assigns a number to this calculation and displays this number.
9. Type the calculation—add the first two columns and put the result in the third: c1 + c2 = c3; then hit <u>return</u>.
10. Other calculations may be entered by repeating steps 6-8.

To make the computations and enter the results into your table you take these actions:

11. The prompt of (5) reappears and you type c to calculate.
12. Another prompt displays: "Column only (DOWN ARROW), Row and Column (ALT SHIFT + ROW OPERATION), Skip row (ALT SHIFT + DOWN ARROW), or Display row (ALT SHIFT + DISP)?"
13. The answer is in a blank line above the table proper. To move it down to the first row of numbers and, press <u>alt-shift</u> and <u>down-arrow</u>.
14. Request each row calculation by pressing <u>down-arrow</u>.
15. Continue this to skip rows (<u>alt-shift</u> and <u>down-arrow</u>) or to calculate (<u>down-arrow</u> alone) until no more rows need calculations.
16. Press <u>cancel</u> twice to conclude.

*Selection by Designation*

Let's review the steps to add columns of numbers and produce a row for an answer, named "row operations" by NBI. First, let's review general operation:

1. Depress <u>mode</u>.
2. Type <u>s</u> (stat).
3. Type <u>e</u> (new calc), <u>return</u>.
4. Type <u>r</u> (for row), <u>return</u>—this totals all columns in the table.
5. Press <u>alt-shift</u> <u>down-arrow</u> to skip this blank line.
6. Enter numbers from the first row by pressing <u>alt-shift</u> <u>enter</u>.
7. Add cells in each numeric row by pressing <u>alt-shift</u> +.

8. To subtract *some* row, press <u>alt</u>-<u>shift</u> –).
9. Move to the "total" row and put total there with <u>alt</u>-<u>shift</u> <u>enter</u>.
10. Press <u>control</u> twice to end things.

Now consider a table where some columns contain numbers to be added while others don't. Maybe this is a report on activity by cities (rows). Columns are used for:

1. Number of sales people
2. Populations
3. Gross sales
4. Cost of materials
5. Commissions
6. Profit
7. Percent profit

It might make sense to find totals only for columns 3 through 6. You specify this in exactly the same way as the previous list with one exception. In step 4 instead of specifying row with <u>r</u>, qualify it by asking for rows 3 through 6 with r[3-6] for NBI.

Each **WP** has its own method. The operator communicates to the system by means of language. The computer is stupid and so the language must be specific and formal. In a formal language, a statement must be perfect to be accepted. The operator has to learn how to do this and that is the problem that faces us: the more complicated the action, the more complicated it is to learn how to describe that action to the system.

### Sequence

Calculations may have to be performed in a particular sequence. For instance, to find the percent of profit for each division one must first find the profit for each division by taking the difference between sales and costs for that division. *Then* the percent of profit is calculated. The math package has to accept specifications for calculations in sequence and then make them in that order. That is the purpose of the number assigned by NBI when you press <u>e</u> (for enter).

### Record the Directions

It would be wasteful to set up a calculation each time it is needed. If a document is recalled for editing or you wish to repeat recorded calculations for a new table, it is thus handy to have them stored. Store the formulas with the table or in a separate document so that they can be requested again. Another way is key stroke recording, examined earlier.

## Recalculate

There might be two reasons why we would wish to revise a table:

1. A mistake was made in entering some part of the table and it has to be recalculated.
2. The table can serve as a prediction tool; fill in predicted values for entries in the table and make the calculation to see how these new figures affect the outcome. Recalculate with other predicted values.

Perform recalculations on a full table. Change some of the entries in the table which already contain values used with previous calculations. Calculated results are no longer correct. Some WPs permit you to call for the calculations, have them redone and the figures entered where they belong to replace existing results.

Here is another use for this capability. A table was constructed, the calculations made by hand, the table filled in and then entered into the WP. The operator checks the calculations by setting up the formulas. When the math program is run, it makes the calculations and replaces inaccuracies with correct results.

## Result Format

For simplicity, there is a default format for results. However, this format is alterable. Some of the specifications which may be at your disposal in your WP are:

1. whether commas are put in results which are large numbers,
2. the number of result digits recorded after the decimal point,
3. whether rounding, up or down, is done,
4. the form of the sign for negative numbers—whether parentheses, prefix or suffix,
5. how zero is displayed—as 0, a blank, a "-", etc.

The result format may apply hereafter or only when a new calculation comes along.

## One Shot Arithmetic

Sometimes you may want to enter results in a report after a single calculation you request is done by the WP. For example, you are typing along "we purchased 28 widgits at $1.81 for a total of ??? on June 17, 1981." It would be nice at this point if there were some way to have the WP do the arithmetic and let you replace the question marks with the right answer; the WP could even do the replacement.

The Xerox 860 has **nontabular math** capability. You must create the document and store it on disk before you enter the math program. You call in the document from the menu. When you need to do arithmetic, you type <u>program</u>; then you type the name of the program which is "screen math", after which you press <u>accpt</u>.

The program takes over and tells you the default options (which you can change). Now you use edit commands to highlight 28, the number of widgits and press <u>accpt</u>. Then the command line displays:

$$28 + - X / \qquad (11.5.1)$$

It is now up to you to indicate which function to perform. Therefore, you type X to indicate multiplication. Next, you highlight 1.81, the price for each widgit, then <u>accpt</u>. Now the command line displays:

$$1.81 + - X / = \qquad (11.5.2)$$

Since you want no more arithmetic, just the result, you type in the equal sign. The command line now reads:

$$TOTAL = 50.68 \ldots PLACE IT WHERE? \qquad (11.5.3)$$

You move the cursor to the place where the answer goes—where the question marks are. You highlight this area and touch <u>accpt</u>. The total on the command line is transferred into the text at the point which you indicated. For the Xerox 860 it is better not to have the question marks; you now have to get rid of them. Instead, just put *nothing* where the answer goes; it is shoved in there, pushing over the existing text to make room.

Should you revise the manuscript and, in particular, any reference to calculations, you should check all occurences of numbers. If you change the price or quantity of widgits, the total cost is now wrong. In this case, go through the same steps again. When you get the answer, highlight and delete the old answer and replace it with the new one.

### Results in Reports

Record processing is discussed in Chapter 12. It provides capabilities which resemble the power available with data processing. Records are established and reports can be generated. Sometimes reports could advantageously use calculation. Then the report program should have this capability so that you can specify the calculations and deposit results into your report during preparation.

# 12
# Record Processing; Programs

This chapter is primarily devoted to records and record processing. Section 12.1 discusses the record and its use: terms are examined and defined. Section 12.2 discusses file processing: how you define, create and use files and records. Section 12.3 discusses subfiles, a portion of the file which you define and for which *you* direct the processing. Section 12.4 discusses report generation: subfiles you have created produce reports or other documents.

Finally, in Section 12.5 we examine programs and programming. This is where word processing and data processing interact. I discuss here the shortcomings of current programming languages and how the situation might be remedied by the vendor in the future.

## 12.1 THE RECORD

### What and Why?

There are many lists which the office keeps. Some of them are obvious candidates for automation, if the word processor can handle them. We have seen how form letters are tailored to a list of customers. The WP can help us organize many lists:

- The names, addresses and telephone numbers of all the employees in the department;
- A list of important contacts for each of the executives in the department;
- A list of vendors of office products, stationery and the like.

I am sure you could add many others to this list of lists.

Most WP vendors provide record processing programs (hereafter simply called the **record processor**) to help you manage your lists. They are of no assistance if you do not understand how they work and keep your lists up to date conscientiously.

The record processor is the closest thing to data processing which is accessible to the office WP operator. It is not as easy as simple text editing and does require a certain amount of training, but its use is immediately rewarding.

**425**

First, record processing assists you in setting up a list. Once a list is established, record processing help you make changes in it. Record processing finds any entry in the list. Record processing prints reports. Besides choosing single items, you can find all those items which have similar specified characteristics.

As with any computerized task, there are rules. Remember, the computer is stupid! It is trained only to accept input in a particular routinized way. Therefore, it is important that you learn the record processing rules for your WP and follow them to the letter.

Vendors have different names for their record processing programs. For instance:

- Lanier calls their program The Records Manager.
- Xerox calls their program Records Processing.
- For the Wang OIS this is List Processing.

Regardless of what your vendor calls it, we refer to this as the record processor.

## Terms

Just what is this thing called a record? A **record** stores all the information that we need to know about an **individual**—a person, a company or a product which is of interest to our company.

Figure 12.1.1 illustrates this. On the left is a group of individuals called a **population**. On the right are rectangles, each representing a record. One individual is associated with one record. The record lists information of importance to us. If it is a vendor's record, it might contain an address but not the number of employees in the plant. For an employee, the job specification may be found but not race or religion. For a product, a product number might be found in the record, but sometimes there is no information about its shape.

### *Field*

Each quality of the individual of interest is found in the record in an area called a **field**; one field describes one quality. With respect to the field, we have two things to consider.

The **field name** is the name assigned to a field to identify it. For instance, one of the fields in our record might be for the zip code; the field name for this field is the zip field. If this is a collection of customer records listing customer names and addresses, then every record contains a zip field. From one record to the next, the contents of this field may differ.

The value found in a field is called the **field value**. It usually differs from one record to the next. (However, there may be some records that have the same field value.) For instance, the zip for one area in New York City is 10010. This value is found for all addresses which lie in that zone.

Recall that for a variable, we had a variable name and a variable value. It is the same situation here: for each field in the record there is a name and a value particular to this record.

*File*

A **file** is a collection of records. In Figure 12.1.1 we see the collection of individuals called the population. It corresponds exactly to the file; there is one record in the file for each individual in the population. A file has a name, the name by which we call it up from the disk. The name generally corresponds to its use or its application: this may be a *vendor file*.

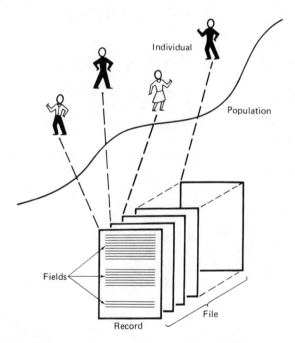

Figure 12.1.1. Relation of files, records, etc to the population.

The records occur in some **sequence**. You may say that the records were put into the file in no particular sequence. This *is* a sequence; it is the sequence by which you entered the record. We could put a record into the file in two ways:

- the last record at the end of the file,
- the last record at the beginning of the file.

Another sequence in which records are kept is determined by some value of a field called a **key**. For instance, all employees have social security numbers. We may use this number as a key to determine the order of the records in the file. Again we have two choices:

- The file is in **ascending** order if records with the highest value come at the end of the file.
- The file is in **descending** value if the records with the lowest key values come at the beginning of the file.

Sometimes we call the key for sorting the **order key**. "Key" is also the name for a field upon which we do a search as we see later on.

## 12.2 FILE PROCESSING

**Requirements**

Figure 12.2.1 shows diagramatically that the record processor:

1. accepts your definition of the file and the record format,
2. helps you create records to make up the file,
3. updates *records* for you by altering values in the fields which make up the record,
4. updates the *file* by adding new records or deleting old or expired records,
5. sorts the file.

**File Definition**

Before you can create records and put them in the file, the record processor requires that you define the file. First you name it; nothing happens until space is allocated for the new file. This space has a name.

The record consists of a number of fields, each named and described unambiguously.

*Field*

To describe the record, you give the characteristics of each field. The record processor may present a field list for you to fill in as with the Wang Office Information

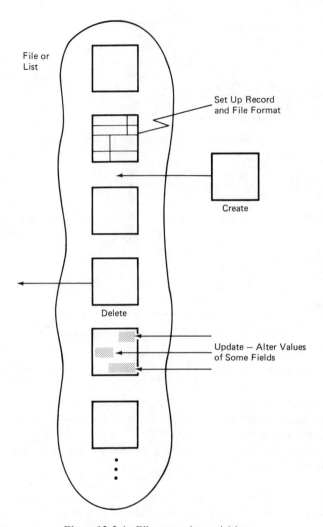

Figure 12.2.1. File processing activities.

System (OIS), Figure 12.2.2. You see 10 fields with blank names each with a field length of 10. You sequence through this definition, supplying names to replace the blanks and field lengths to replace the 10s which appear there. For less than 10 fields, when you have filled them, you may leave unnamed fields sitting in the

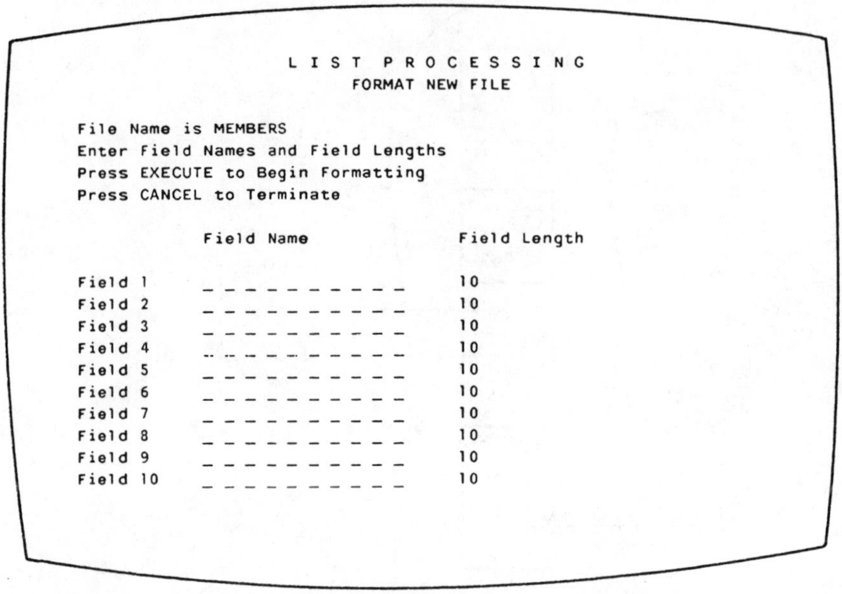

```
                    L I S T   P R O C E S S I N G
                         FORMAT NEW FILE

       File Name is MEMBERS
       Enter Field Names and Field Lengths
       Press EXECUTE to Begin Formatting
       Press CANCEL to Terminate


                    Field Name            Field Length

       Field 1     _ _ _ _ _ _ _ _ _ _    1 0
       Field 2     _ _ _ _ _ _ _ _ _ _    1 0
       Field 3     _ _ _ _ _ _ _ _ _ _    1 0
       Field 4     _ _ _ _ _ _ _ _ _ _    1 0
       Field 5     _ _ _ _ _ _ _ _ _ _    1 0
       Field 6     _ _ _ _ _ _ _ _ _ _    1 0
       Field 7     _ _ _ _ _ _ _ _ _ _    1 0
       Field 8     _ _ _ _ _ _ _ _ _ _    1 0
       Field 9     _ _ _ _ _ _ _ _ _ _    1 0
       Field 10    _ _ _ _ _ _ _ _ _ _    1 0
```

Figure 12.2.2. File definition menu. (Courtesy of Wang).

"menu." For more than 10 you'll get a second (or more) menu. Figure 12.2.3 shows a filled-in record definition.

The length of a field is the maximum length which this field might take up. Most record processors permit variable-length fields, where values may be smaller than the maximum indicated.

Some record processors (not OIS) request that you indicate the kind of information stored in a field. Usually you may designate three kinds of fields:

- alphabetic information, such as a name;
- numeric information, such as a social security number;
- alphanumeric information, letters *and* numerals such as in a part number.

Then these record processors check the data you furnish in creating a record; should you enter the wrong type of information, it notifies you and rejects your entry. Thus, if you put letters in a social security number, you are informed of your mistake.

In what order does the record processor keep your file? In most cases the record processor keeps the file in the order that you supply records. It may be possible to request that the records be kept in reverse order. You may ask the record processor to sort the records and rearrange them. Then records are kept in order by a key field.

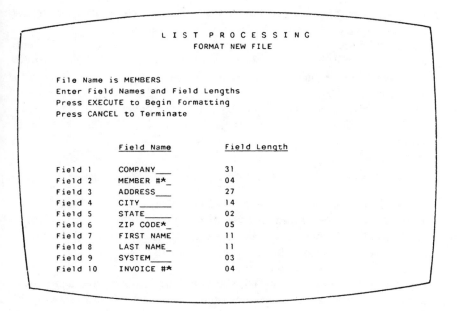

```
                    L I S T   P R O C E S S I N G
                         FORMAT NEW FILE


       File Name is MEMBERS
       Enter Field Names and Field Lengths
       Press EXECUTE to Begin Formatting
       Press CANCEL to Terminate



                     Field Name          Field Length

       Field 1       COMPANY___          31
       Field 2       MEMBER #*_          04
       Field 3       ADDRESS___          27
       Field 4       CITY_____          14
       Field 5       STATE_____          02
       Field 6       ZIP CODE*_          05
       Field 7       FIRST NAME          11
       Field 8       LAST NAME_          11
       Field 9       SYSTEM____          03
       Field 10      INVOICE #*          04
```

Figure 12.2.3. The file menu after a file is defined. (Courtesy of Wang).

## Creation

Though you have specified a record and file format, there are no records in the file. The next step is to create a file. You have a choice of two methods usually:

- Enlist the record processor program to help you create each record.
- Use your WP editing facilities and create each record on the screen.

### Record Processor Assistance

With record processor assistance, the program may both prompt you for field input and monitor each record that you enter. You ask for OIS assistance from the record processor menu after you have set up the file format. The record processor program then presents the field list on the screen just as you set it up (see Figure 12.2.3). After each field name there are as many spaces as you specified for the field. The cursor positions at the first blank of the first field. You enter the field value and a return to signal that you have completed that field. The field is checked and the cursor automatically moves to the first blank of the next field.

Some record processors check each entry after you press return. Of course, it cannot check the way you spell your employee's name nor if you have entered the right social security number. But it can check to see if you put numbers in a name or letters in the social security number. The record processor program does not check the number of characters in the name but if you want, it may check to see if you have provided nine digits for the social security number.

Another feature which accelerates input is the ability to duplicate a field from the last record entered. For example, if you are creating a vendor file and the zip for *this* vendor is the same as that for the last vendor, you can use the *duplicate* key to enter it.

Each record you enter is assigned a sequence number and the record is put at the end of the file. Later you can retrieve this record by specifying its sequence number.

### Word Processor

You can create your records using the word processor. After setting the file format, the record processor menu lets you leave the record processor program and enter the word processor program. You can also close your file now and start creating new records tomorrow. In that case, tomorrow you name a (new) file and create each record as described below.

As you create records under the WP, you have no help from the record processor program. You must remember the format and the requirements and order for each field of each record. You enter the data for the records using the exact sequence of fields and continue until you have created as many records as you wish. You close this file and are ready for the next step, where the record processor program gets this file, checks it out, adds it to the existing file, if any, and makes it available for record processing use.

### Update Records

To **update** a record is to alter some of its fields. Any characteristic of an individual might change over the life of your file. For instance, for a phone list, the extension of one of the employees might change. For an employee file, the number of dependents and hopefully the pay rate may change. A common error is to spell someone's name improperly. Fixing the name spelling is also updating the record.

There are two ways to alter records. One is to enlist the help of the record processor and the other is to edit the file just like text.

### Record Processor Update

To update a record in your file, first ask for the record processor menu. You get a choice of actions for record processor to perform next. You may ask for editing. When you created the file, each record was assigned a record number. If you know this number, you can ask the record processor program to find the record. If you do not know the record number, the procedure is a little more troublesome. For a small file, a simple way to find the record is to ask the record processor to sequence through the file. One record after another flashes on the screen as you press <u>continue</u>.

A third way to reach your record is to "select" the record as you would to create a subfile (described in the next section). You request the select mode and then furnish the key of the record to be changed. For instance, to change a telephone number, enter it; the selected record is found and displayed. What happens next depends on the particular record processor. You may be able to alter the record immediately. Otherwise, note the record number, return to the edit mode and call up that record by number.

In the edit mode, the record is found and all the values of the fields are presented on the screen to examine. Find the field to alter. Move the cursor there and overwrite the old value of the variable with the new value. Then tell the record processor that editing is complete. The updated record is then returned to the file.

*WP Update*

You may use the record file as you would any text file for editing. Call it forth; once text is on the screen you may *search* on the current value of the field to be altered. Or you may *search* for the name or number which identifies the record. Once the record is on the screen, you sequence through it to make alterations. With edit commands you alter the file permanently. When it is called for by the record processor later, the revised copy appears.

**Updating Files**

Whereas updating records alters a record to reflect a change in an individual of the population, updating the file inserts or removes records to show a change in the population. The population changes when new individuals come in or old ones drop out. An employee who leaves is no longer listed in the telephone directory. A new employee gets a phone assigned and should now appear in the telephone directory. File update may be done with or without the aid of the record processor program.

*Record Processor*

Use the menu to request editing. To delete a record, first find that record. When the record is presented on the screen you are given a choice of actions: choose to delete the record and it is removed from the file.

To add a new record, indicate that you want to edit and add a record. The empty fields appear on the screen and you fill in the values as when you create an original record. The record processor program assigns a record number to the new record and places it at the end of the file.

*WP*

You can use the text editor to access any file. To delete a record, first use *search* to find the record. Then be sure to delete all the fields. To add a new record, operate as though you are creating the file. Again, be sure that all fields are entered in the order specified in the definition. You should assign a record number, just like the record processor: check the last record number and assign the next higher number to this record.

### Sort

To sort a file is to put it in order. The file is now kept in order by record number, the order in which you entered the records. For instance, your telephone directory may be entered from a written copy with no particular order. To print out the directory in order of last name, request the sort mode. (The sort options are discussed in the next section.) You name and describe the *last name* field and after a few seconds or minutes, a copy of the file is now in the desired order. You may print it out directly or through a merge program.

## 12.3 SUBFILES

### Need

The record processor can create a subfile and then perform any kind of record processing on it. A **subfile** is a portion of a file, selected according to qualities you choose. The subfile represents a selected group of individuals from the population.
   Innumerable occasions arise for subfiles. You can:

1. select specific employees by their social security number or name,
2. select accounts which have arrears over $100.00,
3. find clients whose zip code indicates they are in the far western states,
4. combine these qualities to find accounts in the far west whose arrears are greater than $100.00,
5. find employees between 40 and 50 years of age.

Figure 12.3.1 shows on the left a file from which records are selected to create the subfile on the right. Once the subfile is selected, it can be operated upon:

A.  All the records in the subfile can be changed in a particular way.
B.  All the records can be removed permanently from the file.
C.  A report can be printed from the subfile.

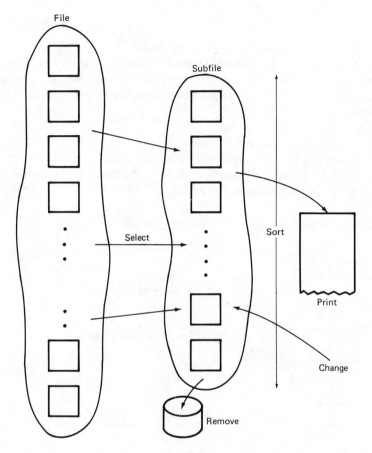

Figure 12.3.1. Subfile activities.

## Selection

Any field(s) in the record can select records for the subfile. The most succinct way to specify records for the subfile is to use a set of formulas or sentences in a formal language. A language for selection, called a **query language**, is popular for dealing with data bases on large computers. A large investment in time is required to learn such a language and to be able to use it adeptly.

The WP alternative to a query language is **interactive** selection. A menu system is the easiest to use. The record processor presents selection criteria; you choose from the menu. Examples in the description which follows are based on the Wang Office Automation System (OIS).

*Field Selection*

For the OIS, the first menu for selection is shown in Figure 12.3.2. At the left is the list of the fields which comprise the record. The cursor is at the first field. By pressing <u>return</u> you move the cursor to the first field for selection. Then press <u>execute</u>. The cursor jumps to the right side of the screen for you to select the type of criterion:

- an upper and lower limit for the field value,
- one specific field value by which records are chosen,
- a field value which excludes records. A record containing any other value for this field is chosen for the subfile.

Move the cursor with <u>return</u> to the applicable line and press <u>execute</u>.

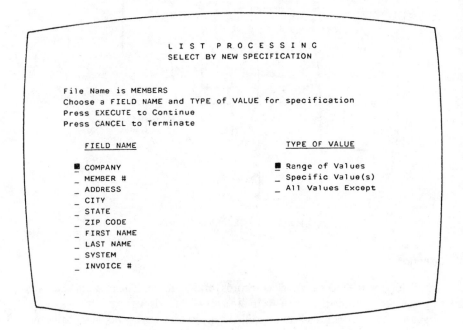

Figure 12.3.2. Selection menu. (Courtesy of Wang).

*Range*

The menu in Figure 12.3.3 appears to set a range of zip codes. You move the cursor to one of the blanks and key a limit value in. Then you set the second limit. The limits may be set in either order. You have established boundary points along the scale of values which the field might assume. Then you may include or exclude

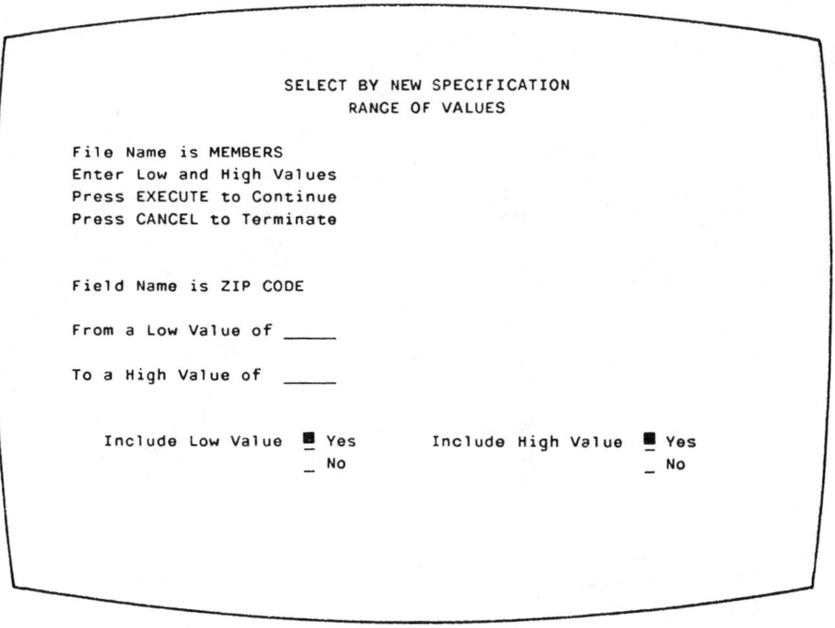

```
              SELECT BY NEW SPECIFICATION
                  RANGE OF VALUES

File Name is MEMBERS
Enter Low and High Values
Press EXECUTE to Continue
Press CANCEL to Terminate


Field Name is ZIP CODE

From a Low Value of _____

To a High Value of _____


   Include Low Value  ▪ Yes      Include High Value  ▪ Yes
                      _ No                           _ No
```

Figure 12.3.3. Menu for selecting a range of values. (Courtesy of Wang).

either boundary at the bottom of Figure 12.3.3. Figure 12.3.4 shows the request for zip code values between 01844 and 28433 *inclusively*.

A range of letter values for another variable could be chosen in the same way. The value you use as a boundary point need not be an actual value of some record in the file. For instance, you could specify that you want records for people with names between N and Q by simply entering "N" for the low value and "Q" for the high value. If "Nevins" were the first name in your file which begins with N, then it would be selected.

Some record processors do not check the file exhaustively. They rely on the assumption that the file has been sorted with regard to the particular field. A sort must precede the selection process for it to work properly. If you have asked for names between N and Q, then as soon as a name starting with R comes along, the record processor assumes there are no more names within the proper range and will stop there. (OIS does not require a sorted file and searches exhaustively.)

*Specific Values*

You can make a request to select records which have a particular value for the key field. In some cases this selects at most one record. For instance, if you specify a social security number, only one worker (or none) should have that number; if

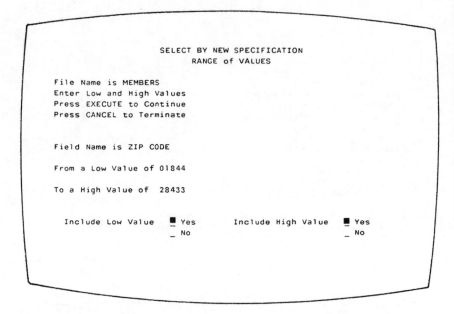

Figure 12.3.4. Selecting a range of zip codes. (Courtesy of Wang).

you use the employee number, the same should be true. It's not so clear if this holds for proper names; there may be more than one John Smith in your firm.

Some qualities are shared among several records in your file, such as the choice of state. You may have several clients from Ohio.

A menu for specific values usually gives you several choices. If you are selecting records on the basis of state, you might thus wish to choose Ohio, Illinois, Michigan and so forth. One precaution: the value that you enter must match the value in the record field itself. If you want to select records from Michigan which the field stores as a two letter value MI, then you must specify MI, not Michigan.

It is clear that any record with a field having *one* of the specified values is acceptable. A request for OH and MI looks for clients who have offices in either Michigan *or* Ohio, not both.

### Exclusive Specification

In some cases it is easier to specify values which you do *not* want rather than ones that you want. Suppose you seek all employees with dependents. You could by the previous method ask for records for which the dependent field contains 1, 2, 3, ..., etc. Instead, wouldn't it be simpler to specify that you want all records, excluding those with no dependents? Here the dependent field value of 0 would exclude that record.

*Multiple Conditions*

You are permitted to set more than one requirement for record selection. Then how is each condition viewed in combination with the others? There are two ways to combine conditions:

1. Require that both conditions prevail in a single record for it to be selected (AND).
2. Require that either one or the other condition prevail in the record for it to be selected (OR).

As an example of the first combination, consider a selection of employees who have no dependents and who make more than $40,000 per year. A record is selected if *both* these conditions are met. To choose clients with an average yearly gross income greater than $1 Million *and* from a western state, the geographical *and* numerical condition are combined with AND. We request a western client *or* a $1 million company with OR.

Each time you complete a selection, the record processor shows you the continuation menu of Figure 12.3.5. This asks whether the next condition you specify is an additional requirement (AND) or an alternative requirement (OR).

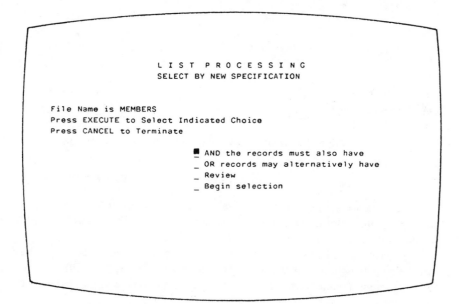

Figure 12.3.5. Adding another selection criterion. (Courtesy of Wang).

*Review*

Once you have set up selection criteria, it is profitable to review them. Selection is complicated and prone to error. From the menu in Figure 12.3.5 you ask to "review." Then the menu in Figure 12.3.6 presents all the conditions that you have proposed. Should you see a discrepancy, you can modify any of the conditions. You may also <u>delete</u> all the conditions and start over from the beginning. If you press <u>cancel</u>, this ends the review and brings you back to the menu of Figure 12.3.5 to add further conditions. When your choice is complete, you initiate the selection activity from the bottom line of Figure 12.3.5. Press <u>return</u> to move the cursor down and execute to get things going.

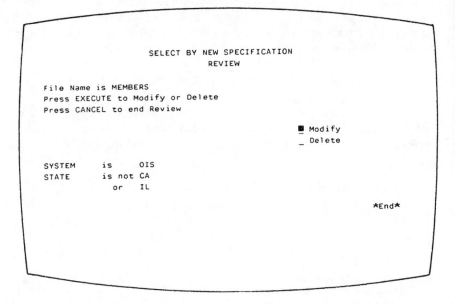

```
                    SELECT BY NEW SPECIFICATION
                              REVIEW

        File Name is MEMBERS
        Press EXECUTE to Modify or Delete
        Press CANCEL to end Review

                                        ▌ Modify
                                        _ Delete


        SYSTEM      is      OIS
        STATE       is not  CA
                     or     IL

                                                 *End*
```

Figure 12.3.6. Reviewing the selection criteria. (Courtesy of Wang).

*Save the Specification*

The record processor gets to work and selects the records you have requested, putting them into a subfile. Once done, the system reports back to you with the menu of Figure 12.3.7.

You have gone to a lot of trouble to make your selection accurately. You may set aside the selection request itself and give it a name: for the Wang OIS you press <u>execute</u>, enter a name for the specification and press <u>execute</u> again. Later if you

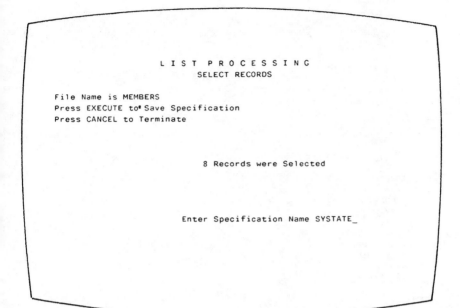

Figure 12.3.7. Saving the criteria specification. (Courtesy of Wang).

wish to apply these criteria to a new version of the file, simply call up this specification by its name.

### Sort

To sort records is to put them in order. A **sort program** does this. One or more fields determines the new order of the records. For a file sorted by employee number, the record for the employee with the lowest number appears first in the file; the record for the employee with the greatest employee number appears last. This is ascending sequence. Sorted files are easiest to use, both for the human and the machine, for some record processing applications.

Most record processors sort either a file or a subfile. The Wang OIS accepts a sort request from the sort menu, a list of fields, together with an empty column in which you can specify the fields used for sorting.

Since a file may be sorted with respect to several fields, you must tell the sort program which to use first, second, etc. Figure 12.3.8 shows the menu for the OIS for a request when the *state* field is first and the *company* field is second. First records are ordered by *state*. Within the set of records for one state, they are further ordered according to the company name.

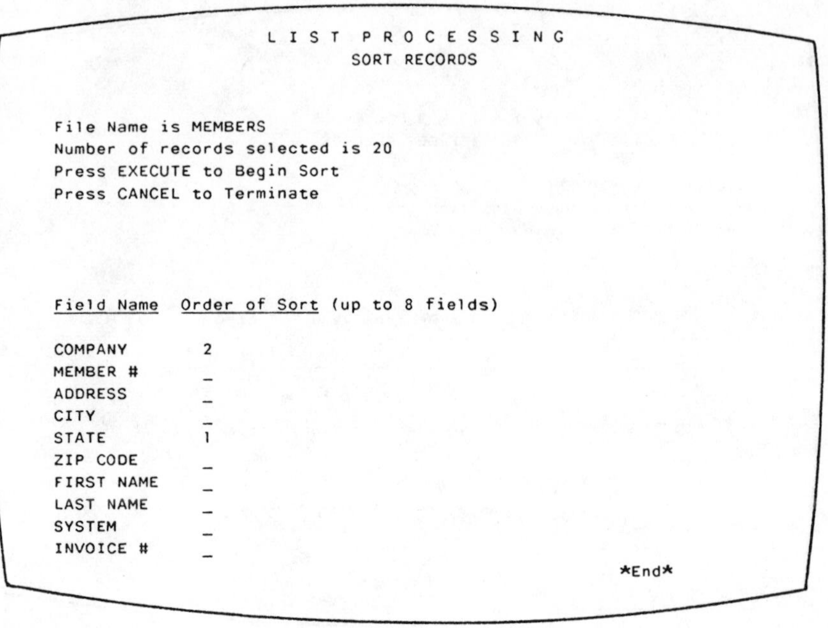

```
                    L I S T   P R O C E S S I N G
                          SORT RECORDS


    File Name is MEMBERS
    Number of records selected is 20
    Press EXECUTE to Begin Sort
    Press CANCEL to Terminate




    Field Name   Order of Sort (up to 8 fields)

    COMPANY          2
    MEMBER #         _
    ADDRESS          _
    CITY             _
    STATE            1
    ZIP CODE         _
    FIRST NAME       _
    LAST NAME        _
    SYSTEM           _
    INVOICE #        _
                                              *End*
```

Figure 12.3.8. A sort request. (Courtesy of Wang).

**Subfile Disposition**

There are at least four things that you can do with the subfile, as displayed in the OIS menu found in Figure 12.3.9.

*Screen Display*

For this choice, each record is presented in its current sequence in the subfile. When presented, it is organized as it was entered: the field name is listed with the field value. Request the next record by pressing next-scrn. Move backward in the subfile to get the next previous record by pressing prev-scrn. During viewing, records are not eligible to be altered.

When you are done viewing records, press cancel.

*Text Document*

The subfile can be stored as a text document. In this format, fields are separated from one another by [tb]s; [cr] terminates each record.

A text document is useful in preparing a report. Sometimes it is desirable to exclude some fields of the record from the report. It is also useful to reorganize

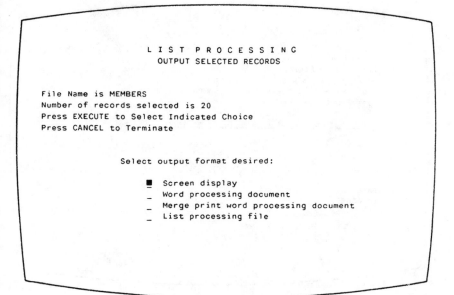

```
                    L I S T   P R O C E S S I N G
                      OUTPUT SELECTED RECORDS


    File Name is MEMBERS
    Number of records selected is 20
    Press EXECUTE to Select Indicated Choice
    Press CANCEL to Terminate


          Select output format desired:

                ■  Screen display
                _  Word processing document
                _  Merge print word processing document
                _  List processing file
```

Figure 12.3.9. Menu to process a subfile. (Courtesy of Wang).

the fields for the report. The menu lets you select fields and specify their order in the report. A field with no number is omitted. Figure 12.3.10 displays a typical choice.

*Record Processor File*

It is possible to pass the subfile over to an existing record processor file different from the one from which it was constructed. There must be complete compatibility between the selected subfile and the destination subfile for this to work. That is, the format of records in each must be identical in respect to the sequence, length and position of each field.

Here is a use for such a facility. Suppose our company keeps records of employees according to their function. There is a separate file for engineering employees, another for clerical workers, a third for management and so forth. Each record contains a field for the department where each employee is assigned. Suppose we would like to extract and create a *departmental* file of employees kept by job category file. After selection, put the selected subfile into the new file for the department. As each selection is made for a category, a new subfile is created; these subfiles are added immediately to the single file for the department.

```
                    OUTPUT SELECTED RECORDS
                  TO WORD PROCESSING DOCUMENT

    File Name is MEMBERS
    Number of records selected is 20
    Enter Values and Press EXECUTE to Begin Output
    Press CANCEL to Terminate


    Field Name   Order of Fields To Be Written

    COMPANY        1__
    MEMBER #       2__
    ADDRESS        ___
    CITY           ___
    STATE          ___
    ZIP CODE       ___
    FIRST NAME     ___
    LAST NAME      ___
    SYSTEM         3__
    INVOICE #      4__
```

Figure 12.3.10. Records go to a WP document. (Courtesy of Wang).

*Document Merge File*

OIS provides a document merge facility. Recall from Section 10.4 that a stencil may be merged with a list to produce a separate merged document for each item on the list.

Merging requires a list in the proper format. OIS uses switch codes. Records consist of fields separated by a vertical double-headed arrow, the merge graphic. Each record is separated from the next by a "don't merge" graphic, which is a double-headed vertical arrow with an underscore.

To do a selective mailing for customers in your mail file, you first select a subfile of records according to some characteristic. From this subfile you may create a merge list by a choice from the menu of Figure 12.3.9. Figure 12.3.11 shows the merge list menu that you get. By entering numbers, you indicate the order that you want for the fields of each record to appear in the merge list; fields without a number are omitted from the merge list.

The record processor selects fields, puts them in the right order and inserts separaters. If you display the list produced, it appears as in Figure 12.3.12. Figure

```
Document  0368Q    Now on Page  1   Line 1    Position  1
⌊1............................................................
9326|4298|Brendan|Stone|Becker Research, Inc.|371 Mason Drive|Chicago|IL |
84372|3942|8423|Thomas|Hennessy|R.W. Lebanon, Inc.|53 Rumfield Avenue|
Watertown|MA|03216|3277|4296|Linda|Sturgis|Boston Tire Company|242 Common
Street|Boston|MA|02187|4835|8435|Janet|Kline|United Media, Inc.| 217
Hanover Street| Hanover|NH |08522|4274|5398|Edward Gray Phillip and Stone,
Inc.|32 First Avenue|New York|NY |32644|3802|4504|Lewis|Waldon|Brewster
Engineering|3921|Ridge Avenue|San Francisco|CA|94267|8436|5321|Stephen|
Lane|Breslin Sports, Inc.| 7 Mountain Lane|Burlington|VT |43657|4077 |4052
Kerry|Robertson|Hospital Supplies, Inc.| 28 Beach Street|Brockton|MA |
```

Figure 12.3.11. Merge list menu. (Courtesy of Wang).

```
                    OUTPUT SELECTED RECORDS
                    TO MERGE PRINT DOCUMENT

File Name is MEMBERS
Number of records selected is 20
Enter Values and Press EXECUTE to Begin Output
Press CANCEL to Terminate


Field Name   Order of Fields To Be Written

COMPANY       5__  ___  ___
MEMBER #      1__  ___  ___
ADDRESS       6__  ___  ___
CITY          7__  ___  ___
STATE         8__  ___  ___
ZIP CODE      9__  ___  ___
FIRST NAME    3__  ___  ___
LAST NAME     4__  ___  ___
SYSTEM         __  ___  ___
INVOICE #     2__  ___  ___

                                              *End*
```

Figure 12.3.12. Subfile set up for merging. (Courtesy of Wang).

12.3.13 shows a stencil with merge codes where information from the merge list goes. Figure 12.3.14 is an example of one merged output document.

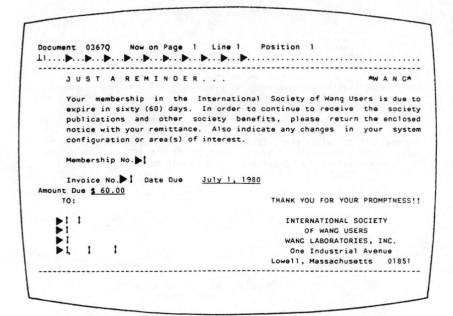

Figure 12.3.13. Stencil into which to merge. (Courtesy of Wang).

Figure 12.3.14. The merged document. (Courtesy of Wang).

**Altering the Main File**

One reason that you select a subfile is to make permanent changes in the original file. There are two kinds of changes. In both, the subfile is applied to alter the file from which it was withdrawn.

*Delete*

You select a subfile to delete records from the main file. These may be employees leaving the firm or customers dropped because their bills are overdue.

Using a procedure specific to your WP, you indicate that the subfile should now be deleted from the file. The record processor looks in the file for records in the subfile and removes them from the file.

*Change*

Instead of going through the main file and changing records individually, you could select them and have the record processor make some change in all the main file records simultaneously. For instance, to reduce risk, we select customers on the basis of the amount they currently owe us and their preferential standing. Although we keep these records in the file, each record is marked as delinquent so that no further goods are shipped to them until their status changes. The selected subfile is matched against records in the file by the record processor, and for each record found, the value of the status field is changed.

## 12.4 REPORTS

**The Report**

A report is one essential output of a data processing application. Produced at fixed periods, it gives the status of the population or a group of individuals in the population. In the latter case, the group is the result of selection. The report is a document of several pages to circulate to management.

There are three ways to produce the report on your word processor:

1. After selecting a subfile, the record processor may print the report directly as we have seen.
2. You can create a stencil which describes the format of the report. This stencil is similar to the document merge stencil. The method is provided by Xerox, Syntrex and Dictaphone.
3. You may write a BASIC program to run on your WP computer as a data processing activity. The program selects fields from each record and reorganizes them to print as required in the report. This concept is examined in Section 12.5.

To generate a complete report in a good format requires many choices along the way. It is not easy to formalize this process and present it either in a number of menus or with a formula for the unskilled operator to understand. A good BASIC programmer can often do this more quickly, using the programming language, than an operator could be expected to do using only the facilities provided by the WP vendor.

A number of report alternatives, from the simple to the complex, are examined:

1. the simple report,
2. mathematics on rows of record fields,
3. a check for changing fields,
4. subtotals,
5. action over field change, suppressing fields.

Examples are included, but with no particular vendor's WP in mind; a combination of the features of several WPs simplifies the presentation.

### Simple Report

The report can be analyzed into several parts. Not all vendors provide for these parts though.

A.  a heading to start the report,
B.  column heads to appear once at the top of each page,
C.  one or more lines of the report that uses the fields of *one* record in the subfile,
D.  bottom notes at the end of each page,
E.  a final message at the end of the report.

Figure 12.4.1 shows this format in practice.

```
COLUMN 1                  COLUMN 2                  COLUMN 3 ...

[start code]
[sf]field 1[ef]           [sf]field 2[ef]           [sf]field 3[ef] ...
[repeat code]

[sf] = start field code;   [ef] = end field code
```

Figure 12.4.1. Report format alternatives.

The report is similar to the document merge. The difference is that a single electronic document is the product of this activity. We may have as many as four electronic documents involved:

1. The subfile contains selected records, the source data for the report.
2. The stencil describes which parts of each record to select and format for the report.
3. The report itself.
4. The set of instructions may accompany the stencil to interpret it for the WP program.

Assume that the subfile has named fields. The stencil in Figure 12.4.1 consists of the heading at the top of each page and the middle lines derived from the file. For the simplest case, one subfile record produces one line in the report.

Commands in the stencil tell the WP program what to do. These commands are shown between square brackets. The first, [start code], tells the WP program that what follows in the stencil is produced once for each record; [repeat code] designates when to start over for the next record.

A repeated line consists simply of field names. Each is between a start field code and an end field code, [sf] and [ef] in the figure. A line could include fixed text; there could be more than one line per record. The WP program uses the stencil as a model to print the report document.

## Mathematics within Rows

Instead of printing a field or a constant in a repeated line(s), you can print the result of arithmetic on one or more fields. Suppose, for example, that one report line shows each item ordered in a purchase order. The record notes the unit price and the number of units. The report might print the extension, the product of the units times the unit cost. Figure 12.4.2 shows an item to print between the starting code [sf] and the end code [ef]: labels for two fields and an operation (multiplication) request that the product of the two fields be printed.

```
[start code]
...
...............        [sf]field n X field m[ef]  ...
.
                          multiply sign
```

Figure 12.4.2. Specifying math.

## Loops

Sometimes it is convenient to provide several records in the file for a single accounting document. For instance, a purchase order may consist of constant information plus a number of different descriptions applying to each item ordered. The constant information, such as the purchase order number, its date and the vendor is kept in every record. There is a separate record for each item ordered with its description, part number, unit cost and quantity.

In the report the constant information should appear only once; there is one line for each item ordered. These items constitute a **group**—one set of constant information and the pertinent fields from records with the same constant information.

Figure 12.4.3 shows a generalized view of a group stencil. A constant heading tops each page. The material between the start code and the end code is used for each group of records in the subfile. Starting a group is a secondary heading and constant information taken from the first record of the group. Directions for each record in the group is preceded by [start loop code] and followed by [end loop code]. These directions name fields and may include arithmetic.

```
{page heading}
[start code]
{secondary headings}
{constant information}
[start loop code]
{item descriptions within loop}
[end loop code]{subtotal and total labels}
[end code]
```

Figure 12.4.3. A general report loop.

Figure 12.4.4 demonstrates how you might specify row and column subtotals and totals. A subtotal appears once for each group; it comes between [change code] *within* a group and [repeat code] *between* groups. A total is taken after all repetition ends.

```
{headings}
[start code]
{group label or field name}
{column description}                          [row total code]
[change code]field name
SUBTOTAL                                      [column total code]
[repeat code]
TOTAL                                         [column total code]
```

Figure 12.4.4. A loop with row math, subtotals and totals.

*Work Report*

Figure 12.4.5 is a work report for the week for each lawyer giving the number of hours that he has worked for each client. There is one or more records for each lawyer for each day of the week; taken together, these records form a group. The constant item is the lawyer's name, extracted from the first group record. Each record in the group produces one line in the report.

Lawyer:  Zablonsky

| Client | Matter | Hours Billed | Hours Unbilled | Total Hours | Percent Hours Billable |
|--------|--------|--------------|----------------|-------------|------------------------|
| Albertson, F. | Contract | 10.0 | 3.0 | 13.0 | 77% |
| Jones, T. | Divorce | 30.0 | 10.0 | 40.0 | 75% |
| Travers, J. | Will | 3.5 | .5 | 4.0 | 88% |
| | Totals: | 43.5 | 13.5 | 57.0 | |

Number of matters:  3

Figure 12.4.5. A legal work report. (Courtesy of Dictaphone).

Figure 12.4.6 is the stencil to produce the report of Figure 12.4.5. The first few lines establish LAWYER as the group field and prints the constant column heads for the group. The repeated lines begin with (**LB**) (for link back) and ends with (**LU,LAWYER**) (LU for link until) to tell the WP that what is included between these points is repeated for each record as long as the lawyer field remains the same.

Lawyer:  **(LAWYER)**
**(0=COUNT)**

| Client | Matter | Hours Billed | Hours Unbilled | Total Hours | Percent Hours Billable |
|--------|--------|--------------|----------------|-------------|------------------------|
| **(LB)(CLIENT)** | **(MATTER)** | **(HB$.9)** | **(HU$.9)((RT)=ROW)(ROW$.9)** | | **(100\*HB/ROW$9)%** |
| **(COUNT+1=COUNT)(LU,LAWYER)** | | | | | |
| | Totals: | **((CT)$.9)** | **((CT)$.9)** | **((CT)$.9)** | |

Number of matters:  **(COUNT$9)**

Figure 12.4.6. Stencil for the report of Figure 12.4.5. (Courtesy of Dictaphone).

## Counters

Further arithmetic may be necessary:

- Keeping totals over a group of records—subtotals,
- Totals over the whole subfile,
- Keeping a count of records in each group,
- Keeping a count of the total number of records processed.

A simple way to keep track of totals and intermediate results is to use labeled counters; formulas in the stencil describe the calculations. Figure 12.4.6 shows one way to specify totals and subtotals for the printout of Figure 12.4.5.

## 12.5 WP/DP; PROGRAMS

**What is WP/DP?**

WP/DP is a popular buzz word. Lots of people use it but nobody really says what is meant. Certainly WP and DP are two distinct activities, but it is really not clear what the range of activities covered by each would be.

This book is devoted almost entirely to word processing; there is no question of what we mean by WP. Data processing is another story. How does processing data differ from processing words?

One way that I distinguish between these two activities is shown in Figure 12.5.1. It seems to me that word processing is more personal. What the computer processes is text, a communication between two people or between one person and a number of other people. Data processing is at the other end of the scale. The computer processes impersonal statistics and records about populations which are kept in an impersonal way. These populations are clients, objects, accounts and so forth. Whatever we do with these statistics, it is a one-way street. All the items in Figure 12.5.1 have been discussed with the exception of the last group. This section is devoted to DP and associated tasks.

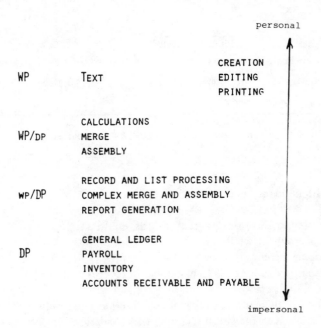

Figure 12.5.1. A continuum of WP and DP activities.

*Requirements*

To make the computer perform any function, it needs a program in memory. To run both word processing and data processing concurrently, both programs must be in memory at the same time: WP programs to process text; a DP program to process data.

*Alternatives*

Start with the proposition that the vendor has furnished a word processor. What alternatives are there for doing data processing. First we list them and then discuss them in order:

0. No capability. The vendor has decided that he does not want to think about data processing. This alternative is numbered 0; no vendor seems to opt for this choice.
1. The vendor furnishes a DP package which you buy as an option and run as a separate program without word processing capability during the DP action.
2. The vendor furnishes a compiler or interpreter as an option. With this facility you can write your own programs and run them without recourse to word processing while they run. The vendor may supply additional optional modules which use the interpreter as a basis for performing data processing.
3. Combined WP and DP may let you run a data processing program *with* word processing capability.
4. Data processing capability is not furnished locally but it is supplied by another computer, either on the premises or at some distant location. The capability provided by the host computer may be used by your WP through its communication program.

**Vendor Packages**

With this method, the vendor writes programs, translates them and sells them to you on disks. To run a DP program, you remove the system disk and mount the one containing the vendor package. When you boot the system, the computer becomes a data processor for the application you have chosen. It is a turnkey system. The system is ready to run.

You have a number of choices for application programs, usually accounting oriented: general ledger, accounts receivable, accounts payable, payroll and so forth.

The problem with this method exists for all turnkey DP application packages for micros and minis as well. You might buy a computer and a few program packages to run in your office. These programs are designed to suit as many offices as possible. They provide you with many options: what data your file contains, how to format each report, how to calculate various intermediate and final results and so forth.

But there is no such thing as a standard office. Each office has its own operating procedure. Each office keeps track of different things and records them a little bit differently. The vendor doesn't expect to fit you into a mold entirely: you take up a seam here, put a tuck in there and so forth. But there may not be enough "cloth" to work with, or too much. The vendor package may actually work for an office that is small and flexible enough to adapt to the program. Otherwise the program must be altered to suit *your* needs. How do you do this?

If the program does not suit you, you can talk with the vendor who may oblige you by tailoring the package. This takes time and programming effort. So you have to pay an additional price to get the program fitted to your needs.

Another possibility is to bring in your own programmer or a consulting firm and have either alter the program to your needs. If the program has been written in a reasonable language, such as BASIC, it may be easy for a professional person to alter it. Assembly language is much harder to cope with.

If you change the program, you take a risk. The program no longer has the guarantee and backing of the vendor because you have made these alterations yourself. You will have to depend on assistance from outside if trouble should develop in running the program.

If you use a package with a number of options, many of which you do not use, then the program may not run efficiently. Since it has many options, it takes time to check if you want each service every time you run the program, even if you never use them. You have to pay in computer running time for unused options. This loss in efficiency is the price you pay for generalization.

**User Programs**

The vendor may supply a procedure oriented programming language along with a compiler or interpreter.

*Use*

To use this facility you place the program disk onto your disk drive. When you bring the system up, you request the interpreter. Let us take as an example the BASIC interpreter provided by Microsoft™. It has a self-contained editor by which you write and check your programs interactively. As soon as you have written part of the program, you can run it and try it out to see if it does what you expect it to do.

You use your WP computer to write programs and run them: the editor program helps you write the program; the interpreter runs it. You need programming talent to do this. This is a specialized activity that you cannot expect the people in your office to be able to do without training.

Many vendors provide BASIC facilities; none provide programmer training as far as I know.

*Packages*

If the only way to take advantage of a BASIC program were to do your own programming, the feature would probably go begging. Many vendors that furnish a program facility also sell program packages that they have created to meet your needs.

*Advantage*

To use the packages, you have to get the interpreter and the packages. What then is the advantage? You now have several choices:

- use packages supplied by the vendor,
- use packages supplied by an independent fabricator,
- modify the packages to suit your needs,
- write your own programs.

There are many programmers who know BASIC; consulting companies do contract programming to meet your specifications. They take your application and write a program suited to it, without the extra options that you don't really need. But do not be misled; there is more to data processing than writing a program. Your office procedures should be examined and analyzed to determine what your needs are. This process is lengthy and expensive. The effort is frequently fruitful and the economy realized is more than trivial. The whole process may be worth its while, but you should be prepared for the effort and expense involved.

An advantage of a different nature also accrues to you. You can buy a vendor's package which is not ideally suited to you. If that package runs in BASIC, then it is much easier to alter by an outside contractor. But the same precautions prevail. Your entire system has to be examined for you to get a good data processing program that suits your office.

### Applying BASIC to Text Files

There are many things that you might like to do with your word processor but are unable to because the vendor's word processing program does not have this particular function. At the present time there is really no way for you to reasonably alter the WP programs.

However, you do have the option of taking text files and applying a BASIC program that you write to alter them. This is essentially what you do when you write a keystroke program (or *glossary* for Wang). You are writing a set of activities to be performed sequentially on text. With the proper knowledge, you could write a BASIC program to do a similar function on your text.

A few examples follow, describing things that I have done to simplify writing this book.

*Glossary*

I hope you find the extensive glossary at the end of this book useful. To prepare it, I went through the book, a chapter at a time, to find the terms to be defined. I defined the terms in a fixed format, in a separate document, entering them at the keyboard of my WP. Naturally the words did not occur in alphabetical order. The same terms might appear several times in the book and I did not want duplicate definitions. Also, you cannot use a glossary where words are in random order.

I set the format of my glossary so that I could use Supersort™ (MicroPro) to put the terms in alphabetical order. Now I could take the ordered glossary and reformat it as I desired.

As I wrote the later chapters, I put the new definitions into a new text file. Then I used Supersort to sort this new file and merge in the old sorted glossary file to get a new sorted glossary.

*Term List*

When I got to the middle of my text, I had 35 or 40 pages of glossary terms. Each time I encountered a questionable term, I had to look it up in this long printout. I thought that it would be convenient to have a list of the terms without definitions on a separate page or two to make look-up easier.

The initial glossary format put each term within quotation marks. Therefore, it was simple to write a BASIC program to find all terms within quotation marks and print them out across the page, keeping them in alphabetical order. Figure 12.5.2 shows an example of the output of this little program.

| | | |
|---|---|---|
| aspect ratio | backspace | belt |
| bidirectional printing | boldface | bursting |
| carriage | carrier | central processing unit |
| chain | character buffer | character generator |
| characters per second | clear | control code |
| cpi | cps | daisy wheel printer |
| dot matrix printer | function key | golf ball |
| hammer register | hardware | home |
| home | increment | justification |
| justification, intercharacter | justification, interword | kern |
| line advance | line advance | line printer |
| lines per minute (lpm) | menu | overstrike |
| paper bai~l | petal register | petal table |
| pin feed | pitch | platen |
| print buffer | print element | print wires |
| program | programmable key | programmer |
| proportional spacing | return | software |
| status line | subscript | superscript |
| tab | tabbing | tractor feed |
| typing ruler | underscore | underscore, broken |
| underscore, double | underscore, unbroken | unit |
| universal key | zoom line | zoom screen |

WP CHAPTER 4

| TERM | PAGE, | ENTRY NO., | CHARACTERS FROM START |
|---|---|---|---|
| volatile | 1 | 1 | 444 |
| External storage | 1 | 2 | 1001 |
| medium | 1 | 3 | 1066 |
| drive | 1 | 4 | 1140 |
| write | 1 | 5 | 1294 |
| read | 1 | 6 | 1382 |
| nondestructive | 1 | 7 | 1484 |
| hold | 2 | 1 | 1719 |
| volume | 2 | 2 | 2805 |
| Reusable | 5 | 1 | 6648 |
| polarized | 5 | 2 | 6697 |
| north | 5 | 3 | 6745 |
| south | 5 | 4 | 6783 |
| substrate | 5 | 5 | 7498 |
| track | 6 | 1 | 7824 |
| gap | 6 | 2 | 8163 |
| core | 6 | 3 | 8215 |
| coil | 6 | 4 | 8305 |
| disk | 9 | 1 | 13011 |
| disk drive | 9 | 2 | 13072 |
| volume | 9 | 3 | 13317 |
| removable | 9 | 4 | 13421 |
| seek | 10 | 1 | 13814 |
| track | 10 | 2 | 14003 |
| tracks per surface | 10 | 3 | 14420 |
| surfaces | 10 | 4 | 14606 |

Figure 12.5.2. A list of terms, the output of an intermediate glossary and an index produced by a BASIC program.

*Index*

Some vendors provide programs which they call index functions. You supply a word and the program will find all the occurrences of that word in your text.

To me an index program should find the occurrence of important words without your telling them *what* words. The probelm lies in determining how to help the program find the words. As you can see in this book, as important words are introduced they are put in boldface. I wrote a small program to locate all occurrences of boldface words; it finds which words are defined in the text and approximately where each is defined. After altering the text, I can now match this printout against the glossary to see if there are any new terms that are not in the glossary.

*Processing Text*

The similarity in all these examples is that a BASIC program is running the computer and operating on text produced by the word processor at some other time. While the BASIC program is running, the word processor is not available. There is no interaction between the two.

### Sharing the WP

As far as I know, there are no provisions made by a vendor to allow a user program to run in such a way that it could use the WP facilities, or vice versa. To make this possible, enough memory is necessary so that both the WP program and user program and the interpreter are held there.

A further help is to be able to split the screen; the WP program uses one half and the user program the other half. Few vendors provide split screens for any purpose, let alone to share programs. Syntrex has a window which allows you to view several documents simultaneously. This is indispensable to run WP and user programs at the same session. The advantages afforded by this capability depend on your needs. An example follows. User programs are an extension of the concept of keystroke programming. However, the full power of the POL allows the user to create functions unique to his needs.

### Remote Host Computer

*Concept*

Here two computers talk together. One does the WP function and the other does the DP function. The simplest way to use the WP computer is as a dumb terminal. The next step is for the operator to interrupt WP action when it is desirable to communicate with the DP computer and for it to provide services to the operator. The last step is an almost complete symbiosis, where each computer has its own role and the operator is merely an observer or caretaker to take over when trouble arises.

*Dumb Terminal*

Most vendors provide a communications package, a program which allows the WP computer to communicate with another computer of the same or different type. All kinds of problems arise when the two computers are of different types and have to talk to each other. But most of these problems have to do with the format of the text. To pass unformatted text between the two poses no problem.

To act as a dumb terminal, the WP computer hardly needs an operating system. Just bring up the communication program. If the two communicate on telephone lines, then the operator dials the host computer and sets up the modem so that the host and the WP can talk to each other.

Now the WP is used like any other *computer* terminal. By keying instructions, files can be sent in either direction. If the host has a data base, inquiries can be made of it. As the name "dumb terminal" implies, no intelligence is required of the WP computer communication program for this application. However, the computer *is* a terminal now; switch to WP and you drop that role and lose the telephone connection. It is one *or* the other.

### Shared-Query Capability

This capability does not exist currently on any WP. It would not be difficult to implement. It is a state-of-the-art capability.

In the memory of the WP computer is:

- the operating system,
- the WP program,
- a communication program,
- a split-screen facility.

The host must also provide services, which Figure 12.5.3 illustrates. It has a communication program and a DP program to interface with the data for the WP.

The best way to explain this capability is through an example. The application is to answer letters of inquiry for charge account customers of a department store. Picture an account adjuster at a terminal. There are a number of letters in the in basket with complaints or requests for information about accounts. Most of them can be answered by form letters, provided that the adjuster has knowledge of the account.

After reading the customer's letter, the adjuster calls forth the appropriate form letter using the WP program. The adjuster now splits the screen and invokes the

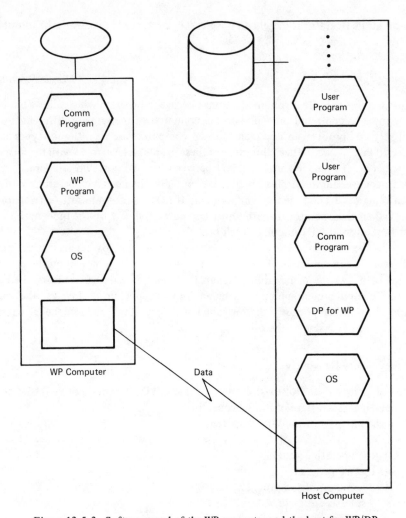

Figure 12.5.3. Software need of the WP computer and the host for WP/DP.

communication program to request the account information. By identifying the customer either by account number, if that is known, or by name, the data base can be integrated. This request is sent (using the communication program) to the host communication program. It talks to the data base manager program. The customer data base is queried and the host computer returns the customer account record, presenting it on the split screen.

The adjuster can scroll through the charge account history to find what is necessary to answer the customer's letter. Name and address information are extracted into the form letter and set up for the envelope. The exact account information acquired from the customer data base can be extracted and transferred into the letter or abstracted as the adjuster sees fit.

Should difficulties or exceptions arise, the adjuster has access to other library paragraphs to fit into the letter to make a sensible reply to the customer's complaint. We might even give the adjuster the ability to alter the customer's account on the data base if it proves to be in error. This privilege should probably be reserved for a supervisor.

### Full Integration

Full integration allows the word processor to access a data base on a host computer automatically. This is a complicated matter requiring considerable local memory in the word processor. However, the day has arrived where WP computers have 100K or even 200K or more of memory to store all the programs required:

- the operating system,
- the word processing program,
- the communication program,
- the interpreter,
- the user source program.

Instead of trying to explain how all these programs could be integrated, let us examine an hypothetical example—a fully personalized correspondence campaign. A large department store wants to send letters only to customers who have purchased cosmetics in the past month or two.

The problem is to personalize a letter, using recent purchases of cosmetics as the basis. A BASIC program is written which inquires of the data base on the main computer which customers have purchased cosmetics in the recent period. The inquiry is based on the account number and examines each customer record, looking for a cosmetic purchase; each sales department uses one or more numbers to show the kind of product bought. Each sale shows such a number, so that it is easy to pick up when a customer has purchased cosmetics.

When the BASIC program running in the WP computer encounters a recent cosmetic customer, it then goes back to the word processor and secures a form letter. It then fills in this form letter from the information from the customer's account, personalizing the letter to mention recent purchases.

The operator merely watches the letters being printed and verifies that the computer is doing its job. If mistakes occur, the operator can catch them and destroy the letters.

We have full integration here, because the user program running under the interpreter is supervising the entire action. It interrogates the host computer and its data base; it activates the word processing program in the WP computer to print the letters; it passes over text to go into each letter.

# III
# EVALUATION AND INTEGRATION

# 13
# The Office System

The office consists of equipment, people and procedures. Each is important in its own right; the system is no better than is weakest link. The aim of this handbook is to give you all the information you need to select and organize a system most appropriate and effective to your office setting. But you don't switch from one system to another in a single move; it is usually a gradual transition.

To introduce word processing judiciously into any office setting, one should be aware of intermediate alternatives to make better use of existing equipment and to insure a smooth transition. A mix of WP, intelligent typewriters and auxiliary is most suitable in some settings.

Section 13.1 examines the intelligent typewriter and its characteristics. It was postponed until the full range of WP functions was examined. This kind of typewriter might find use as:

- an independent device in an office without other WP equipment,
- an alternative for simple document preparation,
- the first step of a full scale edit job as an adjunct for text editing.

Section 13.2 looks at the steps in text preparation from the original to the final document, viewing it as three steps:

1. getting the thoughts into a form where they can be transcribed,
2. putting them into a machine readable form,
3. getting copies of the final edited document.

With alternative forms of equipment and procedures in view, what should you consider in reviewing your office for a new WP system to an extension to an existing one and how do you go about it? Section 13.3 examines:

- evaluation,
- installation,
- training,
- acquisition,

- maintenance,
- systems and procedure.

Finally, to wrap things up, Section 13.4 examines the direction in which technology is moving to see how it may impact the WP field and affect your imminent purchases.

## 13.1 THE INTELLIGENT TYPEWRITER

**What Is It?**

Probably the most popular piece of office equipment in its price category is the typewriter. Millions of them are sold every year; most are electric and some are even portable. There is a considerable difference between the low end of the price range and the high end, which we examine, along with the features that make the difference.

Technology moves relentlessly forward. What was an innovation a few years ago is today a staple. We restrict the review to features of typewriters on the market today. Moreover we exclude features which are outmoded because of advances in technology. The division may not be totally fair.

Mag card typewriters have been on the market for a number of years. They are reliable and are still being sold. Their use is restricted to compatibility with existing equipment. If an office were to buy newer equipment, some documents on mag cards would not be available for use on the new equipment.

We examine the IBM Model 50 and Model 60, Qyx Level 1 through Level 5 and the Olivetti Model 401 and Model 501. Royal and Olympia and perhaps a few other companies make competitive equipment. We ignore the mag card, mag tape cassette and memory typewriters because they seem to be outdated.

*Intelligent Features*

There are four features which distinguish the intelligent typewriter from the standard electric typewriter:

1. An electronic memory for text storage and/or phrases for quick recall during typing. It is volatile, although in some cases a small amount of non-volatile memory is provided for format storage.
2. A microprocessor, together with the required electronics, performs supplementary services to help you edit and format your documents.
3. External storage. Some but not all intelligent typewriters provide external storage, where you place your electronic document for safe keeping to call it up at some future time for editing and type out.
4. Communications may be an option to make the typewriter a remote terminal on the secretary's desk.

Table 13.1 lists competitive equipment and shows the approximate memory, external storage, display and price range.

**Table 13.1. Intelligent Typewriter Characteristics.**

| Vendor and Model | Memory | Phrase | Disk | | Display | Price, $ |
|---|---|---|---|---|---|---|
| IBM Model 50 | 4K | | – | | – | 1700 |
| IBM Model 60 | 4K | 760 | – | | – | 1700 |
| Qyx Model 1 | 80 | – | – | | – | 1400 |
| 2 | 10K | | – | | O | 2400 |
| 3 | 10K | – | 60K | Fixed | O | 4000 |
| 4 | 10K | – | 60K | Removable | O | 5800 |
| 5 | 10K | – | 120K | Removable | O | 7800 |
| Olivetti 401 | 8K | | 8K | Removable | | 5000 |
| 501 | | | | | | |
| Olympia 110 | 6800 | 1000 | – | | – | 2250 |
| 180 | 8K | 2K | 140K | Removable | O | 5500 |
| Royal 5030 | 8K | – | – | | – | 1800 |

## Memory

All intelligent typewriters have some memory. In the lower price range it is not sufficient for much editing. It is most useful for creating a final draft document, prepared, proofread and edited at one sitting. Once the text seems correct, the typewriter puts the document onto paper, but then it no longer stores a copy of the text when you start on the next document.

Most entry errors are observed by the operator shortly after they are made. Often they are a single incorrectly hit key. As for the typewriter, correction consists of removing the incorrect character(s) from the paper and typing the proper one(s) there.

Lower priced models have a short memory span of one or two lines, sufficient for correcting errors you have just caught. The machines have some form of automatic overtype correction: the bad letter is either lifted off the paper or typed over in white. It makes little difference which method is used. The machine remembers one or two lines of typing. If you have messed up the last three letters, for instance, the machine automatically corrects them without your telling it what letters they were. Hitting backspace-correct causes the carriage to back up and remove those letters. Then you type new characters over the corrected area and into memory.

Actually there are two backspace keys, correcting and noncorrecting. The latter simply moves the carriage backward, resetting the internal pointer to the text position. To correct a word three words previous, use (noncorrecting) <u>backspace</u> to move the carriage back to the end of the bad word. Then use the <u>backspace-correct</u> to remove the word. Now key in the new characters.

With the upper level Qyxs and both Olivettis, memory holds a full page. The keyboard gives you flexibility to skip around within the text. Function keys allow you to move backward and forward by word, sentence or paragraph.

There is a communication problem between you and the machine: There is no VDT; the only way to get information from the machine is for it to type on the paper. You direct the machine to position within the text using the function and unit keys to move in either direction by a designated number of characters, words or paragraphs. But the only way to verify your position is by asking the machine to print the text at your present position. One or two words give a good clue to your position. Back up over them to reposition where you were before the printout.

Keeping this in mind, let us examine the steps needed to produce a draft of a one page document with a full page of memory:

a. Put in paper and position it. Start typing your document.
b. When you make a mistake, use the (noncorrecting) <u>backspace</u> to move the carriage backward. This does not remove the bad characters. This is a draft, so you don't care what prints. Just type over the bad letters.
c. When you have finished the draft, remove the paper from the typewriter and proofread it.
d. Put a new piece of scrap paper into the machine. You are now going to correct errors on the first draft. Try to position to each error using keyboard commands. When you believe you are there, print a word or two. If you are at the right spot, make the correction. If it is the incorrect position, you have a lead on where you are in the text and you can reposition properly.
e. When you believe that the text in storage is perfect, you can print it out. Put a good sheet of stock into the machine and advance it to where you want printing to begin. Then ask the machine to replay, print out the document from the beginning, as currently recorded in memory. If you note errors, you go back through the same process and make corrections to get another final draft.

Once you have positioned to make a correction, you can insert or delete just as with a WP. You request delete or insert with the labeled function key. Otherwise the normal entry mode is replacement. Wherever you are, if you start typing, what you key into memory replaces existing text. In insert mode, whatever you key in is entered at this position and pushes existing text over to the right; no text is removed.

You delete text by character, word or paragraph. When you have finished this action, it is a good idea to backspace a short distance and play out the altered text to be sure that it is right.

*Prompts*

During entry or editing, conditions may arise which you should be made aware of. For instance, a large insertion may use up the space allocated to one printed page or use up all the memory space. The system must tell you about this. One way is through small lights on the keyboard. Another way is for the machine to print a message on the paper. While you are typing, characters may come up that you did not enter, a message to you. This will not be a surprise, since the machine will beep at you to let you now that a message is emerging.

*LED Display*

The Olivetti machine comes with a 20 character LED display; the higher levels of Qyx have a display option for $800. It is extremely useful to help with insertions or deletions of more than a couple of characters and to position within the document as described above. You can find out your position by simply looking at the display; the last few characters preceding the pointer position appear there. Further, prompts, messages and questions from the machine are presented on the display instead of being printed on your document (accompanied by a beep, of course).

**External Storage**

Higher priced models provide removable disk storage. In the intermediate range, the Qyx Model 3 provides 60K of fixed storage: the disk is not removable except for repairs and is part of the machine.

Removable disk storage makes possible a library of disks and hence a library of electronic documents, and one of which can be altered or typed out from the ED on the disk.

The fixed disk with 60K of storage provides 15 or 20 pages of text. The operator creates a document and can then store it. In the meantime, the author reviews the document, makes changes in it and returns it for editing. The document is retrieved from the disk, put into memory and edited as above; the new copy is returned to the disk to replace the old copy, if desired.

None of the models allows you to take a portion of one document and insert it in another document. Phrase storage helps make up for this.

*Phrase Storage*

Several machines, including the IBM Model 60, provide phrase storage. This is convenient for repetitive material. The operator uses discretion to determine which phrases to put away. The total phrase storage is limited; you may store one large phrase or many smaller phrases.

### Microcomputer Assistance

One of the most important selling points of the intelligent typewriter is that it assists with page composition and removes the drudgery from a lot of tasks. We are well aware of some of the facilitating actions that are provided with the VDT word processor. Some are found in simplified form in the intelligent typewriter. It seems unimportant how you invoke these aids; what is important is how they can help you. Below we touch on the extent and usefulness of each facility.

*Word Wrap*

Entering a return seems like only one additional keystroke per line. However, it does break up the pattern of typing and makes you wait while the carriage returns. The intelligent typewriter provides word wrap. The method is a little different, since the machine may print at the same time that you enter the text.

As you approach the end of the line and enter the hot zone, it is unclear whether the word you are typing fits on the line, so printing stops. After you have entered enough characters to fill this line and start the next, it is evident to the microprocessor program whether to wrap the last word or leave it there. Computer typing is faster than key entry. So as you continue to input characters, the typewriter prints from memory at full speed, finishing the previous line and continuing until it is caught up.

*Justify*

The greatest departure among the intelligent typewriters is with respect to the implementation of justification. Generally it is available only on replay. But that's when you want it. You don't need the draft to be justified. When the copy is perfect, you replay it and the microprocessor makes calculations so that each line is justified on both sides.

*Center*

One of the biggest typing chores is to center titles. You must count the characters in the title, subtract this from the length, divide by 2, round and then key in the spaces. For the intelligent typewriter, it's a snap. You indicate that you want a title centered and then you key it in. Typing does not start until you enter the full title, signaled when you hit return. The microprocessor makes the calculation and puts spaces in before it starts to print. As you key in the next line, the machine types out the centered title and catches up with you.

*Underscore*

This feature is implemented similarly. You press start-underline and type until the words to be underlined end; then you press end-underline. The type element goes back to the starting point and underlines the words while you continue typing.

*Others*

This discussion is certainly not exhaustive. However, it is worthwhile to mention a few more features that expedite your work and make chores less irksome:

- Column setup   After telling the machine that you want to set up columns at intervals, you type in the largest item in each column. It does not print. The machine sets tabs at the proper distance for these items.
- Column tabs   You can set several sequences of tab values and the machine will store them for you; call them up as you choose.
- Proportional spacing   Some of these machines do proportional spacing. The IBM machine can also backspace the proper interval (the letters you typed are in memory) for you to correct errors anywhere within one or two lines distance.
- Block indents   You can indent a block of material and then return to the former margin setting.
- Subscripts and superscripts   Advance the paper automatically by pressing one key to start and one key to finish.
- Repetitive typing   After entering a form letter into the machine, you can have it retype the letter, pausing as you enter names and addresses in the proper positions.

## 13.2 GETTING THOUGHTS ONTO PAPER

Until now our perspective has been from the point of view of the operator who keys into the WP system and eventually gets a printed document to pass along to its creator. It is important to see the larger process. Communication originates as a thought-and-organization process and eventually comes forth as a document returned to the originator who may then subject it to revision. Creation may use other equipment which stores and alters it in other ways. The text may pass through the hands and minds of several other people. What alternatives are there?

**Phases**

I view the process as consisting of three phases. The first phase is most suitably described by a fancy word, parturition, the point at which the baby emerges from its mother. Human creation consists of conception, pregnancy and parturition. We are not concerned about the first two stages for a written document, but only in what happens when the document leaves its creator.

The next two phases of WP document production consist of getting it into and out of the word processor. Input is usually by keying and output by printing, as we have seen. However, there are variations on this theme to be examined carefully, since they involve equipment other than the word processor itself.

*Parturition*

There are three ways for the creator to give birth to the communication. The first is the physical writing process. This requires good penmanship; it was once the only way to create an original manuscript.

The second means for producing the communication is by voice. There are several variations to this most important alternative which aims at making efficient use of the creator's time.

The final method for producing the communication is the keyboard. The author may enter the document directly into the word processor. Few start this way. A supplementary keyboard or a typewriter is another alternative.

*Input*

Editing and manipulation within the WP require that all characters of the text be in the computer's code set, usually ASCII. The accepted way to get text into the word processor is via the keyboard. But we should not neglect several other alternatives. They include the digital cassette, optical character recognition and a device which came on the market in mid-1981 called IRIS for Intelligent Remote Input Stand. These are discussed below.

*Output*

Direct WP output comes from the printer. But there are other sources. Some WPs connect to typewriters for auxiliary output. Most WP printers produce a single document without copies. Therefore, the copy machine often gets in the act to produce a second or third copy of a document or to produce multiple copies when many recipients are involved. The final extension of this concept involves photo-typesetting, where a plate is produced from which to print copies by offset for a large number of recipients.

### Handwriting

Writing is a late development in both the history of the species and of the individual. Man first communicated with his fellow creature by talking; the first communication between parent and child is by voice, excluding touch and other cues.

In our daily interaction with people, we expect those about us to understand our speech as we understand theirs. We speak several times faster than we write. Since speech seems so much more efficient, why then do any of us chose to write in preference to speaking when the choice arises?

*Advantage in Handwriting*

There is no question that speech is a more effective tool for expressing an immediate feeling. When someone steps on your foot, "Ouch" says right away that you hurt. Writing it out would not be nearly as effective.

A communication for the record should convey thoughts accurately, correctly and unambiguously. To get ideas down without the possibility of their being misunderstood takes time and effort; you need exactly the right words. It is a thinking process. Some of us do our best thinking with pencil and paper. We may sketch and draw, write a few words here and there, connect them together and finally get an approximation of what we want to say. You can write almost anywhere, even under water, they tell me. All you need is the most rudimentary equipment: something to write with and something to write on. You can do it by yourself. Writing is often best done in solitude.

*Disadvantage*

Once you have produced your handwritten document, you may be the only one who can read it. It may be satisfactory as notes to assist you in talking, but it may be hopeless as a document to transcribe onto the printed page. Abbreviations, initials and so forth, which you use to increase your speed and help your thinking, may be unintelligible to someone else. Even after rewriting it totally and in final form, your penmanship may be as poor as mine. How can you expect a stranger to transcribe this accurately and key it into a useful form?

## Voice

The dream of office automation is machine recognition and interpretation of speech. Wouldn't it be fantastic to dictate into a machine and have that machine produce, as output, printed text of what was said? We have machines now which can understand a few spoken words from a specific individual. The more electronics and computer time are put into this project, the more words the machine can understand. It takes considerable equipment to distinguish a few words said by (almost) anyone. Many decades remain before there will be an economically feasible way of converting speech into written material.

There are three ways to use voice for communication. The first of these is simply to communicate by voice to the people to whom the message is intended. This is not of interest to us. An offshoot of this method is electronic voice mail, described in Section 13.4. Here your telephone message is recorded for later delivery.

The two remaining methods involve dictating to a person or to a recording machine.

### Person-to-Person

Person-to-person dictation is better called **stenography**. The author dictates the document to a stenographer, who puts it on paper using shorthand, a phonetic language with brief forms which can be written more rapidly than handwriting. Later, the stenographer transcribes the shorthand document, keying it into the WP system where it is now eligible for editing as a electronic document.

Mechanically aided stenography, stenotyping, has been around for a long time, but it has not caught on in the office. For this specialized art, the stenotypist uses a special shorthand keyboard to put the information on a paper output tape which is later transcribed.

AM Jacquard has a technique for picking up the information from the stenotyping tape machine and bringing it directly into a computer where, with the aid of the stenotypist, the information is converted more quickly into an electronic document.

### Advantages

Stenography has advantages which result from the personal interaction between the author and the stenographer. The first advantage is the exposure of the author to another human being. The second is the contribution of the stenographer to the composition process, which should not be underestimated. A good stenographer can help the author phrase things better or organize thoughts in a way which reads better. When the author mumbles or mispronounces words, the stenographer can question the author and get the exact wording, something that is impossible with a recording.

While composing a piece, an author frequently discovers an omitted point, which should be placed in an earlier position in the text. It is easier for the stenographer to find and enter the new text and the desired position than it is to do the same thing with the recorder.

Sometimes a dictation appointment acts as discipline. The author prepared for the meeting and thus organizes his or her time to make the meeting possible and to be prepared when the time arrives.

*Disadvantages*

There are a number of disadvantages to person-to-person dictation to contrast with its advantages:

1. Two people's time is consumed in the dictation process. The time and naturally the cost of the stenographer are consumed *while* the dictation is given and *again* when it is transcribed.
2. Double time is consumed while the author composes and revises the manuscript with the stenographer.
3. Some people benefit from the interaction with the secretary during composition, but others suffer and are embarrassed to have someone watch them while they think.
4. The stenographer is generally available only during prescribed working hours. The author may find it hard to break free a time slot for composition and dictation because of other engagements during the day. Overtime is not only more costly but it may be more difficult to arrange, since the stenographer may have a personal schedule to fulfill.
5. Since dictation is done during working hours, there are many interruptions from outside sources: fires to put out, meetings to go to, matters which require immediate attention and telephone calls.
6. It is hard to find stenographic help. Secretaries proficient in Gregg, Pittman or Speed Writing are in short supply. And the skill must be *used* to keep up their speed.
7. Stenography, although not as personalized as handwriting, is not universally readable. It is difficult for one stenographer to read the outlines and brief forms of another. Brief forms, abbreviations and penmanship differ considerably. The one who takes the shorthand generally must transcribe it.

These objections may seem insurmountable; their resolution depends upon the position of the author in the firm. A middle level manager may not find it advisable to cope with all the objections. However, a top manager has an executive secretary, all of whose time is totally available.

Dictating machines have been around for several decades. Remember the old Edison cylinders? You recorded on them with a moving stylus. This created a permanent recording, much like a phonograph record, played back with a needle. The cylinders, not reusable, were thrown away when the entire surface was recorded upon.

Technology has moved ahead considerably and now there are many media available, most of which are reusable. Recording is accurate and lifelike, reproducing words and sentences clearly and distinctly, according to how they were spoken into the microphone.

Machines fall into three categories:

- Portable machines fit into a pocket or valise and can be carried on an airplane, taken on a trip or taken home.
- The desk model occupies little space. Most fit into a desk drawer. It can be put to use in a few seconds to jot down a memo either to be transcribed or simply to remind you of something.
- The dial-up machine is reached by the writer by dialing at the telephone. Where direct dial is available, one can telephone from home.

All dictating machines are similar: they are constantly available; they are free from human frailties, although subject to occasional mechanical defects; while in use by the creator, they do not tie up other personnel; none provides easy feedback; that is, the author does not have quick access to alter previous portions of the recorded document without messing up succeeding parts.

*Portable Recorders*

There is a wide range of portable recorders. At the bottom end there is the audio cassette recorder for $30 or $40, which is more frequently used for recording from radio programs. Most can record adequately a dictated document and have a digital counter to tell the approximate amount of remaining tape.

Vendors such as Lanier, Dictaphone and IBM make products especially for the executive with frills which are indeed useful. One of these is a review switch on the hand microphone which lets you reverse the tape and play it back to hear what you have just dictated. This is a necessity when interrupted. If you don't like something that you recently dictated you can go back to a previous point and re-dictate the material from there. Other bells and whistles allow you to give notes to your secretary and pace off the contents of a cassette.

*Dial-In*

With a dial-in dictating facility, your call triggers one of a bank of recording machines. Once this machine is started, you must dictate your entire letter, memo or report. You'd better have it all planned, because most installations do not provide means for stopping the recording, let alone for backing up and correcting a phrase or paragraph that seems incorrect. When you are finished and you hang up the telephone, the recorder at the other end automatically stops. The remaining space on the cassette may become available for other users in a crowded system where cassettes are shared. In a less used system, the next caller gets a different cassette to work with.

Different priority schemes are available to enable a group working on a hot proposal or report to get special service. A telephone number assigned only to this project is one way. It brings in a specific machine(s) assigned to this report. When the WP operators come in early in the morning, they start immediately on the hot proposal, using the machines assigned for the purpose.

Although the system has disadvantages, it also has clear advantages which recommend it in certain situations.

**Input**

We have examined how one creates a document on the word processing system. In the beginning I stressed the difference between creating and editing a document. This difference seems artificial because we often do a certain amount of editing during creation.

The so-called creation process serves two purposes. It gets the document into the WP in electronic form, even if this is a first draft; it also creates a rough draft hard copy document for the originator to modify further if necessary. For the WP, these steps coalesces into a single activity, where creation of the electronic document is immediately followed by printing it. Such need not be the case.

We now examine several alternatives to direct input, some of which separate keying from printing the draft.

    a. The creator and the operator are the same person. The originator, at the WP keyboard, creates and modifies the document and may stop work at any time without printing the draft. The electronic document is recalled later and work continues.

    b. The Aquarius System by Syntrex combines a conventional IBM or Olivetti typewriter with a VDT, a microcomputer and storage at an inexpensive price. You may use the typewriter in the conventional way or flip a switch and it becomes a word processor. Now your keyboard feeds the VDT and creates the electronic document in computer memory. When you are satisfied with the ED, play it back on your typewriter to produce the first draft.

c. Northcom produces IRIS, a combination memory and microprocessor which hooks into an IBM Model 50 or Model 60. Figure 13.2.1 shows what IRIS looks like. Use the intelligent typewriter to create a first draft of your document. Make corrections as you go along, as described in Section 13.1. As you do so, the electronic copy of the document stored in IRIS is similarly updated. When you are satisfied with the document, run off another draft. Then dial up your word processor and send the electronic document from IRIS memory to it at 300 or 600 characters per second.

Figure 13.2.1. An IRIS device. (Courtesy of Northcom).

d. Both Micom and Sony make portable keyboard recorders which have a standard typewriter keyboard. They collapse into a thin case which weighs considerably less than a portable typewriter. The originator keys in a document at any convenient place. When equipped with a battery pack, they can be used in an airplane. There is a LED display which presents the last few characters keyed in. Backspace correction is possible, but not much more in the way of editing. The information is recorded on nonvolatile memory contained in the unit. Sony uses a microfloppy. Sony also permits you to record a voice document. When you have entered your document, you may then connect through a modem to a telephone line after you have dialed into your company. Now the digital or voice recording can be transmitted to another recorder or to a word processing unit. The creator may have a printed copy on the desk upon returning.

*OCR*

OCR stands for **optical character recognition**. The OCR machine accepts a typewritten document produced with either a special OCR print wheel or one with a font which the OCR vendor specifies as acceptable to the machine, such as Courier. Each page submitted is scanned by the machine, converted into digital form and transmitted to the WP system as though the OCR reader were another word processor. Let us see how this device is used to expedite work in the office.

Your office has one or two WP systems. Each has a communication program to enable it to talk to another WP. Your office also has many standard electric typewriters (intelligent or dumb) and does not wish to eliminate these useful machines.

A transcription task is submitted to any typewriter operator to produce a draft with margins, format and typeface acceptable to the OCR reader. It is assigned a document name and returned to the originator to examine and edit.

The originator goes through the document, checks it and notes changes with a special pen with ink which is not picked up by the OCR reader. The hand edited document is returned and is placed into the OCR feeder.

The OCR reader switches are set to make it appear like another word processing system of the same vendor and it is connected to the WP. The reader scans the text, converts the characters on the document into the corresponding codes and transmits them as though as they had been keyed at a terminal, only much faster. The reader notes paragraph ends and converts each into a return for this machine.

The reader is connected by wires to the WP system which is dedicated, at this moment, for use by the reader. The text transmitted by the OCR reader at several pages a minute is received by the communication program in the word processing computer and entered onto a floppy disk or a hard disk. The operator makes certain beforehand that there is enough space on the disk for the incoming document.

Once the document is safely on a floppy disk, it is available to a WP operator for editing. The operator gets the edited manuscript which has just been read in by the OCR reader. Editing marks entered there in ink invisible to the OCR reader are visible to the operator. The changes are now made in the electronic document and then a copy is produced on its printer to return to the originator. Future revisions of this document need not pass through the OCR reader, since an electronic version of the document is now in the WP system.

The OCR reader makes every typewriter a possible source for an electronic document. This means that if you have two WP terminals and ten typewriters, you have twelve possible sources for keying electronic documents. Since much more time is consumed in creating a document than in making simple changes on that document, this makes more effective use of office resources.

An OCR reader costs in the neighborhood of $10,000. This is an economic alternative for an office that has many typewriters and is considering a WP system.

### Output

There is a wide range in the speed of operation of printers. Computerized golf ball typewriters are limited to 15 characters per second; line printers, found in computer installations (also available for WP systems), produce 600 characters per second; laser printers produce several pages per second. This is more than a ratio of 40 to 1. One of the biggest bottlenecks in WP systems is the printer because of its output speed and the fact that high quality seems attainable only with low speed. This is further complicated by the fact that good multiple copies are hard to produce with a letter quality printer.

The most frequently used alternative is the daisy wheel printer, operating at 45 to 60 characters per second, which produces a single original. A copy machine produces one or more copies of similar quality and at the rate of several pages per minute.

Getting multiple copies from the manual feed printer involves considerable operator time. When the printer finishes with one page, the next page must be provided with carbons and onion skin interleaved. This may take as long to set up as the printer takes to produce the page. Multiple sheets are difficult and time consuming to align in the printer.

An attractive alternative practice in an office of reasonable size is to have several printers with different speed ranges and qualities. Draft output can be produced on a high speed printer with moderate quality.

Laser printers are expensive but provide high quality and speed combined. In a medium to large office they are the ideal resource to share. They cannot make copies but their speed makes up for this. They can produce several original *sets* faster than a printer and copier combination can.

Perhaps, in the future, we may be willing to compromise on quality. Some samples of dot matrix multipass printing presented in Chapter 3 seem acceptable to me. Since printers of this caliber can also produce letterheads and logos in a different type font and continuous forms can be used, the printing process can be expedited considerably with only a small sacrifice in quality.

## 13.3 CONSIDERATIONS

Several matters should be given serious thought before deciding upon acquiring or modifying a WP system. A few of these are discussed below.

**When Is Word Processing Necessary?**

In some offices, because of current practice, a WP system provides slight advantage, if any, over the electric typewriter. The typing pool, for example, provides little contact between the creator of the document and its transcriber. The operator may have little knowledge of what the document is all about and may care even less.

Some pools are organized so that the electronic document is not readily available after the first draft is made. This is aggravating to all. The great power of the WP system is flushed down the drain. The corrected draft must be rekeyed. Users might just as well have used a typewriter as a WP system.

The greatest advantage of the WP system is that with sufficient perseverance, you *can* achieve a perfect error-free document. It is ideal where accuracy is more important than speed or productivity. Nothing can really match it. You can eradicate the last error without introducing a new one.

You add productivity to accuracy when repetitious work is involved. The best example is the legal office. The attorney has need for accuracy, but also deals with much repetitive information. There are innumerable legal papers that differ only slightly from one to the next. Since the turn of the century, standard forms have been available for leases, contracts, wills and so forth. You could go into a stationer and choose from a list of hundreds. These same forms are available as electronic documents for the attorney's office for a modest fee.

Instead of having hundreds of forms on hand, the attorney now has their electronic equivalents. Their usefulness has increased considerably. A form, or portion thereof, can be altered and returned to the form library to suit each attorney. On request, paragraphs are withdrawn from the library and assembled into a document in a matter of minutes. What used to take hours to create by typing letter by letter is now recreated momentarily with a good WP system. Since all the excerpts in the library are originals, there is no question about their accuracy.

The case is much less clear cut for the competent executive secretary. This person is experienced, accurate and fast and knows what the boss wants. A WP system may just be a frill.

As a rule of thumb, a WP system can be most effective where:

- accuracy is imperative,
- there is heavy editing and much revision,
- there is boiler plate and repetitious material,
- there are form letters and document assembly,
- tabular and material and multiple columns are an everyday occurrence,
- there are special applications where the WP system is of advantage.

## Evaluation

How do you determine whether a WP system is needed? A decision should be based on the current needs and activities of the office. You should determine what the people in the office are doing and what percent of their time they spend in each activity. This means observation, unless you already have this information. Of primary importance are systems and procedures. How does the system work and what do the people do?

Someone must determine what is going on in your office to make a considered decision. Who does this and how?

*Study*

The objective is to determine how each employee in the office spends his or her time during the day. Each could keep a journal, writing in it the time spent on each activity. In making such observations one tends to see one's time as more productive than it actually is. Even so, a journal may work, provided that a good procedure is developed for reporting what is worked on in detail, so that an accurate estimate is provided.

A better way is an objective survey taken by someone from the outside who observes each employee. This "time-and-motion study" is a prospect which is not greeted amiably.

While such a study could be conducted and manned by in-house personnel, it is less likely that permanent staff people would know what to look for or how to look for it. Such observation requires training and impartiality. It is preferable to get skilled consultants to do the job.

What kinds of things are we looking for? Word processing deals with the preparation and distribution of documents. Each act of this nature is recorded in terms of time spent creating a new document, correcting a document, editing a document, printing a document, copying a document, filing a document and so forth. Another percentage of the time is spent in actions, generally verbal activity, not involved with documents.

The investigator must be alert to the interaction between documents. Preparation of ten identical letters to different people certainly would lend itself to a WP system.

*Analysis*

Once facts are collected, they need to be analyzed. As an example, there might be a large percentage of time spent creating, altering and manipulating tabular information. This is important for the selection process which follows.

Your decision about acquiring or enlarging a WP system depends on what you want to get from it. If you want to improve accuracy and ease of editing, a study is hardly necessary; WP will do these tasks. The questions then become: How many? What unit? Which typewriters do they replace, if any?

If productivity is the aim, then your decision is based on a time-and-activity breakdown. The person-hours per month spent on such activities as making tabular forms, assembling documents, doing complex editing, drafting reports, etc., is determined and broken down accordingly. Overlap, several people doing WP-eligible activity at the same time, is also noted. This helps provide an estimate of the number of work stations needed.

Vendor selection depends upon the WP features required in your office. Other factors must be evaluated individually in the particular office setting. Each factor has several variables to be considered. For instance, maintenance is usually important, but it, in turn, depends on geographical location. Given a particular vendor, one must consider whether the office is located in Omaha, Nebraska or New York City. This topic is touched upon later.

**Installation**

Assuming that you have chosen a vendor and placed an order, you should prepare for the installation of the equipment before it arrives. Here are items to consider:

1. *Furniture* Some equipment is self-contained and free standing. Others, such as the printer, need a bench of the proper height and access to both the front and the rear. There must be a stand for the paper which feeds the printer and for the printed material which comes out of it. There should be space to work with the paper. If this a continuous feed operation, the paper has to be separated or burst apart and assembled into convenient units. If you do not provide table space to do this, employees will be cramped. Each module of the system should be similarly analyzed.

2. *Space* The furniture that you need—tables, chairs and cabinets—occupy space which should be allocated for it before it arrives.

3. *Supplies* There are three important supplies for the WP system:
   Paper is the most important output and it includes envelopes.
   Ribbon is used at a fantastic rate; enough should be on hand for several weeks' consumption.
   Floppy disks store the electronic documents and the number and amount of storage required for them depends upon whether electronic documents are maintained on the disk for any length of time or whether the disks are cleared of the documents at intervals.

4. *Power* WPs are electric devices which consume electric power. There must be outlets convenient to the equipment and electric lines which are not overloaded to power the equipment. Lines, much like telephone lines, interconnect units throughout the office, so you should be prepared to do extra wiring outside of electric power for this purpose. If you are in an

area with brownouts or blackouts you must beware. Recall that memory is volatile, so that any revision which is being worked on in memory will be lost during a brownout. Backup power is sometimes recommended.

5. *Environment* The WP likes to be comfortable. It is reluctant to work in extremes of temperature and humidity, so air conditioning is recommended. Your operators will use CRT screens, so light is an important factor. Too much or too little illumination may degrade their activity. Printers are sometimes noisy. If you notice at the vendor's demonstration that the printer produces excessive noise, you might consider putting it in its own room or getting soundproof enclosures.

6. *Staff* If you have gone through an evaluation procedure, your staff has probably seen strangers on the premises and knows that one or more WP systems is on its way. You may make your selection without an evaluation procedure and your staff may not know until the equipment arrives on the premises. Their astonishment may have repercussions. They are a part of the overall system and if they do not cooperate, the system may fall flat.

## Training

I have found that I can get useful work from an employee with very little training. However, I am well acquainted with the equipment. One or more of your staff must be very knowledgeable about the equipment to make the enterprise work smoothly.

Frequently an office trains its workers to a level of productivity which resembles their previous rate. Since further training seems to take away productive time from the office, management hesitates to make this investment. The effective use of a WP system comes only from knowledge of its capacity to cut down on the drudgery in your office. You make full use of WP equipment only when at least one person knows each and every feature of the equipment and can instruct others properly. One fully trained person is worth a dozen partially trained persons, if the person is a loyal and dedicated employee. What you don't know might hurt you.

Training is most effective when it is integrated with work experience. Several short term training periods are more helpful than one long exposure. Personalized training in the vendor's office is worth any additional cost that it might entail. Do not pin your hopes on cassettes, audio-visual material or self-instructional aids. It is a rare individual that can extract full measure from these devices.

## Acquisition

Usually a vendor offers three plans for acquiring WP equipment:

- buy it,
- rent it at a fixed monthly fee,

- lease it through a third party, often with the option to buy at the end of the contract.

Whichever plan you take, a contract is involved. You want a plan which is advantageous and considers a changing technology. If you buy the equipment, it is yours forever. Renting or leasing allows you to return equipment to get more advanced versions.

You should anticipate changes in your system. The usual approach is to buy less equipment than needed with the expectation that if the system is successful, additional equipment will be added. Most systems do expand. One way is by adding new resources, such as a hard disk. Another way is by buying an additional system or two. Determine if it is necessary for the systems to communicate and how they may do so.

*Second Vendor*

If you consider a second or third system, you may also consider another vendor. You may find that capability is not available in the existing system. There are three facts to face:

1. Two different systems cannot talk easily. You cannot read a disk from one system on another system directly. There are devices to make the format conversion, if this is worth the trouble and the extra cost. Otherwise, one system does not back up the other system.
2. Although the systems may be equivalent in concept and word output, the method of communicating and control functions and keys differ. This means additional training and the difficulty of interchanging operators between the two systems.
3. No one system has all the features that you might desire. A second system from a different vendor may provide a better combination of qualities.

The first two objections may be too strong to consider a second vendor. In this case, when you acquire your first system you must make sure that you can expand gracefully.

## Maintenance

It is difficult to imagine how dependent you can become on a word processing system. The better you have integrated the system, the more the maintenance of the system becomes important. In the legal office, much of the transcription work involves the word processing system. If the system goes down, it is difficult, if not impossible, to return to a manual method of creating a contract or other paper. Therefore, it is essential that you keep the system up and running and that you provide backup for all the important work that is going on. Most WP systems are reliable. The electronic components are not subject to wear. The mechanical devices in the system are more troublesome. The printer is most likely to fail. The head mechanism, the thimble and other moving parts frequently become faulty or inoperative and have to be replaced by the repairman.

### Vendor Contract

When you acquire your system, the customary arrangement is to enter into a maintenance contract with the vendor. Since adequate maintenance is so important, it is desirable to investigate how good the vendor's maintenance practices are. Unfortunately you cannot accept his word for it. He may recommend some of his customers who praise his maintenance practice. You should certainly talk to them and ask them about other customers that they may know. Customers not recommended by the vendor are the best source of this information. They are more likely to be unhappy with and thus more critical of the service supplied.

### Other Sources

The vendor is not the only source of maintenance and service. Agents have sprung up that specialize in maintenance. Repair technicians are hard to find and good service is at a premium.

The ideal arrangement is to call for and pay for service only when you need it. But both vendors and service agents provide maintenance to contract customers first. Only if they have spare time do they give service to a noncontract installation, and then at a high price; they want the steady income that accrues from a contract arrangement.

A maintenance contract is like insurance. You pay for it in the hope that you will not need it. When the occasion does arise, it is imperative that the service be supplied quickly and that the equipment be back in operation at the earliest opportunity.

### Systems and Procedures

The evaluation project which determines whether a WP system is advisable should consider how the WP is integrated into the systems and procedures of the office.

An integration plan which treats the new technology as though it were a one-for-one replacement of old technology does not make good use of the WP system. A plan which scraps the current procedures entirely is equally upsetting. The first extreme would replace each typewriter by a WP system or a terminal; the second system might, for instance, remove all typewriting from individual secretaries to a typing pool where transcription and printing is performed. This is dehumanizing and inefficient. A proper integration plan considers the work flow for each person involved in the current office setting.

Planless acquisition can be deadly. I know of a large broker's office where the printer has neither a tractor feed nor an automatic sheet feed. Thus, when you have finished preparing a fifteen page report on the word processor and want to get a hard copy document, you must stand by the printer for 20 minutes to half an hour entering sheets of paper and collecting printed copy as it comes out of the printer. Poor planning makes poor use of your time.

Bureaucracy and the difficulty of the acquisition process may make it nearly impossible to augment the system to free up your time. All that we need is a simple tractor feed. But then the next person who comes along will have to remove it for single sheet paper.

## 13.4 THINGS TO COME

This section examines the advance of technology as it bears upon the word processing field. What changes in equipment are likely? How will they affect the WP system and the usefulness of the WPs in your office in the near future? This discussion looks at each system component to ask: How might it change? How might this change be put to use? Later portions of the section are devoted to activities related to WP or ones in which the WP system may be involved.

### Printers

The printer seems to be the weakest link in the chain because of the large amount of mechanical motion, linkages and motorized parts in it. This area requires the most work. However the vendor is not doing research in this area, their subcontractors and the original equipment manufacturers are.

Mechanical motion in the printer is inevitable because paper must be moved past a printing area. Printing itself need not be mechanical, so we can hold out some hope there. Another problem is the compromise between quality, speed, cost and availability of multiple copies.

#### Daisy Wheel Printer

The daisy wheel printer is indeed the most popular WP printer because it offers high quality at a reasonable speed of about 50 characters per second. This is really not fast enough for some applications. Only the metal daisy wheel can produce legible multiple copies. Performance has been pushed close to the limit of speed and accuracy. I don't expect speeds to increase above 70 characters per second.

*Matrix Printers*

The matrix printer is frowned upon in the office community. It is associated with low quality printing. Less expensive matrix printers are unreliable and not as fast as they might be. I foresee considerable activity in this area. This printer *can* produce high quality printing when the printhead passes back and forth over the same line several times. This slows down the output, but the printer is already rather fast in some offerings. Within a year or two, reliable, fast, good quality matrix printers may be available with the following characteristics:

- high speed draft quality printing of 200 to 500 characters per second;
- letter quality printing at 60 to 100 characters per second;
- graphics, so that a continuous tractor feed can be used and letterheads with line work in them can be produced by the printer on rag bond paper;
- capability for line drawings;
- multiple fonts to provide italics and other typefaces in the output in a single run without operator intervention; compressed and expanded character sets add further emphasis;
- no problem with multiple copies.

*Line Printers*

The line printer is mostly used in the EDP computer environment. There the device is maintained only to the point that it works. This means that the characters within a line are often misaligned. This is not acceptable in the office, even for a draft. Line printers work fast, but they've been around a long time, so I don't expect that they will make any inroads in the office.

*Ink Jet and Thermal Printers*

These types of printers produce only one copy, so I don't expect them to take hold in the near future.

*Laser Printers*

Here we find one printer which combines high quality and high speed. Only one copy is produced at a time. With the proper software, it is easy to produce a number of copies of the same page; and if the machine has collating ability, it can produce collated, multiple copies of a document or can run several sets in sequence.

The problem with this printer is its price but that may come down in the near future. You *can* run two, three or more complete WP systems on one laser printer. I think that larger offices with several WPs will buy this kind of printer to take advantage of its speed and quality.

## Displays and Keyboards

In most respects, today's keyboards are quite satisfactory. The keys and the switches are fairly reliable. Vendors have taken pains to use the best switches for long life and reliability.

Vendors have done little if any research into optimum key placement, apart from the normal letter and symbol entries. For the special keys, is it better to put the delete key at the left, the right or the top? Which keys should be grouped together? No one seems to have looked into foot switches, such as the organist uses to expand his capability. Let us hope for some research in this area.

*Displays*

There are a large number of display features which are at various levels of use in different vendor products. Hopefully they will find uniform use in the future. Personally I would like to see a larger screen, such as that on the Xerox STAR, but there seems to be resistance both from the vendors and from office personnal themselves. I am not a convert to full page displays; multilevel zoom facility would be quite adequate for most purposes. That is, large type for entry, medium type for editing and small type to show a whole page when necessary. Larger memories within the terminal are easy to come by and would provide full horizontal and vertical scrolling.

I like pan scrolling where the text on the screen seems to move continuously, without the jerky motion that I deplore. A completely responsive screen should be no problem, *and all the features you need should be at your fingertips.*

Within the next few years, when several fonts are available on the printer, I expect those same fonts to display on the screen, as with the Xerox STAR.

I can see little use for color in today's applications, except perhaps to coordinate color keys on the keyboard with colored responses on the screen. Perhaps vendors may tie in color to projected functions, such as multilevel searches or multiple revisions.

## Storage

The WP industry has not yet felt the impact of small, low-priced Winchester drives. A wide variety of these drives is just hitting the market. They range from the small size of 5 inches for 5 megabytes up through 8, 10 and 14 inch models with capacities ranging to 100 megabytes. Most of them are fixed disks;—the medium remains permanently attached. Models with some removable storage are available, but it's questionable whether they can be cost effective.

Within the next year or two, the vendors will be coming out with different combinations of fixed and floppy disks; this is an important development to watch.

Shared resource systems with hard disk drives will become more common. This will lead to management review of text, which I discuss a little later in this section. A good index and directory system is then imperative.

### Memory and Computers

Whether the vendor uses 8 or 16 bit microprocessors will have little effect on the system with respect to the user. What will have an effect is the amount of internal memory that is provided. The difficulty encountered is for 8-bit computers to address more than 64K of memory.

Machines with 100K to 200K of memory are on the market now. Look for even larger memories in the near future. They bring these advantages:

- More text is immediately available without reference to disk and without waiting times as you scroll through.
- There is room to hold several programs simultaneously, so you won't have to switch back and forth between floppy disks as you change programs and start doing record processing.

### Software

Most features that your WP system provides are embodied in the software supplied by the vendor. Every new feature added, such as the ability to handle multiple columns of text, requires new programs. The vendor has a considerable investment in these programs and does not want to scrap any of them. Therefore he usually squeezes in the new program. With larger memories this should be feasible. Expect to see all vendors adding features to their products through additional software, probably at little or no additional cost.

Even when memory is easily available, squeezing a new feature in is not as effective as rewriting the program. Vendors are reluctant to do this because the new programs won't work in the smaller memory of existing computers; rewriting entails cost and is most effective with new products. So in some ways, it is easier for new vendors or new product designs to have features that old ones do not or cannot add.

Some new functions now available are spelling programs, multiple column text capability, windows and more elaborate report generators.

### Related Office Developments

If you are looking for an in-depth discussion of future office automation, you are going to be disappointed. The word processing system will expand and its capabilities will grow to include other areas. Some predictions seem too all-encompassing to me, such as the coming of the cashless society. I tend to be conservative and confine my predictions to the short term.

I contend that current systems provide many facilities which could be better integrated into the present day office if we made a greater effort to educate and train both operators and managers. For example, although some offices have record processing capability in their WP, it is going to waste. Yet they sound as if the thing closest to their heart is data base management, such as is available only on larger computers.

### Electronic Mail

A facility readily available today in one form or another is electonic mail. Lots of people talk about it without defining it. I see electronic mail as falling into three categories:

- local, between terminals in a small office;
- companywide, from any office of the company to any other office,
- nationwide, to almost anyone in the country.

Local electronic mail in the office setting is immediately available. For example, Wang provides MailWay, so that mail can be sent between two communicating word processors. I question whether sending a brief memo down the hall is worth the expense of installing a system of this nature. Local mail works only if users have been regimented to look for and to post electronic letters instead of using their feet or the telephone.

Company-wide electronic mail is indeed useful. It is especially so for a company which is spread out all over the country or is international. A good and effective system falls outside the province of word processing. Systems such as those installed at Hewlett-Packard and General Electric are based on large central computers with local terminals in everybody's office.

A nationwide electronic office mail system where you can contact *anyone* is simply not here yet. It is in the developmental stage and it is at least a decade away. When it arrives, you may be able to tie a WP terminal into the system, but WPs may have changed so much by then that such a possibility is hard to predict.

### Voice Mail

Electronic mail requires that the sender key his letter into a terminal. This may be tedious for one with limited typing ability. Voice mail claims to overcome this difficulty. If you are out, your calls are diverted to be recorded. You can call in later to have the recorded calls played back. This seems to fill an important need for the busy executive.

I have frequently found that I cannot get through to the person that I am calling. The information I need to give to the person is complicated. If I tell a secretary, the message must be relayed to the party. A complex message can be distorted or oversimplified with an unpredictable result. It would be nice if I could leave a recorded message which the receiver could personally examine without any distortions.

I do not understand why we do not press present resources into use for this purpose. I have both a telephone answering machine and a dictating machine. Either one of these can be set to record an incoming telephone message intercepted by a human operator. For example, suppose that I call someone who is out and a secretary answers. I have a complicated message to pass along. The secretary probably has a transcription machine on the desk which could be hooked into the telephone. By pressing the button and starting it, the secretary could record the message directly from the telephone line. A special device for this purpose alone costs only $30 or $40 and could be placed on every receptionist's desk.

When you return to your office you can play back your telephone messages and receive accurate complicated messages without trouble.

### Management Work Stations

I am not very optimistic about the usefulness of management work stations in their present form. It is my impression that top management spends most of its working time interacting with people. Paperwork does get done; often it is taken home, handled on the train or plane or in a hotel room during traveling. The manager is not stationary enough to take advantage of the VDT, nor does he want to be occupied with keys and screens. He or she would rather get a printed sheet of paper to work with, and requests it regardless of the issue.

Middle managers are less reticent to step up to a terminal and key in a few words. The younger generation is growing up with both computers and terminals. Also there is a personal computer explosion upon us. Management will be engulfed with terminals before the millenium, why rush to them?

### Typesetting

How many books, pamphlets, manuals and other material are typeset every year? Many come from handwritten documents or typewritten information. But a rising number of manuscripts are prepared on word processors.

Typesetting has been computerized too. Now most work is done with photocomposition. Directions on character size and font are stored in digital form. Each text character occupies a byte, just as in word processing. In fact, the ASCII code set is commonly used to represent text for typesetting.

The main difference between the electronic document used by your WP system and that for photocomposition is the format statements. The WP system uses relatively few format directives compared with the large number required for photocomposition. Then too, the commands themselves differ. For this reason, the electronic document prepared on the WP is not immediately interchangeable and cannot be fed to the photocomposition machine to make a sensible printed documented. Format statements in the electronic documents prepared on the WP must be stripped and replaced by different format statements. Moreover, new statements must be added to describe how the typeset document should look.

AM Jacquard and Wang have machines which do the job and convert from a WP electronic document to the needed computerized information for typesetting on their machine. Publishers in general do not use this equipment; they have existing equipment that does not mate with the WP system.

More and more authors are producing copy of WP systems. The entire text of a book is already captured in digital form on disks. What a waste to key in all this material again. There are systems and services to convert electronic documents to a usable form for the typesetter. Publishers are reluctant to get involved and provide no incentive for authors for benefits received.

## Summary

Expect massive expansion in the WP market, but no real surprises.

# Appendix A
# Glossary

**acoustic coupler**—A device for coupling the computer to your telephone. You place your telephone headset into the cradle. The computer produces sounds which are gathered by the telephone microphone. It receives sounds from the telephone loud speaker and submits them to your computer.

**action oriented WP**—A WP is so-called when, during editing, you indicate the action to be performed first before you indicate the object upon which it to be performed.

**affix**—Either a prefix or a suffix.

**allocation**—The action of a file manager to assign space on a disk for use by a file.

**allocation bit map**—A map containing a bit for each group of sectors on the medium. A bit is set to 1 for a group which is allocated, and 0 otherwise. The map is computed from the directory entries constructed in memory the first time that the disk is activated. A separate map is kept in memory for each drive known to the operating system.

**alphabet**—The set of symbols (letters, numbers, punctuation and function codes) associated with a code set, for each of which a code exists.

**answer mode**—When two stations are communicating in full duplex by means of modems, one of them is in the answer mode which establishes the choice of a pair of tones used with frequency shift keying. Standard answer mode uses 2225 Hertz for mark and 2025 Hertz for space.

**archive**—An external storage medium containing a number of files which are documents no longer in use. To archive a file is to put it onto such a medium.

**ASCII**—Acronym for American Standard Code for Information Interchange. See Appendix 2 for a table of the code set values.

**aspect ratio**—Ratio of height to width, as in the CRT screen or in a printed document.

**assembly directions**—The directions for automatic document assembly which the WP uses to choose subdocuments to compose the output document.

**automatic document management**—When the WP system maintains each document you create as a complete entity, and you do not have to keep track of the page sequence.

**backspace correction**—For the WP system, to correct the last letter keyed, the operator need press only rub or backspace and enter the new character right over the bad one.

**495**

**backspace**—A key which (1) causes the typewriter carriage to move backward one character position; (2) moves the cursor for the WP backward one position.

**backup**—Copies on an external storage medium of all or most of the files used by a system so that there are alternates on another volume in case of difficulty.

**BASIC**—A procedure oriented programming language in which a user can write a program. This particular language is easy to learn and use.

**belt**—A polyeurethene or fiberglass belt with print slugs cemented to it which rotates at a constant speed within the line printer.

**Binary Synchronous Communication Protocol (BSC or BISYNC)**—A communication protocol in common use for microcomputers.

**bit**—Contraction for "binary digit." An electric signal, a datum or a number which is has exactly two states: on or off, one or zero, yes or no.

**blank**—A character which is entirely white if we are writing with black on white.

**block**—(1) The amount of information read from an input device or written to an output device with a single computer command. For the disk, a block and a sector are the same size. Blocks are numbered consecutively, but the sectors that contain them may be interleaved on the disk under the prevailing skewing discipline. (2) A unit of text defined by the user.

**block movement**—The ability to allocate and move about a block of text within the remainder of the text.

**boldface**—Printing characters emboldened and darker than the rest of the text.

**boot**—Starting up the computer, bringing the operating system into memory and giving it control.

**buffer**—A temporary storage area which holds data.

**buffer, hardware**—A buffer in the form of hardware registers. For example, the printer has a buffer which holds one or even several lines of data (to be printed) and control commands (to which the printer responds.)

**buffer, move**—A buffer assigned to hold a block of information temporarily as it is moved about within the text.

**buffer, number**—A buffer that stores the number of times a search and replace operation should be repeated.

**buffer, option**—A buffer that stores the alternative actions during a search.

**buffer, phrase**—A location where a phrase defined by the user may be stored temporarily and called up for entry at any site in the text.

**buffer, printer**—The hardware memory within the printer.

**buffer, software**—A data storage area in memory, accessible to I/O devices and also to the user program.

**bursting**—The action taken on multiple sheets of a continuous form to separate them into single sheets, keeping them in order.

**bidirectional printing**—The capability of the print carriage to move in either direction horizontally while printing characters.

**bus**—A collection of wires common to many circuits. The computer bus generally consists of three types of wires: data, control and power.

**bus, address**—Control wires in the bus which carry the address.

**byte**—A collection of eight bits.

cable—A set of wires used to connect a device to the main computer chassis.

capacity (disk)—The capacity of a disk or sets of disks which constitute the volume for a disk drive; rated in kilobytes (Kb).

carriage—A platform which holds the ribbon cartridge, the print element and the striking mechanism; horizontally positioned so that the print element strikes the paper to produce letter images.

carriage advance—Movement of the printer or typewriter carriage across the paper.

carriage advance increment—The smallest unit by which the carriage may be advanced. For daisy wheel printers this is 1/120 inch. By varying the number of units the carriage advances, different typefaces and proportional spacing are accommodated.

carriage return—A key on the keyboard, return, and a corresponding code, [cr], which conveys to the computer or typewriter the end of a line or a paragraph, and returns the carriage or cursor to the left margin.

carrier—See *carriage*.

cassette—A plastic container with two hubs and a length of tape wound about one and attached to other. During reading or writing on a cassette recorder, tape is wound off the feed hub, moved past a read/write head and wound onto the takeup hub. The tape may be rewound or advanced at higher speeds than for recording or playback. Most recorder cassettes are reversible; they may be flipped over and put back in the machine. Then they can be read or recorded on another track of the tape. Computer recording does not usually use the second side and records only a single track.

cassette drive—A drive mechanism for recording and reading from a cassette.

cathode ray tube (CRT)—A tube which provides a display screen for presenting alphanumeric information and graphics.

cell—The data at the intersection of a row and column of a table.

central processing unit (CPU)—The portion of the computer which executes one command at a time of the program and does the arithmetic and logical operations which solve a problem. For the microcomputer system, the CPU is contained in a single microprocessor chip on the CPU board.

chain—For the line printer, each metal slug is hooked together in a pivoting arrangement to form an endless chain, the main printing element of the printer.

character buffer—A memory in the line printer similar to the print buffer which contains a character code for each character position on the print line corresponding to the present position of the characters on the chain or train.

character generator—An electronic device with a memory, usually ROM, which contains in encoded form one dot matrix for each character of the font of the screen display or dot matrix printer alphabet.

characters per second (cps)—The number of characters which a printer or typewriter can produce at maximum speed.

clear—A key which causes all the text being displayed to be cleared from the CRT screen.

close—A declaration that the program no longer needs access to this file, which then becomes inaccessible to the program. The file manager then writes back the directory entry of the file to the disk.

code–A collection of bits which represents a letter, numeral or symbol.

code set–A set of codes, one for each letter, numeral or symbol in the alphabet which is to be represented in this data system.

column–Data within a table or text which extends vertically from the upper to the lower limit of the table or page.

column blanking–To remove a column without altering the position of other columns of the table so that blanks appear in that column.

column copy–To make a copy of a column in some other position in this or some other table.

column delete–To remove a column and move over other columns leftward to replace the area that is now missing.

column movement–The ability to move about columns of text within a wide document which is displayed on the screen.

column movement by mask–A mask which the operator sets up to determine how columns will move about the screen.

column movement by save and recall–To move a column in a table, the operator saves the column and then recalls it at the place to which it should move.

column movement, key defined–To move columns the operator enters key strokes which direct their movement.

column swap–Interchanging two columns so that one occupies the position of the other, and vice versa.

command program–On some WPs, a record of a set of key strokes that you enter at the keyboard and assigned to a single key so that the entire set of key strokes is called up with this single key.

compiler–A program which takes another program written in source language and converts it into a machine language program which can then be run on the computer.

computer–A problem solving device, instructed how to solve the problem by a program contained in its memory.

computer system–A computer, a number of devices for bringing data into and removing data from the computer, an operating system and a number of programs which makes it possible to solve a number of problems.

concurrent–The computer can actually do only one thing at a time; however, if it alternates quickly between two or three activities it seems to the observer that these things are going on simultaneously when they actually are occurring concurrently.

configuration–A set of hardware components put together for a particular environment.

continuous form–Paper in the form of a roll or a fanfold with holes punched on either side so that pins may pull the paper through the print mechanism evenly and positively. The paper is perforated horizontally at page length intervals so that it can be torn apart into separate sheets.

control code–A code which does not have a representation on the printer and hence will not cause a character to print; it is used to inform a program of a control action request.

**controller**—Hardware, usually contained on a printed circuit board within the microcomputer cabinet, which controls one or more devices of a particular kind. It mediates control signals from both the computer and the device and regulates the flow of data between the computer memory and the device accordingly.

**copy document**—A document produced from a stencil by replacing a variable by a variable value from a list.

**correction, backspace**—See *backspace correction.*

**counter**—An electronic device that stores a count which can be advanced by entering a pulse at the proper input. Some counters can also have their count decreased by 1 in a similar fashion; others allow a value to be loaded before counting up or down from that value.

**counter, display**—A counter which keeps track of the character position for which the character display is currently being created.

**cpi**—Characters per inch.

**cps**—Characters per second.

**create**—To key in a new document starting with a blank screen.

**cursor**—A marker which appears on the video screen to inform the user where the next key stroke will appear or which function might be selected. The marker might be an underline which is stable or blinks or a rectangle which contains a letter in reverse video, either static or blinking.

**cursor key**—A key which when pressed causes the cursor to move in a designated direction. Five cursor movements are usually provided. Arrows engraved on the keys indicate direction of cursor movement: up, down, right, left or home (top left corner of screen).

**cursor positioning**—Moving the cursor to a desired position on the VDT screen.

**cursor positioning, context**—Positioning the cursor in terms of context units— sentences, paragraphs, etc.

**cursor positioning, express**—Positioning the cursor to the extremes of the VDT screen such as the upper right-hand corner, lower left-hand corner, etc.

**cursor positioning, geometric**—Dictating the position of the cursor in terms of geometric units—character, line, etc.

**cyclic redundancy check (CRC)**—An algorithm or set of operations performed upon a bit stream as it is recorded on, or read from, a sector of the disk. This set of operations is performed on the 0s and 1s which comprise the bit stream to come up with two bytes which are the *check bytes.* For recording, these bytes are added on at the end of a sector and recorded there. Later, when the sector is read back, the identical set of operations is performed on the bit stream. The result should be the same bytes which are written at the end of the sector. If the two check strings do not agree, the data is said to be *invalid.*

**cylinder**—For a multidisk drive, those tracks which are defined by one of the fixed positions of the heads when the arm is not in motion.

**daisy wheel**—A print element for several popular printers, consisting of a plastic or metal disk with spokes radiating from the center. At the end of each spoke is a circular area with a type impression on it. The disk is like the petal of a flower, hence the name.

**daisy wheel printer**—A printer for which the print element is a daisy wheel.

**data terminal**—The name for a remote terminal or a computer when it is used as part of a communication system.

**debug**—To alter a source program which you have written that doesn't work to make it do what it is supposed to do.

**delete**—To remove text from the screen and also from the text image in the WP memory.

**deletion, discretionary**—After pointing out a string for deletion, the operator still has a chance to decide whether deletion is actually to take place.

**deletion, immediate**—Deletion whereby, as soon as the operator signals that a character or string be deleted, the action is actually taken irrevocably.

**density**—The closeness with which information is packed on a medium. It is measured linearly in terms of bits per inch (bpi). It is measured radially on the disk in terms of tracks per inch (tpi).

**descender**—That portion of a letter which lies below the line on which a letter normally sits, such as the tail of the letters j, g, p, etc.

**deserializer**—A device which accepts eight serial bits as input and converts them into a parallel byte as output.

**designate**—To mark a column, word or other quantity of text.

**dictionary, local**—A dictionary used by a spelling program into which the operator inserts questionable words that are found to be correct so that the program will not turn up the words again on this run. A local dictionary lasts only for the examination of a single text document.

**dictionary, supplementary**—A dictionary created by users, containing jargon or technical words related to this particular office practice. When a spelling program is run, the supplementary dictionary is included so that these words will not be tagged as misspelled.

**digram**—A pair of letters which might occur adjacently within a word.

**direct access**—The ability to go directly to any desired portion of a file. This is the case with a disk file provided with a direct-access file manager.

**directory, allocation**—A directory that keeps track of which blocks or other units of external storage are used in sequence to make up the text you compose or the program file you create.

**directory, space**—A directory that keeps track of space on external storage assigned to the file but not yet assigned to portions of text.

**disk**—A thin, circularly shaped disk of plastic coated with magnetic material used for external storage; sometimes called a floppy disk or a diskette.

**disk controller**—Circuitry for controlling one or more disk drives. Usually the controller circuitry is on its own printed circuit board which plugs into a bus; it can control eight or more disk drives, although few systems use more than four drives; two is the usual number. Control signals from the CPU select and direct one of the disk drives. Status signals from the controller tell the CPU the progress of the activity. Data are reorganized by the controller as they pass between the drive and memory.

**disk controller logic**—The disk controller circuitry which includes: a number of registers to keep track of all variables concerned with the drives in question; a serializer and deserializer to convert from a bit stream to byte oriented information, and vice versa; and an arithmetic logic unit to perform incrementing, decrementing and comparison, and to check the CRC to determine if the sector read is valid.

**disk operating system (DOS or OS)**—The microcomputer operating system that mostly runs the computer for the user. It includes drivers for all the peripheral devices in the system. It keeps track of files and manages space on each of the disks. It provides communication with the operator and accepts and interprets commands.

**diskette**—A single removable plastic disk in its own paper envelope which is flexible; also called floppy disk.

**document assembly**—The process of gathering together either manually or automatically a number of subdocuments to form a document for eventual printout.

**document assembly, automatic**—The WP follows your instructions to put together a set of subdocuments to produce an output document.

**document, electronic**—See *electronic document.*

**dot matrix**—A rectangular grid defining the relative placement of visible dots on a display or printout. One matrix is provided for each symbol of the alphabet. Each pattern follows the shape of the printed letter, numeral or symbol. Matrix size is defined by two numbers—the width and height, respectively, in dots. For a given physical character size, increasing matrix size (say, from 5 X 7 to 7 X 9 or 9 X 13) both increases the total number of visible dots in the character and decreases the space between dots, so that the character can contain finer detail.

**dot matrix printer**—A printing device which produces copy by placing down an array of black dots on the paper by means of print wires which hit the ribbon up against the paper to make an impression.

**double density diskette**—The magnetic medium of the first floppy disks allowed recording and reading at a maximum density of about 4,000 flux changes per inch. The encoding methods required at least one flux change for each zero and two flux changes for each 1. Improvements made in the media allow a maximum of 16,400 flux changes per bit. A diskette recorded with the new techniques can hold twice as much data as one recorded at the standard single density.

**double sided diskette**—A diskette that provides two surfaces on which data may be written. This doubles the amount of storage that each diskette provides. It requires that the drive have two heads selectable by the computer.

**drive**—A mechanism for reading from or writing onto an external storage medium.

**drive selection**—When multiple disk drives are attached to a computer only one can transfer data with memory at any given time. The computer *selects* this drive.

**drive, dual**—Disk drive module that contains two disk drives.

**drive, dual head**—A drive where two heads are provided and both sides of the dual-sided floppy disk can be accessed.

**drive, single sided**—A disk drive where the disk can be accessed only from one side because only one head is provided.

**drive, Winchester**—A disk drive which uses one or more rigid disks, some or all of which are not removable.

**driver**—A program which is part of the operating system and controls a device such as the printer or terminal from commands issued by an application program.

**dumb terminal**—A terminal which is not smart. See *smart terminal.*

**duplex**—A communication line which permits transmission in both directions simultaneously.

**EBCDIC**—A code set originally devised by IBM called the Extended Binary Coded Decimal Interchange Code. See Appendix 2 for a table of this code.

**echoplex**—A transmission mode where codes from the keyboard are sent to the computer and echoed over the return line to be presented on the screen. Thus there is no direct connection between the keyboard and the screen; all characters appearing on the screen are those which were received by the computer, thus verifying the transmission.

**ED**—See *electronic document.*

**edit**—To alter an existing (electronic) document so that it differs from the original in some way.

**electronic document**—A document in machine readable form on a disk created by the WP after the operator keys a document into the word processor and is satisfied that the recorded document is correct.

**escape**—A code and on some consoles a key which produces that code. This code often begins a sequence of codes to direct the printer or other device about what movement or action to take.

**extent**—A set of adjacent blocks on a disk.

**external storage**—A combination of a medium and a device which is not part of the CPU and which can store information in large quantities to supplement the CPU memory. The storage is nonvolatile and remains safe when the power goes off.

**field**—The position in a record where one characteristic of the individual, represented by the record, is stored.

**field name**—A name assigned to one field of a record so as to identify the field and make it possible to discuss it.

**field value**—A value that appears in a field of a record where this value describes some characteristic of an individual which this record represents.

**file**—(1) A collection of records, one for each individual of a population; (2) A named collection of data or a program, generally on a volume of a disk. A file is further broken down into chunks of information called records for record processing applications.

**file area**—The area on the disk available to files of data and programming.

**file directory**—The disk area allocated to hold a directory which names and indicates the extents occupied by each file.

**file manager**—An operating system program which manages files for the application program. It finds the file on the medium or acquires space for a new file. On the AP's request it reads blocks or records from a file; it writes blocks or records onto the file when they are passed over by the AP.

**file manager, serial**—A file manager for files kept on a sequential medium or simulating such a medium. A file must be read (written) from one end to the other. Information in between can be skipped over but must be passed through.

**file, subdocument**—A file consisting of subdocuments from which the WP can choose to create an output document for automatic document assembly.

**flag**—A character in the mask which tells the WP what you want to do with one or more columns in your table.

**floppy**—A diskette, usually 8 inches in diameter.

**foot**—Information to appear at the bottom of each page to describe the document to which the page belongs. Also called **footer, footing, trailer**.

**form letter**—A letter which is a copy document produced by inserting variable values from a variable list into a stencil.

**format**—(1) The way that a document appears on the sheet of paper. (2) Entering key strokes at the terminal so as to request that the printed document be in the desired format. (3) The action by which the print formatter program takes the electronic document and prints it as desired on the paper.

**format (disk)**—To write sector information on each track of a soft sectored disk.

**format block**—Encoded instructions within the electronic document indicating the new format for succeeding text.

**format code**—A code which appears in the text area of memory to indicate that the characters which follow are format information.

**format key**—A key which is pressed to enter the format mode or to enable the operator to enter format information and thus reset the format line.

**format line**—A line or ruler which appears on the display to show the setting of the left and right margins and the tab stops and sometimes to indicate alternative margins by which to indent.

**format message**—A set of characters which gives format information to the print format program.

**format parameters**—Information which describes how the document should appear on the printed page.

**format parameters, default**—Parameters to format a page if no other information is furnished.

**format parameters, embedded**—Parameters about the print format keyed in by the operator and displayed on the screen as part of the text but do not print. Instead, they are responded to by the print formatter.

**format parameters, encoded**—Format parameters entered with special keys by the operator. The text editor causes the display to conform with requests. It hides the parameters in the ED. The print formatter finds the parameter in the ED and prints the document to conform.

**format parameters, explicit**—Format information that is entered at the keyboard at print time and to override the default format parameters or those included in the electronic document.

**format parameters, implied**—The electronic document contains no format information at its beginning. The print formatter uses implied default parameters.

**format parameters, included**—Information about how to format a page included in the electronic document.

**format string**—A series of characters, usually preceded by a format code, indicating that format information is imbedded or encoded in the text.

**format, short term**—A format request which remains in force only for a portion of the text development.

**frame**—A complete scan of the screen from top to bottom which writes on the screen the contents of refresh memory.

**function key**—A key which requests the WP to perform a particular function such as delete or insert.

**gigabyte**—One billion bytes.

**global**—Applying to the whole text or applying to the rest of the text from here (where the action is made) onward.

**golf ball**—The print element in a Selectric typewriter.

**graphic**—A special symbol outside the normal character set, which appears on the screen and/or prints to indicate some particular function for the word processor. For instance, a solid triangle is used by some WPs to indicate a carriage return.

**half duplex**—A communication line which permits transmission in either direction but not both simultaneously.

**hammer register**—A 9-bit register in the dot-matrix printer which stores a code where the 1s correspond to hammers which should be hit and the 0s to those hammers which should not be hit to print the vertical of the letter now being scanned.

**hard copy**—A printed document.

**hard sectored**—Refers to when each sector of a disk is marked by a small hole on a circle of constant radius on the disk.

**hard space**—When a hard space appears between two words and word wrap occurs for the second word, the WP brings along both the hard space and the word preceding that space.

**hardware**—The electric and mechanical equipment that goes into a computing system.

**head**—(1) Information which is printed on every page of the document so as to indicate which document each page belongs to. Also called a **header**. (2) The element on a disk or tape drive to read from or write on the medium.

**header insertion, edit time**—A header inserted while the document is edited and not on a separate run.

**highlight**—To make one or more characters displayed on the screen stand out with relation to the others, usually by showing them brighter or dimmer than the others, but sometimes with reverse video or underlining or blinking.

**home**—(1) A known position on the CRT screen; generally the upper left hand corner. Sometimes other home positions are provided, such as the left-hand side of the line or the bottom left hand corner of the screen. (2) A key which causes the cursor to move to a particular and usually distant position on the screen, such as the upper right hand corner or lower left hand corner. (3) For the daisy wheel printer, that petal on the daisy wheel from which all other characters are measured. (4) For the disk, the position where the head is over the outermost track (track 0).

**hot zone**—An area at the right margin used for making hyphenation and word wrap decisions. A word which starts in the hot zone and continues into the right margin is eligible for word wrap or hyphenation.

**hyphen**—A small dash which connects two parts of a compound word. When a word at the end of a line is broken into two parts; the part at the end of the line has a hyphen to end it.

**hyphen, hard**—A hyphen in a compound word which always appears in that word. The two halves of the word may be separated when the word would overrun the margin, leaving the hyphen with the portion on the upper line.

**hyphen, soft**—A hyphen in a simple word used when the word is broken at the end of the line but deleted when the word is not broken.

**hyphen, very hard**—A hyphen which separates a compound word and prohibits that word from being broken or wrapped so that it spreads over two lines.

**hyphenation**—The act of going through the text and inserting hyphens so that words are allocated to lines more evenly.

**hyphenation program**—A program which runs to scan your text and insert hyphens at the proper place in it.

**hyphenation, automatic**—The WP reviews the entire manuscript and inserts hyphens at points where it sees fit, without the need for any human intervention.

**hyphenation, manual**—The operator goes through the electronic document, inserting hyphens wherever they seem to be required.

**hyphenation, system assisted**—The WP scans the text to find any word which straddles the hot zone. It stops and presents the word in context to the operator who can then insert a hyphen where necessary, or accept the word without hyphenation.

**I/O device**—A device which performs input or output or both.

**increment**—The distance in inches by which the movement of the print carriage can be adjusted horizontally. In the industry this is usually 1/120 inch.

**indent**—To move in the margin temporarily by a specified amount. Most WPs provide for indenting from the left margin; a few provide a right indent command also.

**index**—For a list of terms furnished by the user, the pages in the document where these terms appear associated with each term is an index.

**index generator**—A program which examines the text and finds the position of each index term by page and line number.

**index hole**—A hole in the disk and in the envelope containing it, both at the same radius so that as the disk rotates, the two become aligned. That event can be detected optically to produce an index pulse to mark the beginning of every track.

**index pulse**—A pulse produced when the index hole in the disk and in the envelope are aligned and produce the home signal.

**individual**—A person, company, account or object in a population which we want to keep track of and for which we establish a record.

**input**—The process of bringing data into the memory of the computer from the keyboard, a medium or an external source.

**insert**—To enter additional characters somewhere in text displayed on the screen and stored in the WP memory.

**insert by replacement**—Action that is actually insertion and simultaneous deletion; you key in new information which replaces existing text.

**insert, open up**—To insert by this method you hit <u>insert</u> and the WP moves aside the text at the point marked by the cursor, whereupon you may now enter new characters. The text is closed up at your request.

**insert, push aside**—By this method, after hitting <u>insert</u>, the characters that you enter go in at the cursor position, pushing forward the following text.

**interactive**—Reference to an action that takes when the operator and the computer pass information back and forth during the running of the program. For instance, an interactive spelling program finds a word that seems to be misspelled and presents it to the operator for validation. This occurs with each new word. This is in contrast to a batch method, which finds all the words in question and presents them on the screen at once for correction.

**interface**—The circuitry which comes between two devices. In the computer system the interface generally goes between the CPU and an I/O device.

**interpreter**—A program which takes your source language program and operates the computer to perform the actions described by your program.

**interrupt**—The ability of some hardware action to stop a program which is running and give control to another program, usually the operating system. This is necessary to the concept of concurrency, so that when you key in data, the computer stops printing for a fraction of a second and accepts the character.

**justification**—Printing text with uniform margins on both the left and the right sides.

**justification, intercharacter**—Obtaining justification by distributing excess space within the gaps between characters of the line.

**justification, interword**—Obtaining justification by distributing the excess space between words within the line.

**kern**—To reduce the spacing between characters within a line of print.

**key**—(1) A square button such as found on a typewriter. The top is labeled with one, two and sometimes four symbols. When the key is struck, the keyboard generates a set of signals, the code for the character of the code set. Unless some other key is also pressed, the code generated generally corresponds to the bottom letter inscribed on the key. (2) A field which is used to order or sort a file.

**key, control**—The key which when held down and some other key on the keyboard is struck, produces a special code, usually nonprinting. The computer usually interprets this as a request to perform a specific action (such as halting a listing, or rebooting the operating system).

**key, function**—A key which requests a WP function such as <u>insert</u>, <u>delete</u>, <u>format</u>, <u>mark</u>.

**key, hard space**—The key which when pressed inserts a hard space into the text.

**key, shift**—The key which when held down and some other key is pressed causes the code corresponding to the upper symbol engraved on the key to be produced by the keyboard.

**key, special purpose**—A key which when touched causes the keyboard to create a special code, usually nonprinting and conveying a special function such as **backspace**, **linefeed** or **clear** (the CRT screen).

**key, user defined**—A key which when pressed calls forth a sequence of keystrokes previously defined as a command program.

**keyboard**—A set of keys, generally laid out on a rectangular pattern, consisting of five rows and perhaps fifteen or twenty columns. The layout usually corresponds to the standard typewriter keyboard. Additional keys correspond to extra functions required with the computer.

**keyboard program**—See *command program.*

**keyswitch**—A device that produces a signal each time a key is pressed.

**kilobyte (Kb)**—A unit of measurement of 1024 bytes.

**language, assembly**—A low level language by which a programmer can enter commands which resemble machine language commands in their function, but which are easier to use since they are in symbolic form.

**language, higher level**—A language which performs special functions not usually found in POLs. Such languages often incorporate a compiler language as a subset.

**language, machine**—A language consisting of 0s and 1s in which the computer program is stored so it is comprehensible to the computer but not generally to the lay user.

**language, procedure oriented (POL)**—A language for programming whereby procedures for performing logical actions are easily written. Sometimes called a compiler language. Examples of such languages are BASIC, COBOL and FORTRAN.

**language, source**—A language such as BASIC in which a programmer writes the program before it is usable by the computer.

**large scale integration (LSI)**—Placing a large number of circuits, perhaps a hundred or more, on a single chip (the size of a pin head).

**latency**—The time it takes, once the head is positioned at the proper track, to find the desired sector. Latency generally means average latency, the average length of time to reach the desired sector.

**leader**—An additional piece of tape at the beginning and/or end of a cassette or reel of magnetic tape. The leader is made of clear plastic or conductive metal and cannot be recorded upon. The clear plastic provides for optical recognition of the end of tape; the metallic leader provides for electric detection of tape end.

**light emitting diode (LED)**—A component about 1/16 inch in diameter which can be activated to emit light. Single LEDs are used on keyboards to indicate a key which has been pressed. Groups of LEDs are used on some intelligent typewriters to display a few characters of the text which are now pointed to and acted upon.

**light pen**—An input device whereby the console operator can choose among alternatives. When a menu is presented on the screen, for instance, a number of choices are given the operator, each with a box next to it. He positions the light pen to a box representing his choice and then presses the entry button on the pen. The pen contains a light sensor which returns a signal. The time of return of the signal indicates to the computer which choice he has made.

**line advance**—The action of the printer or the typewriter to move the paper up or down within the machine so as to align it for printing on the next or preceding line.

**line printer**—A printer with a print mechanism which is rotating constantly at a high speed. The mechanism might be a drum, a chain, a train, a band or a belt. Printing occurs whenever some print slug arrives at the position at which it should be printed and then a hammer strikes it to make an impression on the paper. Hence, different character positions of the line are printed almost randomly. Only when all the characters for the line have been printed does the paper advance.

**line, folded**—Some WPs take a line from a wide document and display it as two successive half lines on the screen.

**lines per minute (lpm)**—A measurement for the line printer of the number of lines which are printed per minute.

**list, variable**—A list of variable values used with a stencil to produce form letters or copy documents.

**load (disk)**—To load the heads of a disk drive is to release the heads so that they make contact with the disk or ride on the thin film of air created by the rotation of the disk in the case of the hard disk.

**load module**—A module of machine language code which is executable if it is loaded into memory starting at the position incorporated into the module.

**lock key**—A key which when pressed causes the shift to be maintained as though held down through the striking of subsequent letters.

**lock, alpha**—A locking key which when pressed, letter keys pressed thereafter produce uppercase character codes. Numeric keys still produce codes for the numerals.

**lock, shift**—A keyboard lock which when set causes the keyboard to produce the code for the upper symbol on the key when a key is pressed. That is, for an alphabetic key, a capital letter is produced. For a numeric key, a symbol above the numeral is produced.

**log on**—The activities whereby a user makes a work station available for use on the system.

**logical file**—Viewing a file as a collection of sequential blocks.

**lower buffer**—For the typing line WP, there may be additional text which is not displayed in the preview area but is kept in this lower buffer and is obtained when you scroll forward.

**magnetic card**—A thin plastic card about 3" x 9" coated with magnetizable material on which may be recorded the equivalent of page of data.

**magnetic tape**—Thin mylar or plastic tape on which is coated a magnetizible medium. Information is recorded on or read from the tape as it passes beneath a read/write head on the tape drive.

**mainframe**—A large computer for data processing.

**margin**—Blank area on the printed page or on the screen which surrounds the text on the top, bottom, left and right.

**mark**—(1) Designating the beginning or end of a string during editing. (2) Name for 1 in communications jargon.

mask—A ruler line with suitable characters called flags which direct the movement, editing or processing of a column in a table.

matrix printer—An impact printing mechanism with a number of small, thin, flexible rods which make the impression on the paper as a series of vertical dots or undots. A character is formed by combining a number of such verticals.

medium—A material which may be altered or deformed to store data.

medium, physically sequential—A medium which must be read or written in a fixed order dictated by the medium itself. An example is magnetic tape.

Megahertz—A repetition rate of one million times per second.

memory—The portion of the computer which holds the program and data that the computer needs to solve a problem.

memory wraparound—Access to memory where, it is viewed as circular, and data past the bottom of an area is taken from the top of that same area.

memory, random access (RAM)—A memory which can be altered by the computer in a fraction of a microsecond.

memory, read only (ROM)—A memory from which the computer can read information at will but cannot alter or change the information which is stored there.

memory, read only, program, electrically alterable (EAPROM)—A memory which is normally read only, but with a special technique by which the computer can write into it by writing repeatedly a large number of times.

memory, read only, programmable (PROM)—A read only memory into which a program can be written by removing that section of ROM memory from the computer and writing into it by a special process.

memory, read only, programmable, erasable (EPROM)—A read only memory which the user can take out and erase by a special process, usually involving ultraviolet light. By a computer assisted procedure the technician can then enter a new program which is now stored in a read only fashion.

memory, refresh—A memory in the VDT which stores the codes for all the characters which are currently being displayed on the screen.

menu—A list of alternatives presented on the screen from which the operator may choose, usually by hitting a designated key; in this way, many WPs provide the initial choice about whether to create, edit or print a specified document.

MHz—MegaHertz.

microcomputer—A microprocessor and memory of small size and low price which may be used as part of a WP system.

microfloppy—A very small floppy which is 3-1/2 inches in diameter.

microprocessor board (CPU board)—A printed circuit board for which the main component is the microprocessor chip. It contains other components such as those to generate the timing signals and to shape the pulses which are necessary to run the microprocessor.

microsecond—One millionth of a second.

millisecond (ms)—One one thousandth of a second.

minifloppy—A small diskette 5-1/4 inches in diameter.

mnemonic—A set of letters which represents the activity performed by a complete command. It suggests these actions, such as A for add, M for move, so that the programmer can easily recall the letters which represent the command.

**modem**—A device which is capable of both modulating and demodulating a fixed carrier for transmission generally over telephone lines.

**modulation**—Applying a variable signal, such as one that contains data, to a carrier, such as an audible tone, so that intelligence may be transmitted over a considerable distance.

**monitor**—A portion of the resident operating system which gets control when a program fails or when an interrupt occurs.

**motherboard**—A printed circuit board onto which other printed circuit boards attach and to which a bus connects.

**mount**—To place a disk in the disk drive and close the door so it becomes available for use by the computer.

**multiprogramming**—The ability of the computer to perform two programs concurrently.

**nanosecond**—One billionth of a second (one thousandth of a microsecond).

**nesting**—For automatic document assembly on some WPs, permitting one of the subdocuments to be another set of assembly directions which call in a group of subdocuments to replace it in the output document.

**nondestructive**—Information that remains where it was originally stored when reading from a medium or from memory.

**nonvolatile**—Computer memory that retains its content after being turned off and then turned on again.

**object module**—A file containing machine language code produced by a compiler, assembler or other translator, which may or may not be in executable form.

**object oriented WP**—A WP for which you indicate the object which is to be edited by deletion or insertion, etc., before you indicate the action which is to be performed upon it.

**open**—To request in an application program that a file be made available. The file manager creates an FCB from scratch for a new file or from information in the file directory for an existing file.

**operating system**—A group of programs which helps to run the computer. It expedites and facilitates the running of application programs. It does not solve a user problem directly.

**ordinality**—The order of an item in a list. Items in a variable list may replace variables in the stencil in the order of their occurrence, so that the third item replaces the third variable.

**orphan**—The first line(s) of a paragraph which is printed at the bottom of this page and is thus separated from the rest of the paragraph which appears on the succeeding page.

**output**—The action of taking data from the computer memory and putting it onto an external medium or printing it.

**output document**—A set of subdocuments entered into a single final document, the product of automatic document assembly.

**overstrike**—The printing of two characters or symbols, one on top of the other.

**page break**—For a WP system that provides continuous scrolling, a visible indicator on the display which shows the end of one page and the beginning of the next. A *soft* page break is assigned by the system and may move during editing. A *hard* page break is established by the user, and the system may not move it, even after editing would have changed the boundary of a page.

**page break, hard**—A page indicator inserted by the operator so that text thereafter will *always* appear on the next succeeding page.

**page break, soft**—A page break inserted by the system to indicate where it forsees the end of one page and beginning of the next. The soft page break may be moved by the system to suit the format specified.

**page management, manual**—Procedure whereby the operator must make sure that pages follow each other properly during printout. The WP does not automatically keep track of the sequence of pages which constitute the document.

**pagination**—Dividing text into units, each to be printed as a single page.

**pagination, automatic**—The WP, usually using a separate program, scans the text and breaks it up into page size units in terms of the document format selected by the user for hard copy printout.

**pagination, computer aided**—Here the operator and the WP program work together to make decisions about which text is printed on each page.

**pagination, manual**—The operator separates the electronic document into text allocated to each page, making the decisions without any assistance from the WP.

**paging**—The same as scrolling by screen.

**paper bail**—A horizontal rod with rubber rollers to hold the paper against the platen and allow it to move upward smoothly.

**paragraph end**—The indication to the WP that the paragraph is to terminate, generally signaled by hitting return.

**parallel**—A set of wires carries a number of bits simultaneously. Usually *parallel by character* is implied, meaning that the 8 bits of 1 byte are transmitted at once.

**parity**—Reference to the fact that the code for each character contains an odd (even) number of 1s, which provides for checking data transmission. A character is *valid* only if the number of 1s in its code is odd (even).

**parity bit**—An additional bit appended to a character code so that the number of 1s in the code is odd (even). Thus, for instance, any seven bit code set can be made into an eight bit code set with the addition of a parity bit for checking data transmission.

**password**—Reference to documents protected by a requirement that the user supply a previously entered password to either access a document or work on it.

**petal register**—A register in the daisy wheel printer which stores the relative position from home of the last character which was printed.

**petal table**—A table in the daisy wheel printer which indicates the relative position of each character, relative to the home position. See *home*.

**pin feed**—A platen with pins projecting radially at both ends of it so as to move forms positively through the pin feed printer.

**pitch**—The number of horizontal characters per inch to which the printer is set. Pitch is often under the control of the computer.

**platen**—A rubber or rubberlike cylinder in a typewriter or printer which moves the paper vertically by means of friction between it and the paper.

**polarized**—Reference to magnet, which consists of a North and South pole.

**population**—A collection of individuals, each of which has a record appearing in the file.

**port**—A line or set of lines to an input or output device or to a controller from the computer. These lines carry data or control signals or both. A port is selected or addressed by a computer command.

**prefix**—A set of letters which is commonly found at the beginning of a word, such as "de" or "re" or "dis".

**preview area**—The visible portion of the screen below the typing line and not including it.

**print**—The phase of the WP activity by which the electronic document is turned into a printed document.

**print buffer**—Memory within the printer which stores the character codes representing the characters to be printed upon one or more upcoming lines.

**print element**—A mechanical arrangement which hits the ribbon against the paper to make the inked impression of the character upon the paper.

**print formatter (PF)**—The program which takes the electronic document, formats it and prints it out to create the hard document.

**print wheel**—A generic term for print elements such as the daisy wheel and the thimble.

**print wires**—The set of wires in the dot matrix printer, each of which may or may not hit the paper to produce a dot or no dot as part of the character being printed.

**printed circuit board**—A laminated thin plastic board, about a sixteenth of an inch thick on to which wiring is electroplated. This wiring connects components and sockets which are fastened to the board. The sockets receive chips. A printed circuit board comprises a complete functional unit, such as a memory or a processor. One of the edges of the board bears a connector where all wires which leave or enter the board appear as thin printed lines. This edge fits into a receptacle which connects it to other components of the computer.

**printer**—A device for entering characters, numerals and symbols onto paper.

**printing, background**—Printing done in the background where the WP may be doing text editing at the same time it is printing.

**printing, bidirectional**—The ability of a printer to print onto the paper when the carriage is moving either to the right or to the left. This speeds printing because it eliminates carriage returns during which no printing can take place.

**printing, multipass**—The actions of certain higher priced matrix printers to print one line more than once. The second pass of the print mechanism is displaced horizontally and vertically so that now each vertical which makes up a character is printed twice and perhaps slightly differently. This produces a much greater definition and higher quality printing.

**printing, two pass**—Two ability of the print formatter to print all the required material of a full page in one font before the second font is used. The operator changes the type wheel, resets the paper, and the program fills in those characters which were left out during the first pass.

priority—A rule by which requests are given service according to their importance or arrival time such as used for deciding among a number of waiting print requests. Also the relative weight of a pending request.

privacy—For the WP system, the ability to keep a text from being viewed or worked on by other operators that use the system.

program—The directions which tell the computer how to solve a problem.

program, application—A program which solves a user's application, such as editing text, making calculations, keeping track of money and materials, forecasting and so forth.

program, control—The portion of the operating system which is resident in memory and controls the driver and other software.

program, source—A program written in a source language which has to be interpreted or compiled in order to run the computer properly.

programmable key—A key which may be programmed or wired to produce a particular code. Found more commonly on personal computers and mainframe terminals than on WPs.

programmer—The person who writes programs for the computer.

prompt—A symbol presented on the CRT screen to tell you that the program or the operating system requires a new command or line of text to continue.

proportional spacing—Printing where some characters such as an 'M' print considerably larger than other characters, such as the 'i', or the 'period'.

protocol—A set of codes which must be transmitted and received in the proper sequence to guarantee that the participating terminals are hooked together and can talk together as desired.

quad diskette—A diskette which is double sided and records in double density.

query language—A language designed to specify formally the makeup of a subfile.

queue—A waiting line, usually for the printer with requests for text to be printed out.

random access—(1) The ability to read or write data in the same length of time, regardless of its position on the medium or in memory. (2) Sometimes used to describe direct access files.

random file—A file written by a random access file manager where any part of the file is accessible directly.

raster—A sequence of lines swept out by the beam of a cathode ray tube in creating a display. When the beam is turned on, that part of the line is visible. If the beam is turned off, that part of the line is not visible.

read—To copy information from a medium without altering the information on that medium.

real time—Operation of a program that allows the operator to interact while the program is running. For example, a real time spelling program stops when it finds a word which is questionable, displays it to the operator in context and lets the operator decide if it should be changed and how.

record—(1) The amount of text or data that a program sees as a meaningful unit. (2) Data describing one individual.

**record, variable**—A set of items in a variable list used to create one form letter or copy document.

**refresh cycle**—A VDT cycle which presents a frame of information on the screen.

**refresh rate**—The number of frames or refresh cycles which are performed each second to make a steady and constant display. A common refresh rate is 60 cycles per second.

**register, string**—A place in the computer where a string of information is stored temporarily during operation upon it.

**relative track**—An electronic document may be assigned several tracks on external storage. These tracks may not be adjacent. The position of a track with respect to the beginning of the file of text counting *as though* the file occupied adjacent tracks is called its relative track number.

**remote terminal**—A terminal (display and keyboard) which does not have internal computing power and communicates with the computing power by means of communication lines such as telephone lines.

**removable**—Reference to when a medium can be taken from the drive which holds it and stored elsewhere.

**repeat search**—The WP searches for the same string which it looked for in the last search request in succeeding text.

**replace string**—For a search and replace action, this string replaces the search string.

**resident**—Reference to when a program or data is copied into the memory where the program may execute or the data may be processed.

**response time**—(1) The time between when the user requests an action and the action appears completed on the VDT. (2) The keystroke response time is the time between when the user hits a key and the corresponding letter appears on the screen. Generally key response time is a fraction of a second.

**responsive display**—A display which responds to your format directions, showing them on its screen. Thus when you request boldface, the letters appear darker (or lighter) on the screen; if you ask for underline, the letters on the screen are underlined; and so forth.

**return**—A keyboard key which is used to terminate a paragraph.

**return key**—A key, called <u>return</u>, which when pressed serves the function of a carriage *return* except that it is used only to terminate a paragraph for WPs which provide word wrap.

**reusable**—A medium is reusable when new information can be entered there to replace existing data.

**reverse video**—When the normal display shows each character in black on a white background, reverse video shows the letter in white on a black background, and vice versa.

**ribbon cartridge**—A plastic case containing an inked ribbon on one spool and an empty spool on the other side. The cartridge may be installed onto the printer carriage without the operator getting dirty hands.

**ribbon, fabric**—An inked fabric ribbon which is moved back and forth in both directions and thereby may be reused many times until the impression gets too poor.

**ribbon, multistrike**—A coated plastic ribbon on which successive characters strike at overlapping points, moving in one direction until it has been used up and then must be discarded. It cannot be reversed.

**rollover**—When two or more keyboard keys are pressed, the first one released produces a proper code. One or more of the other keys may also produce correct codes.

**rollover, n-key**—Characteristic of a keyboard that when several keys are pressed simultaneously, the first one released produces its *correct code* and then the second, and third, and so forth, up to n.

**row**—(1) The set of scan lines which are required to make up one line of text which might be presented (when referring to the CRT display). The row includes spacing lines in which nothing appears that separate characters on one row from those on the next. (2) Data on one horizontal line of a table between one margin of the table and the other.

**rubout**—A key, called ru̲b, equivalent to the backspace key when used for backspace correction.

**scan line**—One line swept out by the CRT beam as it forms letters and graphics on the screen.

**screenful**—The quantity of the electronic document which can be displayed at any one time on the screen of the VDT.

**scroll**—To cause the text which appears on the VDT to move in some direction so that part of the text disappears and a new part appears, thus enabling the operator to have a new portion of the text accessible.

**scroll, continuous**—Movement of the text continuously across the screen until the operator indicates that scrolling is to stop.

**scroll, horizontal**—Movement of the contents of the screen horizontally to the right or left of a wide document, perhaps revealing more text on either side but not effecting the top or bottom of the screen.

**scroll, incremental**—Continuous scrolling, for which text seems to move smoothly, not by a full line height. Also called **pan scroll**.

**scroll, line**—Movement of the text one line up or down on the screen.

**scroll, pan**—Same as incremental scroll.

**scroll, screen**—Presenting the immediately adjacent screenful of text whether in the forward or backward direction.

**scroll, variable**—Continuous scroll for which the scroll rate is adjustable by operator.

**scroll, vertical**—To move the text displayed on the screen up or down without affecting the text displayed on the right or left of the screen.

**search**—The WP finds the string of characters in the text as you request.

**search and replace**—The WP finds strings which you request and replaces them by a second string you supply.

**search buffer**—A place in memory where the WP stores the search string during a search request.

**search string**—The set of characters for which the WP is looking when it executes the search command.

**search, whole word**—The WP is looks for the entire string as a separate entity and not part of another word.

**sector**—A portion of a track lying between two sector holes or two markers as defined by the formatting process.

**sector hole**—A hole in a hard sectored disk. There are a fixed number of such holes around the circumference of a circle of fixed radius. There is a single hole in the envelope. Each time a sector hole passes underneath this hole in the envelope, a sector pulse is generated optically.

**sector pulse**—A pulse generated by the sector hole as it passes beneath a similar hole in the envelope to mark the sector.

**seek**—The action of the disk drive to position a head to one of a number of discrete positions (over a desired track).

**sequence**—The pattern in which one record follows another.

**sequence, ascending**—An ordered sequence where records for which the key value is larger are at the end of the file.

**sequence, descending**—A sequence by which records with the highest keys are at the beginning of the file.

**sequential access**—A requirement of the file that accessing a record requires scanning through all the intermediate records from the starting position. Sequential access is an inherent feature of a medium such as magnetic tape or punchcards where the medium must be reviewed in a fixed order.

**serial**—Signals represent data by transmitting the bits which represent them over a single pair of wires. Bits appear sequentially in time.

**serif**—A pedestal or squiggle which is part of a typeface design, making it different from other such designs.

**shared logic**—Several VDTs which cannot operate independently but depend upon a small central computer to run them.

**shared resource**—Several stand alone WPs which share a resource such as a printer or a hard disk.

**show phrase**—A capability that exists when it is possible to view a phrase after it is called up but before it is actually inserted into the text.

**sign**—A symbol or symbols which distinguishes a positive from a negative number.

**sign parentheses**—Negative numbers within parentheses, as in some accounting methods.

**sign prefix**—A symbol, usually a plus or minus sign to mark a positive or negative number, respectively.

**sign suffix**—A symbol or set of symbols following a number which indicates its sign, such as CR or *** for a negative number.

**single density disk**—Diskettes, as originally developed, that can read and write at 3200 bits per inch.

**site**—A place in the text which may be the object of a block move activity or other text editing activity.

**skewing**—A method of writing sequentially numbered blocks in nonsequential sectors. Some sectors are skipped so as to improve the efficiency of reading and writing for the disk drive.

smart terminal—A terminal which has capability to do editing and storing data for transmission as a unit. It usually contains a microprocessor chip.

soft sectored—Reference to when sector information is written onto the disk by a format program.

software—The collection of programs required to make the computer work.

sort—The operation by which a group of records, a file or a subfile is put in alphabetical order, usually ascending sequence.

space, hard—See *hard space.*

spacebar—A key, usually a long, thin, horizontal bar, which when pressed produces a code for a blank.

spill area—For manual page management, an area in memory where the WP keeps text which does not fit into one page of external storage and is therefore left over in memory.

split screen—Dividing the screen into different portions, with each portion showing different documents or parts of the same document. Usually both portions are accessible for editing.

stand alone—One VDT and other components to make a single user WP.

start—A signal to initiate the asynchronous transmission of a single character is always a space.

statement, source—One of the statements of an assembly or compiler language.

status line—A portion of the VDT display which constantly presents information about the action that the WP is currently working on, such as the name of the document, the type of function and the mode in which the user is operating.

stencil—A document copied several times but with variable names replaced by variable values so as to produce a copy document, as with form letters.

stencil, form—A stencil that helps the operator to fill in a preprinted form.

string—A continuous sequence of adjacent characters—letters, numerals, punctuation, blanks and alphabetic symbols.

stroke written display—A display for graphics whereby your program indicates the initial and terminal point on the screen for a line which is then written by the display electronics. The graphic and each character are made of a number of such lines.

subdocument—(1) Text on external storage to be assembled with other subdocuments to create a complete document. (2) For document assembly, one piece of text of the many which are to be assembled to create the output document.

subfile—A portion of a file containing some of the records in the original file.

subscript—A letter, numeral or other character printed slightly lower than the other characters on the line.

subtotal—A total taken over only some of a set of numbers or portions of records.

suffix—A set of letters that is commonly found at the end of a word, such as "ing" or "tion."

superscript—A letter, number or symbol printed slightly higher than the other characters on the line.

surface—Each disk, whether large or small, has two physical surfaces. Sometimes only one surface is usable for recording. The technical term applies to a physical surface on which recording can take place.

**switch code**—A symbol, usually a graphic which appears in the stencil instead of a variable name and requests the next ordinal value from the variable list to replace it. It also separates values in the variable list. Hence you are switching from reading the stencil to reading the variable list and back again.

**Synchronous Data Link Control (SDLC)**—A recently developed communication protocol, mainly in use for communication with large computers.

**synchronous recording (or transmission)**—Characters are recorded or transmitted at a continuous timed rate. The activity is preceded by a set of timing pulses which serves to synchronize the reception.

**syntax**—The rules of a formal source language which the programmer must observe. These rules describe which words are proper, what sequence of words is meaningful and where each word must appear with a line.

**tab key**—A key which when pressed causes the cursor to go forward within its current line to the next tab stop; or if there is no further tab stop on this line, to the first tab stop of the next line.

**tab set**—The key or method by which a tab stop is set up on the line.

**tab stop**—The position of the line to which the cursor might proceed when tab is pressed.

**tab, center**—Text entered at the tab stop is centered about this position.

**tab, decimal**—A tab stop that aligns numbers at their decimal point with the integer part being on the left and the decimal part on the right.

**tab, direct**—A set of codes that may be sent by the computer to the printer to cause the carriage on the printer to move to a particular character position on the line, regardless of whether a tab stop has been set at this position.

**tab, express**—See *tab, direct.*

**tab, left flush**—The standard tab which moves the cursor to a position at which text is entered from left to right.

**tab, right flush**—A tab stop whereby text entered is aligned so that the last character appears at the tab stop and preceding characters appear to the left.

**tabbing**—Pressing the tab key so that the carriage or the cursor moves to the next tab stop.

**table**—A rectangular arrangement of text and/or numerical information.

**tag**—A special symbol, usually a graphic, used to prefix a variable name in the stencil.

**telecommunication**—The transmission of intelligence over a distance. In this case we are talking about transmitting data, probably over telephone lines.

**thimble**—A print element much like the daisy wheel, but with spokes all bent upward so that the result looks like a thimble.

**time, average access**—The average time to seek over one third of the tracks on the disk and find the block requested.

**time, head load**—The time required to load the heads after a seek has been performed.

**time, seek**—The time required to move the heads of a disk drive from one position to another to arrive at a requested track.

**time, settling**—The time it takes after a seek for the heads to settle down and stop jiggling.

**time, track-to-track average access**—The average time to find some block on an adjacent track on the disk.

**time, track-to-track positioning**—The time it takes for a head to move from one track to either adjacent track.

**total, intermediate**—A term that applies to a larger subset of all the numbers, as opposed to the grand total, which applies to *all* the numbers, and a subtotal which applies to a small group.

**track**—The circular area swept out by the head when it occupies (seeks to) one of the its standard positions. Tracks are numbered from outside in, starting from 0 and going up to a maximum applicable to that disk.

**tractor feed**—An attachment to a printer whereby pins in this feed mechanism move continuous form paper vertically through the printer by means of sprocket holes punched in the edges of the form. The mechanism is coupled to the printer and advances the paper upon the signal from the computer. The tractor feed is adjustable horizontally for different widths of forms.

**transfer rate**—The rate at which information is transferred from the device to memory, or vice versa for a disk or other peripheral device. The customary unit is kilobits per second (kbs). This should not be confused with kilobytes per second (KBs). A transfer rate for single density diskettes is 250 kilobits per second and that for double density is 500 kilobits per second.

**transparent**—An action that takes place in a computer system about which the user of a system is unaware. For example, the allocation of space to a file is transparent to the WP system user.

**trigram**—A triplet of letters which might occur as a string in a word.

**turnkey system**—A computer system which when plugged in is immediately usable for the function for which it was designed because it contains the corresponding program. The office WP system is a turnkey system.

**typing line**—The particular line of the VDT screen that text must be on for it to be altered and edited, required by some WPs, such as the CPT 8000 and the Magna III.

**typing ruler**—A line displayed on the WP screen which shows margins, tab settings and indents.

**underline**—See *underscore*.

**underscore**—To place a horizontal line under a set of letters on the same line as those letters.

**underscore, broken**—Printing an underscore under letters and numbers but not for spaces between words or punctuation.

**underscore, double**—Printing of a double line beneath a series of characters and spaces.

**underscore, unbroken**—An underscore which continues underneath a group of characters, including spaces and punctuation symbols.

**unit**—(1) A single increment, or 1/120 inch for the standard daisy wheel printer in terms of carriage advance. (2) A set of characters for which there is often a corresponding key to designate a quantity of text such as word, sentence, paragraph, etc.

**universal key**—A key, such as <u>return</u>, found on most WP keyboards, which does not produce a printable character but may produce a universal control code.

**update**—To alter data so as to reflect the state of the real world. You update records to indicate changed characteristics of the individual it represents. You update files to include records for new individuals which have entered your population or remove records for expired individuals which have left the population.

**upper buffer**—For the typing line WP, the text which is invisible but is in memory so that it would appear above the upper screen.

**upper screen**—The text above the typing line and including it.

**utility**—A program which provides a fixed function for the user (such as to copy a disk or to file from one disk to another).

**variable**—A set of symbols in a stencil which names a string in the variable list to be substituted for the variable. The variable usually consists of a graphic followed by a sequence of letters which name it.

**variable value**—The value contained in a variable list which replaces a variable name or a switch code in the stencil.

**VDT**—See *video display terminal.*

**video display terminal (VDT)**—A terminal containing a video display, such as that on a television set, upon which a portion of the document currently being handled by the WP system is displayed for the user.

**volatile**—Refers to a memory where information storage continues only as long as the power is maintained. When the power is turned off, the information in memory is lost.

**volume**—The amount of information which is mounted upon and available from the device. For example, a diskette is a volume for a disk drive; a cassette is the volume for a cassette drive.

**wide document**—A document too wide for a full line to display on the VDT.

**widow**—The last line(s) of a paragraph for which there is insufficient space on this page and hence it is placed on the succeeding page.

**wild card**—A special symbol used in a search string to indicate that any character may appear in this position; only the specified characters in other positions in the search string need to be matched.

**window**—A portion of a display which is characterized differently from the rest of the screen. A window may show letters of magnified size or those from a different area of memory.

**word wrap**—For most WPs the operator types information continuously. Words are placed on the line until the line fills up. If the last word being entered cannot be placed totally on the current line the whole word is taken off and placed at the start of the next line without intervention by the operator and without hitting the <u>return</u> key.

**work area**—An area in the computer memory used by the WP program for storing text which is currently being edited.

**work station**—A terminal in a multiuser WP system.

**WP, line oriented**—A WP system which has a typing line, the only place where corrections can be made in the text.

**wraparound**—See *word wrap*.

**write**—To store information on an external medium.

**write protect**—Each diskette has a notch in one of its corners which is scanned optically to inhibit writing on those disks for which protection is desired. For the floppy (8 inch disk), this notch must be covered to write upon the disk, if the notch is not covered, the disk is protected. The opposite holds for the minifloppy, where a covered notch prevents writing.

**zoom line**—The ability to extract a single line and magnify the letters on that line so that they can be read more easily.

**zoom screen**—The ability for the WP to present the display of text using either larger or smaller type according to which key the operator presses.

# Appendix B
# Standard Computer Codes

**Table B.1. Extended Binary Coded Decimal Interchange Code.**

Most Significant Digits →  /  ↓ Least Significant Digits

| Hex / Binary | 0 / 0000 | 1 / 0001 | 2 / 0010 | 3 / 0011 | 4 / 0100 | 5 / 0101 | 6 / 0110 | 7 / 0111 | 8 / 1000 | 9 / 1001 | A / 1010 | B / 1011 | C / 1100 | D / 1101 | E / 1110 | F / 1111 |
|---|---|---|---|---|---|---|---|---|---|---|---|---|---|---|---|---|
| 0 / 0000 | NUL | DLE | LF only | ESC F | SP | & | - | < |  |  |  | FF | SP |  | - | 0 |
| 1 / 0001 | SOH | X-ON |  | CAN | 7ESC J | ESC D | / | : | a | j |  | ⌐[1] | A | J |  | 1 |
| 2 / 0010 | STX | DC2 | FS | ESC X | ⊥ | □ | Γ | ǀ | b | k | s | {[1] | B | K | S | 2 |
| 3 / 0011 | ETX | X-OFF | GS | ESC P | ESC LF | ESC Z | → | ∀ | c | l | t | }[1] | C | L | T | 3 |
| 4 / 0100 | EOT | DC4 | RS | ESC U | ¬ | ⊤ | ω | | d | m | u | [[1] | D | M | U | 4 |
| 5 / 0101 | HT | LF NL | US | ESC ( | ε | ° | ∩ | Λ | e | n | v | ][1] | E | N | V | 5 |
| 6 / 0110 | ACK | SYN[8] | EM | ESC ) |  |  |  |  | f | o | w | NUL | F | O | W | 6 |
| 7 / 0111 | BEL | ETB | / | ESC T |  |  |  | > | g | p | x |  | G | P | X | 7 |
| 8 / 1000 | EOM BS | CAN | < | ESC S | Δ |  |  |  | h | q | y |  | H | Q | Y | 8 |
| 9 / 1001 | ENQ | EM | = | ESC E | ~ |  |  |  | i | r | z |  | I | R | Z | 9 |
| A / 1010 | NAK | SUB | CR only | ESC C | ¢[2] | ! | ⟨ | ∵ |  |  |  | ⌐[6] |  |  |  | x |
| B / 1011 | VT | ESC | EOT | ESC O | · | $ | % | # |  |  |  |  |  |  |  | ÷ |
| C / 1100 | FF | FS | BS | X-ON | ∨ | * | ▯ | @ |  |  |  | ⌐[6] | 7 |  |  | ↑ |
| D / 1101 | CR | GS | ) | X-OFF | ( | ) | ∧ | ' |  |  |  | Lost 6 Data |  |  |  | ↓ |
| E / 1110 | SO | RS | HT | ESC R | + | ; | ? | = |  |  |  | ⌐[6] |  |  |  |  |
| F / 1111 | SI | US | LF only | ESC CR | | | ¬[2] | ⌐[2] | " |  |  |  |  |  |  |  | DEL |

523

Table B.2. American Standard Code for International Interchange.

| $b_4$ | $b_3$ | $b_2$ | $b_1$ | ROW / COLUMN | $^0{}_0{}_0$ = 0 | $^0{}_0{}_1$ = 1 | $^0{}_1{}_0$ = 2 | $^0{}_1{}_1$ = 3 | $^1{}_0{}_0$ = 4 | $^1{}_0{}_1$ = 5 | $^1{}_1{}_0$ = 6 | $^1{}_1{}_1$ = 7 |
|---|---|---|---|---|---|---|---|---|---|---|---|---|
| 0 | 0 | 0 | 0 | 0 | NUL | DLE | SP | 0 | @ | P | | p |
| 0 | 0 | 0 | 1 | 1 | SOH | DC1 | ! | 1 | A | Q | a | q |
| 0 | 0 | 1 | 0 | 2 | STX | DC2 | " | 2 | B | R | b | r |
| 0 | 0 | 1 | 1 | 3 | ETX | DC3 | # | 3 | C | S | c | s |
| 0 | 1 | 0 | 0 | 4 | EOT | DC4 | $ | 4 | D | T | d | t |
| 0 | 1 | 0 | 1 | 5 | ENQ | NAK | % | 5 | E | U | e | u |
| 0 | 1 | 1 | 0 | 6 | ACK | SYN | & | 6 | F | V | f | v |
| 0 | 1 | 1 | 1 | 7 | BEL | ETB | ' | 7 | G | W | g | w |
| 1 | 0 | 0 | 0 | 8 | BS | CAN | ( | 8 | H | X | h | x |
| 1 | 0 | 0 | 1 | 9 | HT | EM | ) | 9 | I | Y | i | y |
| 1 | 0 | 1 | 0 | 10 | LF | SUB | * | : | J | Z | j | z |
| 1 | 0 | 1 | 1 | 11 | VT | ESC | + | ; | K | [ | k | { |
| 1 | 1 | 0 | 0 | 12 | FF | FS | , | < | L | \ | l | ¦ |
| 1 | 1 | 0 | 1 | 13 | CR | GS | − | = | M | ] | m | } |
| 1 | 1 | 1 | 0 | 14 | SO | RS | . | > | N | ^ | n | ~ |
| 1 | 1 | 1 | 1 | 15 | SI | US | / | ? | O | — | o | DEL |

# Appendix C
# Vendor Names and Addresses

A. B. Dick
Information Products Division
5700 West Touhy Avenue
Chicago, IL 60648
(312) 763-1900

AM/ECRM
205 Burlington Road
Bedford, MA 01730
(617) 275-1760

AM Jacquard
3340 Ocean Park Boulevard
Suite 2000
Santa Monica, CA 90405
(213) 450-1242

BDT Products, Inc.
2315 Otis Street
Santa Ana, CA 92704
(714) 751-2005

Burroughs Corporation
Office Automation Division
95 Horse Block Road
Yaphank, NY 11980
(516) 924-0700

Burroughs/Context
9 Ray Avenue
Burlington, MA 01803
(617) 273-2222

Cado Systems Corp.
2771 Toledo Street
Torrance, CA 90503
(213) 320-9660

Compucorp
1901 South Bundy Drive
Los Angeles, CA 90025
(213) 820-2503

CompuScan
900 Hyler Street
Teterboro, NJ 07608
(201) 288-6000

Concept Industries
1116 Summer Street
Stamford, Conn. 06905
(203) 357-0522

CPT Corporation
8100 Mitchell Road
Eden Prairie, MN 55440
(612) 937-8000

Datamarc
1251 Columbia
Richardson, TX 75081
(214) 783-1691

Diablo Systems
24500 Corporate Ave.
Hayward, CA 94545
(415) 786-5000

Dest Corporation
2380 Bering Drive
San Jose, CA 95131
(408) 946-7100

Dictaphone Corporation
120 Old Post Road
Rye, NY 10580
(914) 967-7300

Digital Equipment Corporation
WP Computer Systems
Continental Boulevard
Merrimack, NH 03054
(603) 884-5111

Exxon Office Systems Company
8 Sparks Avenue
Pelham, NY 10803
(914) 738-4344

G. O. Graphics
179 Bedford Street
Lexington, MA 02173
(617) 861-7757

Greenman-Woodard Co.
200 East Ontario St.
Chicago, IL 60611
(312) 266-2996

Hazeltine Corporation
Commack, NY 11725
(516) 462-5100

Hendrix Corporation
670 North Commercial Street
Manchester, NH 03101
(603) 669-9050

Honeywell Information Systems Inc.
200 Smith Street
Walthan, MA 02154
(617) 895-6000

IBM Data Processing Division
1133 Westchester Avenue
White Plains, NY 10604
(914) 696-1900

IBM General Systems Division
3715 Northside Parkway
P.O. Box 2150
Atlanta, GA 30055
(404) 238-2000

IBM Office Products Division
400 Parson's Pond Drive
Franklin Lakes, NJ 07417
(201) 848-3454

Intelligent Systems Corp.
Intercolor Drive
225 Technology Park
Norcross, GA 30092
(404) 449-5961

Kurzweil Computer Products, Inc.
33 Cambridge Parkway
Cambridge, MA 01242
(617) 864-4700

Lanier Business Products
1700 Chantilly Drive, N.E.
Atlanta, GA 30324
(404) 329-8000

Lexitron Corporation
1840 De Haviland
Thousand Oaks, CA 91359
(805) 499-5911

Lexor Corporation
7100 Hayvenhurst Avenue
Van Nuys, CA 91406
(213) 786-91406

Micom Data Systems, Inc.
4040 McEwen, Suite 100
Dallas, TX 75234
(214) 386-5580

NBI Inc.
1695 38th Street
Boulder, Colorado 80302
(303) 444-5710

Nixdorf Computer Corporation
168 Middlesex Turnpike
Burlington, MA 01803
(617) 273-0480

Northern Telecom Inc.
685A East Middlefield Road
Mountain View, CA 94043
(415) 969-9170

OCR Systems
(A Division of Toyomenka America Inc.)
1 World Trade Center
Suite 4011,
N.Y., NY 10048
(212) 466-4667

Olivetti Peripherals Equipment
505 White Plains Road
Tarrytown, NY 10591
(914) 631-3000

Olympia USA, Inc.
Box 22, Route 22
Somerville, NJ 08876
(201) 722-7000

Racal-Telesystems, Inc.
410 N. Michigan Avenue, Suite 1034
Chicago, Illinois 60611
(312) 329-0700

Radio Shack
One Tandy Center
Ft. Worth, TX 76102
(817) 390-3011

Rutishauser of America, Inc.
9677 Wendall Road
Dallas, Texas 75243
(214) 343-9154

Shaffstall Corp.
5292 East 65th Street
Indianapolis, IN 46220
(317) 842-2077

Shasta General Systems
1329 Moffett Park Drive
Sunnyvale, CA 94086
(408) 734-9360

Sony Corp. of America
Office Products Division
9 West 57th Street
New York, N.Y. 10019
(212) 371-5800

Syntrex Inc.
246 Industrial Way West
Eatontown, N.J. 07729
(800) 526-2829

Vector Graphic, Inc.
31364 Via Colinas
Westlake Village, CA 91362
(213) 991-2302

Voice & Data Systems, Inc.
401 N. Michigan Avenue
Chicago, Illinois 60611
(312) 822-0033

Vydec
9 Vreeland Road
Florham Park, N.J. 07932
(213) 991-2302

Wang Laboratories
One Industrial Avenue
Lowell, MA 01851
(617) 459-5000

Wordplex
141 Triunfo Conyon Road
Westlake Village, CA 91361
(213) 889-4455

Xerox Corporation
Office Products Division
1341 West Mockingbird Lane
Dallas, Texas 75247
(214) 689-6259

Zlyad, Inc.
30 Broad Street
Denville, N.J. 07834
(201) 627-7600

# Vendor Index

# Index

This index was prepared using a BASIC program written by me in MBASIC by Microsoft;
* it was sorted by SuperSort I by MicroPro;
* it was edited with WordStar by MicroPro;
* it was printed by a BASIC program written by me in MBASIC.